CASSELL

# Dictionary of
# SUPERSTITIONS

CASSELL

# Dictionary of
# SUPERSTITIONS

## DAVID PICKERING

CASSELL

**A CASSELL BOOK**

First published 1995 by Cassell
Wellington House, 125 Strand, London WC2R OBB

Copyright © David Pickering 1995

ISBN 0–304–345350

Printed and bound in the United States

# Preface

Superstition continues to flourish around the globe even in the most technologically advanced societies. Some may regard it as a curious relic dating from less scientifically advanced times when human beings sought explanations for the apparently random workings of nature, but to others superstition is an integral and constantly developing part of the richness of life in an increasingly secular, not to say soulless, world. New technologies breed new superstitions, as man grapples with the changes wrought by his own ingenuity.

The startling array of old wives' tales, saws and warnings that survive to this day are a reflection of many preoccupations, ranging from largely historical fears about the welfare of animals and portents of coming weather to psychologically telling omens of marital discord, mistrust of technological innovations and magical ways of probing what the future holds. Sometimes science has demonstrated that certain beliefs, such as those relating to various plants and foods with supposed magical properties, have a basis in reality (though readers who cast their own spells based on recipes or procedures described in the text do so entirely at their own risk). On other occasions there seems no possible rationale behind a notion, but still people everywhere are careful to salute magpies, to avoid walking under ladders and to guard their luck by crossing their fingers, touching wood or spitting.

In this book I have attempted a fairly comprehensive survey of superstitions old and new. Entries are arranged alphabetically and include generic articles on such topics as actors and actresses, birds and sailors, that serve to bring together a host of disparate but related superstitions discussed elsewhere. Copious CROSS-REFERENCES throughout provide links with related articles that may be of interest.

The coverage includes superstitions from many cultures and many eras, with particular emphasis on those of the Western world. Where appropriate I have mentioned the known or speculative origin of superstitions, and have also indicated the country or in some cases the county or state from which they derive; where the superstitions belong to the folklore of more than one culture, however, it would be misleading to be more specific. In order to draw attention to the degree to which superstition flourishes even today, I have paid special attention to curious beliefs that have sprung up in relatively recent times: there are articles discussing the taboos and talismans of astronauts, car drivers, photographers and sports players, to name but a few.

In defining the boundaries of what deserved a place and what did not, I have made a distinction between true superstition and those beliefs that might be more accurately described as folklore, mythology or religion. Sometimes these boundaries are very confused, and when in doubt I have tended to include topics that extend beyond the straightforward old wives' tale if they have seemed of relevance and likely to interest the reader. Thus, many superstitions included here evoke the rituals and ceremonial of the Christian Church, while others are derived apparently from classical legend or from the rites of witchcraft and black magic, subjects that deserve volumes of their own.

Sources consulted have included a large number of reference books on the subject published on both sides of the Atlantic over the past fifty years or so, as well as personal knowledge. Where the authorities have conflicted on the details of superstitions discussed I have tried to include all versions, sometimes indicating the more plausible alternatives and sometimes leaving conclusions on the matter to the reader's discretion. As it is clearly impossible to list every regional variation of some of the most widely known superstitions, I have mostly confined myself to the more universally recognised versions, and my apologies go to those who fail to find a local favourite of their own.

My thanks go, as always, to members of my family and to my friends for their patience, suggestions and assistance while this book was in preparation, and also to the editors and production and design staff at Cassell for their co-operation.

David Pickering

# THE DICTIONARY

# A

**abracadabra** Magical invocation that is now associated chiefly with stage conjurors and pantomime witches but has in fact a much longer history as a cabbalistic CHARM. First mentioned in the writings of the Gnostic physician Quintus Serenus Scammonicus in the second century BC, abracadabra comprises the abbreviated forms of the Hebrew words *Ab* (Father), *Ben* (Son) and *Ruach A Cadsch* (Holy Spirit), though an alternative derivation relates the word to Abraxas, a god with snakes for feet who was worshipped in Alexandria in pre-Christian times.

The charm was said to have special powers against FEVERS, TOOTHACHE and other medical ailments as well as to provide protection against bad luck. Sufferers from such conditions were advised to wear metal AMULETS or pieces of parchment folded into a CROSS and inscribed with the word repeated several times, with the first and last letter removed each time until the last line read just 'A'. According to the thinking behind the charm, the evil force generating the illness would decrease as the word grew shorter. Once the charm had proved effective (after a period of nine days), the wearer was instructed to remove the parchment cross and to throw it backwards into an eastwards-flowing stream before sunrise.

Such charms were, according to Daniel Defoe in his *Journal of the Plague Year* (1722), widely worn in London in the seventeenth century as protection against the plague. Simply saying the word out loud is also said to summon up strong supernatural forces, hence its use by contemporary stage performers and entertainers throughout the West.

**accident** An unintentional misfortune or other occurrence that has no apparent cause, but which the superstitious generally blame upon sinister forces. Echoing the Christian doctrine of an omnipresent God, popular folklore has often attributed accidents to some hidden influence or else to the working of luck, blaming such everyday mishaps as sick ANIMALS and broken pots on ley lines (invisible paths that criss-cross the land and possess strange powers), DEVILS and their agents, such natural phenomena as the phase of the MOON or the flowering of a certain plant, or just the fates in general. In the East Midlands of England, for instance, accidents are said to be most likely when the BEAN plants are in flower. According to some interpretations, outwardly innocent happenings around the home may threaten dire consequences. Thus, a PICTURE that falls off the wall for no obvious reason, or a window blind that comes down without warning, are omens of death that should not be lightly ignored. Even picking up things that have been accidentally dropped on the floor is risky: much better to get someone else to pick them up and then to withhold any word of thanks — then both parties not only avoid ill luck but may also get a pleasant surprise.

Specific examples of accidents that are somewhat perversely good omens include the Japanese belief that if a patient's medicine is accidentally spilt then he or she will shortly recover.

*See also* BREAKAGES; CUTLERY; MIRROR; SALT.

**acorn** The fruit of the OAK, which has been associated with a variety of superstitious beliefs since time immemorial. The oak was venerated by the Druids in pre-Christian times and was similarly revered by many early civilisations, including ancient Rome (the goddess Diana was often depicted wearing a string of acorns). The Norse legend that Thor sheltered from a thunderstorm under an oak tree has led to the belief that having an acorn on a windowsill will prevent a house from being struck by LIGHTNING, hence the popularity of window blind pulls decorated as acorns.

In Britain, one old tradition has it that if a woman carries an acorn on her person it will delay the ageing process and keep her forever young (a reference to the longevity of the oak tree itself). Young lovers, meanwhile, may place two acorns, representing themselves and the object of their affection, in a bowl of water in order to predict whether they have a future together: if the acorns drift towards each other they are certain to marry. Back in the seventeenth century, a juice extracted from acorns was administered to habitual drunkards to cure them of their condition or else to give them the strength to resist another bout of drinking.

**actors and actresses** The theatre has a larger body of time-honoured superstitions than any other branch of the arts, and actors and actresses are renowned for their often obsessive preoccupation with protecting their luck. Many leading performers insist on following the same routine before each appearance and carry charms of various kinds (*see* AMULET; TALISMAN); they may also refuse to change any detail of their costume if they have had success while wearing it. Zsa Zsa Gabor, for instance, though famous for her fabulous jewels and costumes, always wears a worthless child's ring for good luck. WHISTLING in a dressing room is regarded as particularly unwise and the offender may well be asked to leave the room, turn around three times, and spit or swear (*see* SPITTING) before he or she can beg to be allowed back in. This taboo may well date from the days when changes in scenery were signalled by whistles, rather than by tannoy. Similarly, wishing an actor good luck before going on stage is considered to invite disaster by TEMPTING FATE, hence the tradition of telling an actor to 'break a leg' (presumably because worse mishaps than this are unlikely).

Certain plays are said to be especially unlucky, usually because they incorporate supernatural scenes or references to WITCHCRAFT. Actors are almost universally reluctant to quote from or even to name Shakespeare's tragedy *Macbeth*, preferring to refer to it instead as the 'Scottish play'. With its GHOSTS and witches' invocation of supernatural spirits, the play is notorious for the long list of serious (even fatal) accidents that have befallen productions over the years. Incidents blamed on the tragedy have included the destruction by fire of the theatre in Lisbon where it was staged in 1964 and a spate of accidents and illnesses that plagued a production presented by the Royal Shakespeare Company in 1967. The play's unlucky reputation was hardly relieved by the once widespread practice of presenting it as a means of boosting receipts in otherwise unsuccessful repertory seasons. Similar fears surround the pantomimes *Ali Baba and the Forty Thieves*, *Babes in the Wood* and *Bluebeard*, all of which also have undesirable reputations.

The colour GREEN has particularly strong associations with ill fortune in the theatre and many performers refuse to wear it (a particular problem in the case of works featuring Robin Hood in his Lincoln green). Casts have even been known to return scripts bound in this colour. This mistrust may date back to the days when by convention a green carpet was laid down when a tragedy was to be performed, or else to the use of limelight, which cast a greenish glow over the stage and tended to make actors dressed in green invisible to the audience.

Other taboos connected with the theatre include prohibitions on the use of real FLOWERS, drinks and jewellery on stage; never allowing PEACOCK feathers to enter a theatre (or, in the USA, a picture of a peacock or ostrich); never setting CANDLES in groups of three either in the dressing room or on the stage; never allowing performers to be presented with bouquets at the stage door before the play has begun; never wearing BLUE or YELLOW (which has the power to make performers forget their lines); never dropping a COMB or spilling a MAKE-UP box (which must never be tidied up); never looking in another performer's MIRROR while he or she is putting on their make-up; never putting one's SHOES on a chair in the dressing room; never hanging PICTURES in dressing rooms; never using yellow for stage curtains; never siting a peephole to view the audience anywhere but in the middle of the curtain; never allowing knitting in the wings (a superstition associated with the magic of KNOTS); never opening a new show on a Friday (*see* DAYS OF THE WEEK); and never speaking the final line of the script before the first night.

The presence of a cross-eyed person (*see* EVIL EYE; EYE) backstage is considered ominous, and a black CAT crossing the acting area similarly warns of ill luck. A good dress rehearsal is also widely considered a bad omen (probably for the very good reason that it may promote a false sense of security). Picking up a thread of COTTON from the dressing room floor and finding that it will go all the way round one's finger without breaking is said to be good luck among performers and a sign that a contract is in the offing. Other welcome events include an actor's shoes squeaking on his first entrance, discarded shoes landing flat on their soles, finding that one has been given a part that calls for the wearing of a wig, and the first ticket for a production being bought by a relatively elderly man or woman. Somewhat perversely, falling over during the course of a performance is said to bring a production good fortune (as long as it does not happen on a first entrance, in which case the performer is fated to forget his lines). One Continental superstition, incidentally, suggests that lines can be learned more easily if the actor or actress sleeps with the script under his or her pillow.

**adder** Poisonous SNAKE, which, as the only venomous reptile found in the British Isles, has attracted to itself a host of superstitious beliefs. According to ancient British custom, simply coming across an adder is bad luck, unless the snake is killed immediately (anyone killing the first snake seen in the spring is said to be assured of good luck against enemies in the coming season). Another belief has it that an adder cannot be killed before sunset unless beaten with an ASH stick or else rendered helpless by murmuring a special CHARM (the first two verses of Psalm 68). To trap the snake in the first place the procedure is to draw a circle around the creature and then make the sign of the CROSS inside it. The presence of a live adder on the doorstep, moreover, is a sure omen of death in the household, while dreaming of adders is an indication that a person's enemies are plotting against them, according to one ancient Dorset superstition.

Actual adder bites can be treated, according to gipsy lore, by killing the snake and rubbing its body against the site of the wound or else by coating the bite with a paste of fried adder fat (a course of action described by Thomas Hardy in his novel *The Return of the Native*). An alternative treatment suggested in the seventeenth century was to hold a live PIGEON to the wound until it had absorbed all the poison, or else to slaughter a chicken (*see* COCK) or SHEEP and place the bitten part of the body against the still warm carcass (which turned black when the poison had been absorbed). Simpler cures include the application of an ointment comprising ROSEMARY and BETONY mixed with water or the drinking of goosegrass juice and wine. In Wales, the effects of an adder bite can be negated by leaping over water before the snake has disappeared.

More beneficent is the use of a dried or cast-off adder skin, which, wrapped around the affected part, is alleged to have the power to cure RHEUMATISM, HEADACHES or pricks from THORNS and, if hung above the hearth, will protect the whole household from FIRE and ensure good luck. Swallowing a potion containing powdered adder skin will remedy any problems with the spleen or, eaten as a soup with chicken, will cure consumption. Other superstitions concerning adders include the erroneous but commonly held belief that they swallow their young when frightened and the incorrect assumption that they are deaf because they lack visible ears (they detect sound vibrations through the tongue).

**adder stone** A perforated or glass-like stone, naturally occurring, that is traditionally believed to have magical powers. Adder stones were venerated by the Druids and are still thought to be particularly efficacious against diseases of the eye and as charms (*see* AMULET; TALISMAN) guaranteeing protection against evil. Such small stones, of various colours, have been credited with curing children of WHOOPING COUGH (particularly in Scotland), with preventing nightmares, with ensuring success in legal cases and with assisting in recovery from adder bites. Superstition has it that such stones, otherwise known as 'serpent's eggs' or 'snake eggs', are created from the hardened saliva of adders massing together at certain times of the year. According to popular belief, adder stones can be tested by throwing them into a flowing stream – only those that float are the genuine article. The perforations are said to be caused by the tongues of snakes before the stones solidified.

**adder's tongue fern** Small species of FERN that is believed to possess strong healing powers. So named because of its forked spikes, the plant has been credited by British folklore with curing adder bites and countering other evils associated with SNAKES, and was once widely used as an ointment for minor cuts and wounds (the ointment being particularly effective if made from plants gathered when the MOON is on the wane). It is still found in some medicinal lotions and is sometimes drunk as a tea to cleanse the blood.

**afterbirth** The placenta, expelled after CHILDBIRTH, which is held to have certain magic properties. One of the best-known traditions relating to afterbirth concerns the number of lumps in the placenta or the number of 'pops' that are made as it burns: either reveals how many children a woman is going to have. Another old belief links the time the placenta takes to burn to the newly delivered BABY's life expectancy, though it should be noted that some authorities insist that burning the placenta is unlucky and advise that it should be buried instead.

*See also* UMBILICAL CORD.

**agate** An impure variety of quartz, valued as a GEMSTONE and the BIRTHSTONE for June, around which a number of curious beliefs have accumulated since ancient times. Called agate, according to Pliny, because large numbers of such stones were to be found near the River Achates in Sicily, the stone was once thought to have the power to render someone invisible, as well as the strength to turn an enemy's sword against himself. Agate's other alleged properties in different cultures have included defence against the EVIL EYE, the treatment of FEVER and poisons, the cooling of boiling water, the gift of an eloquent tongue, the bestowing of better eyesight (*see* EYE), the promotion of fertility (relating to both childless women and CROPS), protection against STORMS and LIGHTNING, luck in love, and increased athletic prowess (if worn around the neck together with a few strands of LION's hair).

Of the many different forms of agate, jasper is said to staunch bleeding and lessen pain. In former times a piece of jasper was often placed on the stomach of a woman in CHILDBIRTH (it was also respected as a treatment for EPILEPSY and as a means to conjure up RAIN and stop draughts). Red-veined agate is one of the more prized varieties, the red supposedly the ossified blood of the gods, while the possession of green agate is reputed to guarantee the owner a happy life.

**age** The British tradition that it is unlucky, particularly for a woman, to reveal one's age is thought to have originated in the ancient fear of numbering things (the NUMBERS themselves being vulnerable to the influence of evil spirits). A way round this superstition is offered by one old custom, according to which a lover may determine a partner's age by attaching a single HAIR taken from his or her head to a gold RING, suspending it in a GLASS and counting the number of times it strikes the sides (once for each year lived).

*See also* LONGEVITY.

**ague** *see* FEVER.

**aircraft** The crews and passengers of the world's airlines observe innumerable personal superstitions, carrying lucky AMULETS, ritually following the same routine before each flight and so forth. Plane crashes are said to occur in groups of three, though crews are unlikely to comment on this prior to take-off as it is considered unlucky to talk of crashes at this time. Crews also have, as in the theatre, a prejudice against real FLOWERS being allowed on to their aircraft and sometimes ensure that the seatbelts of vacant seats are neatly crossed so as not to provoke invisible evil spirits. Touching the wood of a living tree is generally recognised as a good defence against misfortune in the air, and extra protection will be afforded to a crew member who empties his pockets on to the ground as a sacrificial offering after making a safe landing.

*See also* GREMLIN.

**albatross** Large seabird, capable of long-sustained flight, which has been considered a symbol of ominous portent among SAILORS since time immemorial. The appearance of an albatross, said to be the incarnation of a drowned seafarer's soul, is thought to herald a coming storm and any droppings that the bird deposits on deck cannot be removed but must be left to weather away if luck is to be preserved. Killing an albatross is especially foolhardy and will bring permanent misfortune to both SHIP and crew, a tradition promoted by Coleridge in his *Rime of the Ancient Mariner*. Running somewhat against this tradition, it should be noted, was the sailors' custom of killing them so as to make tobacco pouches out of their large webbed feet. The albatross's gliding flight, meanwhile, has given rise to the popular idea that the bird can actually sleep in mid-air.

The superstitions surrounding the albatross have survived into modern times: Scottish seamen have been known to object to the use of Swan Vesta matches because the SWAN on the box resembles the albatross (swans are traditionally feared in Scotland anyway), while in 1959 the crew of the cargo ship *Calpean Star*, which was carrying an albatross to a German zoo, blamed the bird for a series of mishaps that befell them during the voyage (when the bird died on the ship fifty of the crew demanded immediate release from their work). Such is sailors' fear of the albatross, and by extension of virtually all birds, that in 1958 the crew of the *Queen Elizabeth* demanded and obtained the removal of a budgerigar named Joey who was accused of being the source of various problems that had plagued the ship.

**alectromancy** Method of divination, in which a white COCK is placed in a circle divided into twenty-six segments, each containing a grain of wheat. The order in which the cock eats the grains as a magic incantation is delivered will spell out the answer to any question previously posed, be it an unknown lover's name or the identity of the next ruler. A cock thus employed predicted the coming to power of the Roman Emperor Theodorus in ancient times, and over the centuries the practice has been resurrected for various purposes in many countries.

**All Hallows' Eve**   *see* HALLOWE'EN.

**almond** The almond tree and its blossoms, according to Greek myth, had its origins in a story of doomed love. Briefly, Phyllis was transformed into such a tree after she committed suicide when her betrothed, Demophon, failed to appear on the day set for their marriage (he was in fact merely delayed). The Roman writer Pliny alleged that eating five almonds was a cure for DRUNK-ENNESS, while later authorities have had it that almonds will prove fatal if eaten by FOXES and will also prevent the onset of CANCER if taken on a daily basis.

**amber** Yellowish fossilised vegetable resin, associated with several long-observed superstitions and widely regarded as one of the luckiest GEM-STONES. According to the legends of the ancient world amber originated as the tears of the sisters of the dead Greek hero Meleager, and pieces of amber have been worn in AMULET form since classical times in the belief that they bestow medicinal benefits (particularly on children) and offer protection against WITCHCRAFT and NIGHTMARES. In more recent centuries amber has been especially valued as a preventive against the plague (it was also formerly suggested that wearing amber made a woman smell more desirable to her lover, hence the tradition of mothers giving their daughters a necklace of amber beads as a wedding gift). As late as the twentieth century, amber has been credited with curing such ailments as WHOOPING COUGH and ASTHMA.

**ambulance** The ambulance, though it is a relatively recent innovation, has already gathered to itself a body of superstitions that are widely observed (probably due to the dread that the appearance of such a vehicle often inspires). As early as 1908 children in London were heard chanting variations of the following rhyme:

> Touch your toes, touch your nose,
> Never go in one of those.
> Hold your collar, do not swallow,
> Until you see a dog.

Some people insist that anyone who sees an ambulance should hold their breath and pinch their nose until the vehicle is out of sight, or, as the rhyme suggests, until they catch sight of a DOG (preferably brown or black in colour). Failure to observe this may result in the death of the patient being carried in the ambulance. In flying circles, pilots consider it very unlucky to accept a lift in an ambulance.

*See also* CARS.

**amethyst** GEMSTONE, usually of a deep red-wine colour, that is purported to have particular significance in relation to strong drink (*see* DRUNKENNESS). Taking wine or other liquor from a cup made of amethyst was said, in ancient Greece and Rome, to prevent the drinker becoming drunk, and if the stone was worn as an AMULET it was reputed to cure alcoholism completely. In extension of this, the stone was traditionally worn by priests in the Middle Ages as a symbol of sober living and humility, and was also credited with curing such minor ailments as HEADACHES, TOOTHACHE and GOUT. Engraved amethysts were formerly believed to protect against NIGHTMARES, plagues, locusts, thieves, STORMS, hail, infidelity and other misfortunes and were particularly prized by hunters (an echo of the stone's identification with Diana, the Roman Goddess of the Hunt).

**amulet** A CHARM that is worn as a necklace, bracelet or other decoration about the person in order to benefit from its magical properties. Usually made from a GEMSTONE, bone or other natural material, the amulet (from the Arabic *hamala*, meaning 'to carry', also the name of the neck cord from which the faithful suspended their Koran) has a long history and is known to virtually all cultures. Among the most familiar amulets are the RABBIT's foot, the HORSESHOE, the four-leaf CLOVER, DICE, TEETH, BIRTHSTONES, CORAL and medallions bearing the images of the saints (notably ST CHRISTOPHER), as well as lucky coins, rings, stones, photographs and sundry other items. The ancient Egyptians laid great store in amulets featuring the ankh (a symbol of life) and the eye of Horus (a powerful deity, originally the Sky or Sun God). The early Christians, meanwhile, believed themselves safe if they wore St John's Gospel around the neck, carried relics of the 'true CROSS' or else inserted a slip of paper bearing the Lord's Prayer into one of their shoes.

More recent manifestations of such thinking have included the charm bracelet, to which are attached miniature metal likenesses of such 'lucky' symbols as boots and horseshoes (a custom of late Victorian origin) and a short-lived fad for wearing a violin's D string around the waist in the hope that the wearer would benefit from its harmonious associations. Charms peculiar to specific regions include the red pepper, which is revered for its luck-giving qualities in Italy. The wearing of such amulets is said to bestow general protection against the EVIL EYE and against bad luck, witchcraft and disease rather than against one threat in particular (more accurately the role of the TALISMAN).

**angelica** Plant that is valued in cooking for its aromatic stalks but which also has its uses in superstition. Associated with St Michael the Archangel and sometimes called the 'Root of the Holy Ghost', angelica is also supposed to have various magical properties and was once thought to provide protection against witchcraft as well as against the plague, rabies and other serious illnesses. In keeping with its sacred associations, it is also said to dispel thoughts of lust in the young.

**anglers** The pastime of fishing for pleasure has given birth to several superstitions. Many anglers observe the rite of throwing back the first fish they catch so as to appease unseen spirits, while others spit (*see* SPITTING) on their bait for luck and place lucky COINS on the float. Bad luck is risked by changing rods between casts, discarding a float that has proved lucky, putting the keep net in the water before catching anything, baiting the hook with the left hand, sitting on an upturned bucket or telling another person how many fish one has caught. Right-handed fishermen should never cast over their left shoulder; and if the fish refuse to bite, one remedy, according to the Scottish, is to throw a fellow angler in the water and then haul him out as though he were a fish himself. Swedish anglers also believe that a rod will prove useless if stepped over by a woman.

*See also* FISHERMEN.

**animals** Innumerable species of animal are credited with supernatural powers, including the ability to see the future and kinship with the spirit world (probably a relic of the veneration of certain animals in ancient times). Various animals are feared as omens of misfortune or death (*see* SEVEN WHISTLERS) and may be suspected of being witches' FAMILIARS or the DEVIL in disguise; while others, by way of contrast, are welcomed as harbingers of good fortune or indeed as protectors against evil. Observation of animal behaviour, meanwhile, may furnish the knowledgeable with advance warning of changes in the WEATHER or even of important events in human affairs, such as the imminence of the outbreak of WAR.

Belief in the magical nature of the animal world was once much stronger than it is now, and in many cultures animals were considered almost the equal of humans. This meant that they were sometimes held to be subject to the same laws, and many tales survive from the Middle Ages of animals being blamed for misfortune and even being taken to court for their misdemeanours. As well as livestock and domesticated species, such creatures as rats, caterpillars and even ants, beetles and leeches were called to account for themselves in this way. The proceedings usually culminated in a sentence of death despite the efforts of the defending lawyers (in the case of some leeches tried in Lausanne in 1451 the accused were allowed to live but sternly warned to leave the district within the space of three days). The last such animal trial is said to have taken place in England in 1777, when a dog was brought before a court in Chichester. Other measures against offending animals included exorcism and the use of various CHARMS.

Many superstitions concerning animals have their origin in the folklore of rural communities and are closely connected to the welfare of those involved in animal husbandry or other work on the land. Thus, FRUIT TREES should always be planted with a dead animal of some kind beneath their roots to guarantee a good crop, and farmers will never make any compliment about the condition of an animal entered in a competition but will instead express the hope that it meets with some accident, in order to avoid TEMPTING FATE. Buying and selling an animal are fraught with danger, for fear of offending against the creature's magical potential, and various superstitions are still encountered from time to time even among livestock dealers, such as never refusing a reasonable offer for an animal's purchase so as not to risk its premature death.

In folk medicine, most really effective potions and spells include animal ingredients, as though their consumption or application will allow a patient to benefit from the animal's magical properties. Thus impotent men will be fed parts of a rabbit, famed for its procreative abilities, while sufferers from WHOOPING COUGH will be fed hairs taken from a donkey, which makes a similar braying noise.

Animals attributed with specific magical powers in many societies include the BADGER, the BAT, the BEAR, the BOAR, the BULL, the CAT, the codfish (see FISH), the COW, the CRAB, the CROCODILE, the DEER, the DOG, the DOLPHIN, the EEL, the ELEPHANT, the FLOUNDER, the FOX, the FROG, the GOAT, the HADDOCK, the HARE, the HEDGEHOG, the HERRING, the HORSE, the LAMB, the LION, the LIZARD, the MOLE, the MOUSE, the OYSTER, the PIG, the PORPOISE, the RABBIT, the RAT, SHEEP, the SNAIL, SNAKES of all kinds, the TENCH, the TOAD, the WEASEL, the WOLF and the WORM.

See also BIRDS; FISH; INSECTS.

**Ankou**   see CHURCHYARD WATCHER.

**ant**   The humble but hard-working ant has long exercised a fascination on superstitious people, and numerous beliefs surround it. Among other traditions, it is thought unlucky (in the British Isles at least) to destroy an ants' nest because ants are the reincarnation of children who have died unbaptised. The discovery of ants in the house is sure to be followed by the master of the house falling ill (though, in contrast, considerable prosperity is at hand if ants build a nest close to the door). Treading on ants will trigger a shower of RAIN, and bad WEATHER can be expected if a colony of ants are observed to be unusually active or busily carrying their eggs to a new location.

In Cornwall, where ants are called muryans and are supposed to be either FAIRIES in the last phase of their life on earth or the transmuted souls of ancient Druids punished for refusing to accept Christianity, there is an old belief that a piece of tin left in an ants' nest at a certain period in the MOON's cycle will be magically transformed into SILVER. Elsewhere, it is contended that ants never sleep and that eating ants' eggs with honey is a sure treatment for those suffering from unrequited love. Ants' eggs were once much used in potions for treating various illnesses, and the bodies of crushed ants were particularly valued for their efficacy in curing WARTS when made into a paste with vinegar and a SNAIL. In Scotland, DEAFNESS was sometimes treated by pouring a potion of ants' eggs and onion juice into the affected ear.

**anvil**   *see* BLACKSMITH.

**aphrodisiac**   The quest for a love potion that actually works has preoccupied the superstitious for centuries, and the list of suggested concoctions is virtually endless. These have ranged from various perfumes, some with narcotic effects, to recipes based on such exotic ingredients as MANDRAKE, URINE, human hearts, bulls' testes and semen. SALT is often added to such mixtures to stir the passions, and most have to be prepared while intoning some magic incantation (*see* CHARM). Other foods with allegedly aphrodisiac properties have been said to include APPLES, artichokes, asparagus, CABBAGE, LEEKS, LETTUCE, LIZARDS, OYSTERS, parsnips, partridge, truffles and turnips. Even the humble POTATO and TOMATO have been valued as love stimulants at one time or another.

In order to concentrate the effects upon a particular person, many spells dictate that something containing the 'essence' of that person – a sample of their HAIR, NAIL parings or bodily fluids – must be included in the potion. Other useful ingredients include cantharides (a preparation made from the Spanish fly), cinnamon, ginger, ginseng, MARIGOLD, ONIONS, rhino horn, stag antlers, ST JOHN'S WORT and PERIWINKLES, which should be eaten powdered with earthworms in meat. If impotence is the problem, superstition is not short of a remedy; suggested solutions include eating the fat from a RABBIT's kidneys. To make a rival impotent, however, the procedure is more simple and involves tying KNOTS in a length of string – the person concerned will only regain his virility when the knots are untied.

Superstition also recommends a number of passion-killing preparations, enabling frustrated lovers to forget old affairs and to concentrate on more fulfilling new ones. Among the more challenging 'anaphrodisiacs' are potions incorporating such ingredients as mouse dung and lizards soaked in urine, as well as infusions of POPPY.

*See also* SEX.

**apple**   The apple tree and its fruit are associated with a host of superstitious traditions, many presumably inspired by its central role in the story of the biblical Eden (though the fruit eaten by Adam and Eve is not actually identified as an apple in the original account). Apple trees that produced blossom and fruit simultaneously were one of the features of the Celtic paradise, and the apple is ever-present in the mythology of the Greeks and Romans as well as in Norse legend. Avalon, the paradise to which King Arthur was called, was probably named after the Welsh word *afal*, meaning apple. Later on, in medieval times, a farmer could lay claim to a piece of common land by enclosing it and planting an apple tree on it.

Apple orchards have been regarded as hallowed places since Roman times, and in many parts of the world the destruction of an orchard is an act to be dreaded by all concerned (in the seventh century AD an offender who cut down an apple tree was obliged to pay a fine of one cow). In various parts of England, including the West Country, the old custom of apple-howling or WASSAILING is still sometimes observed, usually on TWELFTH NIGHT. The farmer and his family go into the apple orchards after dark to eat hot cakes and drink cider, some of which is offered to one of the trees. They fire guns into the branches and bang pots and kettles while singing a special apple wassailing song, the aim being to drive away evil spirits and thus guarantee a good crop the following season. Another associated ritual is miming the action of picking up bulging sacks of apples, in the belief that this prophecy will be fulfilled later in the year. In the USA, a glimpse of the SUN on Christmas morning is an encouraging sign that the apple trees will prosper, particularly if the trees are subsequently blessed by rain on ST SWITHIN'S DAY, before which the fruit should never be picked and eaten. The appearance of blossom on an apple tree in the autumn, however, is an omen of death (in some societies an apple is placed in the hands of a child who has died, as a symbol of innocence).

At harvesting time, it is considered most unwise to leave one apple on the tree after the rest have been picked, and if the apple remains there until the following spring a death is sure to occur. Conversely, however, in some areas an apple is always left on the tree to appease unseen spirits. A German superstition, meanwhile, claims that an apple tree will prosper for many years if the first fruit of the season is eaten by a woman who has had many children (it is also said elsewhere that a good year for apples is also a good year for twins).

The apple has always been particularly associated with love and marriage. To reveal a future spouse's identity, a boy or girl should name a few apple pips after intended partners and place them on his or her cheek, the most likely prospect being represented by the last pip to fall. If a solution is still unforthcoming, placing a single apple pip representing a potential partner in a hot fire while intoning 'If you love me, bounce and fly, if you hate me, lie and die', and then observing what happens, might produce the required answer. If the pip bursts with the heat the signs are good – though an opposite conclusion is drawn from this in Sussex, where the quiet burning of the pip promises a successful affair. Squeezing a pip between the fingers until it flies out, and noting where it goes, will indicate the direction in which the home of a future true love is to be found. In Austria, a girl may cut an apple open on St Thomas's Night to examine the pips: if there is an even number of pips she will marry soon, but if one of the pips is cut then trouble can be expected and she may never find a husband.

If the pips have been tried without success, there remains the stalk. Young girls who want to know the initial of their true love's first name twist the stalk once for each letter of the alphabet: it will snap at the right letter. To establish the first initial of his surname the same procedure is followed while tapping the apple with the severed stalk until it pierces the skin.

In other fields of human endeavour, gamblers are said to favour counting the pips of an apple when choosing a lucky number to bet on (see GAMBLING).

A poultice of rotten apples was once recommended for curing rheumy eyes, and potions employing both blossom and fruit were widely used in beauty treatments. Apple blossom, incidentally, should never be brought into the home, or illness will follow. When eating an apple (claimed in a proverb supported by modern scientific thinking to keep the doctor away if consumed daily) superstition dictates that the fruit must always be wiped clean first, otherwise the Devil will appear. Finally, ancient wisdom has it that no bad woman can make good apple sauce.

See also HALLOWE'EN; WART.

**April Fools' Day** The first day of April, on which special licence is given to the playing of practical jokes. Possibly descended from an ancient Roman festival, the custom took hold in France around 1564, when the date of the NEW YEAR was changed from 25 March to 1 January on the adoption of the Gregorian CALENDAR (which replaced the Julian calendar and entailed some rearrangement of the dates of certain festivals). Festivities marking the start of the New Year had for centuries been celebrated on the first day of April, postponed until then because 25 March fell in Holy Week. With the change in the date many French peasants played the trick of arriving unexpectedly on their neighbours on 1 April to fool them into thinking it was still the first day of the New Year. The day subsequently became enshrined worldwide as one on which to test the humour of friends and neighbours, the most popular jokes including sending people on pointless errands (the tradition has been increased in scope in modern times by the sometimes very plausible tricks perpetrated by the media).

Superstition has it that licence for such activities expires at twelve noon, and any jokes attempted after that time will bring bad luck to the originator of them. Anyone who fails to respond to tricks played on them in the proper spirit of tolerance and amusement will also suffer bad luck. It is further said that compensation for being fooled by a pretty girl will come in the form of marriage to, or at least friendship with, the girl in question. Marriage on April Fools' Day is not, however, a good idea for a man, for he will be permanently ruled by his wife. Children born on that day will experience good luck in most matters, but will only meet with disaster when it comes to GAMBLING in any form.

**apron** The apron, as the traditional garb of the working woman, is associated with a number of well-known superstitions. Most familiar is the old belief that putting an apron on back to front by mistake will bring good luck (as will changing the apron round on a day when things are not going to plan). Wishes made when reversing an apron on seeing a new MOON for the first time are almost certain to come true. An apron that falls off is a warning of bad luck or alternatively that the woman wearing it will have a baby within twelve months (in the case of young girls it is taken as an indication that their lover is thinking of them). If a nurse twists her apron strings when putting the garment on she can expect to be involved in some new project very shortly. In Germany, a man who wipes his hands on a girl's apron is, so folklore has it, bound to fall in love with her (though if this happens after the couple are engaged then an argument is sure to follow).

FISHERMEN fear meeting a woman wearing a white apron while on their way to their boat, believing that this will bring them bad luck on the coming voyage. They have even been known to turn back and not set sail until the next tide, by which time the danger is presumed to have passed.

The wearing of aprons by the Freemasons and Rosicrucians (a German Protestant movement with occult overtones) is thought to have had its origins in the apron that Solomon wore when constructing his temple, and similar superstitions do not seem to be attached to the aprons worn by some male workers.

**arch** Both natural and man-made arches of virtually all kinds have been credited with magical powers, generally relating to the belief that persons who are sick may be relieved of their ailments if they are passed under an arch. Arches of BRAMBLE rooted at both ends are particularly effective, as the thorns snag on any evil spirit attempting to go through and thus separate the disease-causing agent from the sufferer. According to some, however, the patient's future health will depend upon the condition of the arch, whether it be of bramble, stone or some other material: if the arch collapses, the patient's health too will go into decline. English folklore places particular value on the arch and credits it with being able to cure a host of conditions, from BOILS and BLACKHEADS to WHOOPING COUGH and RHEUMATISM.

**Ascension Day** In the Christian calendar, the day on which Christ ascended into Heaven (celebrated now on the

Thursday following the fifth Sunday after Easter). According to Welsh superstition it is unlucky to do any work on Ascension Day and those who do so risk accidents (as late as the 1880s miners in the slate quarries refused to go underground in deference to this old belief, and elsewhere even the act of putting out the WASHING was frowned upon as inviting bad luck).

The weather on Ascension Day is also taken as an indication of what is to come: if it is sunny, the summer will be long and hot, but if it rains, CROPS will do badly and livestock, especially cattle, will suffer from disease. It was an ancient belief in Devon that on Ascension Day the clouds always formed into the familiar Christian image of a lamb. EGGS laid on Ascension Day will never go bad and will guarantee the good luck of the household if placed in the roof. RAIN collected on Ascension Day is said to be good for inflamed or diseased EYES, while those suffering from GOITRE are recommended to bite into the bark of a peach tree at midnight on Ascension Day, so that the disease passes to the tree and the sufferer is cured. Finally, gifts to the blind or lame made on this day are sure to be rewarded with great wealth within the following twelve months.

*See also* ROOK.

**ash** The ash has always been of special importance among those trees and plants valued for their magical properties, and to damage an ash in any way is a perilous act. The ash played a crucial role in the mythologies of the Greeks, the Romans and the Nordic peoples (for the latter, in the form of the world tree Yggdrasil, which connects Heaven with Hell and is the source of the material from which the first man, Askr, was made), and was similarly revered in pre-Christian Britain.

Herdsmen and shepherds in the British Isles traditionally favour sticks or crooks made of ash, which they believe provide protection for their livestock against evil (most WALKING STICKS are made of ash to

this day), and diviners use forked ash twigs to detect the presence of underground copper mines. Scottish midwives once fed newborn babies a drop or two of ash sap as their very first drink in order to give them lifelong protection against witchcraft, while burying the parings of a child's FINGERNAILS under an ash tree after they have been trimmed for the first time is said to ensure that the child will have a fine singing voice. Other peoples maintain that the ash is particularly fatal to SNAKES, which detest even its shadow and would rather risk fire than crawl over one of its twigs; in the USA, wearing a sprig of ash in one's hat is considered a safeguard against snakebite.

Where the weather is concerned, if the OAK comes into leaf before the ash a good summer is to be expected, as explained in a traditional English rhyme:

If the ash tree appears before the oak,
Then there'll be a very great soak.
But if the oak comes before the ash,
Then expect a very small splash.

One of the more ominous superstitions connected with the ash tree is that, if its winged seeds fail to appear, a member of the royal family or some other prominent person is sure to die (it is said that no ash tree in England produced seeds in the season preceding the execution of Charles I in 1649). Ash leaves with the same number of divisions on each side, however, are harbingers of good luck and should be worn or carried about the person after chanting the following rhyme:

Even ash, I do thee pluck,
Hoping thus to meet good luck.
If no good luck I get from thee,
I shall wish thee on the tree.

In England a young girl may discover the identity of her future husband by placing an even-leaved sprig of ash in her left shoe or glove, or else in her bosom – she will marry the first man she meets. Alternatively she could sleep with the sprig beneath her pillow, to see her true love in her dreams.

Children prone to BEDWETTING may be cured by gathering and burning ash seeds and placing the remains in the bed with them. In former times passing a child with rickets three times through a newly created cleft in an ash tree at sunrise was widely believed to be an infallible cure for the ailment (though it would return if the tree died). Chips of ash cut at a certain time may be used to treat other conditions, such as WARTS and WHOOPING COUGH, and back in 1688 a two-day nosebleed suffered by James II was reportedly staunched by this means.

*See also* ASHEN FAGGOT; ROWAN.

**ashen faggot** A variation on the YULE LOG custom that was once traditionally observed at CHRISTMAS. A peculiarity of the festive folklore of the West Country, the ashen faggot comprises a bundle of ash sticks bound up with nine bands of green ash, which are set alight on Christmas Eve using a fragment left from the previous Christmas's fire. According to the custom, young girls select one of the bands of green ash as their own and wait for it to burst into flame – the girl whose band is first to catch fire will be the first to marry. This tradition, which is sometimes credited to the Christian myth that Christ was given his first bath before an ashwood fire, but probably has pagan origins, is still maintained in some Devon inns. It is customary for a round of cider to be drunk as each band breaks.

**ashes** The ashes of a spent ritual FIRE have numerous uses in the superstition of many cultures. These are particularly valued as a fertility CHARM, ensuring (when taken from a fire at Easter or Midsummer and scattered over a field or mixed with seeds) that the coming crop will be a good one. In ancient Egypt, the ashes of men with red hair were considered particularly conducive to bountiful harvests. Ashes have even been mixed into the food given to livestock to promote their health.

In Britain and the USA ash provides some protection against witchcraft, and in Wales ashes from fires lit during the Beltane festival (*see* MAYDAY) were formerly placed in shoes to safeguard the wearer from the threat of coming sorrow. In Yorkshire, ashes spread over the hearth on New Year's Eve or St Mark's Eve (or else from the burnt bedstraw on which someone has just died) will give a hint as to what the coming twelve months have in store. Footprints discovered in them the following morning prophesy a death if they lead towards the door, but anticipate a new member of the household if going in some other direction. Many reports exist of people identifying the shape of coffins or wedding rings in the ashes of their fires, giving unmistakeable clues about coming events. Lovers were also formerly known to trace patterns relating to possible partners in the ashes of a fire in the belief that this would help decide their union. In Ireland, the Isle of Man and Lancashire, men could establish who their future wife would be by scattering ashes in a quiet lane at HALLOWE'EN and waiting to see which girl followed the trail first: the ashes would ensure she became his.

According to French tradition, ashes will preserve a household from storm damage if scattered over it, while in South America and elsewhere ashes tossed in the air play an important role in the ritual of rain-making. In the USA, there is a popular prejudice against sweeping out the ashes of a spent fire after four in the afternoon and similarly during Christmas or on a Friday (*see* DAYS OF THE WEEK). The farming communities of North Carolina have also been known to recommend sprinkling livestock with ashes to protect them from infestation by LICE.

The ashes of the dead have great symbolic significance in many cultures throughout the world and are much revered in some regions for their magical properties. In Africa, there are numerous records of human ashes being mixed with food and eaten by relatives in the belief that they will inherit some of the dead man's attributes.

*See also* CINDERS.

**aspen**   Also called the shiver-tree, the aspen is best known for its trembling leaves which stir in the slightest of winds. Folklore has it that the aspen shivers in shame and horror because its wood was used for Christ's CROSS, or because it failed to bow when Christ passed by. The aspen is prized for its efficacy in treating a range of medical ailments, particularly FEVER (in which the patient shivers like the tree). The sufferer pins a lock of his or her HAIR to the nearest aspen while uttering the rhyme: 'Aspen tree, aspen tree, I prithee to shake and shiver instead of me', and must then return home without uttering a word or the charm will not work. An alternative is to cut a small hole in the tree at midnight and place the sufferer's nail-parings into it before closing the hole up and thus trapping the fever permanently (*see* FINGERNAILS). In Cheshire, locals similarly recommend rubbing WARTS with BACON and then hiding the bacon in a slit in an aspen tree: the warts will fade from the sufferer's skin and reappear in the tree's bark.

**ass**   *see* DONKEY.

**asthma**   Respiratory disorder, often the result of an allergy, which has inspired several superstitions of ancient origin. One of the oldest treatments was that recommended to the Romans: twenty or so CRICKETS with a little wine. Many centuries later, sufferers in Cornwall were advised to roll COBWEBS into a ball and to swallow them to effect a cure. In the sixteenth century, cures included consuming a raw CAT, swallowing foam collected from the mouth of a DONKEY or, perhaps a little more appetising, sticking to a diet of boiled CARROTS for the space of two weeks (the vitamin A in carrots may have a beneficial effect on the lungs).

**astrology**   The tradition of 'reading' the stars and predicting from their relative positions what the future holds. Broadly speaking, the months of the year are divided into a ZODIAC of twelve houses, each with its own symbol and characteristics which determine a person's emotional capabilities and ambitions. In 'judicial' astrology the movements of the stars are related to human affairs. The resultant horoscopes published in newspapers and magazines are generally dismissed by the serious scientific establishment, but retain a compulsive fascination for millions who not only know their own star sign but are also versed in their alleged strengths and weaknesses, as dictated by professional astrologers.

The study of the stars has ranked among the intellectual preoccupations of all the world's major civilisations. First developed by the ancient Babylonians, it continues today as a respectable science in the officially approved form of astronomy. Offering some kind of logic behind the apparently random happenings of daily life, astrology, which first fell foul of established scientific thinking in the sixteenth century, suggests that the movements of the planets and the ensuing events are expressions of divine will. Critics claim that it is ludicrous to suggest that one-twelfth of the world's population will all experience 'a pleasant financial surprise' or a 'falling out with a close friend' on the same day, but this is an over-simplification of the system, which depends not just on the day of birth but on the precise hour.

In defiance of all the logical arguments against them the predictions of the astrologers do sometimes impress − perhaps inevitably, due to the law of averages. Examples that have been cited in support of the 'science' of astrology have included the warnings that were signalled by the positions of the planets in November 1963 just before the assassination of President John F. Kennedy. The same stars failed, however, to give any notice of the outbreak of the Second World War in 1939 − though repeated predictions of Allied victory during the course of the war played a big part in boosting morale, to the extent that some Members of Parliament demanded the silencing of the astrologers because their optimism threatened to undermine the willingness of the public to make the necessary sacrifices for the war effort. On the German side, Adolf Hitler was notorious for his reliance upon what his astrologers concluded (as indeed were many other military leaders before him).

The positions of the planets, particularly those of the SUN and the MOON, have long had an occult relevance and are of primary importance in the preparation of innumerable potions and spells. Many plants and other materials only retain their magical properties at given times of the planetary cycles. Back in the fifteenth and sixteenth centuries astrological information was considered particularly useful in medicine: the planets were believed to govern the welfare of the internal organs and the zodiac to influence the surface anatomy. Treatments depended upon analysing the planets' effect upon the four bodily 'humours': blood, black bile, yellow bile and phlegm.

**astronauts** Just as motorists and seafarers have developed their own codes of superstition, so too have the world's space travellers. Many of the superstitions observed are based on much older, time-honoured taboos, such as avoiding the wearing of unlucky COLOURS and considering perfect rehearsals for take-off an ill omen; several astronauts have also been noted for their attachment to good luck mascots. The disaster that nearly befell the Apollo 13 mission was inevitably attributed by many to the unfortunate numbering of the craft (*see* THIRTEEN).

**Aurora Borealis** The coloured lights that often appear in the sky in the extreme Northern Hemisphere as a result of charged solar particles being attracted towards the Earth's magnetic poles. The Aurora Borealis, also known as the Northern Lights, the Burning Spears and the Merry Dancers, is particularly revered by the Eskimo or Inuit peoples, who interpret them as the spirits of the blessed dead sporting in the Heavens. Other peoples have seen in them more ominous portents, and in lands where they only make occasional appearances they have been considered a precursor of WAR (a tradition strengthened when the lights were seen as far south as London in 1939 and again as far south as Cleveland, Ohio just before the Japanese attacked Pearl Harbor). In Northumberland the lights are sometimes called Lord Derwentwater's Lights in memory of the display that occurred on the night of 24 February 1716 when James, Earl of Derwentwater was executed for his part in the failed rebellion of that year.

**axe** As one of the earliest tools invented by man, the axe is associated with several ancient superstitions. Made of IRON, itself considered a magical metal, the axe came to play a prominent role in the rituals of pagan religion and its image is to be found at such sacred sites as Stonehenge. Witches were alleged to 'milk' axes and thereby to steal the milk from all the cows in the area, while others used a piece of AGATE balanced on a red-hot axe blade to search for buried treasure: if the agate stuck to the axe there was nothing to be found, but if it fell off and rolled three times in the grass then treasure lay hidden in the direction that the agate had taken. An upturned axe was also formerly used in the detection of THIEVES. The suspects were obliged to dance in a circle around it until the axe fell over; whoever the haft was pointing towards was regarded as the culprit.

In some European countries it is said that cattle persuaded to step over an axe on their way to the fields in the spring will be impervious to evil influences. In the USA, meanwhile, it is considered unlucky to carry an axe into the home, as this will bring about the death of a member of the family, and bad luck is also to be expected in the wake of any dream in which an axe appears.

# B

**baby** A substantial body of time-honoured superstitions surrounds the subject of babies, many of them reflecting the natural concern of parents for the welfare of their offspring. The superstitious start drawing conclusions the moment a new baby has arrived and take particular note of whether it is born with hands open or clenched shut: if the palms are open, the child will show an honest and generous nature, but if they are closed the child clearly has a mean streak. A baby born with teeth is likely to turn out to be selfish when older or alternatively may die young or become a murderer (in central Europe this may mean that it is a VAMPIRE). A blue vein across the nose, meanwhile, prophesies that the child will die by DROWNING. If the infant has no hair on its head, though, it is sure to grow up quick-witted and intelligent.

By way of greeting the baby into the world the Irish recommend SPITTING on it, while the Welsh suggest rubbing a little honey on its head. In Scotland, placing a KNIFE on the doorstep of the house where the birth has taken place will protect the infant by preventing a witch or other agent of harm from entering the house (no evil spirit can cross over IRON or steel).

Babies should always be nursed for the first time on the right side; if not, they will grow up left-handed. Should the mother experience any difficulty in producing milk, she should drink beer, eat fennel and honey or else apply a poultice of PARSLEY. Wet nurses, meanwhile, may ensure that their milk does not dry up by ignoring calls from outside the house, never burning wood in the hearth and never holding a NEEDLE by the point. If the baby refuses to suck, it has probably been bewitched and measures should be taken to break the spell.

Weaning should start on one of the Church's holy days, ideally on GOOD FRIDAY or failing that when the MOON is on the wane. It should not be attempted in the spring, or the baby will be prematurely grey-haired, and certainly not on CHILDERMAS DAY. Mothers should on no account offer a child the breast once it has been weaned: this will harm the infant's luck in a variety of ways, and in Wales to do so means that the child will swear constantly when grown up.

A baby's first soiled nappy should be left unwashed, and subsequent nappies should not be left out to dry when the moon is up for fear of attracting its baleful influence. Also on the subject of nappies, mothers in the USA are careful not to use old nappies for a new baby, since to do so promises that the child will grow up a thief. In England, it is said that allowing a baby to urinate in a fireplace will hasten toilet-training, and this has the added advantage of ensuring the child's future good behaviour.

Care should be taken not to wash a newborn baby's right hand for the first three days (or, according to some, in the first year of life). Doing so may also wash away the infant's good luck, particularly in financial matters. According to Welsh superstition, the water used to bath a baby should be deposited under a tree in leaf to promote the child's healthy

16

growth (throwing the water from its first bath over the roots of a tree in bloom ensures that the child will be good-looking as an adult). Weighing a baby is not advised in some European cultures. Doing so, they believe, is an insult to God, from whom the child has come; He may therefore take the child back at a young age as a punishment.

Whether born in a hospital or at home it is imperative that the child should be carried upstairs rather than down on leaving the room where the birth has taken place (midwives have even been known to clamber on to furniture placed in the doorway so as to satisfy this requirement when the room where the child has been born is at the top of a house and there are no further stairs). The logic of this particular custom lies in the contention that the babe cannot expect to go up in the world if it heads off downwards at the very start. When a child born in hospital leaves for home, modern superstition dictates that it is unlucky for the baby to be placed on a rear seat and that he or she should be carried instead in the front. Once the baby is safely home, the proud parents are advised to carry the infant three times round the house to provide protection against the colic.

Announcements of birth are widely acknowledged through the observance of various customs. Friends and relatives drink to the health and long life of the new arrival. In some areas anyone who visits a house where there is a newborn baby – whatever his or her business – is not allowed to leave before drinking a TOAST and having something to eat (this sometimes holds true right up to the day of the baby's CHRISTENING).

Saying that the baby is beautiful might seem the polite thing to do, but may be resented in some Jewish households because doing so threatens harm from the EVIL EYE. This has to be countered by chanting, 'Whoever gave you the evil eye may it fall on them' three times in Yiddish. Jewish mothers also suggest that it is unlucky and possibly fatal to the child's health to watch a baby sleeping. Calling a baby an 'angel' is equally unwise as this is TEMPTING FATE to take the child directly to Heaven. Care should also be taken by visitors not to step over a crawling infant, which will stunt its growth. Moreover, tickling the baby on the feet or under the chin will cause it to grow up with a stammer.

Presents traditionally offered to a new baby come in various forms. In northern England it was once customary to give an EGG (representative of the Trinity with its three parts, the shell, the yolk and the white), SALT, and some good BREAD (in some cases also matches to light the way to Heaven, meat and drink) when a baby made its first call on friends or relatives – an occasion known as 'puddening'. Gifts of baby clothes or toys are now more usual, and most babies benefit from gifts of money as a result of the old custom of crossing a baby's palm with SILVER, which is said to fend off evil spirits. New-born babies are themselves thought to be lucky, and those who kiss a newly arrived infant are sure to benefit from its luck-giving qualities (some say the baby will share the temperament of the first person to give it a kiss after its own mother).

Many more superstitions concern the clothing chosen for the very young. In order to confuse the DEVIL and thus to protect young children from his attentions it is considered advisable to dress a baby in the clothes of the opposite sex. Some Irish mothers have been known to continue to dress their boys in petticoats and their girls in trousers up to the age of fourteen. Newborn infants should never be wrapped in new sheets or garments when dressed for the first time, and some midwives used to bring along an old apron or other piece of cloth specifically for this purpose. Additional protection will be afforded a newborn baby who is wrapped in some article belonging to its mother or father (mothers in Ireland and elsewhere sometimes wrapped a pair of trousers belonging to the father around their neck while they were in labour in the belief that this would lessen the pain).

Mothers are advised to dress baby boys in BLUE because the colour, which is associated with the Virgin Mary, provides protection against evil (dressing girls in pink was a later invention with no particular significance). It goes without saying that babies should never be dressed in BLACK, as they will surely die before they have left childhood. When dressing a baby, incidentally, it is thought unlucky to pull clothing over its head and far preferable to start with the feet. After the baby clothes have been grown out of a mother should think twice before disposing of them: if she fails to keep back at least one item then she is certain to bear another child (the same applies to disposing of the CRADLE).

Other superstitions relating to the very young include the traditional notion that a baby's future luck can be foretold by observing which hand the child first uses to pick something up. If it is the right hand, then good luck will attend him or her throughout life, but if it is the left then the baby's future life will be plagued by misfortune. In Louisiana, further information about a baby's future may be obtained by placing before the child a BIBLE, a pack of CARDS and a silver COIN: if the infant reaches for the Bible it has a bright and happy future; if it goes for the cards it will be a gambler; and if it chooses the coin it will do well in business (if a bottle is added as one of the choices and the baby selects it, it is sure to grow up a drunkard).

It is considered particularly unlucky for a baby to be allowed to see its reflection in a MIRROR before the age of six months, and any baby that does so is sure to die before it is a year old. Cutting the baby's nails with SCISSORS before it has reached the age of one also risks misfortune and a life of crime (biting them off with the TEETH, however, guarantees good luck). The child will also die if its HAIR is cut before twelve months have passed. It is also unlucky to place a baby on a TABLE, to carry it in a FUNERAL pro-

cession and, according to US superstition, to toss it playfully in the air (to do so risks the child growing up slow-witted).

Babies should never be passed through an open WINDOW for this will retard their growth, but they will benefit from a good sneeze (*see* SNEEZING), which rids them of evil spirits. Painful teething can be relieved by supplying the baby with a suitable AMULET, which may be in the form of a cowrie shell, a fossil shark's tooth or some other 'magical' item. Sore EYES can be relieved by a few drops of mother's milk, while other conditions such as BIRTHMARKS can be alleviated by the application of saliva. Inhabitants of New England claim that it is a good sign if a baby contrives to fall out of bed three times before the age of one, and even better if it falls downstairs before the same age. Most people agree that the auguries are good if a baby learns to do things in the right order, that is, crawling first, then walking and finally talking (in the USA, it is claimed that giving the child a little water in a thimble will hasten its progress in this last challenge). If a baby smiles in its sleep, it is talking to the angels.

One last cautionary superstition warns that if a baby looks at a woman from between its legs then the latter is fated to become pregnant very shortly.

*See also* AFTERBIRTH; BREAD AND BUTTER; CAUL; CHILDBIRTH; CHILDREN; NAMES; TWINS.

**bachelor's button** Small button-shaped flower, variously identified as double red campion, upright crowfoot, buttercup, white ranunculus and white campion, which was once used by young men as a means of foretelling the success or failure of an intended love affair. According to very ancient rustic tradition, one of these flowers should be picked early in the morning and kept in the pocket for twenty-four hours: if still fresh at the end of that time then a successful outcome could be expected, but if withered the affair would not prosper.

**bacon** In some parts of Europe and the USA bacon is credited with certain healing powers, but only if it has been stolen rather than acquired legitimately. Such purloined bacon is particularly valued for its effectiveness against WARTS, which will disappear when rubbed with a rasher or two, and is also considered of use in treating FEVER and constipation. In Devon it is said that if cooking bacon curls up in the pan a new lover is about to arrive.

*See also* PIG.

**badger** An ancient rustic belief from Yorkshire reasons that the badger has longer legs at the back and shorter legs on one side in order to help it to run across and up a slope. Elsewhere in Europe, badgers' TEETH are particularly prized by gamblers, who claim that carrying one on the person guarantees success in any wager as well as bestowing good luck in general.

**baking** Various superstitious beliefs surround the all-important business of baking BREAD and similar foods, depending as it does upon the apparently magical action of yeast and ovens. Among the most widely observed of these is the superstition that no scraps of uncooked dough or pastry must be left over, or the entire baking will be spoiled and bad luck will follow. Rather than throw away such remnants, cooks are advised to make them into small treats for children. Counting the NUMBER of loaves or cakes as they are removed from the oven is also unlucky and will cause them to go stale quickly. A loaf that emerges from the heat with a cracked crust is a sure sign that a stranger is about to arrive to share in eating it.

Dreaming of yeast, incidentally, is a guarantee of success in one's next project, though it also means that one's wife or lover is pregnant.

**baldness** Superstition offers several treatments for baldness, while warning also that sudden loss of HAIR prophesies the loss of a child, health or property. The problem can be avoided altogether by never cutting the hair when the MOON is on the wane, and in the USA it is said that cutting the hair as short as possible and then singeing the cut ends will encourage regrowth and prevent hair dying. When such things were obtainable, BEAR fat mixed with laudanum and rubbed on the scalp was sure to restore the hair, according to W. Bulleyn's *Book of Simples*. Failing this, a handy substitute is FOX fat or ONION juice, similarly applied. A more drastic remedy recommends rubbing copious amounts of GOOSE dung into bald patches. Rather more simply, a sufferer who stands bareheaded in the RAIN will never suffer complete hair loss.

**ball** According to time-honoured tradition it is possible for children to use an ordinary playing ball to find out what the future has in store for them. Before playing a game of catch, girls in northern England and Scotland may chant the rhyme:

Stottie ba', hinnie ba', tell to me,
How mony bairns am I to hae?
Ane to leeve, and ane to dee,
And ane to sit on the nurse's knee.

The number of times the ball is then caught indicates the number of children that can be expected. Similarly, a young girl may throw a ball against a wall or tree and learn from the number of times it bounces on the ground how old she will be before she meets her true love. A variant in which the ball has to be caught in the hands prophesies that a girl is destined to be an old maid if she catches it an odd number of times and a wife if she manages an even number of catches.

In times gone by, children often made balls of COWSLIPS and, with the words 'Tisty-tosty, tell me true, who shall I be married to?' (or similar), tossed them back and forth while chanting the names of prospective lovers. The name spoken whenever the ball fell was the most likely prospect. In sporting circles, it is considered most unlucky to hold three balls in the hand while serving in TENNIS, and equally unwise to carry a new ball still in its wrapping on to a golf course. Footballers, meanwhile, often like to touch the ball or to bounce it a given number of times before the start of a match.

**ballast**  Reflecting the superstitious ways of seafaring folk, a number of curious customs surround the gathering of STONES for use as ballast in SHIPS. In north-east Scotland there is a particular prejudice against using stones with holes made in them by shellfish, while elsewhere granite and stones that have come from demolished buildings and still have mortar attached are also rejected. Similar prejudices exist against the use of white stones in ballast.

**banana**  In the Caribbean, where they are a major crop, bananas are a particularly lucky fruit. A wish made while cutting a slice from the stalk end of a banana is bound to come true if a Y-shaped mark is revealed.

**banns**  The reading of a couple's banns in church prior to their WEDDING is a formal tradition that has inevitably acquired its own mythology. According to widely held superstition it is very unlucky for a couple to hear their own banns being read and any children they later have are bound to suffer as a result – probably by being born deaf and dumb. It is also unlucky if there is a break in the sequence of the three readings of the banns, which should be heard on three Sundays in succession. Further bad luck is risked if the wedding is called off after the final reading of the banns, an act that was once considered an insult to the Church and could be punished by a fine. In Scotland, couples were formerly advised against having their banns read at the end of a quarter and against arranging the wedding for the start of the following quarter as this was considered unpropitious for the future. After the third reading of the banns the bells in Scottish churches would sometimes be rung to bestow a further blessing on the couple and to drive away evil spirits.

**banshee**  Perpetrator of unearthly wailing that is much feared in Ireland and western Scotland as an omen of approaching death. The banshee is usually heard at night and its supernatural ululations are generally associated with a particular family or clan, who can often detail a history of such warnings from spectral (usually female) guardians. Examples of famous banshees include the one linked to the aristocratic Rossmore family of County Monaghan in Ireland, which was first heard in 1801 and has heralded the death of each successive heir to the baronetcy (including that of the sixth baronet in 1958).

Some claim that the banshee wail is made by the FAIRIES, who sense the coming of death and want to warn the family (*bean si* in Gaelic means 'fairy woman'). Alternatively the banshee is held to be a dead ancestor or perhaps the vengeful spirit of a woman who has suffered some wrong at the family's hands. In some parts of Scotland the banshee is known as the 'washer by the ford' because her figure is seen washing the bloodstained clothes of the person fated to die. Sometimes the banshee is not in the form of a voice, but is heard as a beating DRUM.

**baptism**  *see* CHRISTENING.

**barghest**  *see* DOG.

**barnacle**  Small marine crustacean commonly found on the bottoms of wooden boat hulls and other pieces of timber immersed in the sea for a long time. According to one time-honoured superstition, FISHERMEN claim that BARNACLE GEESE are hatched from barnacles (a belief derived from an older one in which the geese were said to emerge from pieces of waterlogged timber).

**barnacle goose**  The barnacle goose is so called because ancient superstition holds that they begin life as humble BAR-NACLES on ships' keels. Curiosity about the birds' origins was probably provoked in the first place because no one knew where their breeding grounds lay (in fact they are above the Arctic Circle) and no eggs or nests could be discovered. An alternative to the barnacle theory (which was taken quite seriously until the seventeenth century) was that they fell from trees overhanging the water – hence the lack of evidence of nests and shells. Giraldus Cambrensis, writing in his *Topographia Hibernica* in 1186, offered his own view on the subject, explaining that the geese

> are produced from fir timber tossed along the sea and are at first like gum. Afterwards they hang down by their beaks as if they were seaweed attached to the timber, and are surrounded by shells.... They derive their food and growth from the sap of the wood or from the sea, by a secret and most wonderful process of alimentation. I have frequently seen, with my own eyes, more than a thousand of these small birds, hanging down on the sea-shore from one piece of timber, enclosed in their shells and already formed.

Such was the confusion over the creature's genesis that many people were uncertain whether to class barnacle geese as birds or fish. This confusion proved convenient during LENT, when people were allowed to eat fish but not meat.

*See also* GOOSE.

**barren ground**   A patch of ground where nothing will grow, according to superstition because of a curse or because some evil event has taken place there. Ominous sites of this kind can be found all over the world, and there is usually some local legend to account for them. Among the best-known examples in the British Isles are the spot where the drowned body of the British admiral Sir Cloudesley Shovel was temporarily laid in the Scilly Isles after his fleet was wrecked in 1707 with the loss of many

lives (locals claimed he ignored the warnings of one of his seamen about the treacherous coast thereabouts), and the summit of Dragon Hill in Berkshire, where St George is said to have killed the dragon, whose blood permanently poisoned the soil. Other localities boast graves where the grass never grows. Notable among these is the grave in Montgomery churchyard of William Davies, hanged in 1821 for a crime of which he protested his innocence to the last.

*See also* MURDER.

**barring the way**   An ancient WEDDING custom, in which a newly married couple are not allowed to pass on their way after the ceremony until they have paid a small toll. Rarely observed today, the tradition required the couple's path to be barred by a rope or some other obstacle, and it was up to the best man or the groom to pay for it to be removed (the money would then be spent on drinking the health of the newly-weds). Originally, the bride and sometimes also the groom had to jump over the obstacle, which is some cases was a locked gate or a special 'petting stone' set in the earth. The most famous of these is the one on Holy Island: it is still occasionally crossed over by new brides, who must do it in one stride if their marriages are to be fortunate. In some areas the ceremony was accompanied by special verses singing the praises of the happy couple (a practice known in Northumberland as 'saying the noning').

It has been suggested that the custom was symbolic. The bride and groom were making the leap from one situation in life to a new one and the groom was being required to test his ingenuity one last time to prove himself worthy of his new wife – an idea that is still honoured today in the custom of 'nobbling' the car in which he is to drive her away.

**baseball**   The hugely popular US sport of baseball is renowned for the many superstitions observed by players. These apply even before the players reach the ground in the form of various rituals and taboos that can either preserve or destroy their luck. These include never putting a HAT on a bed, avoiding matches scheduled for Fridays and patting the head of any black bellboys in the hotel where the team is staying. If a player meets a member of the CLERGY on the way to the ground then a bad day can be expected, unless the player concerned keeps his fingers crossed until he meets a DOG. Once at the stadium, players are particularly heartened if they catch sight of a truckload of empty barrels passing by – a reference to the lorry that was said to have set the New York Giants on a legendary run of victories many years ago – or if they spot a red-headed woman in the stands (she may well be asked to give a player a HAIRPIN as a token of luck). Players also believe their luck will be improved if their number includes a left-handed pitcher. Among the bad omens are cross-eyed umpires (*see* EVIL EYE) and similarly afflicted women in the crowd, having to play with a damaged bat, finding a bat laid crosswise in front of the team dug-out, losing some item of team clothing and a dog walking on to the field.

In an attempt to safeguard their luck, players sometimes spit in their gloves (*see* SPITTING) and lay them down so that the fingers point to their own dug-out when they go out to bat. They are also reluctant to share their bat with team-mates, in the belief that each bat can produce only a given number of hits and it is unwise to give any of these away. One universally observed taboo concerns never discussing the fact that a pitcher has yet to allow an official hit: this applies to both teams, spectators present at the game and even television viewers at home.

**basil** Herb that is widely used in cooking and to which are attached a range of beliefs that vary from one culture to another. According to the Greeks, basil represents hatred and bad luck, while the Italians by contrast consider it a token of love. Hindus, meanwhile, believe that a leaf of basil placed on a corpse will ensure that the spirit of the dead person reaches Heaven. Elsewhere, it is maintained that the plant gives birth to scorpions.

**bastard** Children born out of wedlock have always been considered lucky. This odd belief may possibly derive from ancient Roman law, which acknowledged such 'natural' children as not bound by the authority of their biological fathers.

**bat** With their nocturnal flight and habit of roosting in secluded shadowy places such as ruins and caves, bats have long been associated with the darker side of superstition; in many cultures they are linked with WITCHCRAFT and death. Children once chanted various rhymes if they saw a bat, urging it to fly away, or, in the case of one old Cornish verse, even offering it bribes:

Airy mouse, airy mouse fly over my
  head,
And you shall have a crust of bread;
And when I brew and when I bake,
You shall have a piece of my wedding
  cake.

The appearance of a bat in a church during a WEDDING ceremony is considered a bad omen, and if a bat flies three times round a house or hits a windowpane this is a sure prophecy of the impending death of someone within. Equally ominous in many countries is the discovery of a bat actually in the house, which again threatens the life of one of the occupants or else is taken as a sign that the human occupants are about to leave. A near miss when a bat flies close by is a warning that the person concerned is threatened by betrayal or witchcraft at the hands of another.

More encouraging is the tradition that the sight of bats flying early in the evening is a portent of good weather, while in the Isle of Man good luck is bound to attend anyone who has a bat drop on them. People have also been known to carry a bat's bone about their person in the belief that it will bring great good luck. If a bat actually collides with a building, then RAIN can be expected. Other traditions suggest that witches sometimes turn themselves into bats in order to enter people's houses and that the sight of bats flying vertically upwards and then dropping back to Earth is a sign that the witching hour has come (*see* WITCHCRAFT). Witches, it is said, often include a few drops of bat's blood in the FLYING OINTMENT they are said to smear on their bodies before taking off on their broomsticks: the idea is that they will then be safe from colliding with anything, as bats appear to be. In order to keep witches away, superstitious people are advised to carry a live bat three times round the outside of the house, then to kill it and nail its dead body beside a window or else to the door of one of their outhouses.

In some countries, such as China and Poland, bats are symbols of long life and happiness, while in Australian aboriginal culture to kill a bat risks shortening a man's life. In Germany, gamblers were once reputed to attach a bat's heart to their arm with a red thread to bring them luck, while in Austria it was said that possession of a bat's right EYE brought with it the gift of invisibility. Elsewhere, bat's blood is often used in black magic, especially in voodoo and in the celebration of the black mass. Other superstitions concerning bats include one promising that anyone who washes their face in bat's blood will be rewarded with the ability to see in the dark. It is also said that slipping a few drops of bat's blood into a lover's drink will promote passion in the drinker. In past centuries, when sides of BACON were hung to mature in chimneys, bats were often blamed if bits of the meat went missing.

Bats' erratic flight paths led people in former times to believe that the creatures were blind – hence the common misconception that they can easily get entangled in a woman's hair, from which they can only be released by being cut free. The Earl of Cranbrook once tested this theory by placing bats in the hair of three female volunteers: the bats easily got themselves free.

*See also* VAMPIRE.

**bathing** The business of WASHING oneself clean is taken very seriously by the superstitious, who warn against certain practices. Particular attention is paid to the time of year when a person bathes, as evidenced by the ancient verse:

He who bathes in May will soon be laid in clay
He who bathes in June will sing a merry tune
But he who bathes in July will dance like a fly.

In various parts of the world it is considered unwise to wash the whole body as this threatens to wash away a person's luck (*see* BABY). Welsh MINERS, meanwhile, are said have a prejudice against washing their backs in the belief that if they do so the roof of the mine will collapse upon them. Bathers are also advised by superstition to begin their ablutions not at the feet but at the head, as this is the 'superior' part of the body (a custom that is backed by medical science because doing so lessens the chance of a headache due to raised blood pressure).

*See also* SINGING.

**bay** In ancient Rome the bay tree (a type of laurel) was sacred to Apollo and Aesculapius, the God of Medicine, and was associated with victory, honour and general good luck. It has retained these associations over the centuries, and until relatively recent times boughs of bay were popular as a form of CHRISTMAS decoration, just as they were when the ancient Romans celebrated the NEW YEAR. In the bay's ability to revive after most other plants would have died Christians saw a symbol of the Resurrection, and took to carrying it at FUNERALS.

The tree's medicinal properties continue to be revered, and bay leaves carried about the person are said to give protection against all manner of disease (just as a bay tree planted near a house was once said to safeguard the occupants from the plague and other ill luck). Bay is also considered an effective defence against evil spirits, GHOSTS and WITCHCRAFT, and remains one of the basic ingredients used by 'white' witches for their spells. The trees are also said to be immune from LIGHTNING strikes and thus offer a safe retreat in a thunderstorm (the Roman Emperor Tiberius always donned a crown of laurel in thundery weather). If a bay tree suddenly withers, however, very bad luck is in the offing – most likely the death of a member of the family. If all the bay trees in a country wither a national catastrophe, such as the death of the king or the arrival of plague, is to be expected.

Bay leaves can also be used as a means of divination. Soothsayers burned bay leaves to study how they were consumed by the flames, or inhaled the smoke as the leaves burned in order to experience the narcotic effects. If bay leaves burn noisily when thrown on to a fire, good luck will ensue; if they burn without a sound, misfortune will surely follow. Pinned to the pillow on the eve of ST VALENTINE'S DAY, bay leaves will also allow a dreamer visions of his or her future sweetheart.

**beans** Since ancient times bean plants have had special magical associations, being particularly linked with death and GHOSTS. Disciples of Pythagoras in ancient Greece observed a taboo against eating them, as did the ancient Egyptians. The Romans offered gifts of beans to the dead on what was called the Bean Calends, and customarily ate them at FUNERALS (beans still featured in British funeral ritual until the nineteenth century). Beans also have special significance in the folklore of various Japanese, Indian and African ethnic groups, and in the Far East bean flowers may be scattered around the house to ward off demons. Several North American Indian tribes also have special bean festivals connected

with ensuring a good crop in the future.

In European culture, the magical properties of beans are reflected by their role in several traditional tales, notably in the fairytale *Jack and the Beanstalk*. They were also once used in certain legal processes to decide a suspect's guilt. The accused was obliged to pick one of two beans from a bag: if the bean was black he was guilty of the crime, if white he was innocent. In former times anyone fearing the influence of evil could protect himself by chanting the tongue-twisting rhyme: 'Three blew beans in a blew bladder, rattle, bladder, rattle' as fast as he could three times in succession without drawing breath.

In the south-west counties of England local superstition insists that kidney beans must be planted on the third day of May if they are to prosper. Elsewhere gardeners are advised to plant their beans on the feast days of St David and St Chad (the first two days in March) or when the leaves of the ELM are as big as a farthing.

As a means of divination, cooks in northern England sometimes concealed a single bean in a peapod when preparing a meal (*see* PEA): whoever got the bean would be the first to marry. On MIDSUMMER'S EVE people were invited to hunt for three hidden beans, one peeled, one partly peeled, and the third unpeeled: finding the peeled bean promised a lifetime of poverty, the half-peeled bean a relatively affluent existence and the unpeeled bean great wealth. Rubbing the white inner lining of a beanpod on a WART is said to be an effective means of treatment, while the consumption of beanpods in wine and vinegar, or of the distilled water of the flowers, is said to promote beauty and improve the complexion.

The flowers of the bean provoke foreboding in many societies, largely through the ancient idea that the souls of the departed lurk in them. In some parts of the British Isles ACCIDENTS are said to be more frequent when the bean plants are in blossom (MINERS in particular are influenced by this tradition) and the appearance of a white bean plant in a bean patch is considered particularly ominous, prophesying imminent death. Superstition warns in particular against sleeping in a beanfield, for this will either bring on nightmares or else rob the sleeper of his sanity. The strong perfume emitted by bean flowers will similarly make a person light-headed or foolish.

*See also* TWELFTH NIGHT.

**bear**   The bear, though long vanished from the wild in most of Europe, is remembered in a variety of ancient superstitions and legends and still plays an active part in the folklore of the USA and Canada and other regions where it continues to thrive. Back in the times when bears were commonly seen at English fairs, trained to dance and tormented in bear-baiting booths, a number of curious beliefs sprang up based on erroneous ideas about the creatures' behaviour.

According to popular superstition, bears obtained their sustenance by sucking on their own paws, and literally licked their newborn cubs into a bear shape when first delivered. Bear fat was highly recommended as a safeguard against mildew and blight in vegetables if garden tools were coated with it, while boiling some bear's fur in aqua vitae and then wrapping it round the feet was said to cure fits. Other recipes involving bear fat offered cures for various aches and pains and also for BALDNESS, and it was said that a child with WHOOPING COUGH would be cured if given a ride on a bear's back. Eating a bear's heart was reputed to endow great courage, while bear's teeth were valued as a charm against TOOTH-ACHE (in the USA bear's teeth were commonly given to teething children). Sleeping on a bearskin, meanwhile, is said to be very beneficial for those suffering from backache.

English superstition also preserves the ancient notion of ghost bears, the most famous of which are alleged to manifest themselves at Worcester Cathedral, at the Tower of London and in Cheyne Walk, Chelsea.

Indian hunters in the USA and Canada revere the creature and always give their apologies to any bear they have killed, laying out the different parts of its carcass according to ancient ritual. Eskimos in particular follow a strict routine after killing a polar bear for fear of offending its spirit, while Lapp hunters who have killed a bear are considered unclean and are obliged to live apart from their fellows for three days. White backwoodsmen once maintained that bears bred only once every seven years, when the commotion was such that cattle for miles around would lose their own unborn calves. In both North America and Scandinavia people are often reluctant to name a bear, preferring such euphemisms as 'the old man' and 'golden feet' in order not to invite an attack.

**beard**   The wearing of beards has inspired extreme reactions in different societies over the centuries. Considered a sign of ungodliness to some early Christians, a symbol of faithfulness to the Sikhs and proof of personal strength to the Mesopotamians, the beard has come and gone according to the dictates of fashion. Taxes imposed on beards by Elizabeth I led to their virtual disappearance for a period during her reign.

In the current century the fact that beards have been sported by more than one British monarch has brought them an association with royalty, encouraging many subjects to grow their own. Modern superstition has it, however, that men with beards are not to be trusted and throughout Europe a man with a red beard is particularly suspect. The same applies to a man whose beard or moustache is one colour and his hair another. A rhyme from the USA expresses this prejudice very succinctly:

Beware of that man
Be he friend or brother,
Whose hair is one colour
And moustache is another.

The beard's power of renewal led to one ancient belief that facial hair was a divine gift and should never be trimmed, because an enemy might obtain the clippings and thus secure power over the wearer.

*See also* HAIR; RAZOR.

**beastins** A COW's first MILK after the birth of her calf, which is particularly prized among some European agricultural communities. According to ancient custom some of the milk is used for making puddings and some presented to favoured neighbours, who are asked to return the bottles unwashed (as cleaning them will endanger the health of the calf). Observing this superstition is said to promote the good luck of the whole herd.

**beauty** Superstition provides an almost endless choice of recipes and rituals designed to preserve and promote physical beauty, many of which may indeed offer some slight benefit. Among specific remedies are treatments for BALDNESS, BIRTHMARKS, BLACKHEADS, BOILS, HAIR, WARTS and many other medical ailments, both serious and trivial. Some are more drastic than others, ranging from concocting potions from wild flowers and herbs to touching a dead man's hand to eradicate skin blemishes (*see* DEAD HAND).

To promote one's overall beauty, European superstition recommends collecting DEW on the first day of May and then bathing in it (in Germany drinking cold COFFEE is said to be equally effective, while VAMPIRE tradition in Hungary recommends taking a bath in human blood). If a person still feels unattractive, one resort worth considering is employing any of a huge range of APHRODISIACS or taking some other secret action to convince a reluctant partner of one's charms. In the case of women, slipping a few leaves of VALERIAN into the UNDERWEAR, for instance, is bound to attract potential lovers and have the desired result.

**bed** The bed, scene of so many crucial human activities, has considerable significance in most cultures. Perhaps the most widely observed superstition today is that it is very unlucky to get out of bed 'on the wrong side' (the other side to the one on which you got into bed the previous evening, or alternatively the LEFT, or DEVIL's, side). Should the sleeper inadvertently get out of bed on the wrong side, the only hope is to make sure that when dressing he or she puts the RIGHT sock and shoe on first (the right foot should in any case always be put down first on getting up). Getting out of bed backwards is deemed lucky in some regions and unlucky in others.

The positioning of a bed in a room is all-important. If it is placed on an east–west axis rather than north–south, the person who sleeps in it is guaranteed to be plagued by NIGHTMARES (though some maintain that the reverse applies). In addition, it should not be placed so that the rays of the MOON fall across it nor so that it points towards the DOOR (because corpses in coffins are carried out feet first). Ancient superstition from the northern British Isles contends that no dying person can expect an easy end if their bed is positioned under the crossbeam of a house or else crosswise over the floorboards. The origins of this curious tradition remain unknown. Sweeping under a sick person's bed, shaving him in bed or moving the patient from one bed to another, meanwhile, are sure to hasten his death.

The business of making a bed is fraught with danger, according to superstition. It is particularly unwise for three or more people to make a bed, as one of them will die during the next twelve months, and mattresses should not be turned on certain days of the week (which days varies from one area to another, though Sunday and Friday are generally regarded as the least auspicious days for such activity). Penalties for turning the mattress on the wrong day range from turning away the affections of a lover to nightmares. In the case of newly delivered mothers, the mattress must not be turned for one month after the birth. In Oxfordshire, those who are anxious to avoid a life alone are advised:

If one day you would be wed,
Turn your bed from foot to head.

To preserve their good luck, bedmakers are also recommended to delay changing a bed that a guest has slept in until at least an hour after the guest has departed. It is unwise, moreover, to turn down the sheets early in the day as this invites evil spirits to rest there. Whatever the system employed, making the bed should be completed in one go, or the rest of the day will be troubled with interruptions and delays. SNEEZING while making a bed is considered unlucky and must be remedied by taking a little straw or stuffing from the mattress and throwing it in the fire. During the Second World War, incidentally, airmen habitually left their beds unmade when going out on a mission in the belief that this would ensure their safe return to them.

Sundry other superstitions connected with beds include placing two buckets of fresh spring WATER underneath to prevent bedsores; checking under the bed before retiring to make sure the Devil is not hiding there (single girls must not do this or they will never marry); never sitting on the bed of a sick person (for fear of being the next in the sickbed); never allowing another woman's children on the bed (unless, that is, the owner of the bed wants children herself); and never wearing a HAT in bed or allowing a hat to rest on it. Straw crosses tied to each corner of a bed will ward off bad dreams.

*See also* BEDWETTING; CHILDBIRTH; DREAM; SLEEP.

**bedwetting** Superstition is quite clear about the best way to eradicate the problem of persistent bedwetting by a child. The remedy is to roast, fry or boil a MOUSE and to feed it to the child concerned baked in a pie. If this fails, the child can be given a bag containing RAT or MOLE droppings, or several roasted slugs, to wear around the neck. If the problem still remains, the child must be taken to a graveyard and encouraged to urinate on the grave of a child of the opposite sex, in which case the difficulty should disappear for good. According to the Scots, children should also be discouraged from playing with FIRE before bedtime as this is held to intensify the problem.

*See also* GRAVE.

**bee** The value placed on bees is reflected by the many superstitions that abound concerning them. Bees are traditionally regarded as the bearers of goodwill from the gods (or by some as the souls of the departed), and the appearance of a swarm of bees in a person's garden is a sign of great prosperity in the offing – though some obstinately claim the reverse and warn that a swarm settling on a roof is an omen that the house will burn down. More ominous is the sight of bees swarming on a dead tree or hedge (or in the CHIMNEY), which all agree is a portent of death.

Exactly when the bees swarm is of significance, as summed up in the rhyme:

A swarm of bees in May
Is worth a load of hay.
A swarm of bees in June
Is worth a silver spoon.
A swarm of bees in July
Is not worth a fly.

Moving bees to a new hive must never be attempted without first informing the swarm of the planned move, in which case they will refrain from stinging the owner. Moreover, bees should only be moved on GOOD FRIDAY, or they will surely die, and they must never be exchanged for cash but must instead be bartered for other goods (stolen bees will fail to prosper). When moving the hive, the bees must never be carried over running WATER, for this will cause them all to perish. Owners of bees are also warned that they must never allow their swarms to be disturbed by the sound of argument or SWEARING, which will offend them and may cause them to leave. Bees who lack their usual industry, meanwhile, are a warning of coming misfortune, while bees who confine themselves to the hive know that RAIN is on the way. If the bees suddenly vacate their hive, death is at hand.

Dreaming of bees is lucky, and a bee flying into the house is an indication that a stranger is coming. If this happens, the bee must not be driven out of the house but allowed to leave of its own accord. A bee alighting on a person's hand is a promise of coming wealth, and in former times superstitious Scots caught the first bee of the season and kept it in their purse in the expectation that this would increase their riches. Another tradition, common to both US and English folklore, holds that bees will never sting a virgin who passes through a swarm.

Reverence for bees pre-dates Christianity, but Christians have also applied their own mythology to the creatures, claiming that the first bees were conceived in Paradise or, according to Breton legend, sprang from the tears of Christ on the CROSS. They also maintain that singing a psalm in front of the hive will give new heart to a swarm that is not doing well, and furthermore that at midnight on Christmas Eve the bees themselves hum Psalm 100 in their hives.

It is most unwise to kill one of these so-called 'Servants of God', and they should be kept informed of all the most important events that take place in the owner's home, particularly news of deaths and marriages within the family (if the bees resume their buzzing after hearing the tidings, they will remain where they are rather than swarming and flying away from their owner). In the case of a death, the bees may be appraised of the news by tapping the hive with the KEY to the front door, turning the hive around, tying black crepe round the hive, or (in Germany) chanting the rhyme:

Little bee your master is dead
Leave me not in my necessity.

When the FUNERAL of the bee's owner takes place, the hives must be 'turned' – that is, lifted an inch or two in the air (in some versions, the coffin must be similarly lifted at the same time). The bees should also be left a morsel of a wedding or funeral cake, and records exist of bees being offered samples of every item partaken by the mourners, including pipes, in powdered form, and tobacco, which apparently they devour with gusto.

Beeswax CANDLES have long been used in churches, especially in funeral services, and beeswax dissolved in water was credited in the Middle Ages as a cure for the condition of erysipelas (it is also said that the ashes of burned bees sprinkled over the shoes will cure flat feet). Finally, the sting of a bee is traditionally considered beneficial in the treatment of RHEUMATISM and neuritis (a notion partly backed by science).

*See also* BUMBLE BEE.

**beech** The beech was revered by the ancient Romans, who grew the tree in the sacred grove of Diana and liked to kiss it, lie in its shadow and pour libations of wine over its trunk. Subsequent generations, however, learned to distrust the tree, alleging that the presence of beechwood in a house causes difficulties in CHILDBIRTH and makes dying doubly traumatic.

*See also* YULE LOG.

**beet** Revered by the ancient Greeks, beets were offered to the gods at the temple of Apollo in Delphi, and continue to be prized for their supposed beneficial effects to this day. In particular, they are credited as a treatment for COLDS and HEADACHES and as a purgative for the liver and spleen. Eating uncooked beet daily is alleged to prevent CANCER.

**beetle** The ancient Egyptians may have revered the scarab beetle as a symbol of the Sun God Ra, but since then relations between man and beetle have rarely been warm. In 1587 a case was even brought before the court in the town of

St Julien in France, in which beetles were charged with wreaking destruction in the local vineyards. In a later generation the havoc caused among crops by the Colorado beetle was such that in the late nineteenth century some desperate US farmers even attempted to have the creature exorcised as if it were an evil spirit.

Most superstitions linked with beetles concern bad luck and prophecies of death. Perhaps the most widely observed tradition is the fear that death is in the offing if a beetle walks over a person's SHOE (it is also a sign of misfortune on the way if a beetle crawls out of a discarded shoe by the door). In Scotland, the appearance of a beetle in a room where the family are all seated is likewise an omen of terrible bad luck, which will be intensified if the creature is killed. Elsewhere in Europe beetles similarly signify death, storms and other kinds of ill fortune.

Of the countless species of beetle, a few have been singled out for special attention. The stag beetle, with its ominous-looking horns, has been linked with the DEVIL, while the burying beetle, said to have betrayed Christ to his pursuers in Egypt, used to be routinely killed by children in Scotland. The dung-beetle, which misled Christ's pursuers by telling them that their quarry had passed by a year previously, is allowed to live but is turned on to its back for telling a lie. Irish superstition has it that when a devil's coach-horse beetle arches its tail it is delivering a curse, while in England the tapping of the death-watch beetle in the timbers of an old house is a warning of imminent death (the tapping is really made to attract a mate). Conversely, though, German superstition claims that it is good luck if a cockchafer beetle (linked with fertility in pre-Christian times) settles on a person's hand. The cockchafer is similarly associated with good fortune in France, where it was formerly carried in processions.

In parts of Africa, throwing beetles into a lake is a ritual associated with rain-making ceremonies, and in many countries killing a beetle is said to bring on RAIN. Arab slave-owners used to tie beetles to an ever-shortening length of THREAD attached to a NAIL to force runaway slaves to return against their will. Finally, according to East Anglian belief, allowing a dead beetle to rot on a thread round a child's neck will cure the infant of WHOOPING COUGH.

**beggar**  Meeting a beggar in the street is said to influence a person's luck for the rest of the day. Whether this will be for better or for worse varies from region to region.

**bell**  Since earliest times bells have been employed in the world's religions and social rituals, and over the centuries have acquired an extensive mythology of their own. Bells in churches are sometimes 'baptised' in special ceremonies, given NAMES and decorated with flowers or engraved with special inscriptions designed to ward off evil. In extension of this tendency to treat bells as living beings, it is further contended that they will refuse to ring if they are insulted and may even exact revenge on anyone who harms them or tries to steal them (according to some authorities, they will sweat blood if terrified).

Bells are almost universally credited with the power of frightening off bad spirits, and in many parts of the world prized animals are fitted with bells to protect them against the EVIL EYE. The sound of bells is said to cause witches riding on broomsticks to plummet to the ground, and also to scare away SNAKES and MICE. In churches, a 'passing bell' is rung on the death of a local person, not only to summon the congregation to prayer but also to drive away any evil spirits lured by the presence of death. Bells also play a crucial role in the ancient Catholic 'bell, book and candle' ritual of excommunication, the bell tolling for the 'dead' sinner.

Ringing church bells at harvest time is recommended as a means of ensuring a bumper crop; their sound might also

**bellows**

cause a storm to abate by distracting the malevolent spirit behind the wind and rain. It was formerly believed that ringing church bells would protect a community from the plague, while in more recent times mothers in the USA have been known to give their children drinks from upturned bells to cure them of stuttering. In Scotland, back in the eighteenth century, a bell at the Chapter of St Fillan was much revered for its efficacy in curing mad people: the afflicted person was dipped in the so-called Saint's Pool and the bell, about one foot in height, was carefully set on his head. Immediately he would get better. Grease taken from bells is recommended for the successful treatment of various skin problems, among other conditions.

On the darker side, a bell that tolls without someone pulling on the rope is a widely feared omen of death, which will strike down a member of the parish within the space of a week. However, bells will also sound under their own volition to indicate the presence of a saint or to give warning of a crime committed nearby.

The image of the bell is widely associated with WEDDINGS, conveying protection from misfortune, and many modern good luck charms come in the form of a miniature bell. None the less, if a bell is heard to toll before the end of a wedding ceremony it may well be deemed a sign of bad luck, probably signifying the premature death of one of the happy couple.

A bell ringing during labour will ease the pains of CHILDBIRTH (expectant mothers have even been known to attach a bell rope round their waists). It is traditionally held that children born as the bell strikes the hour of three, six, nine or twelve will grow up with the gift of second sight and will also be able to see GHOSTS.

Specially cast handbells containing mercury, lead, silver, gold, tin, copper and iron, and buried in a cemetery to 'mature' for seven days, figure prominently in the rituals of necromancy, the black art of calling up the dead to divine the future.

SAILORS are particularly sensitive to the sound of bells and may interpret a bell tolling at the apparent touch of an unseen hand as an omen of shipwreck. Seafarers are similarly nervous of the ringing sound produced by glass tumblers and will quickly silence the noise in the hope of averting disaster. A SHIP's bell, moreover, is supposed to embody the very soul of the vessel and is consequently much respected: it is said that such a bell will never fail to ring, even if securely lashed, if the ship itself goes down.

In the case of handbells, if two bells ring simultaneously in the same house it is said that someone is about to leave. Ringing such a bell while holding it upside down is, according to US superstition, extremely perilous and certain to provoke misfortune of the worst kind.

British folklore in particular gives pride of place to several legends of drowned villages, where the bells of submerged churches can be heard still striking the hour far below the waves. Examples include Bomere in Shropshire; Kilgrimod, near Blackpool; and Caer Wyddno in Cardigan Bay, off the Welsh coast.

**bellows** Perhaps because of their link with the mystical power of FIRE, bellows feature in a number of superstitious beliefs. Giving bellows as a WEDDING present or otherwise lending them out is considered most unwise, and it is widely held that leaving a pair of bellows on a TABLE will lead to a domestic argument or even to a death in the household. On the positive side, one ancient English belief has it that leaning against a pair of bellows will benefit anyone suffering from RHEUMATISM.

**belt** Wearing a belt is said by some to provide protection against witchcraft, and furthermore that wearing a belt blessed by a priest will ease the pains of CHILDBIRTH. Throwing away a belt is, however, unwise, for a witch may use it to acquire control over its former owner. Accidentally twisting a belt when putting it on is supposedly a sign that the wearer is in love, or else (in the case of girls) that the wearer will bear TWINS. If it is twice twisted, this is an omen that the girl concerned will marry a coloured man.

**berry** In rural areas a bumper crop of autumn berries on trees and in hedgerows is a sign of a hard winter ahead, the extra berries being provided by God for the welfare of birds and other animals as well as man. One old Yorkshire saying sums up this belief succinctly: 'Many haws, cold toes'.

**besom** *see* BROOM.

**betony** Plant that has long been valued for its supposed medicinal properties. Apparently named after the biblical Beronice, whose bleeding was staunched by Christ, the plant has been credited over the centuries with preventing NIGHTMARES, promoting SLEEP, overcoming tiredness, safeguarding against witchcraft and, in reverence to the biblical story, stopping haemorrhages. In medieval times, people were advised to take a preparation of a little powdered betony and colewort every morning to prevent DRUNKENNESS.

**Bible** The sacred book of the Christian faith, which has, perhaps inevitably, acquired a reputation as a mystical object in its own right. In acknowledgement of the Bible's great significance in the Christian world, copies of it must always be treated with the utmost respect and anyone who destroys a Bible or otherwise mistreats it is said to put themselves at risk of divine retribution. Similarly, no object should ever be placed on top of a Bible, while trading in Bibles is also considered unlucky.

Simply leaving a Bible open is said to keep evil spirits away, and it was once quite common for busy mothers to leave their BABIES unattended but for the company of an open Bible left in their CRADLE. Sleeping with a Bible under the pillow is said to aid peaceful sleep and also to promote the wisdom and intellectual development of young children. One tradition observed in Yorkshire recommends concealing a page torn from a Bible under the threshold: any THIEVES entering the house will stumble when entering over this, betraying their untrustworthy character and alerting others to their presence. Verses from the Bible may also be worn about the person to provide protection against MADNESS and other maladies, and ailing animals were formerly sometimes fed bits of Bible to assist in their recovery. On the Scottish island of Colonsay it was said that the sick could be cured simply by fanning them with the pages of a Bible.

Perhaps the best-known manifestation of the Bible as a supernatural object is the science of bibliomancy, in which readers employ the book as a means of seeing into the future. Keeping the eyes closed, the reader – presumably confident that his hand is guided by God – stabs a passage at random with a finger, a pin or a SILVER knife, and then divines from the selected verse the answer to a specific query (copies of Homer and Virgil were used like this by the ancient Romans, as is the Koran by some Moslems today). The practice is often observed before noon on New Year's Day to find out what will happen over the following twelve months. One derivative of the custom, popular in the USA, suggests that a lover may divine the true character of a partner by consulting in this way the first chapter of the Book of Proverbs and reading the numbered passage that corresponds to the other's age. It is bad luck, however, for lovers to exchange Bibles as presents.

In a broader sense, the Bible lies at the heart of a vast body of superstition in the Western world, acting somewhat perversely as an authority for the idea of WITCHCRAFT by introducing the figure of SATAN and enumerating the demons who were to become the hierarchy of evil spirits venerated by occultists of later centuries. Though the Bible in its original form does not in fact demand that 'Thou shalt not suffer a witch to live' (a concept based on a mistranslation of the word 'poisoner'), the book has always been quoted as the ultimate sanction against black magic. Back in the Middle Ages, it was not unheard of for witches to be 'tried' by weighing them against the big Bible kept in most parish churches: if the accused witch proved heavier, she was allowed to go free.

*See also* BIBLE AND KEY.

**Bible and key** The use of a copy of the BIBLE and a doorkey in the business of love divination. There is a time-honoured ritual by which a girl may assess whether a suitor is right for her. First she inserts her doorkey between the pages of the Song of Solomon, binding and suspending the Bible with her garter or stocking; then she asks two friends to place their middle fingers on to the protruding keyring and they chant the 'Many waters cannot quench love' verse from the Song of Solomon. If the Bible moves at all during this ritual or falls to the ground, the proposed union is a good one; if nothing happens, the girl will never marry. The same procedure can be followed to determine a lover's faithfulness (the Bible will 'turn' to the right if all is well) or else to find out a future partner's initials, the alphabet being chanted until the Bible turns.

Virtually the same ritual (of which records exist from as early as the fourteenth century) was formerly employed in the detection of THIEVES. The names of the suspects were read out while passages from the Bible were recited; when the book turned, that would indicate who was the guilty party. Alternatively, the key was spun on top of the Bible until it came to rest pointing towards the culprit.

**billhook** A traditional agricultural cutting implement, comprising a curved blade with a hooked end fastened to a wooden handle. Like other old implements it is associated with several taboos,

the most important of which warns against resting a billhook on a TABLE, which invites misfortune.

*See also* SCYTHE.

**birch** Sacred to the Norse god Thor, the birch tree is associated with a host of superstitious beliefs which reflect the wood's usefulness in a wealth of applications from maypoles and brushes to arrows and spoons. The birch has always been respected for its protective powers, and many country people once wore sprigs of it to keep them safe from misfortune. Boughs of birch were formerly placed over doorways to prevent evil spirits from coming in, and the tree was widely credited with warding off wicked fairies and demons, who disliked its magical properties (hence the ancient custom of placing a sprig of birch over a baby's CRADLE). Naughty children were once beaten with birch sticks in the belief that the evil spirits within them would be driven out (just as brooms made of birch would sweep out any dirt). In many areas at Eastertime young girls were lightly struck with bundles of birch twigs decorated with strips of ribbon and silk, in the conviction that this would safeguard them from vermin, flies and back trouble over the coming year; adults once observed a similar practice on other holy days in order to promote each other's youthfulness.

Putting birch sprigs in the places where witches are supposed to gather (dung heaps and so on) will oblige them to hold their covens elsewhere, and adorning livestock with birch will similarly protect them from baleful influences. Planting a birch tree beside the front door is also a good strategy, for any witch meaning to enter must count every leaf on the tree before she can do so – a challenge that all but the most determined witches are likely to decline. The tree must not be allowed to touch or overhang the house, however, as this will only bring sickness and bad luck to those within. In some cultures the birch tree continues to be treated with healthy respect, and it is recommended that any person walking beneath one should cross their fingers to be on the safe side.

**birds** The apparently miraculous power of flight enjoyed by birds has inspired innumerable superstitions over the centuries. The fact that birds seemed literally to inhabit the Heavens prompted many primitive religions to cast their gods in the form of birds of various kinds, and many species have retained particular significance in folklore to this day. Soothsayers in ancient Rome learned to predict the future through their analysis of birdsong, while other cultures credited birds with having their own language and links with the supernatural, the birds themselves often being interpreted as the reincarnation of dead souls.

The appearance of certain birds (particularly those with black and white feathers) may be regarded as an omen of death or some other coming misfortune (*see* SEVEN WHISTLERS), while others are closely associated with WITCHCRAFT and the DEVIL. Some birds of apparently supernatural origin, moreover, appear to have attached themselves to particular families or offices in much the same way as the BANSHEE, appearing when a family member is dying. A famous example is the pair of white birds that appear when a Bishop of Salisbury is dying, supposedly seen as recently as 1911.

Among the best-known superstitions relating to virtually all species is the widely held belief that a bird flying into a room through an open window and then out again is a sure sign of the approaching death of someone in the household, as is the sight of birds flying around a particular house or a bird tapping against the windowpane or coming down the chimney. Apart from domestic poultry, many people refuse to allow a bird, caged or not, or its eggs, into their homes, and it is thought unlucky even to have bird-patterned wallpaper or crockery and other items with pictures of birds on them. Dark-coloured birds that fly around trees without ever seeming to settle are said to be the souls of reincarnated evil-doers, though another popular superstition (from France) maintains that when unbaptised children die they become birds for a time until accepted into Heaven.

Anyone hit by bird droppings can expect ill luck in the near future (though some people claim it is actually lucky), while a person starting on a journey is recommended on setting off to note the position of any birds flying nearby: if they fly to the right a good trip is foretold, but if they fly to the left the traveller would do well to stay at home, particularly if the birds are too many to count. Similarly, in a relic of the 'ornithomancy' of the ancient Romans, much can be gleaned from the direction out of which a bird call comes: if it is from the north, ill luck will ensue; if from the south, a good harvest; if from the west, good luck; and if from the east, love.

The death of a caged bird on the morning of a WEDDING indicates that the marriage will not prosper, and pet birds must be kept informed of important family events or they will languish and die. It is also unlucky to come across a dead bird outside the home and, in Scotland at least, children will spit (*see* SPITTING) on the corpse to ensure, they claim, that they are not given it for their supper. Lastly, parents are warned against feeding too many eggs to their children, which allegedly risks them growing up sexually confused.

*See also* ALBATROSS; BARNACLE GOOSE; BLACKBIRD; CHOUGH; COCK; CROW; CUCKOO; CURLEW; DOVE; EAGLE; HEN; KINGFISHER; LAPWING; LARK; MAGPIE; NEST; NIGHTINGALE; NIGHTJAR; OWL; PEACOCK; RAVEN; ROBIN; ROOK; SEAGULL; SPARROW; STORMY PETREL; SWALLOW; SWAN; THRUSH; WAXWING; WHEATEAR; WREN; YELLOWHAMMER.

**birth** *see* CHILDBIRTH.

**birthday** Echoing traditions relating to the celebration of the NEW YEAR, the progress of events on a person's birthday is said by the superstitious to herald the pattern of fortune he or she will enjoy over the following twelve months. In particular, people are advised not to cry on their birthday, which means they will cry every day of the coming year. Lucky days to be born upon include the first day of a month, a year or a cycle of the MOON.

*See also* BIRTHSTONE; CANDLE; FLOWERS; ZODIAC.

**birthmark** Superstition offers us a number of explanations for the appearance of birthmarks in the newborn, usually blaming them on some shock or evil influence to which the mother has been exposed during PREGNANCY (though this is now discredited). In some cultures birthmarks are considered lucky, the mark of God, while in others they are attributed to the influence of the DEVIL and expectant mothers are advised to sprinkle themselves with black PEPPER to ensure their BABY is not disfigured in this way. It is believed in some quarters that birthmarks will vanish if licked regularly by the mother in the baby's early weeks (a contention that is, extraordinarily enough, backed by science in certain limited circumstances). In the USA, babies who are born with a 'double' birthmark on the head are expected to travel widely and divide their lives between two continents.

**birthstone** The tradition that each month of the year has its own particular precious or semi-precious GEMSTONE or stones has persevered into modern times, fuelled by the vested interest of jewellers, while many other folk customs and beliefs have fallen into disuse. A person's birthstone depends on the month of their birth, and possessing the relevant stone, with its associated qualities, is 'guaranteed' to ensure the owner's continuing good luck. Conversely, it is sometimes maintained that it is unlucky to wear stones associated with other months – opal, in particular, will prove unlucky if worn by anyone not born in October.

Authorities sometimes differ over the exact allocation of the stones to the months, but the following list represents perhaps the most widely agreed version:

January: garnet (truth and constancy).
February: amethyst (sincerity and sobriety).
March: bloodstone (courage and presence of mind).
April: diamond (innocence and light).
May: emerald (success in love).
June: agate (health and longevity) or pearl (purity and tears).
July: carnelian (contentment and friendship) or ruby (courage and purity).
August: sardonyx (marital happiness).
September: sapphire (love) or chrysolite (happiness).
October: opal (hope).
November: topaz (fidelity).
December: turquoise (prosperity).

**black** Of all the colours, black is the one most closely associated with evil and death. In Western culture it is the traditional colour worn at FUNERALS – not so much out of respect for the deceased but as a recognition (dating from Roman times) that everyone is subject to the dominion of death. The DEVIL himself was formerly said to materialise out of choice as a black-skinned man, and up until relatively modern times in some remote areas people turned themselves right round on meeting a black man, just in case he was the Devil in disguise (conversely, it was once held that touching a black man would bring good luck). Witches, meanwhile, are traditionally depicted all in black with a black CAT or RAVEN among their most trusted FAMILIARS, and demons are said to prefer the form of black creatures, be they cats, DOGS or COCKS. On being confronted with an evil spirit, a victim may, it is said, distract the entity by offering the gift of something black, such as a black cock, and thus make good his or her escape.

As well as black cats being somewhat perversely a symbol of good luck, black

SHEEP are considered lucky. Shepherds regard the presence of a black sheep in a flock as a good omen, and general rejoicing traditionally surrounds the birth of a black lamb (though death and bad luck will ensue if the first lamb of the spring is black in colour or if a ewe bears black TWINS).

*See also* BLACK DOG; BLADE-BONE; WHITE.

**blackberry** Prized though the blackberry may be for its succulent fruit, the plant has long been associated with evil. Because the DEVIL is reputed to have cursed it after getting entangled in a blackberry bush when he was cast out of Heaven on what was formerly Michaelmas Day (11 October), it is maintained by some that blackberries should never be picked after that date because the fruit will have been spat on or otherwise fouled by him in retribution for the injuries he received (any remaining fruit is in any case usually well past its best by that date). In France, many people refuse to eat blackberries because of their Satanic links, claiming that it was the Devil himself who made the fruit BLACK in colour.

*See also* BRAMBLE.

**blackbird** In ancient British culture the blackbird was considered a messenger from the dead, and it has retained links with the unknown world of the hereafter ever since. Some families claim that blackbirds appear when the death of a family member is imminent, and such a tradition is thought to have inspired the traditional nursery rhyme about the 'four-and-twenty blackbirds baked in a pie'. Blackbirds are fiercely territorial, so it is perhaps inevitable that the rare sight of two blackbirds sitting together should be considered a good omen (though in Wales such a sighting is a portent of death). Hanging by means of a RED thread a bunch of FEATHERS taken from a blackbird's right wing will discourage strangers from sleeping in the house; if they persist in inflicting their company upon the household, however, slipping a blackbird's heart under the pillow of the sleeping person will oblige the visitor to divulge all his or her secrets. Like the RAVEN and CROW, the blackbird is sometimes depicted as a witch's FAMILIAR.

**Black Dog** Spectral DOG of ancient English tradition, which is reputed to appear at places associated with death. Many churchyards and isolated graves claim a Black Dog in local superstition, and sightings have also been reported at sites where MURDERS have been committed. Descriptions vary, some dogs apparently having huge eyes, while others lack heads altogether. Locals speak fearfully of the howling of the Black Dog, and many claim that the DEVIL himself often manifests in such a form.

**blackhead** A blocked pore leading to spots or other skin blemishes as suffered by many a teenager and post-adolescent despite recourse to soaps and other medication. Superstition suggests its own remedy for the problem, recommending afflicted persons to wait for a sunny day and then to crawl three times through the ARCH made by a BRAMBLE rooted at both ends, ideally moving in an east-to-west direction: if done correctly, the spots are sure to vanish.

**Black Penny** A COIN that was credited with magical powers by the people of Northumberland in the early nineteenth century. Owned by the Turnbull family of Hume Byers, the Black Penny was revered by farmers in the area for its efficacy in treating MADNESS in cattle. The coin was dipped in drinking water that was then given to the livestock, whose condition soon miraculously improved. Lent out by the family on many occasions, the Black Penny was eventually lost in 1827 when a farmer from Morpeth returned it in the post.

**black pudding** A sausage made from various offal products, principally blood, that is supposed to be of some use in divining the future. According to northern English superstition, black puddings should be 'named' after a courting couple before cooking: if the skin remains unbroken when the cooked sausage is removed from the oven, the couple's future together is bright.

**blacksmith** Because the blacksmith works with such mystical things as FIRE, HORSES and IRON, he has always been regarded as a somewhat magical figure himself (according to the Irish, bad luck will never befall anyone who follows that trade). Local legends often speak of ancient standing STONES or spectral horses making annual visits to the smithy in the dead of night, and the blacksmith has often been credited with more knowledge of the supernatural than other men. The blacksmith's anvil is a particular focus of magic, and it was once common for sick children to be taken to the blacksmith so that they could be held over the anvil and thus cured of their ailment. In some areas the patient was laid naked on the anvil while the blacksmith tapped the child lightly with his hammer three times to effect a cure. Blacksmiths were also respected as 'blood-charmers', capable of staunching a haemorrhage through their special knowledge.

Blacksmiths are traditionally reluctant to work on GOOD FRIDAY, claiming that the DEVIL will get them if they hammer NAILS on such an inauspicious day. Lastly, folklore fondly remembers the tradition that until relatively recent times allowed blacksmiths to marry eloping couples over the anvil at Gretna Green and other villages just beyond the Scottish border (though in fact it was not always the blacksmith himself who oversaw these ceremonies).

*See also* HORSESHOE.

**blackthorn** Prickly THORN, from which the Crown of Thorns worn by Christ at the Crucifixion is said to have come. Many people refuse to allow blackthorn into the house for fear that it will bring bad luck (a blossoming blackthorn branch brought into a house will precipitate a death in the family), though crowns of blackthorn, scorched in a fire, were once brought into English homes among the NEW YEAR decorations to guarantee good fortune in the coming year. In Worcestershire, similar crowns were burned to ASHES and then sprinkled over the first- or last-sown wheat to promote a good harvest. Tradition also has it that the blackthorn blossoms at midnight on old Christmas Eve (5 January).

**blade-bone** The shoulder-blade of a SHEEP or GOAT, as once widely used in the business of divining the future. Records exist of shoulder-blades, particularly those of BLACK sheep, being examined for their secrets as early as the twelfth century. A spot on the blade-bone is said to predict a death in the family, while other marks may be deciphered to reveal the truth in certain financial matters or else to find out if adultery is taking place. In the past, some experts even claimed that they could foretell happenings of national importance, such as royal births and the outcome of battles, by such examinations. It is particularly important that the bone, scraped clean of all meat, should not come into contact with anything made of IRON, which will render it useless as a tool for such divination.

One specific use of the blade-bone in divination relates to finding out the sex of an unborn BABY. According to the Welsh, the father should pierce a scorched blade-bone and then suspend it over the back door: the foetus is of the same sex as the first person who comes into the house (excepting members of the immediate family).

Immersing a sheep's blade-bone in a WELL is said to assist magically in the healing of any sick animal that subsequently drinks water from that source. Lovesick humans, meanwhile, are recommended to pierce a sheep's blade-bone with a knife while chanting:

'Tis not this bone I mean to stick,
But my Lover's heart I mean to prick,
Wishing him neither rest not sleep,
Until he comes to me to speak.

Repeating this procedure every night for nine nights in succession on going to bed (or alternatively sleeping with a blade-bone under the pillow) is guaranteed to bring the sleeper a vision of a future partner in his or her dreams.

**blindness** Coming across a blind person in the street is held by many to bring good luck. This fortune will be doubled if help is then offered to the afflicted person, be it in crossing the road or in some other capacity. It is, however, unlucky for a bridal party to meet a blind man on the way to church.

*See also* EYES.

**blood** Long before scientists began to understand the chemical composition of blood and its properties, the folklore of virtually all cultures had recognised its vital role in a host of superstitious beliefs, often based on the idea that blood was the seat of the soul. Sorcerers regarded blood as one of the most potent ingredients in their spell-making and used to it obtain control over others, to subdue demons, to draw magic circles, to drink in certain initiation ceremonies, in CHARMS to release the victims of possession and in potions to safeguard against disease and bad luck.

Pacts with Satan were signed in blood and it was believed by many that the power of witches actually resided in their blood, which was used to suckle their FAMILIARS. Thus the body of an executed witch had to be completely consumed by fire to prevent her powers being passed on to her children. 'Scoring' a witch 'above the breath' (in other words, ripping the skin of her forehead, nose and mouth until she bled) was reputed to rob her of her supernatural powers, and was also said to be effective against WERE-WOLVES. According to medieval authorities, witches might also be restrained by trapping samples of their blood, HAIR, nail trimmings (*see* FINGERNAIL) and URINE in a special 'witch bottle'. Boiling a little blood taken from a bewitched person or animal in a special ceremony at the hour of midnight was reckoned to cause the witch responsible excruciating pain and to cause her to lift the spell.

The Hungarian Countess Elizabeth Bathory believed that BATHING in virgins' blood would preserve her own beauty, while other cultures (such as the Aztecs) offered extravagant sacrifices of blood to their gods in the hope of divine favour. Masai warriors in East Africa drink the blood of LIONS in the conviction that they will thus inherit the animal's courage, just as Norwegian hunters once drank the blood of BEARS in order to share their great strength. Hunters around the world share the ancient custom of smearing themselves with the blood of their prey in order to protect themselves from the dead animal's avenging soul, as in the 'blooding' ceremony in which new members of a fox-hunt are daubed.

The outrage over the shedding of 'innocent' blood, combined with the difficulty entailed in removing dried bloodstains from fabrics and floorboards, has further added to the mythology of blood and several historic sites boast 'ineradicable' bloodstains. Examples include Scotland's Holyroodhouse Palace, where the blood spilled when Mary Stuart's Italian secretary, David Rizzio, was stabbed to death is still visible; a patch of moss marking the scene of an Indian massacre in the US state of Maine, which turns blood-red once a year; and numerous sites where the grass will not grow because of some act of violence perpetrated on the spot (*see* BARREN GROUND). Not unrelated is the notion that the body of a murdered man will bleed if touched or merely approached by the murderer.

Loss of blood was formerly deemed doubly serious, for it implied a loss of 'spirit' as well as a purely physical loss and it was essential to stem the flow as quickly as possible. For centuries people have laid great faith in the idea that nosebleeds and other haemorrhaging can be staunched by muttering certain verses from the

BIBLE. Exactly which these verses are varies, but the most popular include the Lord's Prayer and the sixth verse of the sixteenth chapter of Ezekiel, which must be recited by a member of the opposite sex to the patient. Other treatments include tying a KEY round the sufferer's neck; dressing the wound with ASHES, COBWEBS or snakeskins; applying a SNAIL and a stone to the wound and sprinkling with HOLY WATER. If all else fails, the patient can be brought to a 'blood-charmer', credited with the power of stemming haemorrhages (often the local BLACKSMITH).

Treatments specifically for nosebleeds vary from tying a length of red THREAD around the thumb and dropping an iron key down the sufferer's back to inhaling the ashes of a vinegar-soaked rag; drinking three drops of blood in a glass of water; hanging a dead, dried TOAD in a bag round the neck; and surreptitiously crossing two sticks of STRAW behind the patient. In the USA sufferers are advised to poke a cat's tail up their nostril or, if this fails, to rest the upper lip on a pile of newspapers.

According to ancient Anglo-Saxon belief, bleeding on HALLOWE'EN is an omen that the patient will die in the near future. Menstrual blood was particularly loathed by many primitive societies and some feared that contact with it could even prove fatal, hence the many restrictions placed on women around the world at this stage in the menstrual cycle (see MENSTRUATION).

Blood has, however, been credited with certain healing powers. Lepers, so it was alleged in the British Isles in medieval times, could be cured by WASHING in the blood of children or virgins or else by placing them under the GALLOWS so that the blood of a hanged man dripped upon them. English doctors in the seventeenth century were much taken by the concept of 'sympathetic powder', which was somewhat conveniently applied to a sample of blood taken from the patient, while the sufferer himself remained at home (see also WOUND). Poor circulation, meanwhile, could be improved by eating WALNUT leaves picked before 24 June.

One ancient German superstition underlines the properties of blood as an APHRODISIAC, claiming that a drop of blood from the little finger of a man's left hand slipped into a woman's drink will cause her to fall in love with him. Variations on this spell found elsewhere in the world suggest the same result if a girl offers the object of her affections a drink to which she has added a drop of her menstrual blood.

**blossom** Superstition dictates that care must be taken when it comes to carrying blossom of any kind into the home. Several varieties of blossom, notably BLACKTHORN, BROOM and HAWTHORN, will invite bad luck if brought inside. The same applies to the blossom of any plant or shrub (especially that of FRUIT TREES) that appears out of season, as this may be construed as a sign that there will be sickness and death in the family. If several plants come into blossom out of season at the same time, a hard winter will ensue. Examples of plants that often flower out of season indoors and are consequently prone to triggering misfortune include geraniums.

**blowing out candles** see CANDLE.

**blue** In the language of COLOURS, blue can be interpreted several ways. To some, blue is the colour of the Virgin Mary's dress and thus represents protection and holiness, while to others it is the colour of the sky and thus stands for vigilance (the thinking behind its use in the flag of the USA). The fact that blue is also the colour of the SEA further links it with sadness (hence 'the blues'). People throughout Europe formerly used to decorate themselves and their livestock with blue beads or ribbons in the belief that these would protect them against evil spirits. To this day, BRIDES are advised to wear something blue to safeguard their luck (see WEDDING DRESS).

**boar** Supernatural boars figured in Norse mythology, and boar was the traditional dish eaten by the gods in Valhalla. Subsequently, a boar's head was a highlight of the CHRISTMAS menu in England over many centuries and it is still eaten with great ceremony at Queen's College, Oxford, to the accompaniment of the famous 'Boar's Head Carol'. Superstitions surrounding the boar in the British Isles went largely out of currency after the creature (whose tusks were said to glow red-hot during the chase) became extinct there in the seventeenth century, though the Celtic population once boasted several boar cults. Elsewhere in northern Europe, however, folklore still speaks of spectral boars as part of the ghostly WILD HUNT sometimes seen in the winter sky. In New England and Ireland, meanwhile, the wild boar is alleged to be one of the forms favoured by the DEVIL when he chooses to manifest himself during the meetings of covens.

*See also* PIG.

**boasting** *see* TEMPTING FATE.

**boat** *see* SHIP.

**boil** Folk medicine claims that boils may be cured by crawling three times under an ARCH made of BRAMBLE, in much the same way that BLACKHEADS may be treated. Alternatively, if one wishes to cure a friend's boils (he or she must be of the opposite sex) one must walk six times round a grave dug the previous day and then crawl three times across it on a night when there is no visible MOON.

**bolt** Superstition advises that the bolts of a front DOOR should be left unfastened when someone is dying in the house. If they are left secure then the soul of the deceased person will have trouble departing and the death struggle will be unnecessarily prolonged. By the same token, the WINDOWS are often also opened and, in China, relatives may even go to the extent of making a hole in the roof to ease the soul's flight.

**bone** As in the case of BLOOD, bone was assumed by primitive man to contain something of the essence of the soul and was thus to be treated with respect. Disturbing interred bones risked serious consequences, but conversely obtaining bits of human and animal bone was frequently of considerable importance to witches and sorcerers, for numerous spells and CHARMS require bone as an ingredient. The uses to which bones have been put include divination, for which the BLADE-BONES of sheep and goats are most commonly employed; 'throwing the bones' – tossing them like dice and learning the answer to various queries by observing how they fall; and the delivering of curses (as practised by the aborigines of Australia in a curious 'bone-pointing' ceremony). In various parts of the world great store is placed on the power of musical instruments made of human bone, which are alleged to keep evil influences at bay.

Bones are of considerable use in the treatment of a range of physical ailments. Drinking powdered bone with red wine is said to be a certain cure for dysentery, and GOUT may be treated by applying a paste comprising a mixture of soil and grease scraped from shin-bones found in a graveyard. Carrying a knuckle-bone about one's person, meanwhile, will fend off CRAMP.

British superstition stresses that it is most unwise to throw bones from a meal into the fire, for any person who does so is sure to suffer from TOOTHACHE, RHEUMATISM or some other related malady. Children should also be dissuaded from falling asleep 'upon bones' – that is, upon someone's lap – in order to avoid bad luck.

*See also* SKULL; WISHBONE.

**boot** It is widely acknowledged that putting a pair of boots on a TABLE invites dire misfortune and is likely to lead to an argument between members of the household. In the British Isles it was once alleged that putting someone else's boots on a chair or table would cause the luckless owner to meet his death by hanging. FISHERMEN from Yorkshire have been known to refuse to go to sea if the person bringing their boots carries them over the shoulder rather than under the arm, and some MINERS from the same county will not enter the pit if they get up and find one of their boots has fallen over during the night.

On a more positive note, boots are now generally regarded as symbols of good luck, being particularly associated with WEDDINGS and new ventures of various other kinds and often being depicted on good luck cards and so forth. This tradition dates, in fact, back to biblical times, when old boots and shoes were presented to a bridegroom on the happy day as a symbol of his new responsibilities.

*See also* SHOE.

**borrowing** Apart from discouraging the practice of borrowing altogether in the old proverb 'Neither a lender or borrower be', superstition instructs that there are certain times in the year – the first three days in February and the last three days in March – when it is particularly unlucky to seek a loan of any kind. In Yorkshire, meanwhile, borrowers are recommended to pay back their loans with good grace ('laughing') in order to preserve their good luck. If a KNIFE is borrowed to cut some fruit, then the borrower is advised to offer the owner a little of the fruit itself when the knife is returned. Loans of home-produced MILK or BUTTER should never be made to those suspected of sorcery, for they may enable the person concerned to obtain control over the lender's livestock by means of spells using these ingredients. Neither should FIRE be lent to another person at NEW YEAR. Lastly, superstition recommends that no one should lend money for GAMBLING, for the lender will never win – though conversely, a gambler who succeeds in borrowing money to bet with is bound to do well.

**boxing** In common with other sportsmen, boxers observe their own code of charms and taboos. These include SPITTING on their gloves before the bout begins, trying to be the last to duck under the ropes on the way into the ring, and never wearing new SHOES for an important contest. Fighters are also renowned for their reliance upon all the conventional good luck mascots, ranging from HORSESHOES and RABBIT'S feet to lucky items of clothing. Like other sportsmen, boxers can become very nervous if they catch sight of a HAT lying on a bed or couch just before a match.

**bracken** Evil spirits dislike bracken, apparently because when a bracken stem is cut the patterns within resemble the Greek letter *chi*, the first letter of Christ's name. Others claim that these markings depict the OAK in which the eventual Charles II hid from his enemies, or that they simply spell out the initials of the future partner of the person who severed the stem. Bracken spores are especially prized throughout Europe as they are supposed to bestow the gift of invisibility and of power over all creatures. Gathering these spores is no easy task, however, for it must be done only in the hour before midnight on MIDSUMMER'S EVE and without letting one's hands touch the seeds themselves. To add to the difficulty, demons will try to prevent the seeds being successfully gathered, and few tales survive of anyone managing to obtain them.

**bramble** A bramble bush that is rooted at both ends, thus forming an ARCH through which people can crawl (usually three or more times and preferably in an east-to-west direction), is regarded by superstition as a most effective – if hazardous – tool in the treatment of various ailments. These include BLACKHEADS, BOILS, dysentery, paralysis of livestock, RHEUMATISM, rickets and WHOOPING COUGH. One variant of the superstition, recorded in Herefordshire, advises that the patient should be eating

BREAD AND BUTTER as he undergoes the treatment and that any remaining food should be left behind as an offering. Cornish tradition, furthermore, recommends the application of bramble leaves dipped in HOLY WATER for the treatment of burns and inflammations, to the accompaniment of a special chant.

**brass** Because brass wears so well it was much prized in ancient times and continues to be associated with the qualities of wholeness and constancy. In the Far East, trumpets to frighten away evil spirits were often made of brass, while in the British Isles it has long been customary to include brass fittings in HORSE harnesses in order to give the animal protection from the DEVIL. In France, milk from a COW being milked for the first time is traditionally collected in a brass jug or bowl.

**bread** As the staple diet of many peoples, bread has acquired great significance in the superstitions of a number of cultures. Corn gods once figured highly among the pagan divinities worshipped by rural communities, and bread still has a profound religious significance in Christian countries through its sharing as part of the service of the Eucharist. Many people still think it sinful to throw away unwanted bread: those who do so are destined to go hungry (while to throw bread into the fire is said to be feeding the DEVIL).

The preparation of bread is surrounded by a host of superstitions. In many areas of the world menstruating women are forbidden to touch the dough, in the belief that the mixture will not rise if so handled. If the dough cracks while being shaped into a loaf (or during BAKING) a FUNERAL is imminent, according to Welsh superstition, while in Herefordshire boys are recommended to keep their distance from the women kneading the dough, for should one of these women stroke his face with a doughy hand he will never be able to grow a BEARD. Before the dough goes into the

oven one option is to mark it with a CROSS, which supposedly protects it from evil spirits while baking.

One person alone should put the bread into the oven: if two share the work, they are sure to quarrel. Care should be taken in this task, as a loaf put in upside down – or subsequently toppled over in the oven – is an omen of a death in the house. According to Scottish superstition, there should be no SINGING while the bread is in the oven (nor should baking be attempted if there is a corpse in the house), and it is generally agreed that no bread should be cut with a KNIFE while another batch is baking.

When the bread comes out of the oven, it is significant if some of the loaves stick together. If four loaves come out as one, there will be a marriage in the household. If five emerge stuck together, a funeral is to be expected. The first loaf must be broken open rather than cut, and testing must be done with a skewer rather than a knife or fork in deference to the old proverb:

She that pricks bread with fork or knife
Will never be happy, maid or wife.

The same applies to cakes.

A loaf should always be put on the TABLE for a meal in an upright position or else misfortune is risked (specifically, in some coastal areas, a shipwreck); it must always be sliced from the top edge, never at both ends. In the case of a round loaf, a woman who puts it on the table upside down is betraying the truth that she also spends much time on her back and is really a prostitute. If a loaf or cake breaks in two when it is cut this is a bad omen, warning of anything from a family argument and disappointed marriage hopes to the death of a family member. The discovery of a hollow in a loaf has varying significance in different regions. In some areas this is taken as a sign that the woman who baked the bread is pregnant, while in others the hollow is called a 'coffin' or 'grave' and is a warning that someone will shortly die. Bread must never be passed around on the blade of a knife nor toasted on the point of a knife, otherwise everlasting poverty is risked.

Placing a piece of bread under a child's pillow will protect the infant from evil through the night, and in Ireland in former times bread was often placed in a child's clothing to ensure good luck. In the USA, bread and COFFEE were sometimes placed under the house in the belief that this would prevent GHOSTS from coming in. Bread baked on GOOD FRIDAY or at CHRISTMAS is said to have special healing powers and is sometimes preserved in the house for a whole year to safeguard everyone's welfare and that of the house itself. Records also exist of bread-based recipes for the treatment of such ills as TOOTHACHE, diarrhoea, and WHOOPING COUGH. A feature common to several of these treatments was that the bread should be buried in the ground for a specified number of days before being offered to the patient.

The popular idea that a 'baker's dozen' (THIRTEEN of something) is derived from the custom of baking an extra loaf for the Devil with each batch of twelve is a misconception. In reality the thirteenth loaf is baked in order to compensate for any shrinkage of the other loaves during baking.

Lastly, US superstition has it that anyone who eats a lot of bread will develop a hairy chest.

*See also* BREAD AND BUTTER; DROWNING; DUMB CAKE.

**bread and butter** Buttered BREAD has its own detailed mythology in Western culture. Widely known superstitions concerning bread and butter include the notion that a single girl should never take the last piece of bread and butter on the plate unless it is offered to her, in which case she can enjoy the prospect of 'a handsome husband or £10,000 a year'. Should she take the last piece when it has not been offered, she is fated never to marry at all. A girl who absent-mindedly starts on a second piece of bread and butter before

she has finished the first, meanwhile, can expect to be married soon.

If a piece of bread and butter falls to the ground and lands on the buttered side, bad luck is to be expected; if it falls on the unbuttered side, a stranger will soon appear. In the English Midlands it is said that bread and butter acquired from a posthumous child or from a woman whose married NAME is the same as her maiden name will cure the WHOOPING COUGH, so long as no thanks is given for the food. Finally, the link between bread and butter is recognised in the tradition that two friends parted by another person or some physical object coming between them when they are out WALKING may mend the threatened rift in their friendship by muttering the CHARM 'bread and butter'.

**breakages** According to universal time-honoured tradition, breakages around the home always happen in threes. Deliberately breaking two relatively worthless objects after a first breakage is suggested as a way of protecting more prized items from destruction. Breaking a gift from a lover is particularly unlucky and bodes ill for the affair itself. Similar bad luck also attends the breakage of a MIRROR or of a WEDDING RING.

*See also* ACCIDENT.

**breasts** A woman suffering from sore breasts is recommended in a Devon superstition to go to a church at midnight and purloin a little LEAD from a stained glass window. This lead should then be shaped into a heart and worn around her neck to bring relief to her condition.

*See also* BABY; SEX.

**breath** Many cultures have assumed the last breath of a dying person to convey the soul of the deceased, and various superstitions have been attached to it. In ancient Rome, the closest relative of the dying person was permitted to inhale this last breath and thus to benefit from its supposed spiritually nourishing qualities.

In succeeding eras, the Fijians slaughtered a few men when launching a new boat in the belief that their dying breaths would create a breeze of good luck for the craft, while witch-doctors and medicine-men of various kinds developed the technique of blowing in the ears and mouths of their patients to rid them of evil spirits. Similarly, holding certain BIRDS and ANIMALS close to the mouth and inhaling their breath is reputed to be useful in treating certain respiratory disorders and other ailments. Some societies, meanwhile, have held to the notion that a woman can become pregnant by simply inhaling a man's breath. Breathing on something for luck is a widespread modern manifestation of these ancient ideas, and gamblers often blow on their cards or on the dice before a game.

*See also* ASTHMA; HICCOUGH; SPITTING.

**bride**   *see* WEDDING; WEDDING CAKE; WEDDING DRESS; WEDDING RING.

**bridesmaid**   The original role of the bridesmaid (and the 'best man') was to protect the bride from being carried off by any of the groom's rivals who took a fancy to her before her WEDDING took place. Nowadays the role is primarily decorative, but the conduct of bridesmaids remains significant in terms of superstition. A bridesmaid who trips on her way up the aisle, for instance, is destined to remain a spinster, though if she catches the bride's bouquet she will soon be married herself. Throwing away a PIN on the wedding day is lucky, but a bridesmaid pricked by a pin is a sign of ill luck. Matrons of honour fulfilling the role of bridesmaid are considered especially lucky for the bride, representing as they do the benefits of married life. It is unlucky, however, for a girl to act as bridesmaid too many times. If she is three times a bridesmaid she is fated never to be married – unless she can arrange to serve in the same capacity a further four times. The most propitious colours for a bridesmaid's dress are BLUE, PINK and YELLOW.

**bridge**   Most superstitions connected with bridges suggest they are ominous structures that must be treated with respect, perhaps because for some they symbolise the crossing from life to death. In times gone by, people showed the greatest reluctance to be first to cross a newly finished bridge in the belief that the DEVIL demanded the soul of the first living creature to attempt a crossing, and a bird or small animal was often sent over first. Celtic tradition warns that no one should talk while crossing a bridge or passing beneath one. The notion that two people who part on a bridge will never meet again is universal, and many people throughout Europe will not go under a bridge when a train is going overhead or passing beneath (*see also* RAILWAY).

Builders of bridges sometimes mix a little wine with the mortar around the keystone or otherwise drop a COIN or piece of IRON into the cement to ensure the structure's fortune in the years ahead. None the less, superstitious people may refuse to cross any bridge in the wake of a coffin in the conviction that the bridge will collapse under them.

**brimstone**   Though brimstone (sulphur) is widely associated with Hell and the evils therein, it does have beneficial properties. English superstition advises that if a person suffering from CRAMP carries a piece of brimstone about their person or takes it to bed with them their ailment is sure to be relieved.

**broad beans**   *see* ACCIDENT; BEANS.

**broom**   Yellow-flowering shrub, which is widely considered of ominous portent. Its BLOSSOMS are particularly unwelcome in many British homes during May, in the belief that they invite death into the household. Using a BRUSH made of broom is equally undesirable in that month, as in the old saying:

If you sweep the house with broom in May
You'll sweep the head of that house away.

Thrashing a naughty child with broom was formerly considered to retard the child's growth. The plant did, however, find favour with herbalists in medieval times, and Henry VIII was known to drink the distilled water of broom flowers as a tonic against a range of diseases. It has also been credited with magic powers as an APHRODISIAC, as an aid to SLEEP, and with warding off witches.

**brush** A seemingly innocuous household implement, the brush or broom (once called a besom) is the focus of a wealth of superstitious beliefs. Great care should be taken with household brushes, from the moment they are acquired to the hour of their disposal.

The old saying 'Never buy a brush in May, or you'll brush one of the family away' is still observed in some quarters. This prejudice may even be extended to the purchase of toothbrushes, though the reasons behind it remain obscure. Once acquired, care must be taken about how a brush is used, particularly if it is new or is being used in a new house for the first time. It is especially important that the brush should always be used to sweep dust into the house rather than out – otherwise the luck of the household might go with it (the solution is to carry the collected dust out in a dustpan). Upper rooms must be swept before the hour of midday, after which the carrying of dust downstairs portends that a corpse will soon follow the same route. Old brushes, moreover, should never be taken into new houses; brushes should never be used after dark; and neither should they be borrowed, lent or burned. Furthermore, no one should sweep outside their house before sweeping the inside, nor should they wield a brush when there is a dead body within.

Particularly hazardous is sweeping the room in which an expectant or newly delivered mother is resting. It is especially vital that the area beneath the bed be left unswept or the woman will die. TABLES, meanwhile, should never be swept with a brush and rubbish should be swept away from and not into sunlight (and never out of the front door). On no account must the house be swept on GOOD FRIDAY or at NEW YEAR as this will endanger the life of a relative.

When sweeping is complete, a broom should be rested on its handle, not on its bristles, and should not be left in a corner, unless the owner actually wishes strangers to appear at the house. If it falls over for no apparent reason when a person passes by, misfortune must be anticipated. Bad luck will similarly attend anyone careless enough to step on or over a fallen broom. An unmarried girl should be particularly wary of doing so, as stepping over a broomstick means that she runs the risk of becoming a mother before she becomes a wife. If the handle comes off a broom when it is being used this is also unlucky, and may be interpreted as a sure sign that any person being paid to sweep will not receive their wages.

SAILORS becalmed at sea may burn an old broom or throw a brush lacking its handle overboard in order to summon up a breeze, though it is generally considered most unlucky to lose a broom at sea by accident. Fastening a broomstick to the mast formerly signified that the ship was for sale, and some Indian sailors believe a brush tied to the mast will keep storms away. Horse riders in the USA, meanwhile, will refuse to touch a broom before a race in the fear that they will lose their luck.

Most people are familiar with the age-old superstition that witches fly on broomsticks to their covens (though they were formerly also reputed to use shovels, cleft sticks, eggshells, ANIMALS and other means of flight). Indeed, it is said that a broom accidentally left outside on a Saturday night is likely to disappear of its own accord, accompanying other brooms to sabbath covens whether a witch needs it or not. The usual means of exit for a witch on a broomstick is via the CHIMNEY, possibly an extension of the old custom of showing a broom at the chimney to indicate that the occupier is not at home. In reality few accused witches have ever admitted to flying on broomsticks and the illusion of flight probably owes more to the use of various hallucinatory drugs, although some witches have confessed to performing ritual dances while straddling a stick. Conversely, a broomstick may actually be used to deter witches: when laid across a doorway a broom will prevent a witch from entering the house.

Broomstick WEDDINGS were once a relatively informal marriage ceremony, observed especially in Wales and among gipsies. These weddings were considered lawful once the happy couple had stepped together over a broomstick into the new home they intended to share as man and wife. The marriage could be undone equally simply by reversing the process at any time during the first year.

Lastly, throwing a broom after those setting off on fishing trips or other business is said to bestow good luck.

**bryony** Herbaceous climbing plant that is often mistaken for the magically potent MANDRAKE. Like the mandrake, bryony is credited with a host of properties, being used for its power as an APHRODISIAC and to promote fertility in both men and HORSES as well as for the treatment of RHEUMATISM and various women's problems. In WITCHCRAFT, bryony roots are often substituted when mandrake is unavailable, black bryony being identified as mandrake and white bryony as womandrake. In France, the plant is dubbed the 'herb of beaten wives' because the berries and roots can be used to help reduce bruising. The bryony plant's poisonous flesh also makes it useful as a purgative.

**bubble** A superstition common to both sides of the Atlantic suggests that bubbles floating on the surface of a cup of TEA or COFFEE promise financial good fortune to the drinker.

**bucket** The humble bucket has given rise to a number of superstitions. These include the notion that going past a bucket on leaving the house in the morning will determine the course of the rest of the day: if the bucket is full, good luck will be enjoyed, but if it is empty, the day will be marred by misfortune. An empty bucket is sometimes placed in the doorway at the end of a CHRISTENING celebration and all the married women present are invited to jump over it: anyone who fails to clear the bucket is presumed to be expecting. SAILORS, who read superstitious meaning into a host of everyday occurrences, claim that losing a bucket overboard is sure to provoke bad luck. FISHERMEN, meanwhile, maintain that luck will desert anyone who sits on an upturned bucket.

Young girls are advised that, if they gaze into a bucket of water through a silk handkerchief in the light of the first new MOON of the year, the number of moons they see reflected in the water denotes the number of years that will pass before they marry.

**building** It is widely known that builders will often deliberately leave some detail of a construction unfinished, in the superstitious conviction that perfecting every last bit is TEMPTING FATE. If a fatal accident occurs during the building of a house, it is agreed that the structure will always be attended by ill luck and there will probably be more deaths. Ceremonies held to preserve the fortune of a newly completed construction include the 'topping-out' ritual, in which the topmost point of the structure is decorated with foliage and the builders drink TOASTS in the hope of fending off evil spirits. Nowadays elaborate rituals such as digging the first sod of earth with a SILVER spade and cutting RIBBONS often mark the start of work on (or the opening of) new bridges, shopping centres and so on: all echo the ancient impulse to provide a valuable new structure with magical protection. A curious tradition of relatively recent times claims that it is unlucky for a single woman to witness the laying of a cornerstone of a new building, as this means that she is fated not to be married for at least twelve months after the event.

*See also* HOUSE.

**bull** The great strength and virility of the bull has inspired various superstitions invoking its potential as a source of protection. It is said that bulls are immune from being struck by LIGHTNING, and thus a bull-pen is an excellent place to shelter during a thunderstorm. A bull's heart, stuck with thorns or pins and kept in the chimney-place, meanwhile, will ward off witches. Perhaps influenced by the various bull cults of ancient times, seventeenth-century witches sometimes claimed that the DEVIL appeared at their covens in the form of a bull. As an APHRODISIAC, dishes of bulls' testes were once considered among the most powerful of all recipes intended to enhance sexual performance.

**bumble bee** A bumble bee that is found in the house can signify various different things. British superstition is divided, some claiming that it is a sure sign that a visitor is about to arrive, while others, more ominously, suggest that it is a portent of death. In Scotland, it is said that killing the first bumble bee of the spring and keeping it safe means that the owner will always enjoy good luck and never be reduced to poverty.

*See also* bee.

**bunion** Superstition recommends that bunions be cured by applying a poultice of the DUNG from a COW, mixed with fish oil, and leaving it on the affected part overnight.

**burial** The business of interring the remains of the dead has always exercised great fascination, and the folklore of every culture is heavy with taboos and rituals that must be observed if the souls of the deceased are to prosper and the living are to be untroubled by their GHOSTS.

One of the most widespread traditional beliefs is that the body should be buried in as complete a state as possible. If a limb is missing, for instance, the deceased risks spending the whole of eternity without it, and in the past people often preserved their lost TEETH and so forth so that they might be buried in the GRAVE with the rest of the body when they finally died. In northern England the dead person was often buried with his own BIBLE, hymn book and Sunday School class ticket, and elsewhere even with treasured personal belongings. Some people still baulk, however, at the idea of a wife being buried with her WEDDING RING or with other pieces of jewellery, on the grounds that this will cause offence in Paradise.

The business of transporting a corpse to its final resting place is governed by a welter of taboos (*see* FUNERAL). When it comes to the actual interment yet more superstitions apply. Sites towards the eastern and southern boundaries of a graveyard are the most desirable, the northern quarter (colder and less open to the sun) being reserved in former times for criminals and SUICIDES. In the past, the opening of a new graveyard sometimes posed a significant challenge, for no one would volunteer one of their deceased relatives for the 'honour' of being the first to be interred, despite the free choice of location. The reason for this reluctance was the widespread belief that the DEVIL always claims the soul of the first corpse for his own. The difficulty was usually overcome by burying an animal of some kind first.

In eastern England, the burial of a woman is sometimes regarded as a cause for considerable local concern, reflected in the saying 'If churchyard opens for a she, it will open for three.' In France, meanwhile, the last person to be buried in the year becomes a symbol of death, and their image will be seen by those fated to die the following year.

Most curious of all is the ancient British business of symbolic burial, which involves the faked burial of a living person (usually a sick child) in the belief that this will fool the evil spirits causing the malady and promote the patient's recovery. In Ireland, the custom is particularly linked with children born at WHITSUN, who are allegedly fated to kill or be killed. Similarly, 'dipping' someone repeatedly into an open grave is said to be effective in the treatment of FEVER, WHOOPING COUGH and RHEUMATISM, among other ailments.

Lastly, it is maintained in many societies that great misfortune will attend anyone who destroys a graveyard or otherwise disturbs the dead.

*See also* CHURCHYARD WATCHER; DEATH.

**burn** Superstition suggests several remedies for a burn or scald. Several of these depend on the reciting of a variety of CHARMS while blowing on the site of the injury. A typical example is the following, recorded in the British Isles in 1946:

> There came two angels from the North,
> One was Fire, the other one Frost,
> Out Fire, in Frost,
> In the name of Father, Son and Holy Ghost.

Shropshire tradition recommends a poultice of GOOSE dung and ELDER bark fried in May BUTTER, while those who live in Cheshire suggest laying a piece of church linen over the wound.

**business** Though the common image of a successful businessmen is that of a hard-headed strategist with little sympathy for superstitious thinking, business affairs around the globe are apparently as influenced as any other calling by the preoccupation with luck. As well as reliance upon the ubiquitous charms and taboos observed in the wider world, businessmen have a few superstitions unique to themselves. These include never signing contracts or embarking on business trips on Fridays or on the thirteenth day

of the month, keeping faith with 'lucky' articles of clothing that they wore in their greatest hours of glory, and timing new ventures to coincide with the new MOON. In the USA, leases generally run for an odd number of years, for reasons of luck, and new businesses are traditionally welcomed with floral HORSESHOES.

Particular attention may be paid to the first transaction of the day (called the 'handsel'). It is unlucky to buy anything before something has been sold, but especially encouraging if the first customer of the day is mentally retarded. The first MONEY received in the course of a day's business should be kissed or spat upon for luck so that it brings more money in its wake. It bodes ill, however, if the first transaction of the day does not reach completion, and some traders will go so far as to accept the first offer they get rather than risk losing this first sale altogether.

Other superstitions relating to the world of work include never sweeping out the rubbish from a workshop when there is little new work coming in, as this sweeps away new customers; twisting one's braces in order to employ the magic of KNOTS; and avoiding the use of GREEN in packaging one's products. In times gone by, it was generally thought unlucky for a new housemaid to arrive at her place of employment during daylight, as this was said to bring bad luck both to her and to the household.

Lastly, the window cleaner, who daily has to busy himself with that unluckiest of objects, the LADDER, should take care always to erect his ladder in the same way.

*See also* FISHERMEN; MINERS; SAILORS.

**butter** The process by which MILK is churned into butter is one of those mysterious everyday matters that much engaged the minds of rural peasants in bygone centuries. Those occasions when the milk failed to curdle properly were the source of much anxiety, and superstitious people were not lacking in imagination when it came to seeking the cause. Commonly heard explanations ranged from the TIDES going out instead of coming in to someone in the milking parlour being in love. More often than not, however, the problem was blamed on the malevolent interference of witches.

Whether WITCHCRAFT or some other agency was suspected, it was generally thought that reciting certain magical CHARMS as the churning was in progress would be of help. The following is but one example:

Churn butter, dash,
Cow's gone to t'marsh.
Peter stands at the toll-gate,
Begging butter for his cake,
Come, butter, come.

Other measures that may be taken to ensure that butter churns properly include tossing a pinch of SALT into the fire before commencing work, dropping a SILVER coin or three hairs from the tail of a black CAT into the cream, and using a churn made of ROWAN. The Irish claim that dipping the hand of a dead man in the mixture will prove equally effective (*see* DEAD HAND). If witchcraft is the cause, plunging a red-hot poker (or in New England a heated HORSESHOE) into the cream will give the culprit a nasty burn and enable the churning to continue. Any stranger who arrives during the butter-making must lend a hand in the churning, or the process will not work.

According to the Scottish, butter produced from the milk of cows that have been grazing in a graveyard will cure consumption.

*See also* BREAD AND BUTTER.

**buttercup**  A widespread superstition popular among British children involves holding a buttercup under a friend's chin and fathoming from the reflected yellow glow that the subject is fond of BUTTER. In folk medicine, bags of buttercups were sometimes hung around the necks of those afflicted by MADNESS to effect a cure, while some authorities claim that buttercups may also be used as an ointment in the treatment of blisters.

**butterfly**  In the folklore of many cultures, the butterfly is an incarnation of a man's soul (in some versions, specifically a soul unable to enter Paradise or else that of an unbaptised child). Sicilians claim that good luck will follow if a butterfly comes into the house and will prevent it flying out again, while English and US superstition recommends anyone who needs a new set of clothes to bite the head off a butterfly. In Gloucestershire, it is said that if the first butterfly of the season is white then all will prosper and will feast on fine white bread; if it is brown, then misfortune is in store and humble brown bread will be all there is on offer. It is also unlucky if three butterflies are sighted at the same time. Even more ominously, English tradition warns that a butterfly seen at night warns of coming death, and in some areas the first butterflies of the year were chased and killed to preserve the community's luck. Killing the first butterfly of the season, moreover, guarantees victory over all one's enemies during the rest of the year.

Irish superstition welcomes the appearance of a butterfly near a dying man or his corpse, saying that this bodes well for his soul after death. In Scotland, meanwhile, witches were sometimes suspected of assuming the form of red butterflies.

**button**  It is almost universally acknowledged that doing up the buttons on one's clothes incorrectly is bound to provoke bad luck. The only remedy is to take off the garment and put it on again. Some claim that only an odd NUMBER of buttons should be buttoned on any piece of clothing (if there are three, only the middle one should be fastened). Gifts of buttons bring good luck, and finding a button in the street indicates a new friendship (finding a button with four holes is especially propitious). According to Jewish tradition, a person may resort to counting his buttons if in doubt about something: if he counts an even number he is right, if he counts an odd number he is wrong. In the USA, young girls are advised that they can discover the profession of their future husband by chanting the following rhyme as they count their skirt or blouse buttons:

A doctor, a lawyer, a merchant, a chief,
A rich man, a poor man, a beggarman, a thief.

# C

**cabbage**  A cabbage that sprouts two shoots from a single root is of particular interest to some people, who claim this to be an omen of considerable good luck. One of the now defunct customs associated with HALLOWE'EN involved boys and girls going out to the cabbage patch at midnight and pulling up a cabbage by its roots. The shape of the roots would then be examined to prophesy the quality of the youngster's future partner: if the root was sturdy and long, the person in question would be strong and good-looking; if it was crooked, however, the spouse would be mean-minded, dishonest or otherwise undesirable.

**Caesarean section**  A child who is delivered by Caesarean section will grow up surprisingly strong, according to Cornish superstition. The child will also be endowed with the gift of seeing GHOSTS and may demonstrate the useful ability to find hidden treasure.
*See also* CHILDBIRTH.

**cake**  *see* BREAD.

**calendar**  A superstition that has gathered momentum in relatively recent times is that concerning gifts of calendars at CHRISTMAS. People all over the British Isles are adamant that it is most unlucky to put the calendar up on the wall until the NEW YEAR has actually arrived, presumably because of the danger of TEMPTING FATE. A derivative of this insists that it is also unwise to turn over the page from one day, week or month to the next before the appropriate time has come.

It is widely held that some days in the calendar are unluckier than others. They include the first Monday in April (which marks the birth of Cain and the death of Abel), the second Monday in August (the anniversary of the destruction of Sodom and Gomorrah) and the last Monday in December (when Judas betrayed Christ). Most ill-omened of all is 28 December, which marks the feast of CHILDERMAS. An attempt made by the historian Richard Grafton in 1565 to make a comprehensive list of unlucky days in the year, based on the findings of ASTROLOGY, yielded the following list:

> January: 1, 2, 4, 5, 10, 15, 17, 29 (very unlucky).
> February: 8, 10, 17 (very unlucky); 26, 27, 28 (unlucky).
> March: 16, 17, 20 (very unlucky).
> April: 7, 8, 10, 20 (unlucky); 16, 21 (very unlucky).
> May: 3, 6 (unlucky); 7, 15, 20 (very unlucky).
> June: 4, 8 (very unlucky); 10, 22 (unlucky).
> July: 15, 21 (very unlucky).
> August: 1, 29, 30 (unlucky); 19, 20 (very unlucky).
> September: 3, 4, 21, 23 (unlucky); 6, 7 (very unlucky).
> October: 4, 16, 24 (unlucky); 6 (very unlucky).
> November: 5, 6, 29, 30 (unlucky); 15, 20 (very unlucky).
> December: 6, 7, 9, 28 (very unlucky); 15, 22 (unlucky).

It should be noted that the dates of many important dates in the folkloric calendar were changed when the Gregorian calendar replaced the Julian calendar in Catholic countries in the sixteenth century (1752 in the UK). This change, designed to eliminate the anomalous extra day that occurred every 128 years under the old calendar, meant a recalculation of many significant dates in the Christian year, though popular tradition continued to honour the old festival dates in various ways (*see* APRIL FOOLS' DAY).

*See also* DAYS OF THE WEEK; LEAP YEAR; MONTHS OF THE YEAR; ZODIAC.

**calf**  Rural superstition in the British Isles places a special significance upon calves, claiming that their welfare can magically affect the rest of the herd and that of the farmer. Stroking or patting a calf on the back is ill-advised, for this will bring bad luck to both the animal and the person, while stepping over a calf as it lies on the ground is equally hazardous. TWIN calves are also portents of bad luck, particularly if one of them has a white streak on its back. Conversely, carrying the 'lucky tip' of a calf's TONGUE about the person is said to ensure protection from evil and also to guarantee financial security, while the gift of some MISTLETOE to the first calf of the NEW YEAR will promote the luck of the whole herd.

In times gone by, the link between calves and herd was so close that farmers were known to sacrifice a calf by burning it alive in the belief that this would save the other animals from some threat, such as disease. Hanging a calf's leg or thighbone by the CHIMNEY in the farmhouse was also recommended for the protection of herds of cattle in the Durham area, and, until relatively recent times, farmers sometimes nailed the body of an aborted calf to the wall of the byre to discourage other cows from giving premature birth.

*See also* BEASTINS; COW.

**calling the dead**  A person who calls out the name of a deceased person in a DREAM or FEVER is presumed in both US and African cultures to be close to death.

If a dying person speaks the name of someone living this too is ominous, for the person named will be next to die. German superstition claims that calling out the name of a dead person three times on Christmas Eve is sufficient to cause their GHOST to appear.

**camphor**  According to superstition, camphor has two uses. Firstly, it will safeguard from disease anyone who carries it, and secondly, it will preserve the VIRGINITY of young girls.

**cancer**  Superstition offers no sure treatment for cancer, and the remedies it does suggest are often bizarre. It was formerly suggested that applying the ASHES of the burned head of a mad DOG to a cancer would help the growth (the result of witchcraft or of a SPIDER crawling over the victim's face) to subside. The cancer itself could be 'fed' and thus prevented from harming the patient by placing raw meat on the site itself or at the patient's bedside. Other authorities throughout Europe dreamed up recipes commonly incorporating FROGS and TOADS as ingredients. In Cambridgeshire, a cure for breast cancer involved rubbing a live toad against the affected parts. This is a marginally more appealing course of action than another piece of advice: to swallow small toads and frogs alive in the belief that they would suck out the poison.

**candle**  The almost ubiquitous use of candles in religion is reflected in the importance placed upon them by superstition. A single taper must not be used to light more than two candles, or bad luck will ensue, and it is similarly unlucky, especially in the theatre, to burn three candles together (though in some areas of the British Isles three candles signify a coming wedding). This latter tradition may have its origins in the ancient Christian custom of allowing only a clergyman (*see* CLERGY) to light three candles at the altar.

Difficulty in lighting a candle is a sign that RAIN is on the way. If, once lit, the flame wavers despite there being no detectable draught, then WIND can be expected. On no account should a candle be lit from the hearth: according to the folklore of eastern England, any person who disobeys this dictate is fated to die in poverty. Fire should not be transferred from another candle, either. Candles that burn with a blue flame betray the presence of a supernatural spirit and are an omen of imminent death, as is a candle that gutters and creates a trail or 'winding sheet' of melted wax (this is sometimes taken to apply to the person sitting nearest to it). A sparking wick, on the other hand, promises the arrival of a stranger or of a LETTER (on its way if the spark falls, but only on its way to be posted if the spark sticks to the candle).

Candles should never be left burning in an empty room unless it is Christmas Eve, when a large candle can be left to burn overnight to ensure the prosperity of the household over the following twelve months (a relic of an old story in which candlelight led the infant Jesus through the darkness). Neither should a candle be allowed to burn to the very end, for this invites great misfortune. According to the French and Germans, a dying candle can only be revived by a girl who is a virgin. In other circumstances, an extinguished candle that continues to glow is another omen of misfortune. Knocking a candle out by accident, though, signifies a forthcoming marriage.

Candles are often lit on the occasions of CHILDBIRTH, WEDDINGS and FUNERALS to frighten away evil spirits, and are regularly lit during church services for the same reasons. In Wales, it is said that an altar candle going out during a service is a sure omen of a clergyman's death. Best-known of all is the practice, derived from ancient Greek custom, of lighting candles on a BIRTHDAY cake, usually one for each year. If the person celebrating the birthday succeeds in blowing out every candle with a single breath they are allowed to make a wish, which will surely come true as long as they refuse to divulge it.

Witches have been accused from time to time of employing wax candles in their spells, using them as vehicles to attack their enemies. The usual procedure is to identify a candle as a particular person and then to stick it with PINS and set light to it. Young lovers, meanwhile, may summon the objects of their affection to them by piercing a candle through the wick with two pins and chanting:

'Tis not the candle alone I stick,
But (lover's name)'s heart I mean to
  prick.
Whether he/she be asleep or awake,
I'll have him/her come to me and
  speak.

The person in question will appear before the flame reaches the two pins. Alternatively, if a girl walks backwards downstairs while holding a candle and then turns suddenly on reaching the bottom she will come face to face with her future lover.

See also HAND OF GLORY.

**Candlemas** Christian festival celebrated on 2 February in honour of the Virgin Mary. Marking the anniversary of Christ's first visit to the Temple with his mother, Candlemas has long had significance in the superstitions of the Western world. Witches made Candlemas one of their four annual sabbath dates and in many countries CANDLES blessed during the Christian festival are kept as protection against WITCHCRAFT as well as safeguards against illness and thunderstorms. It is crucial that every last vestige of CHRISTMAS decoration is cleared from churches by Candlemas, for traces of BERRIES, HOLLY and so forth will bring death among the congregation before another year is out.

Particular attention is paid to the state of the WEATHER at Candlemas in different countries. In several regions of the British Isles, good weather at Candlemas is taken to indicate severe winter weather later. In the USA, Candlemas is popularly known as Groundhog Day: if the groundhog sees its shadow when it pops out of its burrow on this day because the sun is shining, it will go back in and the winter will be prolonged by another six weeks. This is also the date on which BEARS emerge from their winter hibernation to inspect the weather: if it is bad they will remain outside, but if it is fine they will reach the pessimistic conclusion that this cannot be expected to last and will retreat to their caves. WOLVES who choose to return to their lairs on Candlemas Day know that the severe weather will continue for another forty days at least.

In France, Candlemas is widely celebrated with the eating of PANCAKES, which must be consumed only after eight o'clock in the evening. Finally, SAILORS are often reluctant to set sail on Candlemas Day, believing that any voyage begun then will end in disaster.

**cane**  In the days when schoolboys were subject to punishment by strokes of the cane, it was widely held that a single strand of horsehair laid across the palm would cause the cane to disintegrate.

*See also* SCHOOL.

**car**  Despite the relatively brief history of motorised transport, the car has already attracted to itself a considerable body of mythology. GREEN cars are widely held to be unlucky and many drivers talk of 'jinxed' vehicles in which they have had numerous accidents (though others will protest that even talking about such mishaps is likely to provoke misfortune). Congratulating oneself on a trouble-free motoring record is also unwise, as this is simply TEMPTING FATE. Particularly suspect are cars bought on the thirteenth of the month or otherwise carrying number plates that in some way add up to the number thirteen.

Stretches of road can be haunted, just as houses can. Drivers on a remote stretch of road in south-west England for instance, have described a spectral pair of hairy hands materialising alongside their own on the steering wheel and attempting to force the vehicle off the road. Other motorists have picked up spectral hitch-hikers and have otherwise been terrorised by ghostly pedestrians suddenly materialising immediately in front of the car. To guard against such dangers, and also against more mundane risks, many drivers carry lucky ST CHRISTOPHER key-fobs or other charms such as lucky DICE, and will transfer these accessories from their old car to their new one in order to preserve their luck. Virtually every driver, meanwhile, will support the contention that WASHING the car is certain to bring on rain.

A rather involved superstition recorded in the USA claims that a girl may employ the 'magic' of cars to hasten the moment when she meets her true love. First she must wait in the same spot until ten red cars have passed, then she must spot a red-haired girl in a purple dress and finally a man in a green tie: the next male who happens along is destined to become her husband.

*See also* AMBULANCE; HEARSE; MAIL VAN; MOTOR-RACING; TAXI.

**cards**  Card players rely largely on their luck for success and are naturally superstitious, carrying the usual array of good luck charms (*see* AMULET) and often sticking to obscure private rituals before a game just as many sportsmen do before a big match. Many players favour lucky cards or numbers during play. The BLACK suits of spades and clubs are considered especially ominous; the ace of spades is the unluckiest card of all, representing disaster and death. A run of black cards is much feared, as this prophesies a death in the player's family. The four of clubs is described by some as the 'Devil's bedstead' and is loathed by many players, who claim that no good hand can include this card, while the nine of diamonds is called the 'curse of Scotland' because the Earl of Stair used the card to signal the massacre of Glencoe in 1692. Any player who finds himself holding two pairs of aces over eights may also sense a *frisson* of fear, for this is the fabled 'dead man's hand' reputedly held by gunman Wild Bill Hickok when he was murdered.

It is unlucky to be touched by a cross-eyed person (*see* EVIL EYE) during a game, and a player should never sit with his legs crossed in case he 'crosses out' his luck though some believe the opposite: *see* CROSS. DOGS are unwelcome at the card table and the table itself must not be bare (ideally it should be covered with luck-giving green cloth). Chips should always be kept in a neat pile on the table and never left in an untidy heap. It is thought best to choose a seat that allows the player to lay his or her cards down 'with' rather than 'against' the grain of the wood on the table. Cards should never be picked up with the left hand (*see* LEFT SIDE) and neither should the cards be touched until the whole hand has been dealt. Bad luck will ensue if a card is dropped on the floor and many players will object if someone looks at their hand over their shoulder, as they fear this will also lessen their chances of success. WHISTLING or SINGING at the card table is also taboo.

To rob an opposing player of luck, the simplest solution (assuming that person is a smoker) is to wait until he or she deposits a used match in the ashtray and then surreptitiously to place another match crosswise over it, thus 'crossing out' the other's good fortune.

Players suffering from a run of bad luck have several options. They may succeed in reversing their fortunes by blowing on the cards as they shuffle them, by sitting on a handkerchief, by getting up and walking round their chair three times or by opening a new pack of cards. They should also be careful not to lose their temper, as this will only worsen their luck. If their luck still shows no sign of improving they must console themselves with the proverb 'Lucky at cards, unlucky in love'.

FISHERMEN and SAILORS are often nervous of playing cards at sea and will throw them overboard if a storm threatens. Pilots and others engaged in dangerous occupations may also have a prejudice against carrying cards around with them. Anyone else who habitually carries playing cards should keep them wrapped in violet silk, which is said to negate their baleful influence. Playing cards should never be thrown away, however, as the only safe way to dispose of them is by FIRE. This should only take place after the replacement pack has been purchased, and the new ones should be passed through the smoke of the burning cards so as to absorb their luck.

Playing cards have been used for the purposes of divination for centuries in the 'science' of cartomancy (though cards used for telling fortunes should never be used in card games – and vice versa). Particularly portentous cards in this context include the jack and the ace of spades, the jack and four of clubs and the even more powerful nine of diamonds, all of which are cards of ill omen. More encouraging is the ace of hearts, which promises great wealth. Fortune-tellers have devised several different approaches to reading cards, the most sophisticated being the use of tarot packs, in which the conventional fifty-three numbered cards are replaced by a set of seventy-eight each with its own meaning and influence upon neighbouring cards.

It is said that burglars will refrain from stealing playing cards on the grounds that if they break this taboo they will certainly be caught.

*See also* GAMBLING.

**carol** The singing of carols at CHRISTMAS is an old tradition, revived by the Victorians but dating back to the festive ring-dances performed on sacred occasions at Stonehenge and other important pre-Christian religious sites. The Victorians held that it was most unlucky to send away carol singers without giving them something, and some still believe that doing so will endanger one's luck in the coming year. It is also considered unlucky to sing carols at any other time of year than Christmas.

**carrot** The carrot is valued in several countries for its magical properties. Best-known is the idea that eating carrots will enable a person to see better in the dark: carrots do indeed assist in the production of vitamin A in the body; this benefits eyesight and can further assist in the treatment of ASTHMA, RHEUMATISM and GALLSTONES. According to Allied propaganda during the Second World War, night pilots were able to outperform their Nazi foes because they feasted regularly on carrots (a story probably put about to deflect attention from the newly developed Allied radar technology). Tradition also prizes the carrot, especially the wild variety, for its alleged power as an APHRODISIAC.

**cat** The cat occupies a central position among animals credited with supernatural powers, and in consequence cats throughout the world are associated with a wealth of superstitions. The ancient Egyptians bestowed divine status on it and in no circumstances would they kill one (a crime punishable by death). Whole households went into official mourning if a cat died and the corpse would be buried with much ceremony. It was from ancient Egyptian superstition, in fact, that the modern belief that a cat has nine lives was derived.

In later centuries the cat became closely identified with WITCHCRAFT throughout Europe and even today no depiction of a traditional witch is complete without her BLACK cat, the form into which sorcerers were often said to transform themselves. Such cats were, it was alleged, fed on the blood of their mistresses. Many people once believed that kittens born in May, a month particularly associated with the dead and with the practice of witchcraft, should be drowned at once. They would also show reluctance to discuss family matters if a cat was present, just in case it was a witch's FAMILIAR or even a witch in disguise. In eastern Europe cats were often marked with a CROSS to prevent them turning into witches, while in France cats suspected of being witches were often caged and burned alive.

Most significant of all is a cat that is entirely black in colour. A black cat that crosses a person's path bestows good fortune and enables the person concerned to make a wish (though the opposite is maintained in the USA, Spain and Belgium, where white and grey cats are preferred and a black cat brings only bad luck). Variants on this belief, however, suggest that a black cat that turns back or is seen from behind may actually be a bad omen. None the less, the symbol of the black cat as a harbinger of good luck is ubiquitous in the British Isles at least, where simply touching such a creature is lucky and where they are a common motif on good luck cards and so forth. White cats are widely distrusted throughout Europe, while stray tortoiseshell cats are most unwelcome in the home for fear that they bring bad luck with them. Cats should never be bought with money, incidentally, for doing so means they will never be good mouse-catchers.

A SNEEZING cat promises RAIN but is generally a good omen, unless it sneezes three times, in which case all the family will suffer COLDS. A cat that sits with its back to the fire knows that a storm or cold weather is on the way, while one scratching a table leg warns of an imminent change in the weather. Cats wash themselves or frolic with abandon when wet weather is in the offing, but if they choose the doorway for their ablutions this is taken as a sure sign in parts of the USA that a member of the CLERGY is about to arrive. If the cat washes its face over the left ear a female visitor is on her way; if it washes over the right ear a man should be expected.

Cats bestow good luck on newly-weds if they appear next to the bride, but must be caught and killed if they jump over a COFFIN, as this is thought to put in peril the soul of the deceased. Killing a cat is ill advised, however, as this is enough to sacrifice one's soul to the DEVIL, and even

kicking a cat lays one open to RHEUMA-
TISM. People are warned, moreover, not
to allow a cat to sleep with their children
for it may, claim ancient authorities,
'suck' their breath and cause them to die.

Folk medicine recommends drawing a
cat's tail across the eyes to cure a sty and
suggests a similar treatment for WARTS
(though only if done in May). Stuffing a
cat's tail up the nostril, meanwhile, will
staunch a nosebleed and pressing a dried
catskin to the face will relieve TOOTH-
ACHE. Dressing WOUNDS with a preparation made from a whole cat boiled in
olive oil was also formerly suggested in
the treatment of more serious injuries,
and gravy made from a stewed black cat
was credited in the southern USA with
curing CONSUMPTION. Other sickness in
the family may be treated by WASHING
the patient and then throwing the water
over the cat, which will take the disease
out of the house with it as it flees. Cats
should be particularly discouraged from
jumping on to pregnant women, as this
may cause the death of the unborn infant.

MINERS are reluctant to say the word
'cat' while down the mine and have been
known to refuse to work underground if
a cat has been seen below and allowed to
live. SAILORS and FISHERMEN, though,
like to take a luck-giving black cat on
their voyages with them, but dislike hearing a cat mewing on board ship as this is a
warning of difficult times ahead – while a
cat that plays excitely is indicative of a
gale. Should a ship's cat be thrown overboard or shown any other cruelty, the
perpetrators are sure to be instantly
punished by a severe storm. Shutting a cat
up in a cupboard or trapping it under a
pot is widely believed to raise up a strong
wind, and the wives of seafarers will often
keep a black cat at home to preserve the
luck of their husbands while at sea.

**caterpillar** The cultures of several
nations allow a small niche for the caterpillar, though in the USA at least the
creature is said to have been a creation of
the DEVIL. In northern England, tossing a

hairy caterpillar over the left shoulder
is said to bring good luck. As a cure
for WHOOPING COUGH, English authorities also placed great store in wearing a
caterpillar in a bag about the neck until
the creature died – the ailment would ease
as the caterpillar perished. Carrying a
caterpillar about the person is also said to
ward off FEVER. Caterpillars themselves
will die if they are approached by women
who are menstruating, and also if it rains
during a Corpus Christi mass. To lure
caterpillars into the open, the garden
should be traversed three times and the
words 'Caterpillars and baby caterpillars,
I am going, follow me' pronounced
aloud.

**cattle**   see BULL; CALF; COW; OX.

**cauff-riddling** An old Yorkshire
custom, in which some chaff is scattered
in a barn at midnight on New Year's Eve
or on some other 'magical' date for the
purposes of divination. If nothing is seen,
all will go well in the coming year, but if a
spectral COFFIN with two bearers is seen
the person concerned is fated to die in the
next twelve months.

**caul** The amniotic membrane that
sometimes covers a newly delivered
BABY's head. Cauls have always been
much prized by the superstitious, especially by SAILORS, who contend that
anyone thus born or in ownership of such
a preserved caul will enjoy good luck,
become an eloquent speaker and, most
importantly of all, be protected from
death by DROWNING. Such was the inten-
sity of belief in this idea that cauls were
regularly advertised in the press in the
eighteenth and nineteenth centuries, and
even in relatively modern times have
often changed hands for quite considerable sums of money. In the Netherlands
and elsewhere people born with cauls are
said to have special psychic powers. The
caul must be carefully looked after or the
health of the person to which it belongs
will suffer. It is maintained by some that a

caul should be buried with its owner when he or she dies, or the ghost of the deceased will walk abroad in search of it.

**cave** Local folklore identifies many a cave as the ancient dwelling-place of a dragon, demon or witch, and most regard them as desolate, forbidding places in which all manner of unseen evil may lurk. Since they were to be avoided few surviving superstitions attach to caves, beyond one old northern English notion that children may be cured of WHOOPING COUGH by taking them to a cave and demanding that the resident spirits relieve the infant of the illness.

**celandine** Herb which is particularly credited in folk medicine as beneficial for the EYES. Herbalists claim that celandine will improve the eyesight of both humans and hawks, in which connection it was often employed by falconers in past centuries. Yellow celandine flowers are also considered effective in the treatment of JAUNDICE and RINGWORM, and their juice may be used to alleviate WARTS according to one old Oxfordshire tradition. Placed in the room of a sick patient, celandine will laugh (in which case the prognosis is not good) or cry out (in which case the patient will recover).

**chain letter** A largely twentieth-century phenomenon, the chain letter – usually a begging letter designed to amass a fortune for the originator by 'blackmailing' recipients into parting with small sums of money and passing the letter on to yet more people – relies upon superstitious sentiment to succeed. The original chain letters were sold by travelling merchants in medieval times, the letters themselves bearing various CHARMS and prayers. The development of modern postal services, however, led to the appearance of a new variety of chain letter to be copied endlessly from one person to another, no person daring to break the chain for fear of the dread misfortune that was promised them if they did so. All such schemes seem to break

down fairly quickly, none the less, without any apparent ill effects (and, incidentally, without anyone making vast sums of money).

**chair** Innocent enough in itself, the humble chair is the object of a number of time-honoured superstitions. A chair that falls over is almost universally regarded as an omen of bad luck (only to be avoided by crossing oneself rapidly five times). If it falls over when a person rises from the TABLE this may suggest that they have been telling lies, and if a chair is passed over the table a quarrel is bound to break out. If it falls over laden with clothing in a HOSPITAL ward, a new patient must be expected. Any single girl who accidentally knocks over a chair is delaying the date of her own WEDDING, perhaps by as much as a year.

Returning a chair to the wall where it stood before a meal was served may seem a helpful act, but to some it simply ensures that the diner will never eat in the house again. Taking a chair that someone else has been sitting on is also unwise, for it suggests that both people will go to the grave in quick succession. In northern England it is also considered unlucky to choose a seat beside an empty chair, while residents of Ohio claim that three chairs placed side by side signify the imminent demise of a member of the household. Turning a chair round three times or walking round it three times is said by gamblers to ensure a change in one's luck when losing at CARDS. On other occasions, chairs should never be turned round as this is sure to spark a family quarrel.

**chalice** The sacred cup used in the Communion or Eucharist services of the Christian Church, which is said by some to have its own special powers. Many people value items of church silver for their healing properties, and in the past children have often been taken to drink from chalices in the belief that this would cure them of WHOOPING COUGH. It was vital that the children did not touch the chalice itself with their hands, and also that the chalice was one used in the Catholic rather than the Protestant service. Until relatively recent times chalices, though made of valuable precious metals, were relatively immune from the attentions of THIEVES, who feared they would suffer extreme misfortune if they included such a sacred object in their haul.

**chamber pot**   The chamber pot features little in the annals of the superstitious, other than at the time of WEDDINGS. In Scottish tradition, the bride's chamber pot was once the first of her belongings brought into the new home, on which occasion it was filled with SALT, some of which was then scattered on the floor for luck. One variant of this custom required the bride and groom to jump three times over the salt-filled pot.

**charm**   An incantion, prayer or other form of words that is supposed to have in itself magical power. Carrying pieces of paper bearing verses from the BIBLE or certain other words or phrases (see ABRACADABRA) about the person was formerly reputed to ward off illness and other forms of evil, while reciting given lines has always been an essential feature of spell-making. Thus, various rhymes may be uttered when attempting to conjure up visions of future lovers, driving away demons or overcoming physical ailments by magical means. The power of the spoken word is such that merely repeating a person's name over and over may be sufficient to cause them to appear in the flesh, while simply uttering a phrase like 'white rabbits' on the first day of the month will guarantee one's luck in the days ahead. Conversely, certain words are regarded with intense misgiving, and seafarers around the globe will resent anyone using words like 'pig' or 'priest' while a vessel is at sea for fear of the consequences. Among the more common instances of charms in everyday usage are those designed to protect one's luck when evil threatens. These include

the various challenges and greetings that should be spoken aloud on sighting a MAGPIE and the simple business of saying 'Bless you' to a person who is SNEEZING.

*See also* AMULET; TALISMAN.

**charm wand**   A slender glass stick with a curved end, sometimes filled with seeds, that is often kept in the home as an ornament but was originally intended to ward off evil during the hours of darkness. The theory runs that any evil attracted to the house will be lured to the wand and distracted from harming the occupants by the challenge of counting the seeds (or the hair lines) in the glass. When morning comes, the charm wand is simply wiped clean of any evil it may have ensnared. A broken charm wand was a cause of some concern and promised ill luck to the whole household.

*See also* WALKING STICK.

**cheek**   Superstition explains that blushing is attributable to the fact that someone somewhere is talking about the person concerned. In Oxfordshire women may respond to a blush with the following charm:

> Right cheek, left cheek, why do you burn?
> Cursed be she that doth me any harm.
> If it be a maid, let her be slayed,
> If it be a wife, let her lose her life,
> And if it be a widow, long let her mourn;
> But if it be my own true love, burn, cheek, burn.

The pseudo-science of PHYSIOGNOMY, in which a person's character is expressed in their appearance, dictates that fat cheeks suggest greed and sensuality, while hollow ones betray envy and meanness or a cold personality. Best of all are those with nicely rounded cheeks, which indicate wisdom and liveliness. A cheek with wrinkles is a symptom of MADNESS.

*See also* DIMPLE.

**cherry**   Growers of cherry trees in Switzerland are advised by superstition to offer the first fruit of a tree to a woman who has recently given birth, for this will ensure that the tree always fruits plentifully. A cherry tree planted in the middle of a vineyard will have a similar effect and guarantee good wine. Other superstitions focus on cherry stones, the most widespread of which is the custom of counting out the stones of consumed cherries one by one while chanting 'This year, next year, some time, never' to find out when one will be married. Others include the rather unsavoury habit of flicking cherry stones towards the ceiling by squeezing them between the fingers: if the ceiling is reached at the first attempt, the marksman is destined to marry shortly. A final superstition from the county of Kent warns anyone walking in a cherry orchard to rub their shoes with a cherry leaf in order to avoid choking on a cherry stone.

**chestnut**  Various beneficial properties are assigned by superstition to both the horse chestnut and the sweet chestnut, and more specifically to their fruits. Carrying two horse chestnuts about the person is said on both sides of the Atlantic to relieve the pain of arthritis, backache and RHEUMATISM. If sweet chestnuts are eaten boiled with honey and glycerine they will also alleviate ASTHMA. Superstition also recommends leaving an offering of a few sweet chestnuts on the table at HALLOWE'EN as gifts for the dead.

**chewing gum**  Sharing a single stick of chewing gum with another person may be a sign of friendship or love, but superstition suggests that in certain circumstances gum may play a more active role in proceedings. Offering another person a stick of gum over which one has expressed a desire to be loved by that person is, according to twentieth-century US mythology, certain to persuade the reluctant lover of the other's charms if accepted and well chewed.

**chicken**  *see* COCK; EGGS; HEN.

**chicory**  Blue-flowered plant, which has long been considered a harbinger of good luck when carried by travellers and explorers. More specifically, it is credited with bestowing the gift of INVISIBILITY and assists in overcoming obstacles of various kinds, including secured locks, if held against them. To work in such a way, however, the chicory must be cut at twelve noon or twelve midnight on St James's Day (25 July) with a gold blade and in complete silence, on pain of death.

**chilblain**  Painful inflammation of the fingers, toes or ears that is caused by prolonged exposure to cold and wet. Superstition offers an impressive range of treatments for this complaint. Chilblains can be cured or prevented, it is alleged, by the wearing or carrying of horse TEETH; by pricking the affected area with HOLLY leaves; by keeping a half-eaten CHRISTMAS cake or the remains of the YULE LOG under the bed; by applying URINE and strawberry juice; by wearing wolfskin gloves and shoes; by circling a mare three times while gripping one's shirt with one's teeth; or by dipping one's hands in manure on 1 May and then clapping them three times on the lid of a bread box. Dipping the affected part in water in which slaughtered PIGS have been immersed is also recommended. Applications of WALNUT oil, carpenter's glue, turnip pulp, soot and vinegar or CANDLE wax will lessen the pain while a choice of more permanent treatment is made.

**childbirth**  The business of childbearing was once much more hazardous than it is today, and superstition was called upon in all its various guises to assist the expectant mother and the unborn BABY. Though medical advances have reduced some of these notions to little more than quaint echoes of bygone eras, others still influence expectant parents and relations (though less often now midwives and doctors).

In remote parts of Europe people will still open all the DOORS in a house and untie KNOTS in the mother-to-be's clothing to make the delivery easier. Other measures to assist the mother in labour include placing a razor-sharp AXE blade edge up under her bed, spilling a little SALT in her palm, placing SILVER coins taken from a church in her mattress and bringing an empty hornets' nest into the room. In Kentucky, birthing assistants may tickle the mother's nose with a feather, while elsewhere in the USA she may be offered a drink partly drunk by another woman or administered a potion made from the powdered rattles of rattlesnakes.

Among the many birthing customs that have fallen into disuse are driving IRON nails into the bed to keep away evil spirits; laying the mother on a bare earth floor from which she might derive extra strength; hanging charms (*see* AMULET) in the bedchamber to ward off witches; and ringing the church BELLS or, if this could not be arranged, tying a piece of bellrope round the mother's waist to summon up divine assistance. Hanging an item of clothing borrowed from a man whose wife is known to be unfaithful to him may also aid the process, according to the Irish. Once the baby is delivered, chicken feathers may be burned under the bed to stop any bleeding (*see also* AFTERBIRTH; UMBILICAL CORD).

Much can be predicted about a baby's future from the circumstances of its birth. A baby born in a wagon, by CAESAREAN SECTION or when the mother's head lies in a northerly direction is deemed especially lucky, as it also is if born with an extra finger or toe. If the baby is born in the breech position (feet first), according to one old English superstition, the child – sometimes called a 'footling' – is fated to be lamed in an accident unless its legs are hastily rubbed with BAY leaves, but will also benefit from special healing powers – as will a baby whose mother dies in giving birth (*see* WHOOPING COUGH). If the father is already dead at the time of the baby's birth it may find consolation in special occult powers.

The timing of the birth is important, according to the science of ASTROLOGY: the phase of the MOON and the state of the TIDES, as well as the date, the day of the week and the hour of the day, all have an influence on the baby's character. Babies born under a new moon are fated to a life of failure (or conversely will grow up very strong). According to the Sicilians a baby's sex is determined by the phase of the moon at the hour of birth: it will be a girl if the moon is on the wane and a boy if it is waxing. If a baby is born with the moon on the wane, it is maintained that the next baby the woman has will be of the opposite sex; if the moon is waxing the next baby will be of the same sex. Babies born when the tide is on the ebb are doomed to die young.

Babies born at CHRISTMAS or NEW YEAR can look forward to a lifetime of good luck. Unluckiest of all are the babies born on CHILDERMAS DAY (28 December) or on 21 March, which, according to US superstition, is a day of particularly bad omen (US custom also suggests that babies born between 23 June and 23 July will be unlucky and those born in May will never enjoy good health).

When it comes to the day of the week, a widely known children's rhyme offers a summary of what may be expected:

Monday's child is fair of face,
Tuesday's child is full of grace,
Wednesday's child is full of woe,
Thursday's child has far to go;
Friday's child is loving and giving,
Saturday's child works hard for a
  living.
But the child born on the Sabbath Day
Is blithe and bonny, good and gay.

It should be noted, however, that this is not the only version: in Cornwall and Scotland, children born on Tuesday are 'solemn and sad' and those arriving on Wednesday are 'merry and glad', while those arriving on a Thursday are 'inclined to thieving'; in Shropshire, moreover, it is Friday's children who are born to sorrow. All are agreed, however, that Sunday's children are especially blessed and will be immune from witchcraft throughout their lives.

Babies arriving at midnight will be able to see GHOSTS, while any 'chime child' born at three, six, nine or twelve noon (the hours when church bells chime) may prove unlucky in life but will be able to see things others cannot and will also be safe from witchcraft. Births that take place at sunrise bode well for the future, but babies born at sunset will be lazy in later life.

Finally, a safely delivered mother is strongly advised to make her first trip out of the house after childbirth to the church, to show thanks for her survival and thus to be cleansed (a ceremony known as 'churching'). If she disobeys this and visits a female friend instead, the latter can expect her own child within the year.

*See also* BIRTHMARK; CHILDREN; PREGNANCY; TWINS; ZODIAC.

**Childermas Day** Holy Innocents' Day, on which the slaughter of the children by Herod is remembered. Commemorated on 28 December, this is widely held to be the unluckiest day of the year. Children born at Childermas are fated to unlucky lives and no new project should be embarked upon on that date, for it will surely end in failure; neither should new clothes be worn for the first time. Superstition warns that even such mundane domestic chores as WASHING and trimming FINGERNAILS should not be attempted. Perhaps in reference to the origins of the festival, though, children's parties were often held on Childermas Day in parts of northern England.

*See also* CALENDAR.

**children** Superstition offers detailed guidance on virtually every aspect of a child's existence in the first few days of life, though once the child has survived the early stages and has acquired a measure of divine protection through the ritual of the CHRISTENING service there are fewer specific taboos and rituals to be observed beyond those in general currency. Most of these may be divided into those that are intended to preserve the child against various illnesses such as WHOOPING COUGH, which have inspired countless remedies in folklore, and those that give some clue about what life holds in store for the infant.

Odd beliefs that have lasted into the twentieth century include the widely held notions that it is lucky to have children on board SHIP, that dreaming of children is an omen of trouble and possibly of death in the offing, and that children prone to blisters on the TONGUE will turn out to be habitual liars. In the USA it was formerly said that any male child who showed a weakness for wearing strings of beads was doomed to die by hanging. A first-born child is reputed by some to be immune from witchcraft, while a seventh child should choose a career as a doctor because he or she will have special healing powers. A tenth child, in deference to the old custom of paying tithes to the Church, should consider a career as a cleric.

*See also* BABY; CHILDBIRTH; NAMES; PRECOCIOUSNESS; TEETH.

**chime child** *see* CHILDBIRTH.

**chimney** The chimney and the hearth, as the focus of family life in past centuries, have always been of mystical significance. FIRE is itself a magical element but also attracts evil spirits, and measures must be taken to ensure that no hostile entity forces its way into the house via the chimney. Tradition has it that witches left for their covens mounted on broomsticks by means of the chimney, and popular folklore in modern times still has Father Christmas entering the house in this way. On the whole, though, chimneys are held to be lucky and may even be touched for luck.

Among the many superstitions concerning chimneys are never using a new chimney for the first time on a FRIDAY; making the sign of the CROSS three times before lighting a fire; throwing three grains of SALT into the fireplace; never allowing a fire to go out unintentionally;

chimney sweep

blessing the fireplace with HOLY WATER, salt and signs of the cross whenever there is a birth or a death in the house; never POINTING at a fireplace nor SPITTING into it; spitting on logs before burning them; and always handling the logs by the larger end. Fire irons and other household implements should always be stored to the right of the hearth and up-ended on special occasions. SOOT coming down the chimney is deemed a bad omen, particularly if it falls during a WEDDING party, while a fire that burns too strongly warns of an argument in the household.

*See also* BELLOWS; POKER.

**chimney sweep**  Just as the CHIMNEY is considered an important focus of magic in the house, so too is the chimney sweep universally regarded as a lucky figure. Receiving a 'lucky' kiss from a black-faced chimney sweep after leaving the church is one of the time-honoured traditions associated with brides in the British Isles, and many people will bow or make a point of greeting a sweep should they meet one in the street (possibly a relic from an old legend about a sweep who saved the life of an English king, who thus acknowledged his assistance). Some people will spit when they see a sweep, and make a wish.

**china ornaments**  Care should be taken when positioning china ornaments depicting animals. In particular, they should not be placed so that they face the door, as this will direct one's luck out of the house.

**cholera**  Though cholera is now rare in Western countries, certain superstitions concerning its detection have survived to the present day. In the British Isles, it is said that a piece of raw meat thrown into the air will instantly turn black if cholera is in the vicinity. Sufferers in Australia are advised to sleep in a churchyard in order to be cured.

**chopstick**  In countries where chopsticks are used as a matter of course, it is widely believed that ill luck will dog anyone who breaks a chopstick. Children, furthermore, are warned that they will be struck dumb if they allow their chopstick to tap anything other than their dish.

*See also* CUTLERY.

**chough**  Large bird of the CROW family, which occupies a special place in Cornish superstition. Legend claims that the soul of King Arthur resides in the chough and that killing one of these birds is a grave error which will bring great misfortune on the perpetrator of the deed.

*See also* RAVEN.

**christening**  The ceremony of baptism into the Christian Church, which is attended by a host of superstitious customs in many countries. The doctrine of original sin decrees that the DEVIL resides in every person until driven out during the christening ceremony, and that those who die unbaptised will be claimed by him in the afterlife (unless they are babies, in which case they are fated to roam restlessly until the Day of Judgement or to be reincarnated as BUTTERFLIES, NIGHTJARS or other creatures).

Various safeguards are thus recommended to mothers before the christening takes place, which ideally should be as soon after the birth as possible. Unchristened babies should, tradition has it, be kept at home until the due date and not allowed into anyone else's house. They should also be protected by AMULETS, which can include GARLIC and IRON and are sometimes used to decorate the CRADLE to fend off evil influences while the baby sleeps. Covering sleeping infants with an item of the father's clothing also provides some protection. Adults are warned, incidentally, not to get between an unchristened baby's cradle and the FIRE, as this invites bad luck.

On the big day itself (preferably a Sunday), the baby should be dressed entirely in WHITE. It is particularly important that none of the ribbons in its clothing is RED, which is very unlucky. Buying new christening robes is frowned upon. Whoever carries the baby must take the shortest route to the church, and on no account must they turn back once they have started (it is also unlucky to cause a christening to be postponed once a date has been set). Members of the christening party in former times sometimes carried with them morsels of cake and BREAD, which were offered to the first stranger of the opposite sex to the baby whom they met on the way to the church: it was very bad luck for the child if these were refused. The church BELLS should ring a full peal in order to protect the child from deafness and to bestow upon it a tuneful voice.

If two children of opposite sex are to be christened together, the boy must go first, according to Scottish authorities, or the girl will grow up with the BEARD the boy would have had. If several children are being christened at once the child who goes first will be especially lucky, though many parents show reluctance to allow their child to be first to be christened in a new church, as an old tradition has it that the DEVIL will seize its soul or else that the child will die prematurely. Some insist that no two children should be baptised in the same WATER, as the second will be washed with the sins of the first. Any child who reaches the font before the priest, meanwhile, will acquire the gift of second sight.

It is vital that the officiating priest (*see* CLERGY) makes no mistake in the course of the ceremony, which invites the interference of evil spirits. If he falters over a word, the child in question will grow up with a stutter. Many people consider it desirable for a baby to cry during baptism to indicate that the Devil has indeed been driven out of its body. By this token, nurses were formerly given to pinching and otherwise maltreating the infants in their care in order to summon up a good wail. If the baby sneezes, however (*see* SNEEZING), this is taken as a bad sign. Water from the font should be allowed to dry and not be wiped from the baby's face, and the child must be allowed to

sleep in its christening robe for the first night after the ceremony (if the child wears a christening bonnet, it must be worn for a further twelve weeks). If a little of the font water is kept and later given as a drink to the infant, the child will be endowed with a fine singing voice.

Christening services should never follow FUNERALS, but extra luck will be enjoyed by children christened in the wake of a WEDDING. Some say the mere fact that a child has been christened will lead to a marked improvement in its physical well-being. All christenings should be followed by a lively party to 'wet the baby's head', thus guaranteeing the child's luck for the future.

Those who remain unbaptised may be doomed to haunt the earth as GHOSTS, and anyone stepping on to the grave of a child who has died unbaptised will die of the same illness, according to ancient English tradition. Lastly, witches sometimes perform ceremonial baptism ceremonies of their own, parodying the Christian ritual, to commit themselves to the DEVIL.

*See also* GODPARENT; NAMES.

**Christmas** As the most popular of all the year's religious festivals, Christmas is governed by a wealth of folk traditions and superstitions applying to virtually every aspect of the festive season. Descended from pagan midwinter celebrations, it remains a diverting occasion that thrives on the disparate elements of material excess and Christian solemnity.

In former times the festivities got into earnest on Christmas Eve, when there was much feasting and jollity and the burning of the YULE LOG took place. Christmas decorations should not be put up until Christmas Eve, but this superstition is now largely ignored and high streets are bedecked with Christmas decorations as early as November in many places. MISTLETOE, according to custom, should not be brought inside until as late as New Year's Eve, but this again is now largely ignored. Centrepiece of the Christmas decorations in virtually every home is the Christmas tree, which was originally revered by the ancient Druids and other pre-Christian societies as a symbol of fertility and has since, like many other evergreen trees and shrubs, come to represent good fortune.

Christmas cakes were usually eaten on Christmas Eve in the nineteenth century, though it was most unlucky to cut into the cake before that day dawned and a portion had to be preserved uneaten until Christmas Day itself. The DOORS of the house used to be opened at midnight to let out any evil spirits, and a Christmas CANDLE was customarily placed in a WINDOW to burn all night long to guarantee the household's luck for another year (it was a bad sign if the candle went out before the family rose). FAIRIES, it was said, held masses in Christ's honour at the bottom of mines at the hour of midnight, and farm animals are still supposed to kneel in homage and are briefly blessed with the power of speech at this time – though it is fatal for a human to overhear what they say.

Christmas Eve is also a time when the supernatural may be consulted about the future. Lovestruck young girls are advised that on Christmas Eve they may be granted a vision of their future partner: all they have to do is walk backwards to a pear tree, around which they must then walk nine times. Alternatively, if a girl taps on a hen-house and gets a reply from the hens inside this means that she will not marry that year; if the COCK cries at her tap then a WEDDING is on the cards. Another course of action is to scatter twelve SAGE leaves in the wind and thus to conjure up the image of a lover-to-be.

St Nicholas, in his modern guise as Father Christmas or Santa Claus, will fill stockings hung on the chimney-breast overnight. This is in remembrance of the legend that St Nicholas tossed three COINS down the chimney of the house lived in by three poor sisters: the coins fell neatly into some stockings that were drying by the hearth. The first person to open the door on Christmas morning to welcome in the spirit of Christmas is very lucky, and further good fortune will attend the household if the first visitor on Christmas morning happens to be a dark man (the arrival of a woman or a redhead is, however, a bad omen). If the sun is shining a fine harvest can be expected the following year. The modern fixation on a 'white Christmas' probably derives from an old notion that this signifies fewer deaths in the year to come. Whatever the weather, it is, however, unlucky to attempt any but the most essential work, such as the feeding of animals, on Christmas Day.

Various superstitions surround the traditional Christmas Day menu, particularly the Christmas pudding. During its preparation this must have been stirred – in an east-to-west direction – by every member of the household, even babies, if the luck of the household is to prosper, and any girl who omits to take part in this ritual can forget her chances of marriage in the coming year. Those who stir the pudding are allowed to make a wish as they do so, but must keep the nature of their wish to themselves if they really want it to come true. Into the mixture may be placed a SILVER coin, which will bestow luck upon the finder, a RING, which will hasten a wedding in the family, and a THIMBLE, for prosperity.

Children born on Christmas Day itself will never be troubled by GHOSTS and are safe from death by DROWNING or hanging. Those born on Christmas Eve are also deemed especially lucky. Though Christmas Day is a popular time for the telling of various horror stories, ghosts will not appear on this one day of the year – though some say that the headless images of those who are fated to die in the following twelve months may be discerned in the shadows cast on the walls by a roaring fire.

In modern times the end of the festive season comes with TWELFTH NIGHT, when all decorations must be taken down on pain of extreme bad luck over the coming year. Those who take their decorations down before Twelfth Night, incidentally, are probably unaware that they are similarly prejudicing their luck over the twelve months ahead and are risking a death in the family. In the past, decorations were often allowed to remain in place until the end of January, when every last trace of them was removed on the eve of CANDLEMAS.

*See also* CAROL; HOLLY; IVY; MINCE PIE; NEW YEAR; WASSAILING.

**church** Various superstitious beliefs have come to be associated with the house of the Lord in all Christian societies. In remote parts of Scotland people shrink from even mentioning the 'kirk' by name, and in many areas the very dust collected from the floor is said to have special healing properties. Similarly, people have been known to scrape powder from stone columns and monuments in churches or to remove fragments of LEAD from the windows for use in potions to cure such ailments as sore BREASTS and FEVER or to ease the passage of death. Rainwater collected from a church roof is similarly credited with mysterious medicinal powers, and for the treatment of various ills the GRASS that grows in a churchyard may be eaten in its natural state or in the form of BUTTER produced by cows that have grazed on it.

Northern English superstition roundly declares that it is impossible to catch a cold from another member of the congregation while in a church. Other widespread superstitions concerning churches include never turning over a hassock, regardless of which way up it is, for fear of suffering twenty unlucky Sundays in a row, and keeping a vigil in the church porch between eleven o'clock at night and one o'clock in the morning on St Mark's Eve, when the spirits of those fated to die over the coming year are said to enter the church. A church door that rattles as though disturbed by an unseen hand is a sure prophecy that a FUNERAL will soon have to be held, as is the sight of a bird perched on a church weathervane. In general, birds that fly into a church are a good omen, but if a ROBIN enters, someone in the congregation is certain to die in the near future.

*See also* BELL; CLOCK.

**churching** *see* CHILDBIRTH.

**churchyard watcher** The spirit of the person most recently buried in a churchyard, whose duty it is to watch over the other people buried there until the time comes to summon another living person to the grave and thus to be relieved. In some rural areas there may be controversy when a churchyard is closed: the relatives of the last person buried there may complain that this means the deceased is condemned to watch over the churchyard forever. In past times unseemly brawls would sometimes break out when two FUNERAL parties met in the churchyard at the same time. Each would try to ensure that their own friend or relative was not the last to be laid to rest and thus delayed from departing this Earth. The sound of the churchyard watcher's cart making its way down country lanes was much feared in many communities. Variants on the tradition around the world include the Ankou figure of Breton folklore, who is said to lay an unseen hand on those who are doomed to die or to scythe down anyone who comes within his reach.

**cigar** A variety of superstitions have attached themselves to the business of smoking a cigar. Among the most frequently encountered are the notions that it is unlucky for a person to be offered a cigar that turns out to be broken, and for a cigar to fail to burn evenly on all sides. Blowing a smoke ring and then catching it and putting it in one's pocket is, however, said to be very lucky. Women should be particularly wary when handling cigars. According to a superstition observed in Salem, Massachusetts, if she accidentally treads on a spent cigar she is fated to marry the next man she meets. The same holds true if a woman takes the last puff of a cigar.

*See also* CIGARETTE; PIPE SMOKING.

**cigarette**  The one really well-known superstition concerning cigarettes is that it is unlucky to light three from the same match. This idea was conceived during the Boer War and became widely current during the First World War, when it was alleged that anyone unwise enough to accept the third light would fall victim to snipers, who, alerted by the lighting of the match in the first place, would by then have had time to find their aim. It has been suggested that the tradition may originally derive from a taboo against priests lighting more than two CANDLES with the same taper. Smoking a cigarette made from the bones of a TOAD, meanwhile, is said to cure insomnia. Tobacco itself will deter SNAKES and may be placed in a baby's CRADLE to ward off evil. Stepping on a cigarette packet bearing the picture of a black CAT or a SAILOR and threatening to tear the packet up is sure to promote one's luck.

*See also* CIGAR; PIPE SMOKING.

**cinders**  A cinder that falls out of a FIRE may sometimes be examined for the purposes of divination. If the cinder is shaped like a purse, riches are in store; if it is shaped like a COFFIN, the tidings are more ominous. A heart-shaped cinder promises the appearance of a new lover, while round, hollow cinders suggest the arrival of a BABY.

*See also* ASHES.

**clergy**  As representatives of divine power, clergymen and religious figures of all descriptions are potent in the superstitions of many cultures. A clergyman met in the street is considered a bad omen, which must be remedied if possible by touching cold IRON. Meeting a nun in the street, however, is deemed lucky, particularly if she is in a group of two or three other nuns. Some people will spit for luck on seeing a nun (*see* SPITTING), but conversely will fear bad luck if she happens to be walking in the opposite direction so that only her back can be seen. Nuns are often less than welcome on board planes, when they are regarded as omens of disaster (*see* AIRCRAFT). In the USA it is said to be unlucky to look at a nunnery.

FISHERMEN are reluctant to set sail if they meet a nun or a clergyman on their way to the harbour, and discussion of priests or churches is discouraged while at sea (even saying the word 'priest' is taboo). SAILORS, moreover, have been known to blame bad voyages on the fact that their vessel was carrying a clergyman or some other representative of the cloth. Gamblers who are experiencing a run of bad luck on the horses, meanwhile, are recommended to kiss the wife of a parson, for this will surely change their luck for the better, according to one old British tradition.

An ancient French superstition of obscure origin claims that priests are more often struck by LIGHTNING than people of other callings.

**clock**  Timepieces are inextricably linked with the coming of death due to the passage of time, so most of the superstitions associated with them are of a dark hue. Many legends talk of clocks that chimed or otherwise stopped at the moment when someone died, and it was once the custom on both sides of the Atlantic for all the clocks in a house to be stopped manually when there was a death in the household. They were not rewound until the body had left the house.

Clocks should never be positioned opposite the fireplace, as this will cause the FIRE to go out. They will, it is claimed, react violently in the presence of any 'unchurched' woman making a visit after CHILDBIRTH, typically by throwing themselves to the floor. To be on the safe side, superstition advises that no one should speak while a clock is striking. Clocks that keep the wrong time are also bad omens, and if London's Big Ben strikes incorrectly at midnight it is said that the royal family will face calamity within three months. Clocks that strike THIRTEEN times, meanwhile, are also considered an ominous sign and some claim that in doing this they conjure up the DEVIL.

A church clock that strikes while a hymn is being sung is an omen of a death in the parish within the week. It is also deemed unlucky if it should strike during a WEDDING service, suggesting the death of one member of the couple within the first year; some brides will refuse to enter the church until the clock has finished chiming. A town hall clock that chimes while church bells are ringing is a warning that a fire will shortly break out in the vicinity. If two clocks strike together, a married couple in the parish will shortly meet their deaths.

**clothing** A number of widely known superstitions apply to the clothes a person wears. The most familiar include the general rule that a person should always begin with the right hand and right foot before the left and the old idea that putting clothes on inside out by mistake puts one at serious risk of misfortune, which can only be avoided by leaving the garment inside out for the rest of the day. In former times the wives of FISHERMEN often wore their blouses inside out deliberately in the hope that this would bring magical assistance to their husbands at sea, and it was frequently said that wearing a coat or shirt in this way would protect the wearer from being led astray by the FAIRIES.

Special rules apply to new clothes. The wearer is invited to make a wish when putting on a new garment for the first time and, in the case of a new coat, is advised to slip a few COINS into the right-hand pocket without delay to ensure that he or she never goes penniless. Brides decking themselves out with their wedding outfits may be wished by a relative 'Health to wear it, strength to tear it, and money to buy another.' New or freshly cleaned or washed clothes should always be first put on when Sunday comes round, to prolong their life, and EASTER must always be honoured by the wearing of new clothing (US authorities stipulate three new items of apparel).

Damaged clothing should never be mended with the wearer still in them. If this taboo is broken the wearer variously risks slander, a parting, a death among friends or relations, loss of wealth or some other instance of bad luck. It is also inadvisable for light-coloured clothes to be patched up with dark-coloured thread. A hole in a sock brings good luck for a day, but bad luck if worn a second day. It is thought unlucky to iron the HEM of garments, for prosperity is ironed away with the creases.

The clothing of a person who has recently died cannot be expected to last long if given away; it will decay just as its former owner's corpse decays. Similarly, some thought is required before lending clothes to the dying – if the latter is buried in them the real owner will go into decline as his or her clothes decay on the corpse. Caution should also be exercised in giving away clothing to strangers, as a witch can use a person's discarded clothes to obtain power over them.

*See also* APRON; BUTTON; CHRISTENING; GLOVES; HAT; SHIRT; SHOE; SOCK; SWEATER; UNDERWEAR.

**clover** Finding a four-leaf clover has always been thought lucky, and many people believe that a person who finds one will meet his or her future lover that day (the luck is doubled if the clover is immediately given to someone else). Superstition has it that they only grow where a mare has foaled and that the four leaflets represent fame, wealth, a faithful lover and good health. They also bestow protection against witchcraft and will prevent any young man who finds one from being drafted into the armed forces. It is further claimed that anyone who wears a four-leaf clover will be able to see

FAIRIES. Wearing a two-leaf clover in the right SHOE is a ruse sometimes favoured by young girls: it is said that they will marry the first man they meet, or someone of the same name. Opinion is mixed about five-leaf clovers: they may guarantee great riches, or they may threaten illness unless given away at once.

Some authorities trace the mystical significance of clover all the way back to the biblical legend that Eve stole some clover as she was expelled from Paradise. Herbalists claim that potions incorporating clover can be used to treat various skin problems.

**coal** The link with the mystical power of FIRE means that coal is considered very lucky and carrying a piece of coal about the person is widely recommended. In the nineteenth century burglars carried a piece of coal as a matter of routine because it was thought to keep them safe from arrest, and soldiers have been known to follow the same practice. Finding a piece of coal in the road is deemed lucky, though some variants of this tradition suggest that it must be tossed over the left shoulder and not spared a backward glance if the luck is to operate. SAILORS, meanwhile, believe that keeping a piece of coal found on the foreshore will protect them from DROWNING.

Coal is one of the items carried in the 'first footing' ritual associated with NEW YEAR celebrations, and a small piece is sometimes included in the gifts put into CHRISTMAS stockings: the coal is then burned on the fire while the recipient makes a wish. One last warning concerns turning a coal over as it burns in the grate – this should never be attempted when poking the fire, as it will only cause bad luck.

**cobweb** The web of a SPIDER is said to have concealed the infant Jesus from Herod's soldiers, and perhaps it is for this reason that cobwebs are regarded as very lucky. In stables and barns they should never be cleared away as they protect the livestock, and it is widely believed that

destroying a cobweb on purpose will only provoke misfortune. No punishment will be exacted against a person who runs into a spider's web by accident, but this may mean that a friend is about to appear. Similarly, US superstition claims that a girl who finds a cobweb on her door is being advised that her lover is unfaithful, while a cobweb in the kitchen reveals to the attentive observer that there is little love in the house. Laying a cobweb on an open WOUND will promote the healing process (this may in fact assist in coagulation and kill bacteria). Cobwebs rolled into small 'pills' are sometimes taken as a treatment for ASTHMA, while rubbing a web over a WART and then burning it is said to destroy the wart itself.

**cock** The crowing of the cock at the break of day links the creature with the SUN, a source of much superstition, and consequently the cock has acquired considerable mystical significance, bolstered by its role in the biblical story of Peter's repudiation of Christ. Cocks have been sacrificed on the altars of many religions and feature as a prime ingredient in various spells. EPILEPSY may be cured, according to Scottish tradition, by burying a cock beneath the sufferer's bed, while sanity may be restored by burying a cock at the point where two estates meet. CONSUMPTION can be treated by preparing a broth that includes parts of a cock, some GOLD and PEARL among more usual ingredients. Simply rubbing an injured part with a live cock and then driving the cock out of the district was said to cure most ills.

Millers used to kill a cock on St Martin's Eve (10 November) and sprinkle its blood over their machinery to protect themselves from accidents in the year ahead. Some claim that, because a cock heralded the birth of Christ, keeping a cock will ward off GHOSTS. White cocks are regarded as especially lucky and as guardians of the farmyard, but black cocks are traditionally associated with evil spirits.

A cock that crows more lustily than usual or while perched on a gate is giving notice of a change in the weather or, if standing in a doorway, of the imminent arrival of a visitor. If it crows in the early evening RAIN can be expected, but if it crows during the night it warns of the coming of death. The crowing of any cock at an inauspicious moment, such as the birth of a child or when someone is about to depart on a journey, is considered a very bad omen. A cock and a hen spied sitting together on the morning of ST VALENTINE'S DAY is a sure prophecy that someone in the house will soon be married. Cocks are also said to crow on Christmas Eve to celebrate the anniversary of Christ's birth, and both real cocks and the cocks on weathervanes on church towers will crow at the Last Judgement to awaken the dead.

*See also* ALECTROMANCY.

**coffee** According to US superstition, much can be learned by observing the movement of BUBBLES on the surface of a cup of coffee. If the bubbles float towards the drinker, prosperous times lie ahead; if they retreat, hard times are promised.

**coffin** European tradition warns that it is reckless in the extreme for anyone to lie in a coffin, even for a joke, before their time has come. In addition, no CORPSE should be laid in the coffin wearing clothing belonging to a living person: as the clothing rots, so the owner of the clothes will suffer a decline in health. It is customary for coffin lids to be nailed shut, but some people prefer to leave them loose, so that their occupants may be able to escape more easily on the day of resurrection. Any chair or table upon which a coffin rests should be tipped over when the coffin is removed, to guard against another death occurring in the household in the near future. AMULETS and RINGS made from the metal fixings of old coffins are said to prevent CRAMP, while coffin NAILS banged into the bedroom door will ward off nightmares.

*See also* BURIAL; FUNERAL.

**coin** There are many people around the world who value coins for their luck-bringing qualities. Tossing a coin into a fountain or pool while making a wish is a universal custom, and many persons carry 'lucky' coins (often ones minted in the year of their birth or ones with holes in). FISHERMEN fix a coin in the wood of their boats and even in their nets for luck, and in former times the poor frequently carried specially made 'touch pieces', which depicted the DEVIL being defeated, to protect them from disease. Particularly lucky are coins given out at Holy Communion and coins found during a rainstorm, on the grounds that these must have fallen from Heaven. It is, incidentally, courting bad luck not to pick up a coin spotted on the ground, and gifts of purses, wallets and coats should never be made without first putting a few coins in them.

Some coins are, however, unlucky. In Britain, the crown or five-shilling piece of pre-decimal currency was disliked in many circles, especially in public houses where it was alleged that any barmaid accepting such a coin would shortly lose her job. In many countries, coins are placed upon the eyes of the dead to prevent them from reopening and looking around for someone to join them in the grave.

*See also* BLACK PENNY; CLOTHING; LEE PENNY; LOCKERBIE PENNY; LUCK PENNY; PENNY; SILVER.

**cold** Superstition offers few remedies for the persistent nuisance of the common cold. Besides asserting that it is impossible to catch a cold in a church, authorities suggest that catching OAK leaves as they fall to earth in the autumn may provide some relief, or else that stuffing the nostrils with thinly cut orange peel might do the trick.

*See also* SNEEZING.

**colours** The symbolic values of the different colours lie at the heart of countless superstitions around the world. Interpretations vary from one culture to the next. Generally speaking, GREEN conjures up the elemental and unpredictable forces of nature (hence the mistrust shown towards the colour by ACTORS AND ACTRESSES and motorists, among many others), while BLACK evokes images of evil and death, WHITE represents purity and innocence, BLUE suggests repose and mystical strength and is generally considered lucky, RED relates to passion and to Hell and YELLOW variously symbolises cowardice and intellectuality.

**comb** Combing the HAIR is a perilous activity in certain circumstances. One ancient eastern European tradition dictates that no one should use a comb that belonged to a dead person; if they do, they will themselves shortly die or at the very least go bald. British custom, moreover, instructs that mothers should never comb their baby's hair before the infant is weaned, or the baby will lose a tooth for every tooth of the comb that breaks (combs made of ivory were much more brittle than the modern plastic variety). Tortoiseshell combs are said to have a calming influence, but dropping a comb brings bad luck.

**comet** Not unnaturally, in centuries past the sight of a comet inspired the deepest foreboding. They are universally recognised as portents of disaster, and over the centuries sightings of particular comets have been linked with such calamities as famine, war, the death of monarchs and, back in 1066, the Norman invasion of England. No one should embark on a new project after seeing a comet, and children born as one appears are fated to die violently. Years in which many comets are sighted are, however, said to be excellent wine years. Some people believe that wishes made on seeing comets or shooting stars (*see* METEORITE) are certain to come true.

**Communion money** *see* RING.

**confetti** The custom of throwing confetti or rice (or in past eras wheat or corn) over newly-weds is derived ulti-mately from pagan fertility rites and is intended as a general blessing upon the pair, specifically to promote their chances of having children. In medieval times the custom was by no means confined to marriage ceremonies, and similar showers of grain greeted the arrival of royalty, magistrates or other dignitaries. Modern paper confetti often comes in the shapes of BELLS and HORSESHOES, meant to bestow further gifts of luck upon the happy couple.

**confirmation** Christian ceremony, which like BAPTISM is said to bestow various benefits not immediately connected to religious salvation. Those who present themselves for confirmation are said to enjoy a marked improvement in health, and in former times those suffering from RHEUMATISM in particular were known to participate in the ceremony on more than one occasion in the hope of a cure. The crucial element in the ceremony as far as healing is concerned is the touch of the bishop's right hand, which effects the cure (being touched by the bishop's left hand is deemed most unlucky).

**consumption** Communicable disease, more often identified in modern times as tuberculosis, which was once a major killer in the Western world (as it still is in the third world). In former times those desperate for a cure were faced with one of the more challenging cures recommended by English superstition: swallowing live baby FROGS before breakfast. Alternatively, the patient had to be carried through a flock of SHEEP as they left their pens first thing in the morning, or else had to sleep where he or she would be exposed to the supposedly beneficent breath of cattle. Other remedies involved drinking broths made by stewing the body of a black CAT or that of a COCK.

**conversation** A lull in the conversation, particularly at mealtime, is traditionally attributed to the fact that an angel is passing over the house. It is further alleged that such lulls usually happen at twenty minutes before or after the hour. If two people say the same thing simultaneously this too has magical significance and is thought to be very lucky: the two parties must not say another word but must link little FINGERS and make a wish, which is sure to come true. An alternative version of this tradition has it that whoever finishes what they are saying first will be the first to get married. Forgetting what one is saying in mid-speech is, however, unlucky and suggests that the speaker is telling lies. In the USA, such an event may precipitate the reciting of the following rhyme:

What goes up the chimney, smoke.
May your word and my word never be broke.

Should a speaker accidentally talk in rhyme, he or she may confidently expect a present before the month is out. If someone appears while others are talking about them, this is a welcome sign that the person concerned is destined to live a long life.

Lastly, it is not unnaturally considered unlucky to engage in any conversation with a witch. If this cannot be avoided it is important that the witch must not be allowed either the first or last word of the conversation.

**cooking** The business of preparing food is much beset with superstitious belief. Among the many taboos relating to the kitchen are: never allowing a pan of WATER to boil over (because in so doing the cook boils his or her lovers away); never sharing such duties as stirring a pot with someone else (for fear of a quarrel); and never stirring mixtures in anything but an east-to-west direction (in imitation of the SUN's movement). Moreover, watched pots, as the old proverb has it, never come to the boil. Secreting such items as rings, sixpences and buttons in cakes, soups and other foods on special occasions is a time-honoured method of divining who is to marry next or who is to enjoy great riches, though such games are now largely confined to the festive

season. Lastly, cooks can expect a long and witch-free life if their PEA soup continues to bubble after being taken off the heat.

*See also* APRON; BAKING; BREAD; CHRISTMAS; MEAT; OVEN; POT; ROLLING-PIN; SALT; SUGAR; WAITING ON TABLE.

**coral** The superstition that coral wards off evil dates back to Roman times, if not beyond, and gifts of coral necklaces are still sometimes offered to youngsters at their CHRISTENING to preserve them from evil and also as an aid, when rubbed against the gums, in teething (they also prevent nightmares). Red coral in particular is said to deter evil and can protect ships and houses from STORMS. It is alleged that red coral worn about the person will turn pale if its owner is ill, regaining its original colour as the patient recovers.

**cork** In various European countries cork is prized for its apparent ability to ward off CRAMP, and some people tie garters of cork around their legs or slip a cork under the pillow when they retire for the night. Others keep the corks from the champagne drunk on a happy occasion, such as a wedding, a twenty-first birthday or a sporting victory, to ensure their good luck in the future, often inserting a COIN into a slit cut into the cork itself.

**corn** A thickened area on the skin of the feet, caused by pressure or friction, which may become painfully sensitive. Superstition recommends treating corns by burying a piece of stolen beef in the ground; as the meat rots, so the corns will vanish.

**corn dolly** Small figure or other shape that is made by plaiting some of the last sheaf of corn stored over the winter to ensure the success of the coming harvest. Corn has been cultivated for some seven thousand years and pagan societies revered a host of corn gods and goddesses. These were kept symbolically alive in such dollies, which were customarily hung up in the chimney-piece – or alternatively by leaving a little corn standing in the fields. The corn dollies found in virtually every craft shop of modern times are usually bought as good luck emblems, though rarely made from the last sheaf of corn as they once were.

**corner house**  An old English superstition warns against living in a HOUSE that stands on a corner, for such buildings (for reasons lost in obscurity) are widely held to be unlucky.

**corpse**  The handling of human corpses is the focus of a myriad of superstitions around the world, most of which have the twofold aim of easing the deceased person's passage to Paradise and allowing the living to continue their lives untroubled by GHOSTS and free of any curse invoked by improper disposal of the dead.

The moment death has taken place superstition insists that the EYES, if still open, be closed, or their gaze will summon another person who is present to accompany the departed to the grave (in some countries the eyes are prevented from reopening by covering them with COINS). Distraught friends and relatives should not allow their tears to fall upon the body, as their distress is believed to trouble the departed soul. Scottish tradition, indeed, discourages mourners from crying at any stage during a FUNERAL.

Touching the corpse is recommended as it brings the living good luck and will, it is alleged, save them from NIGHTMARES in which the dead person appears. The touch of a dead person's hand – particularly one who has died a violent death – may, indeed, prove of benefit to various medical conditions (*see* DEAD HAND). The corpse of a person who has been murdered, however, will bleed if touched by the murderer, thus revealing the latter's guilt.

On no account must an animal of any kind be allowed to jump over the COFFIN: if this happens, the animal must be killed immediately to prevent further deaths in the family. A corpse that remains limp long after rigor mortis should have set in

is a bad omen, warning of another death in the household.

If possible, a corpse should be removed from the house before the weekend, for a body that remains unburied over a Sunday will soon be joined by another in the grave. It is also thought unlucky for a corpse to remain unburied over NEW YEAR's Day. MINERS go further and may refuse to return to work until the body of a colleague killed in an accident is properly laid to rest. SAILORS, too, dislike having a dead body on board SHIP, and if the burial takes place at sea are nervous of watching the body sink for fear that they will follow it.

When the time comes for the body to be carried away it is important that it be removed feet first, in contradiction to the usual manner of birth, or the deceased's ghost may return. Any ground over which the corpse is carried is fated to become barren and, according to one ancient but entirely erroneous tradition, becomes thereby a public right of way. Once the body has gone, the front step should be washed at once to clean it of any ill luck left behind. Linen used to wrap a body is considered very lucky and may be used to relieve HEADACHES if wrapped about the head.

*See also* BURIAL; DEATH; DROWNING; EXHUMATION; HAND OF GLORY; MURDER; SUICIDE.

**corpse-lights**  Spectral lights that glow in places of death, such as churchyards. Norse sagas spoke of such lights at sacred burial spots, and reports of them have continued into modern times. Often the lights hover over the grave of a newly buried person, or else trace the route that the FUNERAL procession is due to take. Sometimes it is said that the lights are warnings sent to the living by dead friends and relatives to advise them that they are soon to die and should make the necessary preparations.

*See also* WILL-O'-THE-WISP.

**cotton**  Stray threads of cotton found on a person's clothes are supposed to foretell that they are about to receive an important LETTER. Close examination of the shape of the thread, futhermore, will reveal the initial of the writer's name.

*See also* ACTORS AND ACTRESSES.

**cough** One cure for a cough suggested by British superstition is to administer to the patient (surreptitiously) barley water in which three SNAILS have been boiled. Alternatively, plucking a HAIR from the patient's head and feeding it to a DOG with the words 'Good luck, you have. May you be sick and I be salve' should successfully transfer the cough from man to beast.

*See also* WHOOPING COUGH.

**counting** *see* NUMBERS.

**couvade** *see* PREGNANCY.

**cow** Cattle have always been a focus of superstitious belief, reflecting their economic importance through the ages. Some societies have venerated the cow, as still happens in India, and the animal has often been said to know the direct path to Heaven (hence the now forgotten German and Scandinavian tradition that a cow should accompany FUNERAL processions). This tradition may explain the long-held notion that a cow trespassing in the garden is a warning of imminent death, while the presence of three cows signifies three deaths in the offing. Other death omens involving cattle include the sound of a cow lowing after midnight and a cow lowing three times directly into a person's face.

The business of milking a cow is not to be taken lightly. The MILK will not flow if anyone sings in the milking shed, and the cows may likewise refuse to co-operate if they spy a new face in the dairy. Those who do the milking must wash their hands when they have finished or there will be no milk next time. Another reason for a poor supply of milk may be that a witch has magically milked the animal already by sucking on the udder in the guise of a HARE or by means of one of various spells. Safeguards that may be taken against witches include fixing a bough of ROWAN wood at the door to the cow shed and, in Ireland at least, sprinkling the floor of the stalls with primroses. In Scotland white cows are regarded as inferior milkers, and it is further considered unlucky to milk any cow being sent to market.

The luck of each individual animal is believed to reside in the rope used to tether it, and cows were traditionally sold complete with their tethers in order to safeguard them from witches or malevolent spirits. Those selling cows are advised to push them backwards out of the barn, or risk the animal proving sterile. It is also most inadvisable to make an offer for an animal not up for sale, as the object of the offer will surely die.

Cows that lift their tails or feed close together know of RAIN on the way, while those whose tails rap against a fence or tree or else lie down to rest on high ground expect fine weather. The breath of a cow was once alleged to be most beneficial to the health and people suffering from CONSUMPTION were often recommended to sleep in the company of cattle; it is still claimed by some that farmhands never contract tuberculosis. A little of the mother's DUNG fed to a CALF will protect the new arrival from evil spirits and may also be used as a poultice for WOUNDS or, in Northumberland, to cure HEADACHES.

In common with other farmyard animals, cattle are said to kneel in homage to Christ on Christmas Eve and to speak with human voices – but anyone who overhears what they say is likely to die forthwith.

*See also* BEASTINS.

**cowslip** Wild flower with a yellow blossom, which is said to spring up only where cow DUNG has fallen. Superstitions concerning the plant include one which claims that if planted upside down the flowers will be red, and another that says cowslips will turn into PRIMROSES. Tossing a ball made of cowslips repeatedly into the air with the words 'Tisty, tosty, tell me true, who shall I be married to?' followed by the names of all one's suitors is sure to provide an answer: the ball will fall to the ground when the future partner's name is pronounced.

Infusions of cowslip flowers are said to improve memory and provide relief for various nervous complaints; cowslip lotions are recommended as a beauty treatment.

**crab** Superstition holds that the crab makes a useful ingredient in various medicinal preparations. A poultice of burned and crushed crab was recommended in Anglo-Saxon England for reducing swellings, while placing the EYES removed from a still-living crab upon the back of a person's neck was sure to relieve the latter's own swollen eyes.

**cradle** The urge to safeguard a BABY from evil influences is answered in superstition in various ways. Decorating a cradle with charms (*see* AMULET), which may range from portions of tobacco and BREAD to pieces of IRON and GARLIC, is sure to ward off malevolent spirits. The child will be further protected if wrapped in one of its father's garments.

Mothers are warned that rocking an empty cradle is a perilous habit: it means either (throughout much of Europe) that the cradle will soon be occupied by a new child, or (in northern England and in the Netherlands) that the last child to sleep in it will shortly die; the first version of events is the one that most people know. It is, incidentally, unlucky to bring a new cradle into the house until the intended occupant is actually born. Visitors to the house are warned not to come between the cradle and the FIRE, which is considered very unlucky. Selling or giving away a cradle when it is finished with will surely result in the former owner becoming pregnant once more, regardless of whether she had thought her family complete. Lastly, bad luck will befall any bailiff who seizes a cradle in distraint of debt.

**cramp** Superstition advises that the pain of cramp can be alleviated by always carrying on one's person or secreting under one's pillow certain animal bones. These vary from the knee joint of a HARE to the fin bone of a HADDOCK and the knuckle-bone (or 'cramp-bone') of a SHEEP, which must never be allowed to come into contact with the ground or it will lose all its power. Garters of CORK or eelskin are reputed to be equally efficacious, while some people have been known to carry a MOLE's paw wrapped in silk or to sleep with a piece of BRIMSTONE in their bed for the same purpose. Others have favoured the wearing of 'cramp RINGS' fashioned from metal taken from old COFFINS, especially if these had been blessed by a monarch (the last English monarch to bless such rings was Mary I). Alternatively, reciting the following CHARM should keep the pain at bay: 'Cramp – be thou painless! As Our Lady was sinless when she bore Jesus'.

**cricket** Just as superstitious as players of any other team game, cricketers at all levels favour 'lucky' bats, clothing, charms and rituals, which may vary from rubbing the ball in a certain way to taking special care that the batsman's pads are never put on the wrong legs. Some batsmen are wary of taking guard twice at the same end, and others consider it fatal to their chances of scoring if, before taking the field, they wash their hands simultaneously with the batsman who is to play at the opposite crease.

**crickets** Superstition places a variety of interpretations upon the appearance of these insects and their chirping 'song'. Crickets in the home are generally regarded as a good omen and it is consequently bad luck to kill one or if one leaves – though some people read their appearance in the home as a portent of evil. White crickets in particular are much feared if they appear on the hearth, as they foretell a death in the household. The sound produced when crickets rub their hind legs together is regarded as a warning of death or else of severe weather, although the sound is welcomed if heard on Christmas Eve as this promises great good fortune. Should a cricket be killed, the perpetrator of the act is likely to find that other crickets have chewed holes in his SOCKS. Yorkshire folklore, meanwhile, insists that a cricket thrown on to a FIRE will not burn.

**crocodile** African and Indian traditions place considerable mystical significance on the crocodile, perhaps reflecting the creature's divine status among the ancient Egyptians. A symbol of treachery, the crocodile is said to weep when it has eaten all but the head of its human victims and these 'crocodile tears' turn magically to jewels to lure further human prey. They may also make pitiful groaning noises to beguile the sympathetic. Crocodile blood is prized for the treatment of snakebites and eye problems, while fried crocodile meat is used to dress WOUNDS; the skin is combined with oil and vinegar as an anaesthetic and the fat also has medicinal properties.

**crooked** British folklore insists that finding anything bent or crooked, be it a COIN, PIN or stick, is lucky and the object should never be parted with. Farmers have been known to plough crooked furrows so that the FAIRIES may not aim their arrows along the ridges towards their horses and oxen.

**crops** Agriculture is much beset by superstition. Farmers are advised to plant rows of seeds on a north–south axis, rather than east-to-west (they will in fact get more sun this way). Ideally, seeds should be planted when there is full MOON as the crops will be ready for harvesting a month earlier than those planted when the moon is on the wane. It is thought very unlucky if a ridge in a field is missed out when the seeding is done, and may be interpreted as a sign that one of the farmer's family will die in the near future. Once the seed is taken out of the barn to the fields it must on no account be

taken back again, even if a sudden change in the weather means it cannot immediately be put on the ground. The fate of a crop may, in fact, be predicted early in the year, according to the old English saying 'A wet March makes for a bad harvest. A dry and cold March will never beg its bread.'

At harvest time, when a person gets his first taste of a particular fruit or other crop that season, he or she may make a wish. Another ancient tradition recommends that when someone first tastes the new season's crop their mouth should be crammed as full as possible, which will ensure that he or she does not go hungry between then and the next harvest.

*See also* CAUFF-RIDDLING; EASTER.

**cross** Central to Christian iconography, the cross has considerable significance among the superstitious, being credited with both the power to ward off evil and certain healing properties. Because of its sacred associations, a cross of STRAW or sticks laid on the ground can be used to detect witches, who are sure to stumble as they walk over it; similar crosses may be placed at doors and windows or over pigsties and beehives to prevent evil entering (the French favour crossed bunches of flowers for this purpose). It is unlucky, however, to leave CUTLERY or SHOES in a cross shape, which is said to be an offence against the Lord (another person must uncross them if the guilty party's luck is to be restored). Similarly, if four friends meet they should avoid crossing each other's arms as they shake hands. Crossing the FINGERS is widely known to ward off evil and so too is crossing the legs, a favourite ploy of superstitious gamblers (but *see also* CARDS). Sitting with legs crossed is said by some to bring luck to a friend in a particular enterprise, but others warn that this may be done to conjure up some hindrance in another's affairs (a reference to the legend that Juno delayed the birth of Alcmene's son Hercules by sitting in such a fashion).

Splinters taken from crosses or even samples of moss growing on a cross are valued in folk medicine. Making the sign of the cross upon one's shoe will cure CRAMP and 'pins-and-needles' in the foot; stitches and other minor ailments may be relieved in much the same way. Marking food, whether it be BREAD or MINCE PIES, with the sign of the cross will similarly protect it from interference by witches or evil spirits.

*See also* EYE.

**crossroads** The intersection of four roads, long regarded as an ominous location. Anything that forms the shape of a CROSS is significant, but crosses made by roads are heavy with symbolic meaning and many people dislike being delayed at such a place for fear of meeting a GHOST, a VAMPIRE or death in person. Primitive peoples often erected their altars where roads met and engaged in human sacrifice there; ever since, crossroads have been associated with death, not least through the traditional erection of the GALLOWS at such spots.

SUICIDES, vampires and criminals were formerly buried at crossroads in the belief that, should they arise from the grave, their vengeful ghosts would not know which of the roads led back home. In modern times witches' covens have sometimes been known to choose lonely crossroads as their meeting-place. Authorities on ley lines, the paths of strange mystic power that criss-cross the land, claim that crossroads which intersect such paths are notorious for CAR accidents and other calamities. Similar traditions also abounded in times gone by about places where the boundaries of three parishes met, though these were usually valued as sites where miraculous cures might be enacted.

**crow** The death-BLACK colouring of the crow, in combination with its intelligence, has led to the bird being regarded as one of the most ominous of all creatures. Once considered a messenger of the gods and later a FAMILIAR of the tradi-tional witch, the crow is now viewed by many as a harbinger of death and disaster, particularly feared if it alights upon a house or taps at a windowpane. A crow settling in a churchyard is likewise deemed an omen that there will be a FUNERAL in the near future.

Crows that leave a wood *en masse* are interpreted as a sign of coming famine, while if they fly at one another it presages the outbreak of WAR. Crows that flock early in the day and fly towards the SUN are a sign of good weather (as is a crow that croaks an even number of times), but bad weather is on the way if they are noisy and active around water at dusk (or if a single crow croaks an odd number of times). In northern England children will see off a single crow with the threat:

Crow, crow, get out of my sight,
Or else I'll eat thy liver and thy lights.

However, a rhyme from the Essex region claims that two crows together will actually bring good luck:

One's unlucky,
Two's lucky;
Three is health,
Four is wealth;
Five is sickness
And six is death.

Should a girl wish to know from what direction her true love will come she has only to throw stones at a crow and to note in which direction it flies off.

*See also* RAVEN; ROOK.

**crying** European superstition offers the parents of children who cry frequently the consolation that a child who 'cries long will live long'. Another superstition of long standing, meanwhile, warns against crying over someone who is dying or at the graveside of someone who has just died, as the soul of the deceased will be robbed of its rest if any tears happen to fall on the grave. Tears shed at WEDDINGS and CHRISTENINGS are, conversely, regarded as a good omen.

*See also* PEARL.

**cuckoo** Virtually all the superstitions surrounding the cuckoo concern its distinctive call, and many people listen out for the 'first cuckoo of the spring'. If this call comes from somewhere to the right of the hearer, good luck may be expected for the coming year; if from the left, bad luck is in store. It is also unlucky to hear the first cuckoo while standing on hard ground, which implies that the hearer will not live to hear next year's bird. If on grass, the person concerned is recommended to roll around on the ground as this will relieve a host of physical ailments. Luckiest of all is the person who hears the first cuckoo on 28 April, of all dates the most propitious for the event, according to Welsh tradition. Ill luck, however, will attend anyone who hears a cuckoo before 6 April or after MIDSUMMER DAY. Superstition also advises that it is unlucky to see a cuckoo before seeing the first SWALLOW of the season, as the rest of the year will be unhappy. More prosaically, Yorkshiremen warn that the cuckoo's call is a warning of approaching RAIN.

Whatever condition a person is in when the first call is heard will remain unchanged for the next twelve months. It is consequently unlucky to hear the cuckoo when hungry or ill in bed; conversely, some people will burst into a run on hearing the sound, reasoning that this will ensure they are busy all year long. Turning over any COINS that happen to be in one's pocket when the cuckoo's song is heard will guarantee prosperity over the ensuing year. It is said, incidentally, that if people remove their left SHOE on hearing their first cuckoo of the year they will find inside a single HAIR of the same colour as that of the person they are destined to marry.

According to the Scots, the number of times a cuckoo calls signifies the number of years a person has left to live, though unmarried people claim that in their case this refers to the years that will pass before their WEDDING. The number of petitions that are made to the bird for information of this nature is said to be the real reason why the bird leaves its EGGS in other birds' nests, having no time to build its own. Lastly, the disappearance of cuckoos in the winter is easily explained by one ancient but persistent tradition: they have all turned into hawks.

**cuckoo flower** Wild flower, also called lady's smock or ragged robin, which is linked by superstition with FAIRIES. Because of this association, it is thought very unlucky to bring a cuckoo flower indoors. It can, however, be used medicinally to purify the blood and to prevent scurvy.

**curlew** Moorland bird with a curved beak and distinctive, eerie cry, which is widely considered a bird of ill omen. The cry of the curlew is much feared by FISHERMEN and other seafarers and is said to portend death or storms, particularly if heard at night. The bird is consequently sometimes identified as the source of the superstition of the SEVEN WHISTLERS. It is also said that a person suffering from JAUNDICE may be cured by gazing into the yellow EYE of the stone curlew.

**cut** *see* WOUND.

**cutlery** In keeping with most other domestic utensils, cutlery boasts its own peculiar associated superstitions. In particular, it is unlucky to lay cutlery on the TABLE so that it forms a CROSS, and if an item of cutlery is accidentally dropped it should be retrieved by another person to avoid bad luck. An old English rhyme advises:

Knife falls, gentleman calls;
Fork falls, lady calls;
Spoon falls, baby squalls.

Dropping a carving knife, it is said, invites a visit by a policeman, while dropping a fork may mean that an ENGAGEMENT will soon be broken off.
*See also* KNIFE; SPOON.

**cyclamen** Ornamental plant once valued for its root, which could be used in

**cyclamen**

various herbal remedies. In particular it was credited as being a purgative and an antidote to poison, and its other uses included hastening the process of CHILD- BIRTH. It was also prized as an APHRO- DISIAC and as an intoxicant. Stuffing the nostrils with cyclamen leaves is said to prevent BALDNESS.

# D

**daddy long legs** On both sides of the Atlantic the daddy long legs is considered a beneficial insect to be respected. In the British Isles, taking care not to harm daddy long legs when reaping the harvest will preserve the luck of crop and reapers alike. In the USA, chanting 'Granddaddy, granddaddy, where did my cows go?' to a daddy long legs will cause the insect to indicate with one of its legs the direction in which any missing cattle will be discovered.

**daffodil** As one of the harbingers of spring, the daffodil is generally considered a lucky flower. In Wales the person who finds the first daffodil of the year will enjoy considerable prosperity throughout the coming months, earning more gold than silver. If, however, the first daffodil hangs its head towards the finder he is fated to suffer an ill-omened year. A single daffodil should never be brought indoors, as this will bring bad luck – although a bunch of daffodils implies no such misfortune. Some say daffodils should never be allowed into the house before the first goslings or chicks have hatched.

**daisy** The daisy is a cheerful little plant, suitably associated with cheerful customs and superstitions. The most familiar is the time-honoured ritual by which a person may pluck the petals from a daisy one by one with the words 'He/she loves me, he/she loves me not' to discover the faithfulness or commitment of a lover (this should really be done at the hour of midday, facing the SUN). Putting daisy roots under one's pillow,

moreover, will produce a dream vision of one's future partner. Eating the first daisy of the season will ensure good luck for the rest of the year; failing this, it should be stepped on to prevent it growing on one's grave before the year is through. Drinking a potion made from daisies will cure MADNESS, and the plant may also be used to treat a myriad of minor ailments from the curing of WARTS to the restoring of HAIR colour. When the petals of the daisy open fully this is taken as a sign of good WEATHER in the offing.

A touching tradition has it that daisy seeds are sown by the spirits of stillborn BABIES as a means of consolation to their sorrowing parents. Another explanation identifies them as having sprouted from the tears of Mary Magdalene.

**dandelion** Of the assorted superstitions that attach to the dandelion the best-known concerns divining the number of years a person must wait before their WEDDING by counting the number of breaths it takes to blow every seed off a dandelion 'clock'. The same process may also be applied to find out the number of children a girl may expect. Ancient traditions variously warn that anyone who picks a dandelion will wet their bed (*see* BEDWETTING), that dandelions will remain closed in the morning if RAIN is in store, and that the summer will be hot but wet if they bloom in April and July. Dandelion tea is highly recommended for purifying the BLOOD, for RHEUMATISM and for liver complaints.

**darts** A popular British pub game, which has thrown up a few unique sporting superstitions. Well-known conventions include a taboo on men playing women, which is considered unlucky, and the habit that many players have of bringing their left foot forward to the line and sweeping it from left to right before throwing the dart.

**days of the week** Each of the seven days of the week has its own character and significance in the world's superstitions. Astrologers have allocated a planetary sign to each day and this largely determines its qualities.

Monday, influenced by the MOON, is not the luckiest of days and is consequently not a good time to sign a contract, expect favours, do any mending, give money or embark on a new project (though, conversely, the Irish prefer Mondays to begin new tasks). The WEATHER on a Monday will be the reverse of what follows during the rest of the week, and should a visitor arrive on a Monday the succeeding six days will be much disrupted by further arrivals. French tradition claims that couples who marry on a Monday will become insane, while in Ireland Monday is a bad time to dig a grave. The first Monday in April, the second Monday in August and the last Monday in December are considered the unluckiest days in the year, marking respectively the anniversaries of Cain's birth, the destruction of Sodom and Gomorrah and the betrayal of Christ by Judas (*see* CALENDAR).

Tuesday, ruled by Mars, is a day for fighting or for the competitive pursuit of BUSINESS. It is also approved as a day for WEDDINGS. Wearing a flower in the lapel is unwise on Tuesdays, and women are further advised to take extra care to avoid FIRE and danger of all kinds and not to present themselves for medical operations on that day. It is risky even for them to trim their FINGERNAILS.

Wednesday, governed by Mercury, is a day of mixed potential. Recommended as a day to embark on courses of medical treatment, to write LETTERS and to ask for favours, it is a bad time to get married, to buy anything expensive or to wear GLOVES. Especially unlucky is a Wednesday that coincides with a new moon (though US superstition somewhat perversely declares Wednesday to be the luckiest day of the week).

Thursday, influenced by Jupiter, is also a day of contrasting fortune. Lucky for weddings, making vital decisions and taking legal advice, it is less ideal for spinning yarn, beginning in a new job, eating chicken, wearing RUBIES and for a child's first day at SCHOOL. In Germany it is regarded as the unluckiest day of the week.

Friday, subject to Venus, is widely held to be unlucky and a day when evil influences are at work – especially if it happens to be the thirteenth day of the month (*see* THIRTEEN). The day that Eve offered the apple to Adam in the Garden of Eden, Friday is favoured for the holding of witches' covens (*see* WITCHCRAFT) and was formerly the customary day for hangings. ACCIDENTS are more frequent on Fridays (though visits to the DOCTOR are not advised), and CLOTHES made on that day will not fit. Projects or trips begun on a Friday will not prosper and any person who laughs on that day, says one old proverb, will cry on Sunday. Many people add that Friday is also an inauspicious day for moving house or for weddings, and formerly in some parts of the British Isles those who courted their lovers on a Friday were hounded by friends and neighbours banging noisily on pans and kettles. According to one old Shropshire superstition, news received on a Friday makes a physical impression upon the hearer in the form of a new wrinkle for every tiding. Children born on Friday will prove unlucky, but will enjoy the gift of second sight and healing powers. Many people claim that the weather on a Friday will be repeated on the following Sunday.

Saturday, ruled by Saturn, is sacred to Jews as the Sabbath and is a good day for setting out on a journey, though not for working. DREAMS told to others on a Saturday are sure to come true, but the day is not recommended for starting new projects, for the performance of good deeds or for leaving HOSPITAL. Scottish superstition states that persons born on a Saturday will be able to see GHOSTS. The weather always includes a fine spell on Saturdays, in remembrance of the fact that it was the day on which God created man. A RAINBOW sighted on a Saturday, however, promises a whole week of rain.

Sunday, influenced by the sun and the holiest day in the Christian week, is the luckiest day of all. Children born on Sundays are especially blessed and are immune from witchcraft; they may also have psychic powers. It is bad luck to work, to make a BED, to cut HAIR or fingernails, to cry, to sew or to court someone on a Sunday, but the day is otherwise ideal for medical treatments, for setting out to sea (see SAILORS) and for the fulfilling of various generous acts. Another English superstition claims that anyone guilty of SINGING out of tune in church on a Sunday will be punished by finding that their dinner has burned.

Forgetting which day of the week it is when a person gets up in the morning has its own consequences, according to one old British rhyme:

Lose a day, you lose a friend,
Gain a day, you gain a friend.

See also GOOD FRIDAY; MONTHS OF THE YEAR.

**dead hand** The hand of a CORPSE, whose touch was once held to have considerable healing powers. This macabre notion applied particularly to the bodies of SUICIDES and newly executed criminals, and in former times patients frequently petitioned executioners to be allowed to touch the body of a recently hanged man, usually paying a small fee for the privilege. The treatment was recommended especially for those suffering from CANCER, scrofula, WARTS, sores and neck and throat problems, the dead man's hand being used to stroke the affected part. Some women also put faith in the procedure as a cure for infertility. RINGS taken from the hand of a dead man can similarly be used to alleviate various minor ailments. The severed hand of a dead man will also assist in the churning of BUTTER if used to stir the milk.

See also HAND OF GLORY.

**deafness** Superstition offers several courses of treatment for deaf people. Irish authorities recommend frequent application of drops of oil rendered from EELS, while the Scots favour a mixture of ant eggs and ONION juice similarly administered. In Gloucestershire it is said that pricking a SNAIL and allowing its juices to drip into the ear will ease earache, while other cures include pouring the URINE of a cow into the ear. Finally, Lincolnshire tradition warns that finding the backbone of an OX in a piece of meat may cause loss of hearing.

**death** As might be expected, death is the focus of a vast body of superstition. Every culture boasts a secret code of omens that warn of imminent death, the most common including the appearance of BLACK creatures such as CROWS, the inexplicable howling of DOGS and the sound of death KNOCKING to gain admittance. Sometimes the threat posed by such phenomena may be evaded by taking certain actions, but at other times there is no escape.

When death approaches, various measures may be taken to ease the process of dying. In many countries friends and relatives will open all the doors and windows (and often drawers and cupboard doors also) when a person lies dying so that the unfettered soul may be allowed to escape unhindered, and may also open any locks and loosen KNOTS in the sick-room for the same reason. Other precautions include never standing at the foot of the dying person's bed, so as not to obstruct the soul's passage; turning MIRRORS to the wall so as not to alarm and confuse the departing spirit; stopping CLOCKS at the moment of death; and

81

allowing a relative to inhale the last dying BREATH. Many coastal communities believe that death will not occur until the TIDE is on the ebb.

In various societies it is deemed wrong to leave the newly dead alone at any time between their death and their FUNERAL, and a constant vigil is kept by friends and relatives. CANDLES may also be lit so that the departed is not frightened by the dark. The ringing of BELLS is reputed to aid the departed by warding off evil spirits: in times gone by a 'passing bell' was rung as the patient approached death, while the 'Nine Tailors' were sounded when death had actually taken place.

A curiosity known in the British Isles is the ancient notion of placing the dying person's bed under a beam to assure them of an easy death. Other largely neglected traditions include laying the TABLE one last time for the dead person, so that the deceased may eat before his final journey, WASHING the dead person's clothing separately from that of the living to prevent another death occurring in the family, and taking care never to be holding a bird or other creature as it dies, whether or not one has actually been responsible for its demise. The idea that one should never speak ill of the dead is still strong in many communities and indeed in public life. This taboo dates back as far as the ancient Romans, and was observed originally not so much out of a desire for 'fair play' towards those who can no longer defend themselves as from fear of provoking their GHOSTS into returning.

While it may seem ominous for someone's death to be incorrectly reported when the person concerned is still alive, such a mistake does have its bright side. According to German superstition, the person concerned is guaranteed an extra ten years of life by way of recompense.

*See also* BANSHEE; BLACK DOG; BURIAL; CORPSE; DEAD HAND; GHOST; HAND OF GLORY; ILLNESS; MURDER; SUICIDE.

**death watch beetle**   *see* BEETLE.

**deer**   Best-known of the superstitions that attach to deer is the widely held belief that they cry on the loss of their horns or when mortally wounded. In former times many people were reluctant to eat venison on the grounds that deer were thought to consume SNAKES in the summer months, and that in consequence their flesh was poisonous. EPILEPTICS were sometimes furnished with a RING containing a fragment of deer's hoof, which was alleged to cure the condition.

*See also* STAG.

**Devil**   The ruler of the Underworld, otherwise called Satan or Lucifer, who is the personification of evil in Christian demonology. Worship of the Devil – the 'Prince of Darkness' or the 'Horned One' – has always been a central feature of European and US WITCHCRAFT and has encompassed such extremes as human sacrifice and orgiastic SEX. Time was when many people were nervous of even speaking his name, preferring instead to refer to 'Old Nick' for fear of provoking dark forces.

Terrifying as he may be, the Devil was often also depicted as slow-witted; many folk tales are based on clever tricks by which he is foiled. Followers of Satan speak of him manifesting in varous forms, his favourite guises including the cloven-hoofed GOAT, reminiscent of the Greek god Pan, the DOG and the MONKEY.

Serious-minded belief in the Devil may have declined since the witchcraft manias of the seventeenth century, but was still sufficiently strong in 1855 for the discovery of the infamous 100-mile-long trail of 'Devil's hoofmarks' in the snow of south Devon to create widespread consternation. Even now the Devil is an indispensable leading protagonist in orthodox religious teaching as well as in horror films.

**dew**   Early morning dew is much prized as an ingredient in a host of preparations recommended by folklore, especially if gathered early on MAYDAY morning. Many people still make a point of WASHING their face in the dew on the first day of May, variously thinking that it is lucky or will in some mysterious way preserve their looks (in times past it was thought best to wash in the dew that collected beneath an OAK). Sickly children were anointed with dew into the nineteenth century, while washing in dew was said to make a person (or livestock) immune from WITCHCRAFT. Used in a lotion, dew is credited with benefiting the eyesight, relieving skin complaints and curing itches, as well as preventing vertigo if taken nasally.

According to a US proverb, the presence of dew is an indication of the WEATHER to come:

When the dew is on the grass,
Rain will never come to pass.
When grass is dry at morning light,
Look for rain before the night.

**diamond** The most sought-after GEMSTONE of all, particularly favoured for engagement RINGS. Appropriately enough, superstition holds that the diamond symbolises conjugal love, inspiring courage in a man and pride in a woman. The superstitious particularly value diamonds that show flashes of colour inside the stone, as these are supposed to be given off by the stone's magical properties which will bring great good luck to the owner. Less desirable, though, is the ownership of such notorious gems as the Hope Diamond and the Koh-i-Noor Diamond, now part of the British royal regalia, on the grounds that both these stones bring bad luck.

**dice** The throwing of dice and placing bets on the outcome, as pursued throughout the USA, is the subject of numerous superstitions. Players insist on blowing on the dice for luck, and may snap their fingers to ward off ill fortune or rub the dice on a red-headed person to ensure they roll in their favour.

Some toss the dice for the purposes of divination. If one spot lies uppermost, an important LETTER is on the way; if two spots show, a forthcoming trip will end in success; if three spots turn up, a major surprise is in the offing; if four show, trouble is brewing; if five lie uppermost, there will be a change at home or a lover will prove untrue; and if six spots show, good luck in financial matters is guaranteed.

**dimple** Superstition has it that dimpled CHEEKS are a sign of God's favour and that such depressions are caused by the touch of His finger or that of one of His angels. In the USA a dimple on the chin (allegedly the imprint of the DEVIL's shoe) is less indicative of good character and suggests that the owner is inclined to bad ways, as stipulated in the rhyme: 'Dimple on the chin – Devil within.' A British variant recorded in Scarborough, north Yorkshire, runs:

Dimple in your chin,
Your living's brought in;
Dimple in your cheek,
Your living's to seek.

**dining table** *see* TABLE.

**dirt** English superstition claims that dirt has luck-giving qualities and that being too worried about cleanliness risks cleaning one's luck away. In some areas bringing mud into the house is a lucky act, particularly in January, while those moving home will leave some small area such as a fireplace uncleaned so that the new occupant does not have to move into a house from which the luck has been entirely brushed out.

*See also* BATHING; BRUSH; CHIMNEY SWEEP; DUNG; WASHING.

**disease** *see* ILLNESS.

**dish** Like many other kitchen utensils, dishes are not without significance among the superstitious. According to the Scottish, it is particularly unlucky if a bride breaks a dish in the course of a WEDDING breakfast and the marriage cannot be expected to prosper. Unmarried people may also employ dishes to see into their futures by the following ritual now associated with HALLOWE'EN. Blind-folded, they are invited to choose between three dishes, one containing clean WATER, another holding dirty water and the last nothing at all. If the person's left hand dips into the clean water, he or she will marry someone who has loved no other; if the dirty water is chosen, marriage to a WIDOW or widow-er will follow; but if the empty dish is selected there will be no marriage at all. The formula sometimes varies, with the dishes containing GOLD, a RING and a THIMBLE (to symbolise respectively a rich marriage, an early marriage and no mar-riage at all).

In times gone by, the ritual of 'disha-loof' was sometimes observed in Scot-land after a death had taken place, with the aim of discovering the condition of the newly departed soul. The ceremony was carried out by three women who laid out three dishes and set between them a sieve into which, with their backs turned, they attempted to place their hands. The first to do so was considered the one who had done most to succour the dead rela-tive or friend, but if none succeeded and the dishes were touched instead, all their efforts were in vain.

**dock** Wild plant, which is widely cre-dited with the power to ease the irritation caused by stinging NETTLES. Superstition has it that, wherever a stinging nettle grows, there too will be found a dock to counter its sting. Children applying dock leaves to the site of a sting sometimes recite the ancient rhyme:

Out nettle, in dock,
Dock shall have a new smock,
But nettle shan't have nothing.

**doctor** Though modern medical practitioners may strive to distance them-selves from superstitious practices, they themselves remain the object of supersti-tious speculation. Among the traditions that survive into modern times are the notions that consulting a doctor on a Friday is ill-advised and may lead to the patient's death; being the first patient in a new clinic or even the first of the morn-ing is a guarantee of a cure; and that a doctor's bill should never be paid in full for fear of TEMPTING FATE. The best doc-tors of all are those who are born the sev-enth child of a seventh child and so have special healing powers.

*See also* HOSPITAL.

**dog** The close relationship between man and the canine species is reflected in a host of time-honoured superstitions, not least in the stories of dogs that have pined to death on the demise of their owners. Dog lovers are inclined to consider meet-ing a dog a lucky event, especially if it is a black and white spotted dog such as a dalmatian, and in sporting circles a grey-hound with a white spot on its forehead is said to guarantee good fortune. Others, however, get very nervous if they are fol-lowed by a dog they do not know, espec-ially if it is BLACK: in Scotland and Lancashire, for instance, this is tanta-mount to an omen of death (though it is lucky according to West Country lore).

The way a dog behaves is alleged to reveal many things. If a dog scratches itself and seems sleepy, a change in the WEATHER is in the offing. If it eats GRASS or rolls in the dust, then RAIN may be expected, but if it produces a bad smell then gales are on the way. According to US authorities, should a dog fall asleep with its paws drawn up and with its tail pointing straight out, the tail indicates the direction in which death will soon appear.

Various superstitions, in fact, link dogs with death and the afterlife. Dogs are widely believed to have psychic suscep-tibilities, and many dog owners tell stor-ies about supposedly haunted locations where their pets regularly refuse to pro-ceed, hackles raised, at some apparition invisible to the human eye (*see* GHOST). In the spectral BLACK DOG or barghest is much feared as a harbinger of death and disaster, and it is also claimed that the

DEVIL sometimes takes the form of a dog in the course of his nefarious activities. Perhaps in connection with this, SAILORS are reluctant even to mention the word 'dog' while at sea, and it is also thought a very bad omen if a dog is allowed to come between a bride and groom just before a WEDDING ceremony (in many places, indeed, dogs are banned from entering churches at any time).

The howling of dogs for no apparent reason is dreaded by many people, who claim that the animals have detected the presence of unseen spirits or evil forces and are warning of someone's imminent demise. In medieval Poland and Germany it was said that dogs howled incessantly *en masse* at the approach of the plague. A howling dog that is driven away but returns to resume its noise is a certain omen of death, while a dog that howls three times and is then silent is a sign that death has already taken place. Some maintain that there is no baulking fate if a dog is heard howling; people living in Staffordshire, however, have the option of taking off their left SHOE, placing it upside down on the ground, SPITTING on it and then treading on it with the left foot, which will both quieten the dog and provide a measure of protection. It was once believed, incidentally, that dogs that howl on Christmas Eve are fated to go mad before the end of the year, and many otherwise healthy animals were formerly destroyed on these grounds.

The risk of rabies has made many people acutely nervous of dogs, and some victims of dog-bites have resorted to bizarre remedies to avoid developing the disease. These have included eating grass from a churchyard, consuming some of the 'HAIR of the dog that bit you' fried in oil with a little rosemary, and even eating parts of the dog itself (typically the heart or the liver). Destruction of a dog that had bitten someone was once automatic: superstition holds that, even if the dog was in good health at the time of the attack, its victim will none the less contract rabies if the dog happens to catch the

disease at a later date. In Scotland, meanwhile, it is said that a dog will never bite an idiot.

In folk medicine, applying a poultice made from a dog's head mixed with a little wine is said to benefit those suffering from JAUNDICE, while the lick of a dog's TONGUE will alleviate sores on the skin and melted dog fat will help against RHEUMATISM. Wearing a dried dog's tongue around the neck, meanwhile, will cure SCROFULA. Some authorities hold that removing a few hairs from a patient suffering from WHOOPING COUGH, or various other complaints, and feeding these to a dog in some BREAD AND BUTTER will successfully cure the patient by transferring the problem to the dog.

*See also* POODLE; WILD HUNT.

**dolphin** The traditionally sympathetic relationship between dolphins and man is reflected by the many legends in which dolphins rush to the aid of men in distress at SEA. According to ancient mythology, dolphins have a weakness for human SINGING and also transport the souls of the dead to the afterlife. Superstitions that have survived to modern times include the curious notion that dolphins change colour when death is near and the general belief that dolphins playing in fine weather or close to shore are a warning of WIND on the way, while the sight of dolphins at play in a turbulent sea indicates that a period of calm is in the offing. Similarly, good weather can be expected if dolphins swim north, while deterioration will ensue if they are spotted swimming south.

*See also* PORPOISE.

**donkey** The humble donkey or ass, upon which Christ is said to have ridden, has inevitably taken an exalted place among the ANIMALS revered by the superstitious. The dark lines across the shoulders of the donkey are said to form the shape of the CROSS, commemorating the animal's role in the biblical story, and as a consequence the DEVIL is unable to disguise himself as this creature. Another version traces the lines back to the Old Testament story of Balaam, who struck his ass and was henceforth reminded of his cruelty by the cross that remained.

Whatever the origins of the markings, it is claimed that plucking three HAIRS from a donkey's shoulders and placing them in a black silk or muslin bag worn around the neck of a person suffering from MEASLES or WHOOPING COUGH – which sounds not unlike the braying of an ass – is certain to cure the disease, as long as the animal is of the opposite sex to the patient (the donkey itself is, however, rendered useless from then on). Alternatively, the patient is passed three times over and under the animal or, in southern England, fed the three hairs, finely chopped, in BREAD AND BUTTER. The right hoof of a donkey, meanwhile, protects against EPILEPSY, and Irish sages formerly treated SCARLET FEVER by forcing hairs from the sufferer down a donkey's throat.

Ancient advice suggests that scorpion stings and snakebites can be treated by simply sitting on a donkey facing its tail, or else by applying the lung of an ass to the wound. Similar action will also relieve TOOTHACHE, and a child is guaranteed permanently trouble-free teeth if it takes its first ride on a donkey. One way to get even with an enemy is to rub his head with donkey hoof clippings, after which his own head will assume the shape of a donkey's.

In many societies, the donkey (which is often believed, incidentally, to be deaf to music) is widely regarded as a lucky animal. It is thought particularly beneficial for a pregnant woman to see a donkey, for it will ensure that her unborn child grows up to be wise and well-behaved. By the same token, farmers often keep donkeys among their cows to preserve the luck of the herd and to help to prevent the loss of CALVES through premature labour. Tradition dictates that no one ever sees a dead donkey because the animals sense their coming demise and hide themselves away. Finding the body of a deceased donkey is conse-

quently particularly lucky, and some people will insist on jumping over it for luck. Lastly, RAIN can be expected if a donkey brays and twitches its ears.

**door** The door is the usual entrance by which luck or evil spirits enter or leave the HOUSE; other options include the WINDOWS and the CHIMNEY. In former times, many householders protected themselves from evil by barring the door magically to malevolent entities. This could be done by such means as knocking NAILS into the door in the shape of a CROSS, hanging a HORSESHOE above the doorway, and concealing various witch-repelling objects, such as an open pair of SCISSORS, under the threshold. Another option was to chalk patterns on the doorstep, joining one door-jamb to the other so that there was no place for the DEVIL to slip through.

Tradition throughout the world dictates that doors be opened at the time of CHILDBIRTH and again at DEATH to cut short any prolonged suffering. Another widespread superstition advises against going out and leaving every door in the house open, and similarly never allowing the front and back doors to remain open together as this facilitates the free passage of malevolent spirits. Doors and windows should, however, be left open during thunderstorms to let LIGHTNING out should it strike the house. In ancient Rome it was thought unlucky for a person to enter a house with his left foot first, and in Germany it is considered unwise to slam the front door in a house where someone has just died for fear of injuring the departing spirit.

In some parts of the world COFFINS bearing the bodies of dead CHILDREN leave the house via a window rather than through the front door. This is to avoid prejudicing the chances of having her own child of any woman who subsequently passes through the door. Mourners returning from a FUNERAL are also advised to come in by a different door or even through a window rather than via the door they used on leaving the house, though other visitors should leave by the same door to avoid taking the household's luck away with them. Once a coffin or a bride has passed through the front door on the way to church, some people immediately wash the doorstep to ensure the luck of those departing and to preserve the luck of those left behind. A new bride is further discouraged from walking over the threshold of her new home and is traditionally carried over it by the groom. Brides and others are also warned that, when entering a new house for the first time, they should always use the front door if they wish to enjoy good luck therein.

Should all the various precautions fail and the house is invaded by evil spirits, one solution is to hang doors the other way round or to brick up existing doorways and create new entrances elsewhere, a course of action that is bound to confuse any agent of misfortune.

**double fruit** According to British superstition, any person finding a fruit that has grown as 'double' will enjoy good luck, and if the fruit is shared with another person then both may make a wish. In Austria, pregnant women finding double fruit are advised to expect TWINS.

**dove** The dove's association with the Holy Ghost of Christian teaching has meant that the bird is widely linked with the qualities of purity and holiness. No evil spirit may assume the form of a dove or obtain control over one. Some people, though, fear the appearance of a dove as it can be associated with death. MINERS have been known to refuse to go underground on seeing a dove, and some say that a dove circling someone is a sure sign that the person concerned is fated to die in the near future – though he may well be destined for happiness in the afterlife. Another widely held superstition, however, asserts that no person can die peacefully while lying on a mattress or pillow that contains dove feathers, and in the past stricken people were deliberately laid

on such feathers in order to delay the moment of death until various friends and relatives could be reached.

Scottish superstition advises that the innards torn from a living dove can be used as a laxative for cattle, though other authorities warn that great misfortune will befall anyone who kills a dove. US superstition advises that placing a dead dove on the chest will alleviate pneumonia and, further, that turtle-doves making their nests near a person's house will protect that person from RHEUMATISM (though they will also render anyone who touches them infertile).

**dragonfly** An old superstition claims that anyone who catches a dragonfly will marry within the year. An angler may observe from the position of a dragonfly where the fish are. This will only work, however, if the angler is of good character: if he is not, the dragonfly will mislead him by hovering over empty water.

**dream** The interpretation of dreams and their psychological meaning has attracted many academics in modern times, but superstition has long had its own thoughts about the subject. In the ancient world, long before Freud and Jung set about their analyses of the dream-state, it was thought that dreams provided a doorway to the supernatural and that much about the present and the future might be divined from their study.

Virtually every dream is said to have its own particular significance. Among the more commonly held superstitions are the notions that dreaming the same dream three nights in succession means it will almost certainly come true, and that it is lucky to forget the dream you had the previous night. If a dream is remembered its nature should not be divulged, according to British tradition, until after breakfast. Dreams experienced on a Friday night and discussed with others on a Saturday (see DAYS OF THE WEEK) are sure to come true.

In both the West and the Orient it is said that, if a person dreams something, exactly the opposite will happen to them in real life. If one dreams of death, therefore, this bodes well for the living, but if one dreams of a WEDDING a FUNERAL is likely to follow.

Dreaming of the future is promoted by sleeping with a HORSESHOE, a LEAF or a KEY under the pillow. Various procedures, such as slipping a BLADE-BONE beneath the pillow on retiring to bed, will enable the sleeper to dream of a future lover.

*See also* NIGHTMARE.

**dress**  *see* CLOTHES.

**drink**  Ancient British superstition advises that it is lucky to have WINE or beer spilled on one's person by accident, but that it is unwise for two people to drink from the same cup unless they are married, as this will inextricably entangle their future lives with one another. Stirring one's drink with a KNIFE, moreover, is a sure way to wind up with indigestion.

*See also* COFFEE; TEA; WATER.

**dropsy**  Cures for dropsy, in which watery fluids collect in the tissues or in a body cavity, are among the least appealing devised by superstition. Back in the sixteenth century it was recommended that sufferers behead three earthworms, store their remains with sugar and licorice in jars of HOLY WATER for nine days, and then take a sip of this delightful cordial once a day for another nine days. In Devon, meanwhile, a spoonful of TOAD ashes taken every morning for three days while the MOON was waxing was once regarded as an infallible cure.

**drowning**  Death by drowning is the greatest fear of every seafarer, and there are many superstitions concerned with safeguarding their welfare at sea. Most people are familiar with the old idea that drowning people see their whole life flit before them as death approaches – and also with the notion that they cannot drown until they have surfaced three times. In fact, the time it takes to drown varies according to the salinity of the

water, salt water taking longer to be absorbed by the lung walls than fresh water. Also widely held is the tradition that a drowned body will rise to the surface after seven (alternatively eight or nine) days.

The location of drowned persons is often a difficult task, and superstition is not wanting in suggesting ways to make this easier. Solutions include firing off guns over the water (the report will supposedly burst the gall bladder of the CORPSE and allow it to rise) and floating a lighted CANDLE or a loaf of BREAD containing some SILVER or mercury on the water in the belief that this will infallibly drift to where the body lies.

One rather perverse old British superstition claims that it is unlucky to rescue a drowning man, for he will certainly become his rescuer's enemy. Furthermore, every river, according to Irish and Scottish folklore, demands at least one human life every year. If this is denied, the life of the rescuer may be claimed as recompense. The sea may also claim another life, according to the inhabitants of the Hebrides, if a drowned person is buried too far beyond the waterline.

Discussion of drowning is forbidden by many SAILORS and FISHERMEN, and some refuse to learn to swim on the grounds that if the sea is going to claim them it is better not to prolong the agony of death but to resign themselves to their fate. They also claim that the souls of drowned seafarers can be heard when the wind is high, and these spirits may reveal themselves to the living to warn them of their own imminent deaths.

*See also* CAUL; SEVEN WHISTLERS; SWEATER.

**drums**  British folklore boasts a number of spectral drums, whose sound heralds some dire event. Most famous of these is Drake's Drum, which is said to roll when war is about to break out. Once the property of Sir Francis Drake and now kept at his old home, Buckland

Abbey, near Plymouth in Devon, it is said to have beaten a roll in 1914, at the start of the First World War; again at the end of the conflict, in 1918, when it was heard on board British ships at anchor in Scapa Flow in the north of Scotland; and reportedly once more during the evacuation of Dunkirk in 1940.

Another celebrated spectral drum was that which belonged to an itinerant drummer who was arrested for vagrancy in Tedworth (now Tidworth) in Wiltshire back in 1661. After the owner was parted from his drum and had been sentenced to transportation, the drum continued to beat to an unseen hand and the entire village was much troubled by supernatural interference. The Airlie family of Cortachy Castle in Kirriemuir, Angus, claim to have a 'drum of death' alleged to sound whenever the demise of the head of the family is imminent.

It is presumed that these drum stories owe much to primitive pagan belief, in which the beating of drums was supposed to dispel any lurking evil spirits.

**drunkenness** Superstition proposes numerous cures for this condition, many of which depend upon slipping something unappetising into the drink of the person concerned. These extra ingredients vary from OWL eggs and a few drops of the drunkard's own BLOOD to the powder of a dead man's bones and live EELS. To sober someone up quickly the best remedy is to roll him in manure and make him drink olive oil, then force him to smell his own URINE and bind his genitals with a vinegar-soaked cloth.

According to the Welsh, conversely, eating the roast lungs of a PIG enables people to go on drinking all day long without getting drunk.

See also HEATHER.

**duck** Perhaps the best-known tradition involving ducks is that if they lay EGGS of a dark brown colour this is a very bad omen, only to be remedied by destroying the duck that has laid them and hanging it head down so that the evil

spirits responsible fall from its beak. Owners of ducks are also recommended to bring duck eggs into the house before sunset, for any brought in after that hour will fail to hatch. An old British treatment for the condition of thrush is to allow the patient to breathe directly from the open beak of a white duck or drake (see BREATH). Ducks that flap their wings while they swim are a warning of approaching RAIN.

**dumb cake** In the British Isles, a special cake that is prepared in complete silence so that it may be used for the purposes of divination. The ingredients of flour, WATER, EGGS and SALT are mixed by one or more persons and then placed on the hearthstone, the upper surface of the cake being pricked with the initials of one of those present. If all is done correctly and in complete silence, the future partner of the person concerned will appear and similarly prick his or her own initials on the cake. Variants of the tradition suggest that it may only be performed at midnight on Christmas Eve, HALLOWE'EN or other auspicious dates, and, further, that portions of the cake must actually be eaten by those wishing to know their future partners. In some regions it is stipulated that the petitioners must walk backwards to their beds after eating the cake, when they will be pursued by apparitions of eager lovers-to-be.

**dung** The droppings of various animals are an essential ingredient in a range of potions and preparations recommended to the superstitious. In the British Isles, poultices of OX and COW dung are credited with excellent healing powers, while GOAT droppings mixed with vinegar are said to cure WARTS and BOILS. Smearing a concoction of MOUSE droppings and honey on the head, meanwhile, is one of several similar cures for BALDNESS. Lumps of dung left around the house are guaranteed to promote the luck of all the inhabitants, and stepping in a cowpat or in DOG dirt (which can be dried and used to treat dysentery) is similarly lucky – as long as it is the left foot that has been soiled and it is not done on purpose. Similarly, it is thought lucky by many people to be hit by droppings from a passing BIRD. In times gone by, it was thought by some burglars that if they defecated at the scene of their crimes they would be safe from discovery.

**dust**  *see* BRUSH; DIRT.

**dwarf**  People in Britain, Canada and India are agreed that meeting a dwarf of the opposite sex is very lucky. This tradition probably derives from the ancient idea that dwarfs are guardians of precious metals, which themselves have magical powers. Among their other attributes, dwarfs are reputed to be able to see into the future and to make themselves invisible at will.

*See also* MINERS.

**dyspepsia**  Irish superstition offers its own solution to the problem of dyspepsia or indigestion if conventional remedies fail. The sufferer is advised to fix a small CANDLE to a COIN and to place this on the affected area. The candle is then lit and a glass placed over it so that a vacuum is created and the skin is drawn up. This is said to be an infallible method of drawing out the evil influence that has caused pain.

# E

**eagle** Associated with the gods of both the ancient Greeks and Romans, the eagle has always been linked with strength, divinity and immortality. The ancient Egyptians, who worshipped the eagle-headed Horus, believed that the human soul took the form of an eagle after death. Christians, too, see the eagle as a symbol of resurrection. Irish tradition claims that Adam and Eve were turned into eagles and live to this day on an island off the coast of Galway. In Wales, the eagles of Snowdon were said to raise whirlwinds throughout the land by the flapping of their wings.

Seeing several eagles flying together is said to be a sign of peace, but if the birds remain motionless on rocky outcrops they are a warning of an enemy's approach. It is widely held that eagles never grow old and that they renew their youth by flying so close to the SUN that their feathers catch light and then plunging into the sea, from which they emerge rejuvenated. Their flesh, feathers, EGGS and BLOOD are consequently valued as ingredients in the WITCHCRAFT of many countries. The eagle is now protected by law and those who persist in plotting to steal an eagle's eggs (which bestow great good luck and protection against witchcraft if eaten by two people) are warned that, if successful, they will never again enjoy peace of mind. Many dislike hearing the piercing cry of an eagle, which is taken as an omen of death, and likewise become nervous if they see an eagle hovering for a long time over a particular spot as this too is interpreted as a warning of imminent demise. The heart of an eagle can be used to concoct an effective APHRODISIAC, while its gall bladder should be mixed with honey as a remedy for poor eyesight (*see* EYE) and its marrow is credited by some as having strong powers as a contraceptive. Eating the still warm brains of a dead eagle is said to conjure up fabulous illusions.

**eagle-stone** A hollow oval of clay ironstone, which was once credited with magical powers. Transported to the West from the Orient in increasing numbers in the seventeenth and eighteenth centuries, such stones were reputedly recovered from the nests of EAGLES, who used them to facilitate laying eggs. It was said that wearing eagle-stones as AMULETS would ease the process of CHILDBIRTH: records exist of women wearing them tied to the thigh during labour as far back as the thirteenth century, though the practice more or less died out in the British Isles in the early nineteenth century.

**ear** According to the ancient science of PHYSIOGNOMY, much can be learned about a person's character by an examination of their ears. If they are small, the owner is naturally mean, but if large this is a sign of generosity. Flat ears indicate a lack of refinement in the owner, while square-shaped ears are proof of a noble heart. The wise, meanwhile, can be distinguished by their long ears. Any vertical lines or creases in the ear apparently warn of a heart condition.

If a person's ears tingle, this is a sure indication that someone somewhere is talking about them. If it is the right ear that tingles, good things are being said; if the left, the gossip is malicious. Pinching a tingling left ear or making the sign of the CROSS over it will immediately cause the slanderer to bite his tongue. A traditional English rhyme goes one step further and actually identifies the person:

Left your mother,
Right your lover.

Hearing a ringing in the ears has its own significance. British superstition claims that, because the sound resembles that of distant church BELLS, it warns of the imminent death of a friend or a member of the family. The noise may, however, be turned to a person's advantage: if on hearing the ringing a person requests a friend to choose a letter at random from the alphabet (or else a number that corresponds to a certain letter) that letter is assuredly the first letter of the name of the person's future spouse.

*See also* DEAFNESS; EAR-RING.

**ear-ring** Some people wear ear-rings for reasons other than mere physical adornment. It is a widespread superstition that piercing the earlobes will improve poor eyesight (*see* EYES), though there is no medical evidence to support this, and SAILORS maintain, for reasons lost in antiquity, that wearing a gold ear-ring will protect them from death by DROWNING.

**earth** *see* SOIL.

**earthquake** The fear associated with earthquakes means that all the superstitions attached to them are of foreboding and death. A traditional English rhyme dictates:

There are things
An earthquake brings:
At nine of the bell
They sickness foretell;
At five and seven they betoken rain;
At four the sky
Is cleared thereby;
At six and eight comes wind again.

All over the world domestic and wild animals are said to signal imminent earthquakes by changes in their behaviour.

Anyone who dreams of an earthquake, meanwhile, is advised to take particular care as he goes about the day's business.

**Easter** As the holiest season in the Christian calendar, Easter has become a time of great significance among superstitious people in all Western countries. Easter was originally a pagan festival in praise of the Germanic Goddess of Spring, Ostera, and it is from this more ancient tradition that such customs as the eating of Easter eggs ultimately derive. Timed to coincide with the first Sunday following the full MOON of the vernal equinox, Easter is now marked by a host of rituals and customs that combine Christian and pagan elements.

Among the most familiar of these superstitions is the idea that the SUN dances as it appears on Easter morning to celebrate Christ's resurrection. If looked at through a darkened lens, it is said that on Easter morning the sun bears the imprint of a LAMB and FLAG, two images which have symbolic associations in Christian mythology. This is not the only weather myth connected with the day, however, for it is also claimed that a WIND that blows on Easter Day will continue to blow throughout the year, while a shower of RAIN that day promises a good crop of grass, but little hay.

Most people know the old custom of wearing new clothes on Easter Day, or at least the tradition of the 'Easter bonnet'. This practice originated in the habit of wearing the same set of clothes throughout LENT, finally discarding them for a new set on Easter Day itself. Those who do not wear at least one new item of clothing on Easter Day risk their existing clothing being soiled by birds or, worse, being spat upon by passing DOGS or having their eyes pecked out by CROWS.

Children born on Easter Day are deemed especially fortunate, and HOLY WATER saved from the Easter service is said to be particularly effective as a cure for a wide range of physical ills. Less well-known is an ancient German superstition that RABBITS lay eggs on Easter Day (hence the widely recognised figure of the Easter Bunny).

The chocolate Easter eggs of modern times, incidentally, hark back to the hard-boiled eggs that used to be dyed RED in memory of Christ's blood and were given to children in former times to preserve their health over the ensuing twelve months. The egg imagery is further passed down to the present time through the various egg-rolling rituals and egg-hunting games still carried out in many rural areas; all were originally meant to ensure good fortune in the coming months.

**eclipse**  People around the world have long feared the eclipse of the SUN or MOON, not infrequently attributing the happening to evil spirits trying to rob the Earth of light. Eclipses have often been interpreted as omens of the death of some high-ranking person such as a monarch – among them the Roman Emperor Nero and Catherine of Aragon, first wife of King Henry VIII of England, in 1536. Alternatively, they may presage some dreadful national calamity, such as the coming of the Black Death in 1348 and the outbreak of the First World War in 1914. Considerable panic has accompanied predictions that eclipses mark the start of the end of the world. Making a great deal of noise, by banging on drums, discharging guns in the air and so forth, is customary in many countries when an eclipse takes place, the idea being that the cacophony will frighten away the malevolent spirit responsible for the phenomenon.

**eel**  The sinister snake-like appearance of the eel has undoubtedly contributed to the many superstitious beliefs that surround it. A northern English tradition claims that eels actually suck the blood of anyone who swims among them, and ignorance about their breeding habits has led to several bizarre theories about their origins. These have included the notions that they form from horsehairs that come into contact with water, and that they

spring from the slime of other FISH. Further eccentric ideas include the superstition recorded in the Ozark Mountains of the USA that a cooked eel will become raw again if left uneaten.

Eels are alleged to have several uses in medicine. These include feeding expectant mothers powdered eel livers during a difficult birth, rubbing eel's blood on WARTS, using a whole eel to cure DEAFNESS, wearing garters of eelskin to prevent CRAMP (a treatment particularly favoured by swimmers) and slipping one into a drunkard's glass to cure alcoholism. Eel fat can be used to make an ointment that will render FAIRIES visible to human sight, while eating an eel's heart will enable a person to see into the future. Should the whole eel be consumed, however, the diner will be struck dumb.

Thunderstorms are said to disturb eels, and stormy weather is thus the best time to undertake an eel-fishing trip. It was once thought that witches and sorcerers clad themselves in jackets made of eelskin in the belief that these were impervious to gunfire.

**egg**  The humble chicken's egg is the object of a host of superstitions reflecting its importance as food, symbol of life and Christian icon. The first egg laid by a pullet is thought to be lucky, and in former times farmhands would present these to their sweethearts. If the pullet in question is brown, a wish may be made when the egg is eaten. If the bird is white and the egg is slipped beneath the pillow, the sleeper will be vouchsafed a vision of his or her future lover. If the same thing is done with the egg of a black hen, the person who consumes it will be protected from fever for the next twelve months.

Setting eggs to be hatched is a complicated business. Eggs should always be set under the hen in odd numbers and never when there is a new MOON or on a Friday or Sunday (*see* DAYS OF THE WEEK). To protect them from WEASELS and witches it is best to mark each egg with a small black CROSS.

The collection of eggs is not to be lightly undertaken and certain taboos must be observed. It is thought particularly unlucky to collect eggs and take them indoors after sunset; similarly, requests to buy eggs after nightfall may well be turned down. Finding an egg that is unusually small (often the case with the last one that a hen lays before sitting) is even more to be feared, for such eggs are said to have been laid by COCKS and are an omen of death only to be negated by throwing the offending egg over the barn roof. If such 'cock's eggs' are allowed to hatch, a serpent will emerge. Somewhat against expectation, it is also considered an omen of misfortune if a single hen is discovered to have laid two eggs in one day.

Having collected the eggs, care should be taken in carrying them. An old English rhyme runs:

Break an egg, break your leg;
Break three, woe to thee;
Break two, your love's true.

Furthermore, carrying new-laid eggs over running WATER means that none of them will hatch.

The everlasting question about which end of an egg should be cracked open when eating it is one which has vexed many people over the centuries (as satirised in Swift's *Gulliver's Travels*). Superstition advises that the correct end is the larger one; to break into the smaller end betokens only disappointment of one's hopes. Finding that one's egg has a double yolk is open to differing interpretations: in northern England this warns of a coming death, but in Somerset at least it signifies a WEDDING. Eating an egg every morning for forty days is recommended by the men of Morocco as an excellent way to improve one's sexual performance (*see* APHRODISIAC).

Rather then eating them, some people choose to pour three drops of egg white into a glass of water for the purposes of divination. Sometimes performed on Midsummer Day (*see* MIDSUMMER'S EVE) or on some other 'magical' day of the year, this ritual allows a person to divine from the shape that the white assumes the profession of their future partner or something else about their prospects in the coming months. Those who have tried the experiment have reported seeing such shapes as churches, coffins, ships and school desks.

Alternatively, to get a glimpse of a future lover a person should remove the yolk of a boiled egg and fill the hollow with SALT, then consume it without having anything to drink before going to bed. If all goes well this will bring on a raging thirst during the night, and the apparition of a future partner will appear in the person's dreams with water to soothe it.

Some thought should be given to the disposal of the eggshell. It is important to break the shell up once the contents are consumed, as a witch may use the empty shell to obtain power over the person who has fed from it by means of spells, or else use the shells as boats in which to set sail and wreck ships at SEA. It is bad luck, however, to push one's spoon through the bottom of the egg. Eggshells should never be burned, moreover, for to do so prejudices the laying of more eggs by one's hens. Feeding ground eggshells in milk or water to small children will, it is alleged in Lincolnshire, cure them of BEDWETTING, but older siblings should be discouraged from keeping decorative 'blown' eggs in the house, as these invite bad luck (it is all right, however, to keep them in an outhouse or garage). Some chicken farmers hang up empty eggshells near the chicken coop in the belief that this will protect the hens from predatory kites and preserve their good health. In Japan, women are warned never to step over an eggshell; if they do so they will surely go mad.

Other miscellaneous superstitions concerning eggs include the notion shared by seagoing FISHERMEN that it is very unlucky to have eggs on board ship or even to mention the word 'egg'. If they really must be discussed then some other term, such as 'roundabout', should be used instead. Jockeys are also nervous of eating eggs as they are held to constitute a mysterious threat to the health of their mounts. In the USA, it is said that rubbing a BIRTHMARK with an egg every morning and then burying the egg under the doorstep will cause the blemish to disappear. Dreaming of eggs is held to portend a death in the family.

*See also* EASTER.

**elbow**  British and US superstition is agreed that an itching elbow constitutes a prophecy that the person concerned will shortly be changing his or her bed companion. The agony of banging one's 'funny bone' is literally doubled by the knowledge that this is a warning of bad luck only to be avoided by deliberately banging the other elbow as well. A neglected English superstition, incidentally, suggests that if one succeeds in biting one's own elbow then one's enemy will immediately be soaked in a downpour or even killed.

**elder**  The elder or Judas tree, from which Judas is said to have hanged himself and from which the CROSS may have been constructed, has an unlucky reputation which probably pre-dates Christianity. Though it offers protection in a thunderstorm, as LIGHTNING will never strike it, the tree is most unwelcome indoors and should never be used as firewood, as this will bring the DEVIL himself down the chimney. If it is used to build boats, they will sink; if it is used as a murder weapon, the dead man's hand will emerge from his grave to point out the murderer; if it is used to make a CRADLE, any baby placed in it will fall prey to evil spirits. Neither should small children or animals be struck with a stick of elder, for this will retard their growth.

A bough of elder picked on the last day of April and hung over the doorway will, however, protect the household from evil over the coming year, and AMULETS made of elder will fend off witches (*see*

WITCHCRAFT). None the less, while disliking the tree's pungent smell, witches favour elder for their wands. Horsemen to this day will sometimes carry a small twig of elder to fend off saddle-sores. Cutting live elder wood should never be attempted, though, without first asking the permission of the 'Elder Mother', otherwise known as the 'Old Gal', lest she take offence and strike the woodcutter down.

Remedies involving the elder range from treatments for WARTS and fits to cures for RHEUMATISM, the usual procedure being to carry a stick of elder continually about one's person. Elder leaves collected on the eve of MAYDAY have special healing powers. If boiled in milk, the bark will relieve JAUNDICE, and if boiled in water it will cure EPILEPSY, according to long-established English tradition.

Dwarf elder is said to have originated in the blood of England's slaughtered Danish invaders and is sometimes still termed 'Dane's Blood'. The red colour of the stems is said to betray the fact that real blood flows within them, and cutting the stem will cause a real injury to any witch in the vicinity. This 'bloody' quality is undoubtedly the reason why the plant is a frequent ingredient in traditional witchcraft recipes.

**elephant**  Symbolic of long life and patient strength, the elephant is a popular good luck emblem. In African and Indian culture it occupies a special place, and many of these traditions have been taken up into the folklore of countries where the elephant is not indigenous. Ganesh, the elephant-headed Indian god, is venerated for his power to bestow great riches upon those he favours and may also grant success in a particular enterprise, especially one of a commercial nature. Thus, good luck cards in the West are often decorated with pictures of elephants, whether the event in question is a WEDDING, a school exam or a driving test. Similarly, miniature elephants are often to be found on charm bracelets and as brooches, all meant to promote the wearer's good fortune (just as, in Africa, people wear rings or bracelets of elephant HAIR for luck).

Ornaments and pictures of elephants should always face the DOOR if they are to operate successfully in attracting luck to the household, as elephants are naturally curious animals and like to know of any comings and goings. Perhaps because it seems so unlikely, it is said to be particularly lucky if a bride and groom encounter an elephant on their wedding day. Finally, one entirely incorrect superstition once commonly expressed in the West was that the elephant was unable to kneel.

**elf-shot**   In rural tradition, the condition of a COW or other livestock that goes into decline allegedly because it has become a target of the arrows that are supposedly fired by malicious FAIRIES and other spirits. Agricultural communities throughout the British Isles once attributed many a sudden death or outbreak of illness among their animals to the interference of evil spirits and talked of them being 'elf-shot'. Often a local expert on such matters was summoned to find the offending missile and to treat the ailing animal if he could. In fact, the many arrowheads found and identified as elf-shot turn out to be flint arrowheads dating from prehistoric times.

**elm**   The long-lived elm tree was revered in Norse mythology as the source of the first woman, Embla, and is still associated with a number of ancient traditions. Among these is the superstition that one's livestock is sure to suffer from disease if the leaves from an elm tree fall in their vicinity. Farmers in south-west England claim that barley should not be planted until the elm leaves are the size of a MOUSE's ear, while in the USA elm bark is recommended for the treatment of bed sores and BURNS.

**emerald**   A precious GREEN-coloured gemstone, generally associated with good luck. The BIRTHSTONE for those born in May, emeralds make a good choice for WEDDING presents as they confer happiness upon married couples. It is important, however, that emeralds are never given on a Monday (*see* DAYS OF THE WEEK) lest they lose their luck-giving properties. In some parts of the world the emerald is considered an APHRODISIAC. It is also claimed that secreting an emerald beneath the TONGUE will give a person the power to conjure up evil spirits.

Wearing an emerald ring is said to ease the pain of CHILDBIRTH, to cure EPILEPSY and dysentery, to negate the effects of snakebite and to ward off witches. It is also a good idea to wear an emerald if one has to answer a case in court, as this will ensure victory. Simply touching an emerald is alleged to benefit those suffering from BLINDNESS.

**emu**   Flightless Australasian bird, which is considered very lucky in its native land. New Zealanders insist that emu meat will cure many physical ailments, but warn that killing one of these creatures invites misfortune.

**engagement**   The announcement that two people are to marry, which, like the WEDDING ceremony itself, has its own peculiar taboos and traditions. The most crucial ritual of the modern betrothal is the buying of an engagement RING, which is conventionally more ornate than the plain gold band favoured by the majority of brides and grooms as a WEDDING RING, though jewelled engagement rings were rare in the past. The luckiest stones for engagement rings include DIAMONDS, SAPPHIRES, EMERALDS and RUBIES and others among the more precious of the BIRTHSTONES. PEARLS should be avoided because they represent tears, as should OPAL, unless the wearer was actually born in October.

According to US custom, some thought should be given to the day upon which the transaction takes place (*see* DAYS OF THE WEEK). If on a Monday, the couple can expect an eventful life together; if on a Tuesday, they will live in peace and harmony; if on a Wednesday, they will never quarrel; if on a Thursday, they will realise all their ambitions; if on a Friday, they will have to work hard for their eventual rewards; if on a Saturday, they will enjoy a life of pleasure together. The place is also relevant: proposals of marriage should never be made in public places or while travelling in a train or on a bus. Girls may rest assured about receiving proposals when at a dance, since even if they refuse they will enjoy an improvement in their luck.

It is unlucky if the ring fails to fit and has to be adjusted, and even more ominous if the ring gets lost or broken before the wedding. On no account should another person be allowed to try on the engagement ring, although friends may be allowed to slip it on to the end of their finger and make a wish, which will come true so long as they do not say 'thank you' afterwards.

The actual betrothal is nowadays an informal affair and few suitors drop on one knee. In times gone by, however, the business was much guided by superstitious belief. The betrothal request itself was often delivered by a third party, who had to pay particular attention to such omens as the ANIMALS he met in the street, and would turn back if he felt the signs were not good. The engagement would only be considered official after the couple had drunk a TOAST together, their little fingers locked as they drank from the same glass. They would then break some plates and glasses to symbolise the break they were making with their past lives. Dowries, meanwhile, were often ritually refused before final 'reluctant' acceptance.

Having announced their engagement, it is considered unlucky for the happy couple to go to church to hear their BANNS being read. Instead, they might like to break a BAY twig into two pieces and keep half each as a souvenir: for as long as they keep the twigs carefully their love will prosper. They are also advised by superstition not to stand together as GODPARENTS during their engagement, for this means they will never reach the altar. It is also unlucky (though in these times virtually unavoidable) for them to have their PHOTOGRAPH taken together.

Should the girl change her mind before the wedding, all she has to do, according to superstition, is present the other party with a KNIFE – and he will get the message. It is, however, unwise to get engaged too often as the DEVIL is entitled to claim a person's soul on the occasion of their third engagement.

**epilepsy** In ancient times epileptics were regarded as somehow in contact with the gods and people were thus very wary of the disease, around which many bizarre theories evolved. In later centuries fits of epilepsy were blamed on WITCHCRAFT and other external influences. Among the cures suggested were burying alive a black COCK at the point where the fit took place, or else piercing the ground with a NAIL, wearing a RING fashioned from a half-crown given during a service of Holy Communion, drinking a potion made from MISTLETOE and consuming the heart and blood of a CROW on nine successive days.

**epitaphs** Collectors of graveyard epitaphs are warned by one US superstition that this is a risky business, as the person concerned may be deprived of all powers of memory.

**evil eye** The power to influence another's health or well-being for the worse by simply looking at them. Since ancient times people with green or blue EYES have been widely supposed to be able to harm their enemies with no more than a severe look. The notion reached its climax during the witchcraft panic of the seventeenth century, when many European witches were accused of the practice of 'overlooking' their victims. Anyone with uneven or deep-set eyes, eyes of different colours, cross-eyes or a squint may still be suspected of possessing the evil eye, even though the person himself may have no wish to profit by such powers. Nowadays the evil eye is associated primarily with gipsies, who may employ it against anyone who does not offer them money when approached.

Such was the belief in the powers of the evil eye in former times that many people hung glass 'witch balls' in their windows in the hope that these would deflect and negate any malevolent influence. Particularly at risk are CHILDREN and ANIMALS: they may be protected by pieces of CORAL, red RIBBONS, HORSE-SHOES, necklaces of BETONY leaves and knotted cords and with AMULETS, often in the shape of an eye or a TOAD or in the form of a necklace of blue beads. Mediterranean FISHERMEN traditionally decorate their boats with an eye device to guard against such malicious interference. The fleur-de-lis pattern familiar from coats-of-arms is also reputed to fend off the evil eye.

SPITTING in the eye of someone suspected of 'overlooking' is said to provide further protection, while other alternatives include burning the body of any animal killed in this way – which will cause the culprit excruciating agony – or simply making the sign of the CROSS. Sticking PINS into an effigy of the accused person will similarly lift the curse. Children threatened by the evil eye can be safeguarded by holding them upside down for a few moments every morning or by WASHING them from a basin of water in which a SILVER coin borrowed from a neighbour has been placed. Best known of all the defences is probably the 'Devil's horns' or 'fig sign', made by holding down the middle two fingers of the hand with the thumb and directing the horns at anyone suspected of threatening the evil eye.

**exhumation** Perhaps not surprisingly it is widely held to be unlucky to dig up a body that has been interred. Punishment for so rash an act may extend to the death of one of the surviving members of the deceased's family.

*See also* BURIAL; CORPSE; GRAVE.

**eye** The colour of a person's eyes is said to reveal much about their character. An old US rhyme details precisely the significance of several different colours:

Blue-eye beauty, do your mammy's duty,
Black-eye, pick a pie,
Run around and tell a lie;
Grey-eye, greedy-gut
Eat all the world up.

Meeting a cross-eyed person in the street is lucky as long as the person concerned is of the opposite sex: if not, it is wise to spit as the person goes by to avoid ill luck. Itching eyes, meanwhile, are an indication of what the future has in store: if it is the right eye that itches, good luck is in the offing, but if it is the left eye then the tide of luck will run against the person concerned. An itching right eyelid is also deemed lucky in men, but unlucky in women. If the itching becomes unbearable, then the eyes should be bathed in rainwater gathered from the leaves of a teazel or collected on Holy Thursday or Ascension Day.

Superstition offers all manner of treatments for eyes that are sore, infected or otherwise in less than perfect condition. A sty, for instance, can be cured by rubbing it nine times with a gold WEDDING RING or (when there is a new MOON) with the tip of a CAT's tail after one hair has been pulled out – or else by washing the eye in cow's URINE or rubbing it with green GARLIC. Most curiously of all, a sty was said to disappear if one rang a doorbell and ran off before the door was opened.

Cataracts may be treated by burning a CAT's head and blowing the ASHES into the affected eye. Conjunctivitis may be relieved by applying a lotion of powdered vine shoots or a piece of cold veal. Egg yolk, curdled milk and urine are all recommended as eyewashes.

*See also* BLINDNESS; CORPSE; EVIL EYE; EYEBROW; EYELASH; SPECTACLES; WINKING.

**eyebrow** Superstition claims that the shape of a person's eyebrows is determined by their character. Everyone knows that a person whose eyebrows join is not be trusted, though alternative interpretations suggest that this is a sign of good luck and a woman whose eyebrows join is fated to a happy marriage. In times past eyebrows that join were thought to be evidence that the person concerned was a WEREWOLF or witch.

**eyelash** A single lash that falls from the eye may be placed on the back of the left hand and then struck with the right hand or blown at as a wish is made: if the eyelash vanishes at the blow or breath, then it has disappeared to arrange for the wish to be granted. Eyelashes that curl downwards have their own significance. If the right eyelashes curl down this is a good omen in the case of men, but the reverse for women.

# F

**fairy** The magical and traditionally malevolent 'little people' to whom many misfortunes and supernatural happenings are frequently attributed. Including such unearthly creatures as goblins, pixies, elves, changelings and gnomes, the fairies are an ancient tradition in folklore much beloved by children and now largely associated with a more romantic age when farmers and knights in armour often encountered these beings. There was something of a resurgence of interest in fairies in the early years of the twentieth century with the success of J. M. Barrie's children's book *Peter Pan*, which was furthered by the famous (but now discredited) photographs of the 'Cottingley fairies', a hoax perpetrated by two sisters. The Irish, meanwhile, continue to keep alive stories and customs concerning the related figure of the leprechaun.

Fairies are associated with Arcadian landscapes of streams and woods, though they may also be attached to the history of certain families. They are often depicted as mischievous and vain. According to different accounts, fairies are fallen angels, the spirits of the prematurely dead or the last survivors of a race of tiny beings who inhabited Celtic lands long ago.

Threatening small children that the fairies would come and get them was a favourite ruse of parents for many centuries, but adults themselves much feared the interference of the little people, who had the power to injure their livestock and to cause terrible misfortune if crossed, either accidentally or on purpose.

Back in the seventeenth century it was thought unlucky even to mention the word 'fairy', and such euphemisms as 'the good neighbour' were preferred. Inhabitants of rural areas learned to shun places where fairies were reputed to gather, but greatly prized any fossil sea-urchins they found, believing that these were really 'fairy loaves'.

Great care should be taken to avoid dark green 'fairy rings' in the grass, which mark the place where the fairies have held a circular dance at midnight (the rings are actually made by a fungus). It is said that these may even indicate the whereabouts of a fairy village. It is thought very dangerous to sleep in one of these rings or even to step into one after nightfall – especially on the eve of MAYDAY or on HALLOWE'EN – and livestock are also reputed to keep their distance from these phenomena. To be on the safe side, passers-by should reverse their HATS to confuse any fairies who might attempt to make them join in their dread dance. A more daring person may hear the sound of the fairies laughing and talking if he or she runs nine times round such a ring, though this must always be in the direction that the SUN takes, or the runner will fall prey to the fairies' power. Destruction of a fairy ring is extremely foolhardy and is in any case futile, as the ring will regenerate itself.

**familiar** The supernatural spirit agent of a witch or sorcerer. The familiar is a feature primarily of the witchcraft tradition of England and Scotland, for few records exist of such unworldly assistants elsewhere. Familiars typically took the form of domestic ANIMALS, most often CATS, DOGS and black BIRDS, but witches examined by witchfinders of the seventeenth century admitted to harbouring all manner of demons, which they were said to feed with their own blood. Admissions such as this were once sufficient 'proof' for a witch to be condemned to death, and many old and ignorant women died because they had not the wits to deny associating with such imps.

The widespread fear of such familiars, which might enter a house and perform deeds ranging from souring the MILK to committing MURDER, lay at the root of much superstition concerning various species of animal.

**feather** Just as BIRDS are associated with a host of superstitious beliefs around the world, so too are their feathers regarded as objects of considerable magical potential. The ancient Egyptian god Osiris wore a cloak of feathers, while American Indians have always prized the feathers of the EAGLE. In the British Isles it is said to be unlucky to pass by a black feather lying on the ground without sticking it upright into the soil, in which case good luck will follow. SAILORS sometimes carry a WREN feather on their voyages in the belief that this will protect them from shipwreck.

Care should be taken if a person sleeps on a mattress stuffed with feathers. The bed should never be turned on a Sunday as this will provoke NIGHTMARES for a whole week and, according to authorities from Devon, may even lead to the death of a member of the household. In particular, mattresses containing the feathers of DOVES or PIGEONS are said to cause the dying to suffer protracted and painful deaths instead of slipping easily away.

**feet** On the whole, feet are associated with good luck. Scottish tradition has it that BABIES born feet first have special healing powers that may be exercised by treading on the affected limbs of those suffering from such conditions as RHEUMATISM and lumbago. Anyone born with an extra toe or with webbed feet is considered unusually lucky, though according to the Scots a man whose second toe is longer than his big toe will prove a cruel husband. Conversely, a woman whose second toe is longer than the first toe will bully her husband. Accidentally scraping the right foot on the ground while walking promises a meeting with a friend (though a disappointment is in store if one stumbles on the left foot). Soles that itch, meanwhile, are a sign that the person concerned is about to embark on an unplanned trip.

Flat-footed people are unlucky, and it is deemed unfortunate to meet a flat-footed man in the street on a Monday morning (see DAYS OF THE WEEK) or when setting about some important BUSINESS, and even worse if someone with flat feet enters the house on NEW YEAR's Day. The Scottish and Irish attach similar misgivings to meeting anybody with bare feet, especially if the person concerned also has red HAIR. Should such a person be met in the street the only remedy is to return home for a drink and something to eat and then begin the journey again. A high instep, conversely, is held to be lucky and in Massachusetts an instep high enough to let water flow underneath it is an indication of good breeding.

In many places visitors take care to enter houses right foot first, since entering on the left bodes ill for the household. The same applies when setting out on any journey from home; and, when dressing, the right foot should always be shod first. Bad luck will follow if a person accidentally attempts to put their left foot into their right shoe.

Back in the fifteenth and sixteenth centuries the authorities sometimes took the precaution of preventing condemned witches from touching the earth with their feet after being sentenced, for fear that this would enable them to escape by magic and bring further harm to their enemies.

**fern** British superstition credits the fern with a range of magic powers. Sometimes referred to rather ominously as the 'Devil's brushes', ferns are variously reputed to be evil plants that will bring harm if cut or even touched, or else luck-giving plants that will ward off evil influences if used to decorate a HORSE's head or collar. If brought into the house they will provide protection against LIGHTNING, but if they are cut or burned then RAIN will surely follow.

Walking on ferns is ill-advised as this will cause a person to lose his bearings and become lost. Plucking and carrying a fern leaf is also a bad idea, as the leaf will attract ADDERS. Tossing a fern flower in the air and observing where it falls, however, may indicate the whereabouts of buried treasure, and carrying a fern flower offers a safeguard against WITCHCRAFT.

Particular superstitions attach to the spores of the fern, which are said to bestow the power of INVISIBILITY if collected on MIDSUMMER'S EVE and carried about the person. Keeping some fern seed in a pocket or handbag will also promote the enduring faithfulness of a lover. Consuming spores crushed in water, meanwhile, is said to be a sure remedy for stomach ache if they are gathered from a fern growing on an OAK, and various other potions and lotions based on fern seed are recommended for the treatment of minor WOUNDS, COUGHS and inflamed EYES among other conditions. Sleeping on a mattress or pillow containing ferns is alleged to cure RHEUMATISM and rickets.

*See also* ADDER'S TONGUE FERN; BRACKEN; MALE FERN; MOONWORT.

**ferret** Though not the best-loved of animals, the ferret does have the redeeming feature of being able to cure WHOOPING COUGH, according to ancient English and Irish tradition. The procedure recommended is to let a ferret drink from a bowl of MILK and then to feed the remainder to the patient.

**fever** Superstition offers several courses to those who are struck down with fever. The consumption of SPIDERS is considered one of the best treatments, the insects being eaten alive in slices of apple or with jam or treacle. Alternatively, COBWEBS may be rolled up into pills and eaten or a spider may be hung in a small box or bag around the neck until it dies. For those with more delicate stomachs, the solution may be to bury a newly laid egg at a CROSSROADS in the middle of the night on five nights in succession, the idea being that the fever will be buried with the eggs. A more convenient treatment is to wear two sets of UNDERWEAR and to have friends or relatives daily tear off a piece of the one worn nearest the skin until no more garments remain.

Feeding a salted bran cake to a DOG may successfully transfer the complaint to the animal, and secreting beneath the doorstep of the house next door a bag of HAIR clippings and nail trimmings (*see* FINGERNAIL) taken from a dead man will similarly cause the symptoms to transfer to the luckless neighbour. Chanting such charms as 'Ague, farewell, till we meet in Hell' and 'Ague, ague, I do thee defy, make me well for Jesu's sake' may also cause the fever to subside, as will chalking three CROSSES on the chimney-breast and allowing them to be obliterated by SOOT from the FIRE.

Sufferers of fevers in Wales should cross water to reach a hollow WILLOW tree and then breathe three times into the hollow trunk to rid themselves of their malady (see BREATH), while patients in Lincolnshire may nail three HORSESHOES to the end of their bed to effect a cure.

**fig sign** *see* EVIL EYE.

**figurehead** A carved wooden figure, often depicting a naked woman, that formerly adorned the prows of most big ocean-going vessels and was thought to embody the soul of the SHIP. The custom of attaching such figureheads probably had its roots in the ancient practice of dedicating ships to particular goddesses, which is why the majority of figureheads were female despite the tradition that it is unlucky to have women on board ship. SAILORS always placed great faith in figureheads, claiming that they helped to protect the ship, and they were consequently treated with great respect. Perhaps the most widespread superstition was that no ship could sink without its figurehead. Though few modern ships are decorated with such figures except in a very truncated form, the idea is perhaps kept alive through the many MASCOTS, bunches of lucky HEATHER and other emblematic objects that are attached by drivers to the front of trucks and private cars.

**finger** Almost as much may be gleaned about a person's character from their fingers as from a study of their face. The many superstitions concerning their shape and magical properties are detailed in the pseudo-sciences of PALMISTRY and chiromancy.

English superstition warns that a person with short fat fingers is dim-witted and intemperate, while those with long fingers may well have 'artist's hands' and be intelligent but will prove foolish with money and, according to Scottish authorities, may well turn out to be thieves. If the fingers are so short that a person cannot encircle his own wrist with the THUMB and forefinger, this is, according to Canadians, a sure sign that he or she is a glutton. Persons with long forefingers are also to be mistrusted, especially if this first finger is actually longer than the middle one. The forefinger of the right hand is, incidentally, sometimes called the 'Poison Finger' and is thought to be venomous, so should never used to rub ointment into a WOUND (though it may be used to rub spittle on to RINGWORM patches). The third finger of the left hand, usually the finger upon which WEDDING RINGS are worn, is the luckiest of them all and has special healing powers. Tradition has it that a vein runs directly from this finger straight to the heart. A little finger

that is crooked is said to indicate that its owner will die rich. Those born with extra fingers will enjoy a lifetime of good luck, but those with bent fingers will be burdened with an ill-tempered nature.

Crossing the index and middle fingers behind the back while telling a 'white lie' will protect a person from retribution. Similarly, many people around the world cross their fingers to ward off bad luck at the moment of realisation of some project or undertaking, be it the outcome of a horse race or opening a set of examination papers. This may also be done to negate the ill effects of breaking some taboo, such as walking under a LADDER.

POINTING a finger at someone or something is considered rude in some circles. This attitude may have its origins in the old notion that pointing a finger at a SHIP as it leaves harbour will cause it to sink or in the general taboo against pointing at people in case this causes them harm by invoking the power of the EVIL EYE. Pointing at a FUNERAL is especially to be discouraged, for it may lead to the premature death of the person doing the pointing.

Pulling the finger joints to see if they 'crack' is a test of love: if they make the desired sound, the person concerned can be certain that he or she is in someone else's thoughts. Alternatively, pulling every finger and counting the cracks made will reveal the number of one's lovers or else the number of children one is destined to have.

Finally, if two people coincidentally utter the same word together, they should immediately link both pairs of little fingers and make a wish. This is sure to come true so long as everything is done in complete silence. In one variant they must recite together:

I say chimney, you say smoke,
Then our wish will never be broke.

*See also* FINGERNAIL; V SIGN.

**fingernail** In terms of shape, fingernails that bulge in the middle are a sign that the person concerned will die early, while fingernails that are crooked betray an evil, greedy nature. The white crescent that shows at the base of the fingernails, meanwhile, indicates life expectancy: the larger these crescents are the more years are left to that person. White spots in the nail are regarded as omens of good luck, while black spots signify ill luck and yellow spots threaten death. In the case of white spots, more detail is offered by a traditional English rhyme, which may be chanted beginning with the index finger and working round to the little finger:

A friend,
A foe,
Money to come,
A journey to go.

A spot on the THUMB apparently means that a gift is shortly to be expected.

The nails should ideally be trimmed on a Monday or Tuesday but never on a Friday or Sunday, as this is unlucky (*see* DAYS OF THE WEEK). Another old English rhyme, known in several slightly different forms, runs:

Cut them on Monday, you cut them for health;
Cut them on Tuesday, you cut them for wealth;
Cut them on Wednesday, you cut them for news;
Cut them on Thursday, a new pair of shoes;
Cut them on Friday, you cut them for sorrow;
Cut them on Saturday, see your true-love tomorrow;
Cut them on Sunday, the devil will be with you all the week.

The fingernails of BABIES should not be cut until the infant is at least a year old or the child will become a THIEF in later life (it is, however, all right to bite them short). According to authorities in northern England, a woman who can manage the feat of trimming her right fingernails using her left hand is likely to prove the dominant partner in marriage. SAILORS, meanwhile, claim that it is unwise to trim the nails (or to cut the HAIR) while at sea, for fear that it will summon up a storm.

Great care should be employed in disposing of the fingernails, for – like hair clippings – they are much sought after for use in witches' spells. Superstition holds that all fingernails are unique to their owners, so if a witch gains possession of any trimmings she will be able to use them as ingredients and acquire influence over a person. To be absolutely sure that parings are destroyed for the purposes of WITCHCRAFT, they should each be cut into three pieces or else spat upon (*see* SPITTING). If acquired intact by a malevolent agent, nail trimmings may be hidden so that anyone who walks over them will fall immediately under the power of that agent. If the person concerned happens to be a pregnant woman, she will lose her child. If they are buried beneath a person's doorstep, that person will be struck down at once by illness, which will continue until the parings are taken away.

In contrast, fingernail clippings feature in many time-honoured remedies, often being ritually burned or buried in the belief that by so doing a patient will be relieved of whatever ails them.

**fir**   The fir tree or pine, with its evergreen foliage, was sacred to the ancient Greeks and Romans and came to symbolise such qualities as immortality and fertility. The Scandinavians sometimes place boughs of fir on COFFINS before a burial, while German tradition in former times dictated a special ceremony for newly married couples in which they carried fir tree branches decorated with CANDLES.

Among the best-known superstitions relating to the fir tree are the British belief that the owner of one will die not long after his tree is struck by LIGHTNING or otherwise destroyed, and the US taboo against planting firs in lines on the grounds that one member of the family who owns the trees will die for each tree thus planted. Dreaming of such trees signifies the arrival of suffering, but such dreams may be prevented by decorating the foot of the bed with a bough of fir.

Closed fir cones have their own significance, representing virginity to the ancient Romans, and the tree's sap has always been popular in the making of incense.

**fire**  As one of the four elemental forces once thought to govern the Earth (alongside air, earth and water), fire has long represented many things, including renewal and life itself. In ancient times it was thought that fire was a gift from the gods, and so most of the dead and living religions of the world feature fire in their rituals. Some surviving beliefs about fire that are common to British and US tradition originated with the Druids, while others were engendered by the work of medieval alchemists, who sought to turn base metals into gold by exposing them to heat.

Ceremonial bonfires were once a common sight on certain set days of the year, and were usually intended to preserve the luck of livestock and crops. In the British Isles, the tradition lives on in the popular festivity known as Bonfire Night. This occasion for big communal bonfires and firework displays purports to commemorate the discovery of the Gunpowder Plot to burn the Houses of Parliament in 1605, but undoubtedly has its origins in the fires that were once lit at HALLOWE'EN to mark the end of the summer.

The fireplace is widely considered to contain the collective soul of the household. Innumerable superstitions surround the business of anointing hearths and lighting fires as well as observing the flames, smoke and ASHES for the purposes of divination. A fire should not be kindled by two people, as they are sure to quarrel. Some people will draw the curtains on lighting a fire, believing that it will not 'catch' in the direct light of the SUN, which is deemed to be jealous of such imitation. In some households only residents are permitted to poke the coals for fear of offending the gods of the hearth, though an acquaintance will be allowed to perform this service if he has been a friend for seven years or has been drunk in the company of his hosts at least three times. A fire that bursts into life very quickly or suddenly flares for no apparent reason is said to be a portent of visitors arriving very shortly, while fires that are reluctant to burn are showing sensitivity to someone being in a bad temper or else are bewitched by evil spirits. One remedy in the latter case is to place the poker upright against the grate so that a CROSS is formed. Difficulty in lighting the fire on CHRISTMAS morning is particularly unwelcome, as this presages an unlucky year ahead.

If a fire burns on one side of the grate only, a WEDDING may well be on the cards; however it may also signify a parting and even a death in the house. If a fire crackles noisily, cold weather is to be expected. According to Scottish superstition, flames that burn blue are spectres of the fire and if there are many of these bad weather is on the way. Cheerful fires are said to reflect the mood of the household and mean that any absent members are prospering. A fire that spits and roars fiercely, however, warns of an imminent argument; and, in Wales at least, a fire that collapses in the middle suggests that a grave will soon have to be dug. If the fire burns with new strength on being poked this means that the lover or spouse of the person present is in a happy frame of mind. Sparks that glow at the back of the fire are a sign that important tidings are to be expected, and are said by some to represent letters on the way.

It was formerly considered very unlucky to leave dead embers unswept on retiring for the night, and soot falling down the chimney was once said to warn of a terrible calamity in the offing. Should a fire from the previous evening still be burning in the morning this is taken as a bad sign in some quarters, threatening illness and even death. It is also deemed unlucky to spit into a fire or to allow a fire to be left burning when a CORPSE is present. In former times it was folly of the highest order to permit a neighbour or anyone else to take fire out of the house during the NEW YEAR festivities, for instance by lighting a taper at the fire in order to return home and relight a fire that had gone out. Allowing this to happen virtually guaranteed ill luck, most likely the death of one of the family.

**first foot** *see* CHRISTENING; NEW YEAR; WEDDING.

**fish** Those who pursue the business of fishing as a livelihood and those who go angling for pleasure observe numerous taboos and associate many species of fish with particular superstitions. It is still widely believed that eating fish is good for the brain, a relic of an ancient belief in the wisdom of all fishes, and many types of fish are further valued for the treatment of a range of medical conditions. In the USA the TENCH is popularly nicknamed 'Doctor Fish' because of its efficacy against JAUNDICE, while in the British Isles the trout has a time-honoured reputation as a cure for WHOOPING COUGH, a live fish being placed either in or close to the sufferer's mouth so that the latter gets the full benefit of its healing BREATH. An alternative cure for whooping cough involves laying a flat fish on the patient's chest and keeping it there until it dies.

Fish living in sacred pools and rivers were once themselves held to be sacred, and the dried EYE of the cod is sometimes carried for luck. Northern English superstition dictates that it is unlucky to burn fishbones. When eating a fish it is generally advised to start at the tail and work up to the head, as the reverse procedure will warn other shoals away from the shore and back into deep water.

It is not just the edible fish that are luck-bearers. Included among them is the inedible fiddle fish, which is welcomed in fishing nets: crews will often pick these out and attach them to lines so that they may be towed along behind the boat on subsequent voyages, thus ensuring a good catch.

*See also* ANGLERS; DOLPHIN; EEL; FISHERMEN; FLOUNDER; HADDOCK; HERRING; PORPOISE; SALMON; SHARK.

**fishermen** Those who make their living as professional fishermen rank alongside other seafarers as arguably the most superstitious of all the world's workers, a reputation which reflects the dangers inherent in making a living on the high seas. Most of these beliefs are firmly linked to preserving the welfare of crews, offering the kind of reassurance that all SAILORS seek.

The fortunes of a fishing trip may be decided by various omens before a crew assembles on a vessel or even before the members of the crew leave their houses. If a fisherman treads on the fire tongs he can forget hopes of catching anything at all, but if he has a quarrel with his wife before leaving the house the portents are good, especially if the quarrel turns into a fight and the fisherman draws blood from his spouse. Observing various taboos while preparing lines and NETS may also improve the chances of a good haul. Extreme ill fortune is threatened, however, if a fisherman meets a cross-eyed man (*see* EVIL EYE), a representative of the CLERGY or a woman in a white APRON when he is on his way to the harbour. Many a fisherman has been known to abandon fishing for the day if any of these events take place, returning home until the next TIDE. In the past, fishermen have gone so far as to pursue and kill any DOG they meet on their way to the harbour, for fear that it will endanger their catch.

Another tradition dictates that no fisherman should venture out to sea at the start of the season before he has shed a few drops of his own blood in a fight or some accident. In addition to this, fishermen should not fish day in day out every day of the week, in order to avoid offending the gods of the sea by their greed.

Once at sea, fishermen believe that their catch will be small if an evil event, such as a MURDER or SUICIDE, has recently happened on the coast close to the fishing grounds; fish are widely believed to sense such happenings ashore and therefore retreat from coastal waters. The haul will likewise be disappointing if the first fish caught is male. To encourage a good catch some fishermen throw the first fish back or nail it to the mast, or else insert a COIN into one of the floats on their nets as payment to Neptune for the ocean's bounty. If desperate for a good catch, Scottish fishermen recommend throwing one of the crew overboard and then hauling him back in, believing the fish will follow suit. If a man falls overboard by accident and starts to drown, however, his crew-mates may show reluctance to save him, mindful of the old tradition that the gods of the sea will not be deprived of a soul once they have one in their clutches and may demand the life of the man's rescuer instead (see DROWNING).

In common with sailors, fishermen are nervous of using certain words while at sea for fear of disaster. These include all mention of PIGS, the Church and other things connected with the land; in Scotland it is also deemed unwise to take the name of God in vain. If such a word is mentioned, the only remedy is for all the people aboard to touch something made of IRON. It is also unlucky to count the fish as they are caught; this job is often left until the boat is safely back in harbour, or else the crew use their own code to avoid speaking recognisable NUMBERS.

It is thought to be a wise precaution to change the crew of a boat every year in order to protect the vessel's luck.

See also ANGLERS.

**flag** The flags and banners of armies and SHIPS have always been treated with special reverence and are still considered almost magical items, able to restore fighting spirit in hard situations and acting as rallying points in the confusion of battle or even as symbols of national unity. The loss of a regiment's colours in battle has always brought with it the worst disgrace, and many soldiers have sacrificed their lives in their attempts to get their colours back from the enemy. Tearing a flag is regarded as desperately unlucky, especially so in the case of a SHIP's colours, which must never, incidentally, be passed from one man to another through the rungs of a LADDER. Specific instances of flags of magical origins include the finely woven 'faery flag' that was said to have been given by the 'little people' (see FAIRIES) to the Macleods of Dunvegan Castle in Skye, where it is still preserved.

**flea** Various superstitions surround the flea and its highly irritant bite. Fleas are alleged to bite more often than usual when RAIN is expected. If they suddenly abandon a body they had previously infested for some time, it may be interpreted as an omen of the person's imminent death. In Germany, however, a flea bite on the hand may actually be welcomed, since it prophesies that the person concerned will shortly receive a kiss or some item of good news. Householders anxious to rid their houses of fleas are advised to get up early on 1 March, close the windows and clean the house thoroughly, sweeping the door lintel and any cracks where fleas might hide; if this is done properly, no fleas will return that year.

According to European tradition, fleas will never enter a bed that has been well aired on Maundy Thursday and will shun the bed of a monk. Soil collected from beneath the right foot when the first CUCKOO of the year is heard is said to work well as a flea repellent. Other objects reputed to repel fleas include boughs of WALNUT and FOXGLOVES. Alternatively, a flea-ridden person may drive away the insects by leaping over a Midsummer bonfire (see MIDSUMMER'S EVE), by bringing a SHEEP or GOAT into the house, or by decorating a picture of the Virgin Mary on Easter Sunday as the Resurrection bell strikes while intoning the words, 'Depart, all animals without bones.'

**flounder** Flat fish, with both eyes located on the upper side of its distorted face, whose odd appearance has inspired a handful of superstitions. It is said that the flounder acquired its somewhat grotesque appearance as punishment for its jealousy when the herring was chosen as 'king of the sea'. Alternatively, the Scots maintain that the flounder fell into the habit of making faces at rock cod and eventually stayed that way.

**flowers** Superstition honours virtually every well-known wild flower with its particular mystical attributes and uses in folk medicine and spell-making. Giving people bunches of flowers (preferably an odd number of them) has always been considered a loving gesture and one liable to bring good luck with it. Flowers are, for instance, almost everywhere carried by brides as symbols of good fortune and fruitfulness (see WEDDING DRESS).

Every month of the year has its designated flower which will bring luck to those born at that time:

January: carnation and primrose.
February: primrose.
March: daffodil and violet.
April: daisy.
May: hawthorn and lily of the valley.
June: rose and honeysuckle.
July: water lily.
August: gladioli and poppy.
September: aster and convolvulus.
October: dahlia and goldenrod.
November: chrysanthemum.
December: holly.

Caution must be taken in giving flowers in certain circumstances, however. It is very unlucky to take flowers that bloom out of season into the house, because it threatens a death in the family. It is also most unwise to give white flowers of any kind to a sick person: these too foretell death, even if only seen in a dream, as they are said to shelter the souls of the dead. Even worse are bunches of mixed red and white flowers, which are considered so ominous that many British nurses will not allow them into HOSPITAL wards for fear that a person on the ward, not necessarily the recipient of the flowers, will die as a result. Red flowers on their own are, however, perfectly acceptable as they symbolise life-blood, as are violet, yellow and orange blooms – though they should never be laid on the patient's bed.

Another popular tradition holds that nurses will remove flowers from a ward before settling their patients for the night, on the grounds that the flowers will deprive the sick of health-giving oxygen (in fact, in most modern hospitals flowers are only removed if they are considered to represent a risk of infection). When the patient recovers and leaves hospital, superstition recommends that any flowers given remain behind or the patient will soon be back again.

ACTORS AND ACTRESSES dislike the use of real flowers on stage, maintaining that they are unlucky. Dead flowers found lying in the road should on no account be picked up: doing so will communicate whatever has contaminated the blooms. Similarly, it is unwise to throw aside a flower left on a GRAVE as this may cause the place where the flower falls to become haunted (see GHOST). Moreover, detecting the smell of flowers when there are none present is widely considered an omen of death.

Flowers with yellow centres are generally approved of as they are said to provide protection against WITCHCRAFT, and the bright yellow sunflower will bring luck to the whole garden. Gardeners are advised that flowers planted when the MOON is waxing will do best, and that sowing seeds on Palm Sunday will result in all the flowers growing double.

See also BACHELOR'S BUTTON; BROOM; DAFFODIL; DAISY; DANDELION; GORSE; HEATHER; KNAPWEED; MOONWORT; MOTHER-DIE; PEONY; PLANTAIN; PRIMROSE; ROSE; SPEEDWELL; TREES.

**fly** Despite the fact that few people like flies, a fly falling into someone's drink is supposed to be lucky. Solitary flies found in the house during the CHRISTMAS season, when few still survive, are also thought to be lucky and are therefore sometimes left unmolested. Measures that may be taken to deter flies throughout the year include hanging three EGGS over the front door on ASH WEDNESDAY and suspending a HERRING from the ceiling on GOOD FRIDAY. If a fly is present in the room when a woman gives birth, the baby is sure to be a girl.

The irritating persistence of flies is said by some to have originated in the fact that their kind were excommunicated by St Bernard and have ever since sought vengeance.

**flying ointment** The magical ointment that witches are supposed to smear on themselves to acquire the power of flight. According to widespread tradition, witches rub this ointment all over their bodies and then fly naked to their sabbaths on their broomsticks or other vehicles. Alleged ingredients of such ointments include the fat of BABIES, the blood of BATS, SOOT, and samples of aconite, HELLEBORE, HEMLOCK and belladonna.

*See also* BRUSH; WITCHCRAFT.

**fog** Misty weather may often strike those caught in it as eerie and ominous, especially at sea, but superstition offers little opinion on the origins and portents of fogs in general. An ancient British rhyme also known in the USA does, however, suggest that the location of a fog predicts forthcoming WEATHER patterns:

Fog on the hill
Brings water to the mill;
Fog on the moor
Brings sun to the door.

Another superstition dictates that hanging a dead FROG in an orchard or vineyard will keep damaging fogs at bay.

**food** Various foods have their own unique magical properties as AMULETS, as APHRODISIACS and as medicinal restoratives. Some superstitions, though, relate to food in general. In some fishing communities, for instance, it is held unlucky to give away FISH as this might prejudice future catches. Similarly, in the days when farmers often treated their neighbours to free meals of pig's fry or cow's BEASTINS, it was important that the plates were returned unwashed.

It is still believed unlucky to drop food on the floor while eating and similarly undesirable to leave any food on the plate at the end of the meal (in prison circles this means that the diner will one day return to prison to finish the meal). It is also deemed unwise to leave the remains of supper on the table overnight, as this gives witches and evil spirits the opportunity to interfere with it.

*See also* BAKING; BLACK PUDDING; BREAD; BREAD AND BUTTER; BUTTER; CHRISTMAS; COFFEE; COOKING; CUTLERY; EGG; MEAT; MILK; PIE; PIG; SALT; SUGAR; TEA.

**football** Modern organised football dates back little over a hundred years, but variations have been played around the world for many centuries and the game has acquired many time-honoured myths and superstitions. Some taboos and rituals are peculiar to certain clubs or players. In the UK, Newcastle United consider it a good omen if the players catch sight of a WEDDING on their way to a match but fear the sight of a FUNERAL, while in Italy fans of Napoli scatter SALT on the pitch and clash cymbals on the sidelines before the game to frighten away evil spirits. Some grounds are considered deeply unlucky, notably Derby County's Baseball Ground, which is said to have been cursed when resident gipsies were moved from the site, and Wembley itself, which has witnessed more than its fair share of injuries over the years.

Goalkeepers, remembering an incident when Arsenal's keeper failed to make a Cup Final save back in 1927 because he was wearing a shiny new jersey, often refuse to take the field in new tops, while other players stick to lucky foods and carry a variety of good luck charms. Almost every club has its lucky MASCOT, which may vary from animals to small boys and girls. In more distant parts of the world, pre-match rituals include sacrificing animals and calling on the help of witch-doctors to cast spells over the defending team's goal-line. In 1979, for instance, members of the Peruvian team Melgar, believing they were being plagued by a curse made by a former player, resorted to soaking their shirts in a special potion said to ward off such influences – and subsequently enjoyed an immediate change in their fortunes.

Other superstitions echo taboos in more general currency and include always putting on the right boot before the left, bouncing the BALL between the youngest and the oldest players on the team, touching the ball for luck and bouncing the ball three times on the centre-spot. The rattles and banners of the fans, furthermore, are sometimes interpreted in terms of magical charms designed to protect the favoured team from evil.

**footling**   *see* CHILDBIRTH.

**four-leaf clover**   *see* CLOVER.

**fox**   Universally considered an animal of great cunning, the fox is generally identified with evil and as an animal to be feared. In former times witches were often alleged to have the power to turn themselves into foxes, and in Scotland at least farmers sometimes nailed a severed fox's head to the barn door to warn off any prowling witches (*see* WITCHCRAFT). In Wales it is said that spying a lone fox is lucky, but seeing several at once is an omen of misfortune. Foxes are also unwelcome in the vicinity of the home as they signify the coming of disaster and death. In parts of eastern England it is claimed that a fox-bite will have fatal consequences, and anyone bitten cannot expect to live more than seven years.

Elsewhere it is claimed that when there is a shower of RAIN while the sun is shining this is a sure sign that a foxes' wedding is taking place (in other parts of the world the animal thus honoured may be the monkey, the jackal or poultry).

One widely known example of the fox's legendary cunning concerns the animal's supposed method of ridding itself of FLEAS. The creature holds a ball of wool or grass in its mouth and then swims into a river; as the water rises the fleas (somewhat in the manner of the children's character the Gingerbread Man) climb on to the fox's head and then on to the wool, which is released to float downstream.

Though maligned in rural districts for the damage it does on poultry farms, the fox is prized as the source of ingredients in a range of folk remedies. The TONGUE may be laid on the skin at bedtime to extract a deeply embedded thorn, and can also be applied to the EYES to cure cataracts. It may also be cooked and eaten or else carried about one to improve the courage of a person who is naturally shy. Carrying a fox's TOOTH will help to treat an inflamed leg, while the liver and lights, dried and sugared, prevent COUGHS. Drinking the ASHES of a fox in wine is said to benefit the liver and to cure respiratory problems, while fox fat rubbed on the scalp will apparently combat BALD-NESS. Finishing a bowl of MILK partly drunk by a fox is reputed to be a cure for WHOOPING COUGH.

**foxglove**   Distinctive tall wild plant which is intimately connected with FAIRY lore throughout the British Isles. The facts that parts of the plant are poisonous and that it is often found in the deepest and most secluded parts of woods have no doubt done much to give the foxglove its rather ominous magical reputation. Few people will dare to risk their luck by taking a foxglove into the house and SAILORS are traditionally reluctant to allow this flower on board ship. Foxglove tea, on the other hand, has long been valued as a cure for DROPSY and it was this tradition that drew the attention of conventional medicine to the properties of digitalis, which is now widely used in the treatment of heart conditions.

**Friday** *see* DAYS OF THE WEEK; GOOD FRIDAY; THIRTEEN.

**frog** The frog, with its amphibious lifestyle and glistening skin, features in a wealth of superstitions and folk remedies. The animal enjoyed divine status in pre-Christian Rome and has ever since been credited with great magical potency. Simply observing a frog and noting its behaviour will reveal what WEATHER is in store. If the frog's skin is shiny, fine weather is in the offing, but if it is dull RAIN is due. Rain will soon fall in answer to the croak of a frog and, before the development of adult frogs from tadpoles was understood, it was said that frogs themselves came to Earth in showers of rain. Frogspawn deposited at the edge of a pond promises STORMS. The appearance of a frog in the house, meanwhile, is deemed most unnatural and is therefore unlucky, possibly even a death portent, though it is lucky to come across a frog outside.

Some people have been known to place great store in carrying a particular bone taken from a frog (or TOAD) that has been ritually killed. The procedure that has to be followed is to bury a live frog or toad in an anthill for a month until the new MOON, then to strip off the remaining flesh by placing the body in a stream. As the water does its work the sought-after bone will start to float upstream while uttering unearthly shrieks. The bone must then be taken to a stable on three nights in succession, on the last of which the owner may be required to do battle with the DEVIL himself before the spell is deemed complete. Possession of such a magic bone brings with it the power to control HORSES and PIGS and the ability to cure WARTS, among other gifts.

Other superstitions, however, warn against killing frogs as they are said to be the reincarnation of dead children (hence their sometimes child-like cry). Placing the TONGUE of a frog on someone while they sleep will oblige the sleeper to reveal his or her secrets, but some authorities warn that anyone who actually touches a frog will become instantly infertile.

In folk medicine the frog has many uses. Putting a live frog on a skewer and rubbing its body against a wart will cause the wart to disappear as the frog dies. Trapping a live frog in a bag and hanging the bag in the CHIMNEY until the frog perishes will cure WHOOPING COUGH, as will feeding the unknowing patient frog soup, while holding a live frog in a patient's mouth will cure thrush by transferring the disease to the unfortunate amphibian. In times gone by, sufferers from CONSUMPTION and CANCER favoured eating a few live baby frogs before breakfast. Back in the seventeenth century powdered frog livers were also alleged to cure EPILEPSY. In the case of EYE problems the recommended procedure involves a volunteer licking first the eyes of a frog and then the eyes of the patient.

**fruit tree** The well-being of a fruit tree is important not only to the economic welfare of its owner but also to the household's fortunes, according to various widely held superstitions. New fruit trees should always be planted with the body of some dead animal at their roots in order to ensure good crops, according to one time-honoured British custom. Fruit trees that bloom twice in one season, meanwhile, are a dire omen, warning of the imminent death of a family member.

Much fun may be had by divining one's future through the counting of the number of stones or pips left on the plate after eating fruit. Though there are regional variations, the usual way of doing this is to count the stones off while chanting the words 'Tinker, tailor, soldier, sailor, rich man, poor man, beggarman, thief', in order to find out the occupation of a future spouse (or to discover one's future career). If some stones remain uncounted, some people will start the rhyme again from the beginning or will add 'ploughboy, cowboy, doctor, dentist' to increase the choice. Another alternative is to add 'This year, next year, some time, never' to find out when one is to be married, or when some hoped-for event is to take place. In former times, the same ruse was tried when counting the BUTTONS on one's clothing.

**funeral** The sombre business of interring the dead is naturally enough the focus of many superstitious beliefs. Most are concerned with ensuring that the deceased person is allowed to rest in peace, leaving the living to go about their daily lives untroubled by GHOSTS.

Firstly, it is held to be lucky if RAIN falls while a funeral is taking place, as an old English saying attests:

Happy is the bride that the sun shines on,

Happy is the corpse that the rain rains on.

Less propitious is a funeral that takes place on a Sunday (see DAYS OF THE WEEK) or, even worse, at NEW YEAR. It is no better, though, to postpone a funeral because of the weather, the date set or any other reason, as this may offend death and persuade him to seek out new victims in the same neighbourhood.

The COFFIN should always leave the dead person's house by the front door (or by the WINDOW if that is the only alternative to using the back door). If the back door is used, the deceased's soul will be in terrible jeopardy in the afterlife. Ideally the body will be transported in an east-to-west direction (see SUNWISE TURN), and once the journey has been started it must on no account be delayed or abandoned (though modern traffic lights can make this requirement difficult). In times gone by, if a deceased woman was a virgin this was marked by the mourners dressing in white and by a pair of symbolic

white gloves being carried at the head of the funeral procession (see MAIDEN'S GARLAND).

Care should be taken by the mourners that they do not break certain taboos, which may mark them out as the next to die. In particular, they should keep behind the coffin as it proceeds to the church, avoid standing in a ray of direct sunlight during the ceremony, and finally be careful not to enter the home of the deceased before the next of kin go in after the service is over. If the gathered mourners make an odd number, one of them will shortly be joining the deceased in the grave. According to US authorities it is very unlucky to 'gatecrash' a funeral uninvited, and pregnant women and children under the age of a year may not be welcome in the mourning party. It has been suggested, incidentally, that mourners wear black clothes in order to confuse the DEVIL, but it is unwise to wear these after the funeral as this invites further attention from death.

Not unnaturally it is considered bad luck to meet a funeral procession in the street, particularly so if the person concerned is a bride on her way to church or anyone else setting out on an important journey. The only sure remedy in this case is for the person to walk a few steps with the funeral party, though some might on reflection find the presence of bride in full regalia a somewhat grotesque presence in such circumstances. Other possible precautions include SPITTING after the hearse, crossing the FINGERS and removing one's HAT. It is further said that the sex of the first person the funeral party meets determines the sex of the next person fated to die.

It is unlucky to catch a glimpse of a funeral through a window or through the door and better to watch openly from the pavement, and it is perilous indeed to attempt to count the number of CARS following the coffin as, according to US superstition, this determines the number of years the person counting has left to live. Irish superstition, however, suggests that some good can come of meeting a funeral procession: if the person concerned throws a stone after the coffin and invokes the name of the Trinity while calling out the dead person's name he may rid himself of his WARTS by wishing them upon the corpse.

The tradition of feeding the mourners at the home of the deceased after the funeral is over is also significant as a superstitious rite, and it was formerly accepted that every mourner should wash and dry his hands in the house. The towel used was then thrown over the roof or otherwise given up to the WIND. Lastly, the happier the atmosphere at the wake, the better the prospects for living and dead.

*See also* BURIAL; COFFIN; CORPSE; DEATH; HEARSE; MOURNING.

**furniture** Many examples of domestic furnishings, such as CHAIRS and TABLES, boast their own unique traditions, reflecting the tendency for the bulk of superstitions to focus on the mundane objects of everyday usage. In general terms, it is said that if furniture moves by itself, for instance chairs toppling over and PICTURES falling off walls, this is a portent of death as well as an indication of possible poltergeist activity (interference by unseen supernatural entities). One device occasionally resorted to when death has visited the household is to change the positions of the furnishings in a dead person's bedroom while the FUNERAL is taking place: should the dead person's GHOST return to the house it will be confused by the new layout and depart very quickly. Some people, moreover, prefer to arrange furniture parallel with the lines of the room and the house so as to avoid forming too many CROSSES.

Scottish authorities claim that creaking furniture warns of an imminent change in prevailing WEATHER conditions, while others see in this a portent of death.

*See also* MIRROR.

# G

**Gabriel's hounds** Spectral pack of DOGS that haunts the skies of northern Europe in company with the WILD HUNT. Anyone hearing or seeing the hounds, who are particularly associated with stormy WEATHER, is doomed to die in the near future.

*See also* SEVEN WHISTLERS.

**gallows** Historical sites of execution, often located at CROSSROADS (which are themselves locations associated with evil), are not unnaturally regarded with the deepest suspicion by most people and various folk traditions surround the gallows itself. Though few ancient 'gallow-trees', often made from ELDER wood, survive intact they continue to be associated with powerful forces and a splinter taken from a gibbet is to this day considered a potent object. In particular such splinters, worn in a little bag round the neck, may be used to ease TOOTHACHE or more rarely to cure FEVER.

*See also* HANGMAN'S ROPE.

**gallstones** Superstition offers a radical cure for gallstones. The treatment suggested involves boiling SHEEP droppings in fresh MILK and drinking the resulting concoction daily until the problem is resolved.

**gambling** The pursuit of gambling is surrounded by a wealth of superstitions intended to preserve and indeed improve a gambler's luck. Specific tips and taboos relate to such pastimes as gambling on HORSES and DICE and playing at CARDS, but several traditions are relevant to gambling in any form. These include the general taboo against playing for money before 6 p.m. on a Friday, the widespread belief that the presence of a woman or DOG will always ruin one's chances of winning, and the notion that meeting a HUNCHBACK or cross-eyed man (*see* EVIL EYE) on the way to play is a very good omen. First-time gamblers always win, according to another widely held superstition, on the strength of 'beginners' luck', and gamblers who play with borrowed money are equally blessed by Lady Luck. Many gamblers place great faith in various CHARMS and AMULETS and strive to keep their temper in the face of the tide turning against them, knowing that displays of emotion will only tempt further setbacks.

**garlic** Most people schooled in modern horror films know that garlic is an effective safeguard against VAMPIRES, though in fact it has long been considered to give protection against a much wider range of evil spirits. The plant was considered a gift from the gods by the ancient Egyptians, although Christian mythology has it that the first garlic sprang up where Satan's left foot stepped when he left the Garden of Eden (an ONION grew where his right foot fell). In medieval times roasted garlic cloves were shared among French families at MID-SUMMER'S EVE parties in the belief that they would preserve all the members of the household from harm. The plant is also regarded as a counter to WITCHCRAFT and evil in many Oriental countries. For repelling vampires, garlic gathered in May is thought to be the most effective and should be used to guard the WINDOWS and worn in the form of a necklace. Garlic may also be fixed to a child's CRADLE to protect the infant from malevolent spirits, and Sicilians may slip garlic into the beds of women in labour to ease the pain of CHILDBIRTH.

As a tool of the herbalist, garlic is prized for its effectiveness against infestations of WORMS, in treating sunstroke, against DROPSY, in relieving such life-threatening diseases as SMALLPOX, plague and leprosy, and in easing minor ailments like TOOTHACHE, earache (*see* EAR) and BEDWETTING. It may also be administered to calm hysterics or placed in the SOCKS of children afflicted with WHOOPING COUGH. In remoter parts of the USA, garlic poultices are recommended for the treatment of rattlesnake bites and scorpion stings. Scientists, meanwhile, have identified garlic as one of the most effective natural mosquito repellents.

Nor is superstition wanting when it comes to advice for masking the smell of garlic on the breath. The problem is solved quite simply by eating a mint leaf, a raw bean, some aniseed, parsley or a coffee bean.

**garter** Most surviving superstitions relating to the garter are now linked to the WEDDING ceremony: many brides include a single garter in their wedding outfit. It is sometimes hurled to unmarried male guests as the bride leaves on her honeymoon, and the man who catches it is said to secure lasting good luck. In former times it was the object of a lively romp in which the men tried to take the already loosened garter from the bride by force; the winner wore the garter in his HAT before presenting it to the girl of his choice. Should a bride lose a garter during her honeymoon, though, this is an omen that the marriage will not prosper.

More neglected now is the tradition that a virgin may wear a garter of STRAW or shells on the eve of her wedding to promote her chances of becoming pregnant. Wheat straw will guarantee that she will have a boy, a garter of oat straw that she will have a daughter. Any girl who sleeps with a garter under her pillow, meanwhile, will be granted a vision of her future partner in her dreams. Alternatively, she may enjoy the same result by attaching her garter to the bedroom wall, setting her SHOES at right angles and saying the following rhyme before getting silently into bed:

I pin my garters to the wall,
And put my shoes in the shape of a T,
In hopes my true love for to see,
Not in his apparel nor in his array,
But in the clothes he wears every day.
If I am his bride to be,
If I am his clothes to wear,
If I am his children to bear,
I hope he'll turn his face to me,
But if I am not his bride to be,
If I am not his clothes to wear,
If I am not his children to bear,
I hope he'll turn his back to me.

People suffering from RHEUMATISM are advised to slip on red garters, while those afflicted by CRAMP may benefit from wearing garters made of CORK or the skin of an EEL. Should a garter slip down by accident, this is widely taken as a sign that a girl's lover is thinking of her.

Ceremonial garters are also worn by the high priestesses of many covens as an indication of their high status (*see* WITCHCRAFT).

**gas** An example of a superstition of relatively recent coinage is the widely held European belief that carrying a child through a gasworks will benefit any respiratory problems it has.

**gate** Most spells offering the unmarried the chance to catch a glimpse of their future partner seem particularly aimed at females, but a gate provides the single male a rare chance to enjoy the same privilege. A tradition recorded in Shropshire says that if a man marks three notches on a five-barred gate on nine consecutive nights he will be rewarded by a vision of his future partner on the last occasion.

*See also* DOOR.

**gemstone** Precious and semi-precious stones have long been held to have their own special properties. Most people know their own BIRTHSTONE and many wear RINGS and other items of jewellery containing these gems in the belief that doing so will bring them luck (whereas wearing a stone not connected with one's birth month is said to be unlucky, especially in the case of OPAL). Other superstitions concerning gemstones in general include the notion that dipping them in honey makes them shine all the more brilliantly. It is also alleged that any man who obtains for himself a jewel incorporating DIAMONDS, LODE-STONE and SAPPHIRES will enjoy powerful influence over women.

*See also* AGATE; AMBER; AMETHYST; CORAL; EMERALD; JADE; JASPER; OPAL; PEARL; RUBY; SARDONYX; TOPAZ; TURQUOISE.

**ghost** The spirit of someone who is dead, around which idea numerous superstitions have evolved. Whether a ghost manifests itself as a visible apparition, as an invisible poltergeist who disturbs the FURNITURE or merely as a 'presence' felt by those particularly sensitive to such entities, most people are terrified at the thought of meeting one and fear the ramifications of such an encounter. Superstition holds that spirits, which may include apparitions of animals, return to Earth for a variety of reasons. These include seeking vengeance for their deaths, warning others of danger, and seeing to some unfinished business that must be put right before they can enjoy eternal repose.

Disregarding many of the taboos insisted upon by superstition may result in the calling up of the dead and the appearance of ghosts, and even lingering in the vicinity of such ominous locations as CROSS-ROADS may be enough in itself to summon the attentions of the supernatural. Crossroads are, incidentally, the traditional burial-place of executed criminals and SUICIDES, largely because their vengeful ghosts will be confused by the choice of ways open to them and are thus less likely to find their way home and cause trouble to surviving relatives. Measures that may be taken against encountering ghosts include, according to Scottish tradition, wearing a CROSS of ROWAN wood fastened with red thread and concealed in the lining of one's coat.

**glass** The superstitious have always been fascinated by the curious properties of glass and the material has come to be associated with a wide range of offbeat notions. It is traditionally held in Britain to be unlucky to look at someone through a pane of broken glass, since this means that a quarrel between the two will shortly break out. To this day many people also advise against looking at a new MOON through glass, as this will bring on extreme bad luck. Glass balls, ideally made in the light of a full moon, have, however, been used for the purposes of divination for many centuries. Smaller versions were once worn about the person to prevent NIGHTMARES, cure illnesses in livestock and otherwise provide protection against harm.

Drinking glasses should never be handed to newly arrived guests but should instead be set down so that the visitors can pick them up. In Russia guests are often expected to break their glasses by throwing them over their shoulder – a gesture meant to appease the gods. One ruse known in several folklore traditions is to take a surreptitious sip from someone else's glass in the belief that it will enable one to read the other person's thoughts. Drinking from a glass at four opposite 'corners', that is in the shape of the CROSS, is recommended as a means of curing oneself of illness. If a glass breaks, someone in the household is near to death. Similarly, a drinking glass that emits a high-pitched ringing sound for no apparent reason is recognised by many as a death omen and is particularly feared by SAILORS, who will attempt to stifle the noise at once. Anyone who is worried that someone is trying to poison them should always drink out of Venetian glassware, incidentally, as this will shatter the moment anyone puts poison in it.

Should a glass vase be accidentally broken this is, surprisingly, a good omen, promising seven years of good fortune – in marked contrast to the seven years of bad luck that will befall someone who breaks a MIRROR.

*See also* SPECTACLES; WINDOW.

**glove**  In the days when people wore gloves much more than they now do, they were considered symbols of both authority and love; surviving superstitions reflect this history. Most people know that if they drop a glove it is unlucky to pick it up themselves and preferable to allow a friend to do so for them, a custom that probably originated in the ancient courtship ritual of a woman dropping a glove and waiting to see if a desired but as yet unproven lover deigned to retrieve it. Gifts of gloves are traditional between lovers, though an English variant of this suggests that they are in fact ill-advised as presents because they signify that the two people will soon be parted, possibly by a quarrel. Few people are now aware of the tradition that it is unlucky to wear gloves on a Wednesday (*see* DAYS OF THE WEEK), but many still observe the ancient taboo against shaking hands without removing a glove first.

Losing a glove is naturally enough unlucky, and if a pair of gloves is left at a friend's house it is important to follow the correct procedure in order to keep that friend. When the owner has retraced his steps he must refrain from picking the gloves up until he has first sat down, and he must not put them on until he has stood up again. Losing a pair of gloves that subsequently fall into the possession of a witch is worst of all, for the witch will be able to use them to acquire evil influence over their owner (*see* WITCHCRAFT). Finding a pair of gloves is, however, thought to be very lucky, especially if the gloves are found on a Sunday, in which case the person concerned is guaranteed a successful week at work.

**glow-worm**  Superstition offers the humble glow-worm a modicum of protection from human harm. An ancient tradition warns that anyone who kills a glow-worm risks ending a love affair and possibly even the death of their lover. Keeping a glow-worm in the house is said among farmers to ensure that their cows will give consistently good yields of MILK.

**gnat**  The gnat is a lucky insect and should be welcomed into the home if anyone is ill: gnats allowed to enter the sick-room at sunset will absorb the patient's ailment and take it with them when they leave. If gnats fly close to the ground, RAIN is on the way; but if they fly high in the air fine weather is to be expected.

**goat**  The goat has always been associated with virility and the darker supernatural forces, in ancient times often being identified with Pan, who was half man and half goat, and subsequently with the DEVIL himself, who is said to have a goat's cloven hooves and is sometimes depicted with a goat's head. Satan's favourite disguise, the goat shows its allegiance to the Prince of Darkness by visiting him once every twenty-four hours to have its BEARD combed. The primitive notion that sins and diseases could be transferred to a 'scapegoat' is reflected in the still-observed tradition that a farmer should always keep a goat or two to absorb the physical ills that would otherwise afflict his other livestock; the stronger the smell of a billy goat, the less likelihood there is of any COWS or HORSES falling sick.

The goat's connections with the supernatural mean that the flesh, skin and milk of the animal are valued in folk medicine. Rubbing sore feet, eyes and heads with fresh goat's cheese was recommended in Anglo-Saxon times and its brains, passed through a golden RING, were sometimes fed to children suffering from EPILEPSY. Some people carry goat's feet and HAIRS from a goat's beard as lucky AMULETS, while SAILORS have been known to fix a goatskin – or even a whole goat – to the mast to ward off foul WEATHER. A goat's horn slipped under the pillow will cure insomnia.

It is good luck to meet a goat when setting out on an important journey, and encountering a black goat on a bridle path suggests that treasure is hidden nearby.

**godparent** The friend or relation who stands as godparent at a CHRISTENING ceremony may often have only a hazy idea of what is expected and still less awareness of the superstitions that surround the role. In former times the Church forbade godparents from marrying one another and there is still a prejudice against inviting married or engaged couples to stand as godparents together, as this is said to result in the couple parting company within three months. Historically at least, it was also rare, particularly in Germany, for pregnant women to be asked to act as godmothers for fear that this would cause them to have a miscarriage. Godparents who have already lost a godchild are also unpopular choices: some parents fear that the same fate will strike their own child.

On a more positive note, godparents acquire certain healing powers by virtue of filling the role, and their SHOELACES or GARTERS may well prove beneficial if lent to those suffering from WHOOPING COUGH and worn round the neck. Any godparent who is tempted to look into the font during a christening is advised that the baby will grow up looking like him or her.

**goitre** Modern medicine offers treatment with iodine to remove the unsightly growths known as goitres, but before iodine deficiency was identified as the cause superstition recommended its own solutions. The more radical of these included arranging for the DEAD HAND of a CORPSE to make the sign of the CROSS over the goitre. Alternatively, early on May morning the patient was required to visit the grave of the young man most recently buried in a churchyard, to pass a hand three times through the DEW collected on his grave and then to press the dew to the affected part. For those nervous of such procedures, superstition also suggested that binding a HAIR from a HORSE's tail round a goitre would make it disappear.

**gold** Universally prized for its monetary worth, gold is also valued by the superstitious for certain intrinsic powers connected with it. Records survive from a thousand years ago to the effect that gold is particularly efficacious in treating EYE problems, and even today some people claim that rubbing a sore eye with a gold WEDDING RING will cause a sty to disappear. Apparently the time-honoured tradition that seafarers pierce their ears to wear gold EAR-RINGS is somehow connected with this belief (it is also popularly held that SAILORS who wear gold ear-rings will never go down with their ship). Certainly it was once an accepted practice for children with sore eyes to have their ears pierced so that they could wear twists of gold wire in them.

Rubbing the eyelids with gold even when one does not have a sty is said to bring good fortune to whoever tries it. When other treatments against illness prove ineffective, one option remaining is to pour a little WATER over a gold (or SILVER) coin and then to give the water to the patient to drink: the ailment is sure to disappear. Women having a difficult time in CHILDBIRTH, meanwhile, may be encouraged to remove any gold jewellery they are wearing, as this is sometimes blamed for such problems. Those troubled by WARTS may find that rapping them with gold will do the trick.

Anyone wishing to strike it lucky by digging for gold ore is advised to search for it by means of a HAZEL divining rod, the prongs of which have been wrapped with IRON.

**golden plover**  Shore bird of the PLOVER family, whose eerie, high-pitched cry has attracted a reputation as a harbinger of death in Wales and other regions. The gloomy associations of the golden plover are intensified by the widespread tradition that the souls of the seven Jews who assisted in the crucifixion of Christ are now entrapped in these birds and doomed to wander the Earth for the rest of time. The golden plover is one of several candidates for the source of the SEVEN WHISTLERS legend. More cheerful is the superstition from Cheshire which claims that golden plovers are kind-hearted birds whose cries are meant to warn SHEEP of any lurking danger (hence their nickname of 'Sheep's Guide').

**golf**  Those who play golf are as superstitious as any other sportsmen and cherish a good number of taboos and traditions. These include carrying a lucky club around in one's bag even if one never intends to use it, never changing one's mind about which club to use after taking one out of the bag, never approaching a tee from the front, always teeing off with a BALL numbered three or five and with the manufacturer's name towards the player, never cleaning a ball when one's luck is in, never unwrapping a new ball after play has begun and, of course, taking particular care when playing the thirteenth hole. There is also a taboo against using the word 'shank', as hitting the ball with the shank, of the club is clearly not a good idea.

Many golfers dislike starting a round before one o'clock, but modern match schedules often make it impossible to respect this preference. In Scotland, where the game originated, it is still held that whoever wins the first hole is sure to win the match. On top of all these traditions, golfers share with other sportsmen the usual irrational faiths in lucky garments, pre-match rituals and MASCOTS.

**Good Friday**  As one of the most sacred days in the Christian calendar, Good Friday is associated with many superstitions throughout the Christian world. It is in fact a day of mixed blessings. Any BABY born on Good Friday is to be pitied as this is unlucky, according to the Welsh, but it is conversely a good day to wean an infant because he or she will grow up healthy and prosperous. CROPS should not be planted on Good Friday (though it is all right to sow garden seeds) as the ground should not be disturbed on this day, and nobody should attempt to do any WASHING as the clothes will never come clean (a reference to the legend that Christ cursed Good Friday washing after he was slapped in the face by a wet garment while being led to the Crucifixion).

BLACKSMITHS, mindful of Christ's suffering on the CROSS, may decline to hammer NAILS on this day; likewise children tempted to climb TREES are warned not to do so. On the whole, in fact, work of any kind is not a good idea as it will only have to be done all over again, according to the inhabitants of Norfolk. Wishes made in prayers said at the stroke of three o'clock in the afternoon, the hour of Christ's death, are sure to be granted.

BREAD and buns baked on Good Friday will never go mouldy – as is the case with Good Friday EGGS – and have beneficial healing properties if fed to those suffering from WHOOPING COUGH and other ailments. In past centuries, indeed, well-cooked Good Friday bread was sometimes kept for many years, a little of it being grated off and administered to the sick as necessary. A hot cross bun kept over from one Good Friday to the next, meanwhile, will prevent the house from catching fire.

Sundry other Good Friday traditions include the notion that boys who wear long trousers for the first time on this day will have happy marriages, and that this day is the one time in the year when bees may be taken from their hives without causing them harm.

**goose** The goose was in former times the traditional dish served up on Michaelmas Day, and it was widely held that any household where goose was eaten on this day would enjoy prosperity times in the coming year and not fall into debt. If the meat proved to have a brown tint this meant that a mild winter was in store; if it was pure white or bluish in colour, the winter would be severe. Geese were once seen in every farmyard, and in Wales it is still said that if the geese leave a farm there will shortly be a FIRE. The Welsh also maintain that it is an ill omen if a goose lays two EGGS in a single day or produces one hard egg and one soft one. Geese that fly in the air, it is claimed, are a prophecy of good weather; if they fly near the Earth then STORMS may be on the way.

Goose grease mixed with turpentine and rubbed on the chest is valued in US folk medicine as a cure for COUGHS and COLDS and is also used in the treatment of RHEUMATISM and earache (see EAR).

See also BARNACLE GOOSE.

**gooseberry** Inquisitive children are still to this day informed by some parents that BABIES (specifically baby boys) are found under gooseberry bushes, though quite where this particular old wives' tale came from is unclear. It seems to be a relatively recent invention which may not date back beyond the nineteenth century. Gooseberry bushes do, however, feature in a centuries-old tradition which suggests that piercing a sty or WART with a gooseberry prickle will cause it to disappear.

See also PARSLEY.

**gorse** The gorse bush, with its unfriendly spikes, is an unlucky plant.

Many people will refuse to allow a sprig of gorse blossom into the house, maintaining that to do so invites the death of one of the family or some other dire misfortune.

See also HAWTHORN.

**gout** Modern medicine has made gout largely an ailment of historical curiosity, but sufferers once had only superstition to turn to. Cures ranged from putting toenail clippings and a few HAIRS from the affected leg into a hole in an OAK, which was then sealed with cow DUNG, to eating the powdered head of a red gurnard (a fish) or wrapping the foot in deerskin and applying to it a SPIDER whose own legs had been carefully removed.

**grass** The British, who boast the finest lawns in the world, have just two traditions relating to the mystical properties of grass. The first holds that when animals such as CATS and DOGS nibble grass RAIN is on the way (actually they do it to aid the digestion). According to the second, a stalk of seed-bearing rye grass may be plucked by an unmarried girl for the purposes of divination, the seeds being counted off to the well-known formula 'Tinker, tailor, soldier, sailor, rich man, poor man, beggarman, thief' to reveal the occupation of her future husband.

See also HAY.

**grave** The burial sites of the dead are not unnaturally the object of much superstitious belief and few people would care to be seen flying in the face of these for fear of offending the deceased. Numerous taboos surround the digging of a grave. A grave must always be dug so that the body may be laid in it on an east–west axis, the head towards the west to facilitate the CORPSE's rise on Judgement Day. Once dug, a grave should not be left empty over a Sunday or someone else must die to fill it; if this is unavoidable, the gaping hole should at least be covered over as though it is occupied. Accidentally dropping something such as a hat into the hole is ominous, and suggests that the owner too will be shortly be laid in the earth. Graves positioned on the south side of the churchyard are generally the most sought after as these areas usually get the most sunshine; the chillier north side is traditionally reserved for SUICIDES and criminals.

Not surprisingly, it is generally thought unlucky to plough anywhere near a grave, even one of ancient origins, and some people still react with horror to the idea of a 'ploughed' graveyard in which the remains of the long-dead are deliberately churned up together so that new graves may be dug. CROPS planted where bodies have been buried will fail to flourish, and many localities boast patches of ground where nothing will grow because they are a grave site (*see* BARREN GROUND).

Robbing a grave of its contents, even if only to transfer a corpse to a grander tomb, is extremely reckless and may call up the vengeful spirit of the person whose remains are disturbed. Walking on or stepping over a grave is frowned upon in many European countries, particularly if the grave contains the body of an unbaptised child, and the offender may be punished by catching a fatal disease popularly called 'grave-scab'. If a pregnant or married woman walks on a grave, any child she subsequently has will be born with a club foot. It is very unlucky to pick a flower growing on a grave, especially if the flower is then given to someone in HOSPITAL.

Builders who remove gravestones for use in new structures are warned that anything they build is sure to collapse, and if bits of gravestone are used in making a road that stretch will become notorious for accidents (*see* CAR). Despite these taboos, however, many gravestones and monuments have suffered over the years because chips of stone have been removed by shepherds, who maintain that feeding them in powdered form to their SHEEP will cure various diseases. Some authorities also detail a variety of procedures involving walking round graves, crawling over them and even eating the grass that grows over them to relieve BOILS, TOOTHACHE and other ailments. One folk remedy from Lincolnshire that is almost guaranteed to cause offence recommends that children given to BEDWETTING be allowed to urinate on the grave of a child of the opposite sex.

*See also* BURIAL; CHURCHYARD WATCHER; COFFIN; DEATH; EXHUMATION; FUNERAL.

**green** The colour of nature, green has many powerful and ancient associations and, though it is supposed to represent hope and immortality, it is generally thought on both sides of the Atlantic to be among the most unlucky of all COLOURS (though it is lucky in some European countries). FAIRIES and other malicious wood spirits are said to wear green, and it is suggested that anyone who dons green or otherwise favours the colour will come under their evil influence. Even today many motorists will think twice before choosing a green CAR, while ACTORS AND ACTRESSES are famous for their dislike of the colour on stage. Issues of green stamps have not fared well in the past, and it is said that whenever the Post Office releases stamps of this colour some national catastrophe quickly follows. Brides are particularly advised against wearing anything coloured green; in times gone by the guests at a WEDDING would also avoid the colour, and no green vegetables would be included on the menu at the reception. One pessimistic traditional saying still occasionally heard in the British Isles warns that anyone who wears green will have to wear black soon afterwards.

**gremlin** A mythical creature whose interference with the workings of a machine is often blamed for any mechanical fault that develops. The gremlin was an invention of a British Royal Air Force bomber squadron stationed on the north-west frontier of India shortly before the Second World War. The squadron had been much plagued by minor technical problems and the officers accordingly invented the gremlin as the source of these woes, the name being a conflation of the Brothers Grimm and Fremlin's Brewery, whose beer was the only brand stocked in the squadron bar. The idea quickly caught on with Royal Air Force units during the war after the squadron was posted back to the UK, and the gremlin has remained a familiar figure in the popular imagination, being blamed for breakdowns not only in aircraft but also in cars, trains and virtually any other kind of machine. The only way to foil the activities of gremlins, apparently, is to lay an empty beer bottle nearby – the mischievous creatures will crawl inside and stay there.

**groaning cake**  A special cake (or sometimes a cheese) that is made to celebrate the birth of a child and to ensure the good luck of the new arrival (*see* CHILD-BIRTH). Rarely seen in modern times, the groaning cake (so called in reference to the noises a mother makes in labour) should be cut by the father or else by the attending doctor, who must take care not to cut himself as this is an omen that the baby will die before it is a year old. Refusing a piece will bring the infant bad luck and rob it of charm.

A groaning cheese may be cut from the middle until the hole is large enough for the baby to be passed through it for luck (usually done on the day of the CHRIS-TENING). Unmarried girls may choose to keep their slice of cake or cheese and slip it under their pillow in the expectation of seeing their future lover in their dreams.

**growing stone**  A small pebble, of the type that litters many a field and garden. The difficulty involved in clearing a plot of land of such small stones has led to the popular English superstition that they actually grow from the earth, a notion that explains why they always seem to reappear when the ground is supposed to have been swept clear of them.

**guinea fowl**  The guinea fowl, with its repeated unchanging cry, is said to bring sunshine to a farmyard, according to one northern English superstition, and is otherwise considered an excellent bird to have around to promote the luck of a farm.

**gull**  *see* SEAGULL.

# H

**haddock** Various superstitions surround the haddock, most of which attempt to explain how the fish acquired its black gill spots. According to one of these, the spots are the fingerprints of Christ himself, imprinted on the fish when he held it aloft at the feeding of the five thousand. Another tradition links the haddock to St Peter, the marks of his fingers being left on the fish's skin after he held it to receive the tribute money that the fish brought. One Yorkshire legend claims that the haddock acquired its spots after it was seized by the DEVIL, who picked it up by mistake after he dropped his hammer in the sea while constructing the rock outcrop at Filey Brigg (otherwise known as the Devil's Bridge). The Scots refrain from burning the bones of the haddock because the fish once warned that if this happened it would cease to frequent Scottish shores.

**hair** Superstition insists that hair retains a mystical link with the body even after it is cut off. It therefore has great potential in folk magic and there are numerous associated taboos and traditions. To begin with, the colour of the hair is said to communicate information about character. A red-haired person is widely held to have an irascible temper (perhaps in reference to the red-haired Judas Iscariot or to the red-haired Norse invaders of Britain), though he or she may also be courageous and it is considered lucky to run one's fingers through someone's red hair. Fair hair is a sign of a weak nature, while black hair suggests great strength and virility and is also lucky. Whatever the hair's colour, however, it remains unwise to pluck out any odd grey hairs that appear as ten more will grow for every one so removed.

People with straight hair are said to be cunning, while those with curly hair are of good temper. Those whose hair forms a 'cowlick' curl are said to be naturally lucky, but any woman who suddenly develops curls at the temples where her hair was previously straight is warned to look to her husband's health, for he has not long to live. Those who would like curly hair, meanwhile, are advised to eat the crusts of newly baked BREAD. Girls with exceptionally long hair were once warned that 'with hair below the knee ne'er a bride will she be', and too bushy a growth of hair suggests that the wearer may be dim-witted because the hair is diverting nourishment that should go to the brain.

The Welsh claim that a child with two crowns will be lucky in money matters, while the Scottish believe the child will never drown; the English say it means that the infant will live in more than one country. A woman whose hair grows into a point on the forehead is said to have a 'widow's peak', an ill omen which indicates that she is destined to become a widow. The same conclusion may be drawn from a parting that suddenly appears in a girl's hair where there was previously none.

In men, a hairy chest or luxuriant facial hair is widely held to be a sign of strength and is therefore lucky (which is why in ancient times victorious soldiers some-

times hacked the beards off their enemies). Those with a lot of hair on the arms
and on the backs of the hands are destined
to enjoy considerable wealth. Hair on the
palms of the hand is, however, a sign of
MADNESS.

Looking after the hair involves the
observance of various taboos. The Scottish say that a woman must never COMB
her hair after dark if she has friends and
relations at SEA, as this will bring them
into terrible danger; elsewhere similar
taboos exist about using combs after the
day has ended, though it is usually all right
to use a hairbrush. In the USA it is considered vital that HATS should not be too
tight, for this will cause the hair to thin.

Hair that is trimmed when the MOON is
waxing will grow back quickly, but hair
that is cut when the moon is on the wane
will stay short and may lose its shine. On
no account should hair be trimmed on
GOOD FRIDAY, and in some areas hair-
cutting should also be avoided on Thurs-
days, Fridays, Saturdays and Sundays (*see*
DAYS OF THE WEEK). One old English
rhyme advises:

> Best never enjoyed if Sunday shorn,
> And likewise leave out Monday.
> Cut Thursday and you'll never grow
> rich,
> Likewise on a Saturday.
> But live long if shorn on a Tuesday
> And best of all is Friday.

Cutting one's own hair is unlucky, and
seafarers are warned that cutting their
hair while at sea will summon up a storm.

Disposal of cut hair is of paramount
importance for, in common with nail
clippings and various bodily fluids, a
small amount may be used by a witch to
obtain control over the person from
whom it came because of the enduring
psychic link with the rest of the body.
Simply boiling a strand of hair will oblige
the owner to come to the witch or
sorcerer, whether he wants to or not. By
burning the hair in a ritual ceremony a
witch might cause the person from
whom it has come excruciating pain.

One variant involves including a few
strands of hair in a wax image representing the person from whom the hair has
come, and then holding the figure in a
flame to inflict intense burning pain and
even to cause death. A defence against
such a threat is to cut off some hair or,
more drastically, part of a finger as a sacrifice to ward off further harm. Witches
themselves were sometimes shorn of all
their body hair in accordance with a
superstition that this would rob them of
their supernatural powers.

The safest method to dispose of cut hair
is to bury it. This is better than burning it,
as the soul of the person to whom it
belonged will still need it on Judgement
Day. Perhaps because of the threat of
witchcraft no person should keep a lock
of his or her own hair or that of their
children, for this promises them a premature death. If a BIRD obtains so much as a
single human hair to help make its nest,
the person from whom the hair came will
be afflicted with a severe HEADACHE. If
the bird is a MAGPIE, according to the
folklore of Devon, that person will die
within the year.

Some people claim that a single strand
of hair plucked from the head may be
used for the purposes of divination. The
procedure is to draw the hair tight
between the nails of the forefinger and
thumb and then to release it: if the hair
curls up this is taken as a proof of pride or
else as a prophecy that the person concerned will enjoy considerable riches. In
Scotland, the number of bends in the hair
indicates the number of spouses the
person will have.

Alternatively, two girls may secretly
meet in complete silence between the
hours of midnight and one o'clock in the
morning and pluck out a hair for each
year they have so far lived. These hairs are
then burned on the fire one by one while
the girls speak the words: 'I offer this my
sacrifice to him most precious in my eyes,
I charge thee now come forth to me that I
this minute may thee see', upon which an
apparition of each girl's future husband

will materialise. Observing how a strand of hair burns when thrown into the fire will also reveal how long a person has to live: if the hair burns quickly and brightly, then the person concerned has many years left to go. If the hair refuses to burn this may be taken as a sign that the owner is fated to die by DROWNING.

In folk medicine hair can be used in curing WHOOPING COUGH and is also a useful ingredient in love potions (*see* APHRODISIAC). Lovers often exchange locks of each other's hair, possibly to show their confidence that the other will not misuse it as a witch might. Further myths concerning hair include the persistent idea that it continues to grow even in the grave, and the notion that finding a stray hair on one's shoulders indicates an important LETTER on its way.

*See also* BALDNESS; BEARD; HAIRPIN; SCISSORS.

**hairpin** Because of its association with HAIR, the humble hairpin is not without magical significance. Finding a hairpin promises making a new friend; losing one is more ominous, suggesting that an enemy is close at hand. If a hairpin works its way loose in the hair this is taken as an indication that someone has that person in their thoughts – though in Germany this may signify the end of a love affair.

**Hallowe'en** Festival, celebrated on 31 October, when GHOSTS roam abroad and witches traditionally hold their sabbaths (*see* WITCHCRAFT). Originally a pagan festival of the dead, Hallowe'en marked the end of the Celtic year. It was said that the SUN itself entered the gates of Hell on this date, providing an opportunity for evil spirits to slip out and menace the Earth for forty-eight hours – hence the ominous associations of the modern version of the festival. Attempts to Christianise the festival by making it the eve of All Hallows' Day or All Saints' Day, when Christian saints and martyrs are commemorated, have failed to obliterate its essentially pagan character, empha-

sised by the now ubiquitous imagery of broomstick-riding witches and grotesque masks fashioned from hollowed-out pumpkins which are meant to scare away demons.

Hallowe'en is the one time of year when the supernatural holds sway over the Earth, and numerous superstitions are associated with it. These range from protective rituals to keep evil spirits at bay to means of divining what the future has in store. One of the most widely held notions connected with the festival is the blood-chilling idea that on this date the souls of the dead make their way back to their earthly homes to warm themselves at their old firesides. In many quarters it is thought dangerous to attempt to hinder the dead from returning in this way, and Hallowe'en is generally considered a time when extra care should be taken not to linger in churchyards or do anything that might offend the FAIRIES or other malicious sprites.

If a person is walking down a road, for instance, and hears someone walking close behind it is important that they do not look round (it is likely to be death himself, and looking into his face will hasten the living person's own demise). It is also risky to look at one's own SHADOW in the moonlight and most inadvisable to go on a hunting expedition on Hallowe'en, as one may accidentally wound a wandering spirit. Children born on Hallowe'en will, however, enjoy lifelong protection against evil spirits and will also be endowed with the gift of second sight. In rural areas farmers may circle their fields with lighted torches in the belief that doing so will safeguard the following year's harvest, or else drive their livestock between branches of ROWAN to keep them safe from evil influences.

Most surviving Hallowe'en superstitions concern the business of foretelling the future, in particular getting a glimpse of a future partner. According to Welsh tradition, anyone going to a CROSSROADS on Hallowe'en and listening carefully to the WIND may learn what the next year has in store and, when the church CLOCK strikes midnight, will hear a list of the names of those who are to die in the locality over the next twelve months.

Several of the most widely known Hallowe'en divination rituals relate to APPLES. Superstition suggests that, if a girl stands before a MIRROR while eating an apple and combing her HAIR at midnight on Hallowe'en, her future husband's image will be reflected in the glass over her left shoulder. A variant dictates that she must cut the apple into nine pieces, each of which must be stuck on the point of the KNIFE and held over the left shoulder. Moreover, if she peels an apple in one long piece, and then tosses the peel over her left shoulder or into a bowl of water, she will be able to read the first initial of her future partner's name in the shape assumed by the discarded peel. Alternatively the peel is hung on a nail by the front door and the initials of the first man to enter will be the same as those of the unknown lover.

Hallowe'en is also the occasion on which groups of unmarried boys and girls twirl apples on strings over a fire, the order in which the apples fall off the strings indicates the order in which they will be married (the owner of the last apple to drop will remain unmarried). Yet another Hallowe'en custom is the game of ducking apples: without using their hands, children attempt to take bites out of apples floating in a bowl of water or suspended on a string. Superstition has it that they are fated to marry the owner of the apple they manage to bite. Alternatively the winner of the game takes their apple to bed and sleeps with it under their pillow so as to get a vision of a future spouse in their dreams.

Other customs involve blindfolded girls pulling up CABBAGES and examining the shape of the root to make conclusions about a future spouse, throwing NUTS into the fire to see if they jump (if they do, a lover will prove unfaithful), sprinking letters cut out of a newspaper on to some water to see what name they

form (that of a future lover) and inviting a blindfolded person to place their left hand on one of three DISHES, one filled with clean water, another with foul water and the last empty. If the clean water is chosen, the person's future partner will be attractive and desirable; if the foul water is selected, he or she will already have been married; if the empty dish is chosen, there will be no partner at all.

Some girls may be tempted to follow the ritual of eating a salted HERRING before retiring for the night: the resulting thirst will summon up the sympathetic spirit of a future partner who will come with a drink of water. More complicated is the ancient procedure in which a person dips their sleeve in a stream at a point where land belonging to three people meets, and then goes home and hangs the sleeve in front of the fire: during the night the spirit of a future spouse will materialise and turn the sleeve to allow the other side to dry.

*See also* CANDLE; CAUFF-RIDDLING; DUMB CAKE; EGG; FIRE; GARLIC; HEMP SEED; SNAIL.

**hammer** One of the principal tools of the BLACKSMITH, the hammer is said to facilitate the soul's flight to Heaven if one is laid on the brow of a newly deceased person. Furthermore, any husband who wishes to ensure that his opinions hold sway in his own household is advised to purchase a hammer before he buys anything else.

**hand** The hand, as the instrument of so many human actions, has its own superstitions. In common with the face, much may be learned from the physical characteristics of someone's hand. People often talk of 'artist's hands', and it is generally held that people with long, slender hands are more talented and sensitive than those with less elegant, stubby hands. Moist hands, meanwhile, are a sign of a passionate disposition, while cold hands suggest a warm heart.

The right hand is said to belong to God while the left belongs to the DEVIL, and it is accordingly the right hand that is raised in swearing oaths. Left-handed people are supposed to be lucky if met in the street (though not, according to northern English superstition, on Tuesdays, when they will bring bad luck), while ambidextrous people are thought to be untrustworthy and cunning.

Itchy PALMS have their own significance: if it is the right palm that itches, the owner is about to receive some money or some important news; if it is the left palm, he or she is fated to part with money in the near future unless they take the precaution of TOUCHING WOOD. Another tradition claims that an itching palm allows a wish to be made and further counsels, 'Rub it on brass, it's sure to come to pass.'

If someone has recently enjoyed a run of luck, friends and relations may clamour to rub their hands in the hope that a little of this luck will rub off on them. Shaking hands with the left hand is unlucky, as is shaking hands across a table or over a person, and if two couples cross arms while shaking hands there is going to be a surprise WEDDING. Should the same two people shake hands twice by mistake, they should shake hands once more to avoid any bad luck befalling them. Engaged women are warned not to allow their left hands to touch their right hands until they are safely wedded, or the marriage will be unhappy.

In past times some mothers refused to wash their BABY's hands until the child was a year old, for fear of washing the infant's luck away. It is also deemed unlucky for two people to wash their hands in the same basin together: they will quarrel unless they also spit into the water (see SPITTING). Washing the hands in URINE, though, will protect a person from WITCHCRAFT.

The touch of certain hands was formerly reputed to have special healing properties, particularly if the hand belonged to a king or a dead man, and many people paid for the privilege to cure such ailments as scrofula (see KING'S TOUCH) and GOITRE. In some parts of Europe

people still carry small hand-shaped AMULETS in the belief that these ward off evil.

Finally, a grisly superstition of ancient origins claims that a hand that has committed some dire act, such as MURDER or striking a parent, will by way of punishment protrude from the grave when the guilty party finally comes to be buried – and, in some versions of this belief, a puppy DOG will come and urinate on it.

*See also* CORPSE; DEAD HAND; FINGER; FINGERNAIL; GLOVE; HAND OF GLORY.

**handkerchief**   A handkerchief is frequently carried on the person and is therefore considered to have considerable magical properties. If someone drops their handkerchief it is unwise for them to pick it up themselves and better if they can persuade someone else to retrieve it for them (perhaps a reference to the courtship rituals of medieval chivalry). Handkerchiefs should never be put into the pocket still folded, and on no account should one be borrowed from someone else because this signifies 'borrowing tears' as well. Neither should handkerchiefs be given as presents to a lover, as this means the affair is doomed to end. Tying a KNOT in a handkerchief is intended to prevent the DEVIL making one forget something important.

A quaint US superstition allows the handkerchief to be used for divination. A handkerchief is hung on a bush on the eve of MAYDAY and left there overnight. In the morning the initials of a future spouse will be written on the handkerchief in DEW.

**Hand of Glory**   The hand of an executed criminal, which was once reputed to have various magical powers.

The Hand of Glory was particularly prized by witches throughout Europe as part of the paraphernalia of black magic and also by THIEVES, who valued its alleged ability to make the occupants of a house fall into a deep entranced sleep while they went about their nefarious business.

**handsel**

The Hand of Glory was prepared by severing the hand of a hanged felon while the body was still on the GALLOWS, pickling it for fifteen days, drying it till it was hard and then fixing between the fingers a CANDLE made from virgin wax mixed with the fat of a hanged man and sesame. When the candle thus mounted was lit everyone in the vicinity, with the exception of the owner of the gruesome object, would fall into a profound slumber from which they could not be roused, however much noise was made. Records exist of such a Hand of Glory being employed during a foiled burglary in rural Ireland as late as 1831. In some cases no candle was fixed in the hand, but one of the fingers was lit instead; if the finger would not light this was a warning that someone in the house was still awake.

One antidote to the power of the Hand of Glory involved smearing the threshold of the house, the WINDOWS and other entrances with a special ointment, the ingredients of which included the gall of a black CAT, the fat of a white HEN and the blood of a screech-owl.

**handsel**  *see* BUSINESS.

**hangman's rope**  The ROPE used to hang a man was in former times considered to have its own special properties. As far back as the ancient Romans it was claimed that wrapping such a rope round the temples would relieve a HEADACHE, and this tradition persisted almost as long as capital punishment in the British Isles at least. Possession of a hangman's rope or even a single strand of it was also reputed to fend off all manner of fits and FEVERS, the rope being worn somewhat ironically around the neck. GAMBLERS also greatly prized these ropes in the belief that they improved their luck. Time was when hangmen made a tidy profit from selling off portions of their rope, though pieces of rope used by SUICIDES were considered equally effective.

**hare**  The superstitions associated with the hare mark it out as an ominous creature closely linked with dark forces. It was worshipped in Britain in pre-Christian times and this, together with the animal's eerie cry and habit of standing on its back legs almost like a human, may have contributed to its otherworldly reputation that has persisted into modern times.

The animal was formerly widely regarded as one of the favourite disguises of witches, so in rural communities many people feared its appearance anywhere in the vicinity of their livestock. Countless stories survive of hares that have been shot at with SILVER bullets (ordinary bullets were said to have no effect) and of some crone in the district shortly afterwards appearing with a fresh bandage on some part of her body. Witches disguised as hares were alleged to MILK cattle dry, and the sight of a hare crossing someone's path was considered deeply unlucky, to the extent that FISHERMEN would turn back for home and brides would postpone their WEDDINGS. STORMS, mining disasters (*see* MINERS) and FIRES (which are sure to follow if a hare runs down the main street of a village) have all been blamed on sightings of hares, and SAILORS will not suffer even the word 'hare' to be mentioned while at sea.

Dreaming of hares is similarly said to warn of imminent catastrophe, often a death. In some regions, however, it is only WHITE hares – the reincarnations of lovers who have died of grief, according to the Cornish – that are unlucky, and seeing a brown hare is actually said to be a good omen which provides an opportunity to make a wish. In modern times, indeed, most people have somewhat perversely come to associate the hare with good luck, chiefly through the time-honoured tradition that carrying a hare's foot, now usually in the form of a keyfob, is very lucky.

Other miscellaneous superstitions connected with hares include the notions that they change their sex every year, that killing them is unlucky, that they never sleep and that they will cause deep melancholy and timidity in anyone who consumes their flesh. The hare's celebrated fertility, meanwhile, has linked it with the season of EASTER, though this tradition has gradually been undermined by the equally fecund RABBIT, which shares many of the same traditions.

In folk medicine, hare's blood rubbed into the skin is recommended as a cure for freckles, while carrying a hare's foot will ward off RHEUMATISM. One very ancient English remedy suggests that eating hare's brains in wine will stop one over-sleeping.

*See also* HARE-LIP.

**hare-lip** Superstition blames the birth of a BABY with a hare-lip upon events that take place during the PREG-NANCY. It is said that any pregnant woman who is startled by a HARE or RABBIT is likely to give birth to a child with a hare-lip; expectant mothers may also be warned to avoid walking over the animals' burrows, which may have the same result. The only remedy open to a woman who unwittingly breaks this latter taboo is immediately to drop two stones into the hole to forestall the mis-fortune, or else to bend down and make a long tear in her skirt.

**hat** As with other items of CLOTHING, superstition demands that care be taken when putting a hat on. Anyone who makes the mistake of putting a hat on the wrong way round is fated to suffer ill luck for the rest of the day, a situation that can only be reversed by going out and buying a new hat. Some sportsmen will, how-ever, deliberately wear their hats reversed for luck. Hats should never be worn indoors as this will bring on a HEADACHE and care should be taken to ensure that they are the right size; if a hat is too tight the wearer may suffer HAIR loss. It is unlucky for women to remove their hats in church, but men should always take off their hats if a FUNERAL passes by, on pain of becoming the next person to die. Hats must never be laid down on BEDS or TABLES as this invites extreme bad luck,

especially in sporting circles. According to US superstition, a woman who puts on a man's hat is conveying a desire to be kissed, while a bridegroom who forgets his hat will prove an unreliable and unfaithful husband.

**hawthorn** In common with other THORN trees the hawthorn has dark supernatural associations, probably because it is thought by many that the crown of thorns placed on Christ's head during the Crucifixion came from the hawthorn. Hawthorn blossom should therefore never be brought into the home because it brings death with it, and spikes of hawthorn are sometimes used in black magic rituals intended to bring pain to some unwitting victim, the thorns being pressed into the heart of a SHEEP or BAT (*see* WITCHCRAFT). The sickly smell of the hawthorn blossom is said to be exactly like that which accompanied the Great Plague in London in 1665, and many people claim that the smell of the plant is the smell of death itself.

It is most unwise to sit under a haw-thorn on HALLOWE'EN or one of the other dates when malevolent spirits roam the Earth; this risks enchantment by FAIR-IES, who are apparently often found in the vicinity of the tree. It is thus very unlucky to cut a hawthorn down, unless the permission of the fairies has been requested first.

The tree (sometimes called May blos-som) is, however, also linked with the more optimistic ceremonies traditional to MAYDAY and is believed to protect livestock and people from evil influences as well as from LIGHTNING. In times gone by the taboo against bringing hawthorn into the home does not seem to have applied, and many people decorated their rooms with hawthorn blossom to protect the household: the theory was that witch-es would get tangled up in the spikes. Newly married couples were once offered boughs of hawthorn for their protection, while babies' CRADLES were often adorned with hawthorn cuttings. In the English Midlands a 'globe' of hawthorn was suspended in farmhouse kitchens at NEW YEAR and and kept there for a year before being burned over the ridges in the fields to guarantee a good harvest in the succeeding year. Hawthorn trees also symbolise fertility, and the scent of the hawthorn is widely considered an APHRODISIAC.

Legend has it that the very first hawthorn was the one that took root at Glastonbury when St Joseph of Arimathea struck the ground with his staff. The tree, which always blossomed at midnight on Christmas Eve, was destroyed in the seventeenth century but was replanted from the many cuttings taken from it and is still considered holy.

**hay** A loaded hay wagon encountered on the road may be considered unlucky, especially by the impatient motorist, but this is only true if it is going away from whoever sees it (it is particularly unlucky if the load turns off the road while still in sight, and if this seems likely to happen the observer should look away). If the wagon is approaching the observer this is an excellent sign of good luck and a wish may be made. One ancient English superstition claims that young men and women should be encouraged to sleep in new hay ricks; this ensured that the hay would be sweet, and also that the girls would become pregnant.

*See also* GRASS.

**hazel** The hazel is thought to be particularly effective as a defence against WITCHCRAFT and evil spirits, and was considered sacred in Celtic mythology. It will also cure RHEUMATISM and lumbago, among other diseases. Because of the tree's varied magical powers forked hazel twigs are among the favoured tools of dowsers and diviners. Anyone who cuts a length of hazel on MIDSUMMER'S EVE, taking care to approach the plant backwards and cutting the twig using both hands between the legs, will be able to use it to divine for hidden treasure (to check that the twig is working it should be held

over WATER until it gives a high-pitched squeal). For the same reason, both sorcerers' wands and royal sceptres were once made of hazel wood. In former times the tree also symbolised fertility and immortality, and so hazel twigs were frequently carried at WEDDINGS.

Welsh superstition has it that anyone who wears leaves and twigs of hazel in their cap will enjoy particularly good luck and have their wishes granted. SAILORS, meanwhile, believe that taking a bit of hazel to sea with them will protect them from shipwreck, and hardened drinkers believe that if they cut a piece of hazel at midnight on HALLOWE'EN and keep it in their pocket they will never get drunk however much alcohol they consume (*see* DRUNKENNESS). Hazelnuts may also be used for divination at Hallowe'en. If the nuts are placed in the fire and jump in the air, one's lover is unfaithful.

The nuts, like the tree itself, represent fertility, and years when there is a good crop of nuts are said to be good years for the birth of many BABIES – and also for large numbers of PROSTITUTES.

**headache** Superstition can offer a variety of treatments for people who suffer from debilitating headaches. These include wrapping the skin of a SNAKE or a HANGMAN'S ROPE around the temples, holding tightly on to some scraped horseradish and pressing one's thumb against the roof of one's mouth. More elaborate is the remedy that involves drying and powdering some moss found growing in a human SKULL and inhaling it like snuff. In the north of England a poultice of cow's DUNG may be heartily recommended as a cure.

**hearse** The business of burying the dead is fraught with superstitious belief which extends to the vehicle in which the CORPSE is carried. Many people show nervousness on catching sight of a hearse, whether it is carrying a COFFIN or not. In fact the sight of an empty hearse is considered especially unlucky by some, as it suggests that death is looking for someone to fill it. A hearse that pauses even momentarily outside one's door is an omen that someone in that house will die in the near future; similarly, it is deemed a bad sign if a hearse has to be reversed or turned round, because this will offend the dead person and lead to the demise of another member of his or her family. Undertakers themselves are warned that it is unlucky to be the first person to drive a new hearse as, so the story goes, the driver will shortly be carried in one himself.

*See also* BURIAL; FUNERAL.

**heart**   As the traditional seat of the soul, the heart has particular significance in the superstitions and traditions of WITCHCRAFT. In former times, if a farmer suspected one of his animals had died as the result of being bewitched the solution was to cut out the creature's heart and pierce it with PINS or THORNS; the witch or sorcerer responsible would be afflicted by terrible pain or would otherwise be obliged to make his or her identity known. The lovesick are advised that removing the heart of a live PIGEON and sticking it with pins will oblige a reluctant lover to fall passionately in love. If the lover still proves unwilling, sticking a HARE's heart with pins and burying it near a newly dug grave will cause the unconsenting party to experience a sudden decline in health, culminating in death.

**heartburn**   Modern medicine presents various simple chemical solutions to the problem of heartburn, but superstition offers its own alternatives. One involves drinking the juices of a ST JOHN'S WORT plant that has been picked at daybreak on St John's Day, while others recommend sucking on a lump of COAL and the consumption of powdered toenails (*see* FINGERNAIL).

*See also* DYSPEPSIA.

**hearth**   *see* CHIMNEY; FIRE.

**heather**   Most people are familiar with the notion of heather being a lucky plant, and it is quite common for drivers to stick a sprig of white or even purple heather in the grille of their car radiator to protect their fortune or for gipsies to sell sprigs of it for good luck. White heather is traditionally the lucky variety as, so the legend goes, this is the only variety not tainted by the blood of the ancient Pictish inhabitants of the northern lands. The Scots, however, have had reservations about white heather ever since 1745, when a sprig of it was presented to the luckless Bonnie Prince Charlie. Another legend of Scottish origins claims that heather, the traditional flower of Scotland, will never grow over the graves of the clansmen. Other properties of the plant are said to include the power to prevent a drunkard from taking alcohol.

**hedgehog**   Superstition maintains that the generally endearing hedgehog is actually an unlucky animal and a favourite disguise of witches (*see* WITCHCRAFT). To be absolutely sure of preserving one's luck in the presence of a hedgehog the safest course is to kill it at once, especially if it is about to enter the house, which is a particularly bad omen. Farmers in remote parts of Europe claim that the hedgehog robs milk from their COWS, so they seek to exterminate it as they would any other vermin. Another trick attributed to the animal is rolling on APPLES so that the fruit are impaled on the spikes and can be easily carried off by the creature.

According to an ancient British weather superstition the hedgehog emerges from hibernation at CANDLEMAS (2 February) to see if the winter is over: if it returns to its den, at least another six weeks' worth of severe weather is in store. In the USA the same traditions apply to the groundhog or woodchuck. An eighteenth-century American rhyme advises:

Observe which way the hedgehog builds her nest,
To front the north or south, or east or west;

For if 'tis true what common
people say,
The wind will blow quite contrary
way.

Eating hedgehog meat, a delicacy
associated with gipsies, is said to cure fits,
and the creature's jaw is sometimes used
in treating RHEUMATISM. Consuming the
left EYE fried in oil is alleged to cure
insomnia. Finally, pregnant women are
warned against accidentally treading on
such a creature, for if this happens they
are fated to give birth to a hedgehog (*see*
PREGNANCY).

**hellebore** The different kinds of
hellebore were credited with various
magical properties in medieval times and
are still associated with a variety of superstitions. Black hellebore will bring
extreme bad luck to any person who
picks it, but white hellebore is much
prized as a cure for MADNESS and other
maladies and was fed to children before
breakfast to promote intelligence. White
hellebore flowers are alleged to be effective against leprosy, rabies and EPILEPSY
and may also guard against MISCAR-
RIAGE. If the hellebore plant bears four
tufts it is said that the harvest will be a
good one, but if there are just two tufts
the crops will fail.

**hem** A hem that turns up on a garment should be welcomed: it is said to be
a certain indication that the wearer will
shortly acquire a new garment of the
same type. It is commonly believed that if
the hem of a woman's skirt gets turned up
she is about to enjoy a piece of good fortune, possibly receiving money or some
other gift. On no account should she turn
the hem down again, or the surprise will
not arrive.
*See also* CLOTHING.

**hemlock** As one of the most notorious of all poisonous plants, hemlock is
widely associated with the DEVIL and
other evil influences. Witches were formerly alleged to list hemlock as an ingredient in their evil-working spells (*see*

WITCHCRAFT) and hemlock was variously credited with having the power to
summon demons, part lovers, induce
MADNESS and make animals infertile. It
was also said to be one of the ingredients
of witches' FLYING OINTMENT. Children
who so much as touch the plant may, so
they are warned in parts of northern
England, be whisked instantly away by
the Devil's cohorts.

The potency of hemlock does, however, make it invaluable in folk medicine.
In particular, hemlock poultices are supposed to relieve RHEUMATISM, while the
roots can be used in treating various EYE
complaints.

**hempseed** The chief use of hempseed
in superstition lies in the business of divination. According to ancient English tradition, girls wishing to get a glimpse of
their future husband are advised to go to a
churchyard at midnight on a propitious
date (sometimes at HALLOWE'EN) and,
while tossing hempseed over the left
shoulder, intone the following:

Hempseed I sow, hempseed, grow.
He that is to marry me,
Come after me and mow.

If the charm works, the spirit of the girl's
husband-to-be will appear with a
SCYTHE, cutting short the grass. If no one
appears the girl will not get married, at
least in the near future, and if a COFFIN
materialises the unfortunate girl is fated
to die before she can be wed to anyone.

**hen** Despite the obvious economic
value of the hen, superstitions surrounding it are generally negative. A hen that
crows like a COCK or grows feathers
resembling those of the male bird is an
extremely bad omen and the creature
should be killed at once (BLACK hens,
incidentally, are often selected for ritual
sacrifice). A hen that roosts at an odd time
is also liable to alarm its keepers as this is a
DEATH omen. Slightly less threatening
are the notion that if a hen comes into the
house this is a warning that an important
visitor is on the way, and the now archaic

tradition of taking a cackling hen into the home of newly-weds to guarantee their happiness. Sharing with the hens a little fruit from the farmhouse at NEW YEAR is recommended to ensure that they continue to lay well through the year (*see* FRUIT TREE). Perhaps best known is the general belief that, if hens gather together on a mound and start to preen their feathers, RAIN is in store.

*See also* EGG.

**henbane** The poisonous qualities of henbane have caused it to be listed among the much-distrusted plants allegedly favoured by witches in their spells (*see* WITCHCRAFT). Burning henbane is said to summon up evil spirits, and eating any part of the plant may lead to insanity and death. The plant is, however, useful in folk medicine and is credited with killing the pain of TOOTHACHE if smoked, though this practice may have fatal consequences; alternatively, it may be mixed with vinegar and sluiced round the mouth. The plant may also be employed in a variety of love charms (*see* APHRODISIAC) and to soothe the injuries caused by witches' spells.

**heron** The heron is, according to British superstition at least, an ill-omened bird. Its appearance near a house is enough to make many people anxious, but few people will dare to kill one for this risks the direst ill luck.

**herring** The herring once formed a major part of the diet in Christian countries during LENT, when meat was forbidden but FISH was not. Superstitions associated with herrings include the Scottish idea that they are sensitive to violence and will desert a stretch of water if any blood is shed on land nearby. FISHERMEN, meanwhile, are wary of washing herring scales from the boat or from their boots while still at sea, in the belief that this will harm their luck. In times when herrings were scarce one old solution was to 'raise the herring' in a special ceremony: a cooper donned a flannel shirt and a tall hat adorned with the fish and paraded the streets. Fishermen still maintain that the sex of the first herring caught in the season is crucial: if it is female the season will be a good one, but if it is male then catches will be meagre. Sea anemones are sometimes referred to as 'herring shine' in the mistaken belief that they will one day turn into herrings.

Salted herrings may be used in love divination rituals at HALLOWE'EN. If a person consumes a whole salted herring, complete with bones, in three mouthfuls and retires immediately to bed without uttering a word or taking a drink, he or she will be rewarded with visions of a future spouse materialising with a drink to assuage their thirst. The white membrane of a herring, located beneath the backbone, may also be used by girls for purposes of divination: if this is thrown against a wall and sticks to it without adopting a crooked shape, a future husband will prove attractive and trustworthy; but if it fails to stick or sticks crookedly the future spouse will be undesirable and untrue.

The Irish claim that laying a salted herring on the feet will relieve a sore throat, while others maintain that suspending a herring from the ceiling on GOOD FRIDAY will keep the house free of FLIES throughout the summer.

**hiccough** European superstition explains that if a person suffers an attack of hiccoughs this is a sure indication that someone is thinking of them, possibly unkindly. Cures vary from region to region. In Greece the sufferer must identify the person who has them in their thoughts, while Germans recommend placing a dampened paper CROSS on the forehead; the standard British cures are to count to a hundred without taking a breath, or to drop a cold KEY down the sufferer's back. US authorities prefer the ruse of surprising the sufferer out of his hiccoughs by making a sudden loud noise. Other alternatives include grasping the left THUMB firmly in the right hand or reciting one of various CHARMS. Anyone who has hiccoughs in church is, according to common belief, temporarily possessed by the DEVIL.

**holed stones**   Natural holes in stones – and indeed in trees – have always been regarded as having special healing properties. All around the world the idea persists that passing a sick person through such a hole with appropriate ceremony will cure them of ailments ranging from rickets and WHOOPING COUGH to BOILS. Barren women passed through such a hole will find themselves fertile. Once a person has been passed through such a hole and cured they must protect the stone or tree in question, as their fates are now interlinked and any future misfortune that befalls it will be reflected in their own well-being.

Smaller stones and pebbles with holes in them have always been considered lucky and are often carried about the person to ward off witchcraft and other evils. Keeping one of these on the bedstead will prevent NIGHTMARES and guard against RHEUMATISM.

*See also* ADDER STONES.

**holly**   Traditionally hung in most homes as part of the CHRISTMAS decorations, holly is supposed to have special protective powers and is generally considered a lucky plant. It is claimed by some that holly wood was used in the construction of the CROSS on which Christ was crucified, and the red berries of the holly (previously yellow) are thought to be so coloured in remembrance of Christ's blood. The evergreen leaves, meanwhile, represent eternal life.

Hanging holly in the house protects all within from witchcraft and other misfortunes. Some say the holly must be picked before Christmas Eve (but not taken inside until that day) and that the prickly male variety is especially lucky for men while the smooth-leaved female version is lucky for women – though the latter will bring only bad luck if carried by the 'first footer' at NEW YEAR. One English

tradition has it that if the holly is male the man of the house will get his way at home over the coming year, but if it is female his wife will rule the roost during that time. When the festive season is over some people retain one small sprig of holly, and keep it in the house for the rest of the year to protect it from LIGHTNING. Discarded holly boughs must not be burned while the leaves are still green: to do so is extremely unlucky and may bring about a death in the household. It is also unlucky to step on a holly berry and very unlucky to cut down the tree itself.

A very well-known WEATHER superstition is that the holly tree will bear many berries if severe winter weather is in the offing. Leaves from the plant may be used in a variety of charms intended to reward young girls and boys with glimpses of their future mates. A young girl may also divine her future by counting off the number of prickles on a holly leaf while reciting 'Girl, wife, widow, nun' and noting the word on which she reaches the last prickle.

Drinking MILK from a cup made of holly wood is said to cure WHOOPING COUGH in children, and placing a garland of holly round a HORSE's neck will prevent the animal suffering NIGHTMARES. Thrashing the feet with sprigs of holly is alleged to be an effective, if painful, cure for CHILBLAINS.

**holy water**   The WATER blessed and used in religious services inevitably has applications outside the church. The fact that many fonts still boast lids with locks attached is evidence of the enthusiasm with which people once believed that holy water could drive out evil and heal virtually any ailment. Sprinkled in three corners of a bedroom, for instance, holy water will force RATS to vacate the room via the unsprinkled fourth corner. If kept over from an EASTER service holy water has the power to ward off witches and other evil spirits, and if preserved from Palm Sunday it will prevent STORMS. Holy water may also be used to test witches: if a witch is suspected of having turned herself into a CAT, the animal should be placed in the bowl used for the water – if it tries to escape, it is undoubtedly a witch in disguise. Finally, WASHING in holy water will eradicate WARTS.

**honeymoon**  The business of getting married is much complicated by the countless taboos laid down by time-honoured tradition, but the newly-weds are generally left to their own devices when safely on their honeymoon. What taboos there are relate almost exclusively to honey. Revered in ancient times as a symbol of fertility and sexuality, honey is still considered an APHRODISIAC – hence its connection with marriage. In former times newly-weds were expected to drink mead and honey daily for the first thirty days of the marriage while the MOON went through a complete cycle (hence 'honeymoon'). In some parts of Europe the bride is given gifts of pots of honey, and it has always been the custom for bees to be informed of any WEDDING that takes place in the family. In the South African Thonga tribe new bridegrooms are prohibited from eating honey (at least openly) until their wives have given birth to their first child. In Turkey the genitalia of bride and groom were in former times smeared with honey to make them more attractive to each other.

Other miscellaneous superstitions relating to honeymoons include the contention that when retiring to bed on the wedding night it should be the groom who locks the front door – if the wife does it, the couple will argue before morning. Most sobering of all, though, is the notion that whichever of the couple falls asleep first on that initial night will also be first to die.

**hops**  Hanging a bunch of hops over the mantelpiece or over the hearth is, according to old English superstition, a good way to safeguard the household's luck until the next hop-picking season.

**horn**  Animal horns, in ancient times symbols of fertility, have a number of uses in superstition according to some authorities. Although it is considered unlucky to allow a horn into the house, possession of one may help to give protection against the DEVIL (the 'Horned God'), especially – in the USA – if it has come from an OX. The effects of the EVIL EYE, moreover, will be negated if a person keeps the horn of a STAG, at least according to a shared British and Spanish tradition, and 'making horns' with the fingers by pointing the index and little fingers is said to ward off evil forces.

**horse**  The horse has always been credited with various magical powers, some of which may have originated in the horse cults of pre-Christian eras. The economic value of the creature in former times meant that horse-owners were especially nervous of any threat posed by witches against their animals, which had to be defended with HORSEBRASSES and other CHARMS and AMULETS. Horses found to be sweaty in the morning were rumoured to have been 'hag-ridden', that is, used as mounts by witches going to sabbaths during the night. This was regarded as a serious calamity and horse-owners often placed a HOLED STONE or some other magical safeguard in the stable to prevent this happening. Alternatively, the horse's tail might be carefully plaited with RIBBONS to deter witches. Horses are also widely supposed to be able to see GHOSTS, and there are many stories of horses refusing to proceed when they reach a supposedly haunted location.

The magical potency of the horse both as a means of protection and as a symbol of fertility meant that horse bones were often buried in the foundations of new HOUSES, and the creature is frequently a character in the mumming plays and ceremonies that mark certain auspicious dates in the folk calendar, such as MAYDAY.

BLACK horses and horses with WHITE 'stockings' on their legs are considered especially lucky, though, according to one old rhyme from Devon, the number of white legs is crucial:

If you have a horse with four white
legs,
Keep him not a day;
If you have a horse with three white
legs,
Send him far away;
If you have a horse with two white
legs,
Sell him to a friend;
And if you have a horse with one white
leg,
Keep him to his end.

White horses are often thought to be
harbingers of ill fortune, particularly (in
the USA at least) if ridden by a red-
headed girl, and anyone who encounters
one is advised to spit immediately on the
ground (*see* SPITTING). Piebald horses are
generally considered lucky, and if one is
seen a wish may be made while crossing
one's fingers (though it is unlucky to see
the tail of a piebald horse). It is also said
that the riders of piebald horses are excellent people to consult for advice concerning various folk cures: whatever
treatment they suggest will prove infallible, however implausible it seems.

Going to a stable and inhaling horses'
BREATH is recommended as a cure for a
host of minor ailments, including
WHOOPING COUGH. Eating a single HAIR
from a horse's forelock with BREAD AND
BUTTER will cure anyone suffering from
WORMS, while one taken from the tail can
be bound round a GOITRE to make it disappear. A preparation of horses' hooves is
said to alleviate FEVER, horse TEETH may
be used to counter NIGHTMARES and to
treat CHILBLAINS, and powdered horse
spur (a horny substance commonly found
on horses' legs) drunk with warm milk
and beer was once said to combat
CANCER. Least appealing of all is the
remedy for sore throats that advises the
sufferer to drink a concoction comprising
the juice of live CRABS and foam from a
horse's mouth.

Other miscellaneous superstitions
relating to horses include the notions that
if they stand in a group with their backs to
a hedge it is a warning of imminent RAIN,
that if a horse comes out of its stable right
foot first there is nothing to fear, and that
a journey will turn out well if the horse
one is riding snorts a lot. Last but not
least, it is deemed very bad luck to change
a horse's name.

*See also* EEL; GAMBLING; HORSEMAN'S
WORD; HORSESHOE; JOCKEYS.

**horsebrass** Now collected simply as
decorative pieces, horsebrasses were originally made to protect valuable HORSES
from the threat of witchcraft and the EVIL
EYE. The earliest recorded brasses date
back some five thousand years and the
idea is common to many of the world's
cultures. The metal designs, which
include such evocative motifs as ACORNS
and SWASTIKAS, should always be kept
very shiny, the theory being that they
will dazzle any malevolent being which
comes too close.

**horseman's word** According to
British and European superstition, certain privileged people have access to a
highly secret word that allows them
immediate and total control over HORSES
in their charge. This very useful word is
handed down from one generation of
horse-handlers and BLACKSMITHS to the
next and is never divulged to outsiders. In
centuries gone by, societies were formed
in many rural districts by the few experts
to whom the magical word was known.
Many of these characters became local
legends for their seemingly miraculous
ability to calm excitable horses with a
mere whisper.

**horse-racing** The noble sport of
HORSE-racing has its own mythology and
superstitions. Gamblers on horses are
notorious for their faith in good luck
charms and rituals and will bet on lucky
numbers, owner's colours and even at
random, using a pin to select a runner. It is
generally held that betting on a horse
which has had its name changed is
unlucky and, as with performers in the
theatre, that it is courting disaster to wish
a jockey good luck before the race starts.

The riders themselves observe various taboos, relying on lucky MASCOTS and crops (which must never be dropped). They are also sensitive to being addressed as a 'jockey' before the race starts, preferring people to use their real names, and dislike finding their BOOTS resting on the floor rather than on a shelf when the time comes to dress. Even the idea of discussing the topic of superstitions is anathema to professional jockeys.

*See also* GAMBLING.

**horseshoe** Of all lucky charms and AMULETS guaranteed to ward off evil, the horseshoe is perhaps the best known. The origins of the beliefs surrounding it are uncertain, but they may be linked to ancient horse worship or to primitive sex cults. Alternatively, the special properties of the horseshoe may have been derived from its crescent shape, revered by pre-Christian MOON worshippers, or else from the fact that it was made from IRON, one of the most magical of metals.

Finding a horseshoe by chance is very lucky, though it is doubtful that a horseshoe that is bought has any lucky properties. Especially lucky is a horseshoe that has been cast from the near hind leg of a grey mare and has seven NAIL holes, particularly if some of the nails are still in place (*see* NUMBERS). Horseshoes found in this manner can be either spat upon and tossed over the left shoulder while making a wish, or can be taken home to be nailed above a doorway to bring good luck to anyone passing beneath. Opinion is divided over which way round the horseshoe should be fixed, though most people hold that the prongs should point upwards in order to keep the good luck from falling out. Others, however, have been known to allow the prongs to point downwards in order, they explain, to direct the good luck at those passing beneath. Once in place, the horseshoe will not only protect the good luck of the household but will also deter witches.

The horseshoe is now one of the most widely recognised emblems of good luck, being particularly associated with WEDDINGS (modern CONFETTI is often cut into horseshoe shapes); it is also commonly depicted on good luck cards relevant to many other undertakings such as examinations and driving tests. Many athletes, performing artists and others carry their own miniature horseshoes and are distraught if they lose them. Horatio Nelson was just one of many Royal Navy commanders past and present who have had a horseshoe nailed to the mast of their ship (in his case, the *Victory*) to safeguard the luck of the ship's company and keep the vessel safe from STORMS.

Other superstitious beliefs associated with the horseshoe relate to folk medicine. It is said that the water in which newly made red-hot horseshoes are dowsed acquires the power to cure impotence, while in Germany food served on a plate branded by a horseshoe is said to cure WHOOPING COUGH. Nailed in groups of three to the bedstead, horseshoes are also alleged to fend off the threat of FEVER.

**hospital** Most people dislike the thought of being in hospital and the whole subject is hedged in with various superstitious beliefs, of which several are still in common currency. The day on which a person is admitted to hospital is itself of significance: if the patient is allowed a free choice, he or she may well prefer a Wednesday (*see* DAYS OF THE WEEK), which is reputed to be the best day to start a course of medical treatment.

Finding out what happened to the previous occupant of one's bed is a good idea, as any new patient is likely to share the same fate. Once one is settled in a ward, the behaviour of the nurses should be carefully observed. If a nurse twists her APRON strings when putting the garment on this is merely an indication that she will soon be transferred to new duties, but if she knocks over a CHAIR a new patient is to be expected and if she unthinkingly piles bedclothes on to a chair this is an omen that someone in the ward is about to die (this superstition recalls the days when corpses were wrapped in blankets prior to being placed in a COFFIN).

Pills that are RED or pink are likely to do a sick person's health a lot of good, but superstitious patients should on no account consent to swallowing BLACK pills. Visitors arriving on the ward should be carefully scrutinised if they bring gifts of FLOWERS. Bunches of mixed red and white flowers should be immediately removed, because these are the colours of death. Convalescents who feel they are able to take the air for the first time are warned to walk in the direction of the sun, since walking in the opposite direction (WIDDERSHINS) risks retarding one's recovery.

If, in the face of the many risks that superstition reveals, the patient finally recovers enough to leave hospital he or she is advised to make their departure (leaving their flowers behind them) on any other day than a Saturday – a patient who leaves for home on that day will soon be coming back.

*See also* ILLNESS.

**hot cross bun**  Small buns marked with a CROSS, a traditional EASTER food. In fact, the hot cross bun has its origins in the buns that were eaten at various pre-Christian pagan festivals, the cross being added later to make the link with the Crucifixion and to keep evil spirits at bay. If baked on the morning of GOOD FRIDAY these buns are supposed to have special magical properties, and in days gone by some were always kept aside to be hung up in the house to preserve its luck through the year (it is said they will never go mouldy). If someone fell ill, a little of the bun was grated off, mixed with milk or water and administered to the patient in the belief that this would soon cure such ailments as WHOOPING COUGH and dysentery. SAILORS in former times often took a hot cross bun to sea with them as a lucky charm, and farmers have been known to keep them to protect their granaries from RATS.

**house**  Superstition decrees that there are a number of things a new occupant of a house can do to ensure that he or she will prosper. It is essential to make one's peace with any spirits already residing in the house and also to safeguard the home from invasion by evil spirits. To quiet any existing presences the new home-owner is advised to carry a loaf of BREAD and some SALT into every room to demonstrate that no threat is being made. In some areas it is said to be important that a BIBLE is the first thing brought into the new home. To block the entry of evil from outside, DOORS and WINDOWS may be protected by means ranging from placing HORSESHOES and iron NAILS over entrances to scratching chalk patterns on the doorstep.

In ancient times it was thought that the first person to cross the threshold would die, and various sacrifices were required to prevent this happening. Special attention would also be paid to venerating the cornerstones and foundations of the building, as still observed in the construction of many modern civic and commercial edifices. To protect the home against the threat of FIRE it may be wise to bury the blouse of a virgin in a jar. In times gone by, living animals were sometimes buried in the foundations of a new house to appease hostile spirits; many existing buildings stand on foundations that include offerings of coins and other items.

Having settled in, the occupant is encouraged to make sure that any guests always leave by the same door that they came in by or they may unwittingly take some of the household's luck away with them. Another precaution concerns the procedure that must be followed if the occupant manages to get locked out and has to force entry through a window: he or she must open the front door, go back through the window and then enter properly through the front door as originally intended. Housewarming gifts, incidentally, are good for the luck of the new occupant, though any presents should be for the house, rather than the individual; among the luckiest are gifts of salt and COAL. To encourage family pets to settle in quickly, many people smear the paws of cats and dogs with butter in the belief that this will distract them from exploring too far afield.

Other miscellaneous superstitions concerning houses include the notion that any young woman who moves house is likely to become pregnant in the near future and the theory that things for church should never be made in an upstairs room, as the feast of the Passover took place in an upper room.

*See also* BUILDING; CORNER HOUSE; HOUSELEEK; SPRING CLEANING; STAIRS; THATCH.

**houseleek** Small plant that is often found growing on walls and house roofs. According to Welsh tradition, disturbing houseleeks growing on a roof is very unwise as they bring luck to the household and protect the occupants from disease. The English maintain that the plant deters LIGHTNING and that it also protects against FIRE. Any house-owner would therefore do well to plant some house-leeks on his roof as one of the first jobs he undertakes on moving to a new home.

The plant is also useful in folk medicine, the juice of its leaves being used to cool burns and treat ulcers, sores, corns, ringworm and other minor ailments.

**hunchback** Widespread tradition suggests that meeting a hunchback is very lucky and managing to touch the hunch itself (preferably surreptitiously) is luckier still. This superstition, which continues to flourish among gamblers in particular (*see* GAMBLING), has its roots in the ancient belief that hunchbacks are essentially evil but that touching them allows a person to 'borrow' something of their psychic powers (which is why hunchbacks were often included in the retinue of medieval kings and queens).

**hydrangea** Flowering shrub much prized by gardeners but mistrusted by some people as a somewhat unlucky plant. In particular, hydrangeas should not be allowed too near the house as this means that one's daughters will never marry.

# I

**illness** Countless superstitions are intended to alleviate the sufferings of the ill, or to fend off the threat of sickness. These include a whole range of AMULETS and CHARMS reputed to provide protection against specific maladies, or against one illness in particular, be it the plague, rabies or other communicable disease. Many treatments operate on the theory that it is possible, by certain actions, to transfer one's symptoms to another person, to an animal or to some other living thing, often a tree. Others attempt to treat the problem by listing as ingredients body parts of ANIMALS that have in some way a quality that may counter the illness (thus a bird with a fine singing voice may be named in treatments for sore throats or an amphibian with a slimy skin may be recommended in the treatment of WARTS).

Some remedies have been proved by science to have some basis in fact. Chewing on a bit of WILLOW, for instance, may release the acids that have since been used in the synthesis of aspirin, while CARROTS, with their high vitamin content, may indeed aid the eyesight as superstition has long claimed (*see* EYE). Far more remedies appear to have no connection with reality – or at least not with any reality that a contemporary scientist would care to put his name to.

One of the most curious of all types of cure, applicable to a wide range of illnesses, is the idea that one may 'sell' one's malady to another person. Still occasionally tried in relatively modern times, the procedure is to sell the patient to a neighbour or friend for some paltry sum and thus, by the change in 'ownership', to confuse the evil spirit responsible for the problem – and thus to effect a cure. The patient may then be 'bought' back when recovery is complete.

Certain signs may be 'read' as warnings of imminent epidemics. These include VIOLETS blooming out of season, white COMETS appearing in the Heavens and BAY trees suddenly withering.

*See also* ASTHMA; BLACKHEAD; BLINDNESS; BLOOD; BOIL; BREATH; BUNION; BURN; CANCER; CHILBLAINS; CHOLERA; COLD; CONSUMPTION; COUGH; CRAMP; DEAFNESS; DEATH; DOCTOR; DROPSY; DYSPEPSIA; EPILEPSY; FEVER; GALLSTONES; GOITRE; GOUT; HARE-LIP; HEADACHE; HEARTBURN; HICCOUGH; HOSPITAL; INFLUENZA; JAUNDICE; KING'S TOUCH; LAMENESS; MADNESS; MEASLES; MENSTRUATION; MISCARRIAGE; PALPITATIONS; PIMPLE; PREGNANCY; RHEUMATISM; RINGWORM; SCARLET FEVER; SCIATICA; SHIVERING; SMALLPOX; SNEEZING; SPLINTER; SPRAIN; TOOTHACHE; ULCER; WHOOPING COUGH; WOUND.

**image** The use of images of living people in WITCHCRAFT is an ancient tradition, allowing the sorcerer's magic to be directed – for good or ill – at any person of his or her choosing. Superstition dictates that such an image, usually made of clay or wax, does not have to be a particularly good likeness so long as it is finished off with something that has been in close contact with the victim or patient. This may be anything from a strand of HAIR or FINGERNAIL clippings to a HANDKERCHIEF or a shred of CLOTH-ING. The underlying idea is that the image and the real person are mystically linked, and anything done to the image will be duplicated in the living person.

PINS or THORNS stuck into a wax or clay image will cause the victim excruciating pain; if the image is melted, placed in a fast-flowing stream or otherwise destroyed, so too will the real person perish. In the superstitions of Afro-Caribbean voodoo the figure is actually sent to the victim. Alternatively, the witch or sorcerer may use such means to influence a person's financial prosperity, health or love life. The victim's only defence is to locate the image and burn it. The effects need not be badly intentioned, however, and some witches will use such figures to help overcome a person's infertility, assist in reuniting them with a lost lover and so forth.

*See also* PHOTOGRAPH; PICTURE.

**indigestion**  *see* DYSPEPSIA; HEART-BURN.

**influenza**  Modern medicine still has trouble dealing with flu epidemics and in former times the imaginations of the superstitious were taxed to the full in trying to find cures for what was all too often a fatal complaint. Among the many remedies that were suggested were feeding a patient spoonsful of HOLY WATER, applying to the chest poultices of cow DUNG or clay chipped from the threshold of the door, wrapping the patient in warm and still bloody animal skins, placing a hot brick soaked in vinegar and rubbed with GARLIC on the patient's chest, and SPITTING into the FIRE and burning eggshells and CABBAGE hearts in the flames.

Several treatments had to be taken orally and demanded a very strong stomach indeed. These included concoctions of FERNS and CHICORY root mixed with honey and licorice, a few drops of the blood of a male GOAT, egg yolks spiced up with a few live LICE (or, failing that, the URINE of a seven-year-old girl or a little SOOT) and finally a few fat slugs and DOG faeces, which could if desired be made more palatable by combining them with OYSTERS dissolved in milk and wine.

*See also* COLD; SNEEZING.

**initials**  It is usual now for parents to take care that the initials they give their offspring do not spell some unfortunate word, but in US superstition at least this is not necessary: anyone who boasts initials that spell a word of any kind is deemed very lucky and is sure to become rich and famous.

*See also* NAMES.

**ink**  In former times, when virtually every LETTER and transaction was written in ink with often unreliable pens, everyone was familiar with the mythology of the ink blot. Contrary to expectation, an ink blot that appears by accident while writing a letter is actually very lucky. If the letter is to a lover, the blot ensures that the recipient will have warm thoughts about the sender. Another taboo warns against trying to hasten the drying of the ink by holding the letter close to the fire or by using blotting paper. This is considered most unlucky – it is better to let the ink dry in its own time. Tipping the inkwell over is, not surprisingly, deemed an unlucky act which may amount to an omen of death.

**insect**  Man has always been fascinated by the insect world, although he has also often been repelled by it. Superstitions about insects reflect this ambivalent attitude, ranging from the affectionate myths surrounding such creatures as BEES and LADYBIRDS to soul-chilling taboos relating to SPIDERS, LICE and BEETLES. In ancient Egyptian times the scarab beetle was accorded divine status as the representative of the Sun God Ra, the source of all life on Earth. In other eras and cultures insects have been treated as sentient beings who should bear the same responsibilities as humans, hence the extraordinary medieval trials of errant beetles and other hapless creatures.

Many WITCHCRAFT potions and folk remedies include insect ingredients, while some species may be 'consulted' to reveal the truth about love affairs or the financial future and yet others continue to be loathed and feared as portents of death.

*See also* ANT; BUTTERFLY; CRICKET; DADDY LONG LEGS; DRAGONFLY; FLEA; GLOW-WORM; GNAT; MOTH; SPIDER.

**invisibility** The gift of making oneself invisible would doubtless be of use to most people from time to time, and superstition offers just about the only chance of achieving this state. Recommended procedures include carrying a piece of AGATE about one's person, collecting under specified conditions and at considerable risk the seeds of FERN or BRACKEN, and secreting a BAT's right eye about one's person. If all these measures fail to have the desired effect, the only option is to dig up a dead body and swap shirts with it.

**Iona stone** A small greenish stone found on the shores of western Scotland and believed by many to have the power of granting wishes. The story goes that such stones received a blessing from St Columba and may grant one wish each to anyone who wears them; it is also claimed that anyone who wears such a stone will always be safe from DROWNING.

**Irish stone** An old British superstition claims that certain stones brought over from Ireland have special healing properties, and stories about miraculous cures effected by touching such stones have persisted into relatively recent times. Irish stones are supposed to be particularly effective in healing injuries if a person of Irish birth applies them to the affected part. Because there are no SNAKES in Ireland, it is said that Irish stones will kill such creatures and, if kept indoors, will prevent any snakes or TOADS from entering the house.

**iron** Because iron is associated with FIRE and has been one of the principal materials used by man since time immemorial, it is the most supernaturally potent of all metals. The ancient Egyptians believed that iron had the power to repel evil forces, and it is still considered a strong defence against malevolent forces and simple bad luck. A witch, for instance, cannot cross over iron, so laying a pair of SCISSORS or a KNIFE under the doormat will stop one entering the house. Many people touch iron to avoid the threat of the EVIL EYE and various objects made of iron, such as HORSESHOES and NAILS, are considered highly effective as luck-preserving AMULETS.

Among the many specific superstitions involving iron are the notions that biting on a piece of iron the day before EASTER will prevent TOOTHACHE for the rest of the year; that plunging a red-hot iron POKER into a churn will help BUTTER to form; that putting a poker in an outside corner of a room will promote luck; and the idea that a sick person may rest a piece of iron on the afflicted area and then nail the iron to a TREE in order to be cured of the problem (*see* ILLNESS). If someone in the household dies, all the foodstuffs should be pricked with something made of iron to prevent death corrupting them. If a BABY arrives, a piece of iron should be put in the CRADLE to keep evil at bay.

Even rusty iron has its uses: keeping a rusty SWORD beside the bed will ward off CRAMP, while an old SCYTHE over the bed will keep witches out of the bedroom. In contrast, though, some say dulled old iron (which is not shiny enough to scare away evil spirits) should never be brought into the house for fear of bringing misfortune in with it; and iron must never be allowed to come into contact with a plant picked for its medicinal properties, especially MISTLETOE, for this will cause any beneficial qualities to be lost.

Many BLACKSMITHS refuse to work iron on GOOD FRIDAY in remembrance of the nails used on the CROSS.

**ivory** Because ivory is an animal product it has its own significance to the superstitious. It is said that any jewellery or trinket made of ivory is lucky and it is also credited with the power of warding off corruption of various kinds, notably CANCER.

**ivy** The evergreen ivy has been considered a sacred plant since pre-Christian times and – though the Romans linked the plant with the revel-loving god Bacchus – it has fairly gloomy associations for most people and is often used for FUNERAL wreaths. Poisonous and suitably funereal in colour, it is none the less valued as a protection against evil and has many applications in folk medicine. Ivy can cure or prevent DRUNKENNESS and can also be used to treat CORNS, running noses (*see* COLD) and rashes. Drinking out of a cup of ivy wood will cure a child of WHOOPING COUGH.

Growing on the walls of a house, ivy will protect the occupants inside from evil; however if it dies their bad luck will be doubled. Ivy plants should not be allowed inside the house, however, because they invite misfortune and death. Neither should they be given as gifts as this will end the friendship.

Any young man who wants to get a glimpse of a future lover is recommended to take ten ivy leaves and sleep with them under his pillow in order to see his lover in his dreams. Girls, meanwhile, must place the leaves in their bosom and chant the following lines:

Ivy, ivy, I love thee,
In my bosom I'll put thee,
And the first young man that speaks to me
Shall be my love and marry me.

# J

**jackdaw**  Like the CROW and other large BLACK birds, the jackdaw is widely considered a creature of ill omen. If a jackdaw settles on a particular house, death is likely to strike one of the occupants; this is even more certain if it comes down the CHIMNEY (though in some European countries a jackdaw perched on a rooftop is more optimistically a prophecy of a new arrival within the family). As with the MAGPIE, it is deemed unlucky to see a single jackdaw but less ominous to see several together. Jackdaws that fly noisily in an unceasing circle, meanwhile, are a warning of coming RAIN, and if they are slow to return to their roosts in the evening severe weather should be expected.

**jade**  Semi-precious GEMSTONE prized for its magical properties in many different cultures. Jade is thought to be very lucky in the Orient, while in Africa it is said that it will conjure up RAIN; in South America it is used to cure spleen problems, and in New Zealand fertility symbols are made from it.

**japonica**  Flowering shrub related to the quince; according to one Kent tradition, this was the original 'forbidden fruit' of the Garden of Eden. In consequence it is thought highly inadvisable to pick japonica fruit, though elsewhere in the country many people make jam or jelly from them with no apparent ill effects.

**jasper**  *see* AGATE.

**jaundice**  Medical condition in which the blood contains an unusually high proportion of bile pigment, which gives the sufferer's skin a yellowish tint. The colour connected with jaundice has inevitably led to a number of superstitions and a variety of cures have been suggested. Remedies range from eating nine LICE on BREAD AND BUTTER and drinking HEN's droppings in white wine to drinking the URINE of a young boy daily and urinating on a NETTLE at daybreak for nine days in succession. Alternatively, the sufferer can wear a crushed hardboiled EGG in a little bag round the neck or in the armpit, or has the option of eating a hollowed-out CARROT in which his own urine has been allowed to evaporate while hanging in the fireplace.

**jockey**  *see* HORSE-RACING.

**journey**  *see* TRAVEL.

**juniper**  In the folklore of many countries the juniper is considered to have protective powers. The infant Christ was hidden from pursuing soldiers by the foliage of a juniper tree, according to legend; ever since it has been noted for its merciful and magical nature, with FOXES and HARES frequently sheltering in it to escape the hunt. Juniper smoke will ward off evil spirits and disease, and in former times the plant was often used to decorate cowsheds as a safeguard for livestock. The berries will also deter SNAKES.

On a more gloomy note, anyone who cuts down a juniper tree will die within the year or lose a close relation, according to the Welsh, and any person who dreams of a juniper tree may experience a decline in luck and, if ill, will almost certainly die. It is all right, though, to dream of juniper berries as this foretells success and possibly the birth of a male child.

In folk medicine, potions made from juniper are credited with relieving RHEU-MATISM, EPILEPSY and liver complaints among other illnesses, and are also alleged to help rejuvenate the elderly.

# K

**kettle** According to one much neglected superstition, it is most inadvisable for an unmarried girl to position a kettle so that the spout faces the wall. If she allows this to happen, she will never find a husband.

**key** Various superstitions surround locks and keys, no doubt inspired by their symbolic qualities. It is thought to be very bad luck to drop a key, and even worse to break one. Possessing keys that go rusty despite all attempts to prevent this occurrence is, however, a good omen: in the English Midlands it is said to suggest that someone is about to leave the owner an inheritance in their will. The luck-preserving powers of keys are also reflected in an old European tradition that slipping a key under a child's pillow will keep the infant safe from evil while asleep.

Indeed, because keys were traditionally made of IRON, touching a key when danger threatens is considered a sensible precaution against all manner of evil. If a person is uncertain about which way to go on coming to a CROSSROADS, meanwhile, one solution is to toss a bunch of keys over the left shoulder and observe how they fall: the longest key in the bunch will point out the right direction to take. All owners of bunches of keys are warned against jangling them on Wednesdays, as this will make the owner go mad.

*See also* BIBLE AND KEY.

**kingfisher** The kingfisher figured in ancient Greek legend in the legend of the tragic lovers Halcyone and her husband King Ceyx who, after Ceyx was drowned, were reunited as kingfishers. The bird was originally known as the halcyon (meaning 'brooding on the sea') because it was erroneously believed that the bird made floating nests out of fishbones. The gods ensured that the weather would always be calm when the kingfisher was on its water-borne nest, and seafarers often talk of 'halcyon' periods when the sea remains calm for days at a time. Another old superstition alleges that a dead kingfisher suspended from a roof will act as a weathervane, turning to point its beak into the wind.

Kingfishers owe their bright plumage to the fact that a kingfisher – hitherto grey – was the first bird sent out from Noah's ark: the bird flew higher and higher, acquiring the colours of the sky itself and then scorching its breast and tail-feathers in the heat of the SUN. When the bird tried to return to the ark the boat had floated elsewhere, and some say kingfishers seen skimming the surface of lakes and rivers are still in search of it.

In medieval times it was said that kingfishers would never decay, and dead birds were sometimes placed among CLOTHING to keep it fresh and moth-free. Seeing a kingfisher is thought to be lucky, though a variant of this is that it is only lucky (especially in business matters) if the bird approaches from the right of the observer; if the bird flies from the left, misfortune will follow. Wearing kingfisher feathers is reputed to promote by magic the beauty of any woman, and in some European countries people sew kingfisher feathers into their clothing to guarantee good fortune.

**king's touch** For centuries it was widely believed that the touch of a reigning monarch had special healing powers, in particular in the treatment of scrofula – the 'king's evil'. Reminiscent of the healing power attributed to Christ's touch, the king's touch was revered in ancient Rome and subsequently came to be associated with many of the great ruling families of Europe. In England, the first monarch thought to have been credited with such healing powers was Edward the Confessor, before the Norman Conquest, while the last was Queen Anne (who failed to bring Samuel Johnson relief from the condition when she honoured him with her touch in 1712).

The procedure involved the sufferer being touched while the words 'I touch, but God healeth' were pronounced, and then being presented with a small gold or silver medallion that the patient was obliged to wear around the neck for the rest of his or her days. The superstition reached its height during the reign of Charles II, who bestowed the king's touch upon some hundred thousand scrofula victims. Even in the late twentieth century there are records of people bringing new babies to Windsor, one of the seats of the modern royal family, 'for luck'.

**kiss** The act of kissing someone or something has always been thought to signify something more than affection alone. Kissing HANDS and RINGS has long been a feature of civic and religious ceremonies, representing declarations of loyalty and humility as well as love and spiritual unity. A kiss is also thought to convey something magical, and many people will kiss AMULETS and other luck-giving objects to promote their own good fortune. It is thus far from unusual for gamblers to kiss betting slips or pools coupons in the hope that this will increase their chances of winning.

Sundry superstitions surround the kisses exchanged between lovers and friends. Contrary to what some politicians might think, it is unlucky to kiss BABIES, and young children should be discouraged from kissing one another until they are old enough to speak. If not, they will grow up to bestow their favours too liberally and will be considered foolish, or may be struck deaf and dumb. Another ancient tradition has it that young virgin girls will become pregnant if kissed fully on the mouth.

It is unlucky to kiss anyone on the NOSE, as this will lead to a quarrel, and also inadvisable to lean over someone's shoulder to kiss them on the CHEEK – such a kiss will be followed by a KNIFE in the back, according to one old superstition. Kissing a man with a moustache should not be lightly undertaken either, for if a hair becomes detached and is affixed to the other party's lips, the latter will never get married. An unexpected kiss from a man who has a dark complexion, however, is certain to be followed by a proposal of marriage.

*See also* MISTLETOE.

**knapweed** English superstition advises that the humble knapweed or cornflower has its uses when choosing between a number of potential lovers. A girl should pluck the flower from the head of a knapweed plant and secrete what remains in her bosom for a time. After an hour the severed plant will produce another flower if the lover she is thinking of is a good choice.

**knee** According to English superstition, an itching knee means that the person concerned will shortly be kneeling in a strange church, although a variant US explanation holds that it is a sign of the owner being jealous of someone.

**knife** Being made traditionally of IRON and having a wide range of uses, knives are naturally the object of much superstitious speculation. The fact that knives may be employed for evil purposes as well as for mundane domestic chores means that they must always be treated with respect. Gifts of knives, especially as WEDDING presents, are ill advised as these threaten to sever the friendship and may even split the couple asunder. To be absolutely secure, the knives should be given 'on permanent loan'; better still, a token amount of money should be given in exchange, as though the knives had been paid for in the usual way. The same applies to penknives and SCISSORS.

At the TABLE, knives should on no account be allowed to cross each other (see CUTLERY), either when laid out at the start of the meal or when placed on the plate at the end. If this happens, remedies vary from throwing the knives on the floor to knocking the table three times with the handle of the vertically held knife. Neither should knives be spun on the table top or used to toast or to pass BREAD with. Some say it is lucky if a knife comes to rest blade upwards on being laid out, but many more protest that this will cut the feet of the FAIRIES and should be corrected at once. If a knife drops from the table this spells the imminent end of a love affair, or else prophesies some misfortune or the arrival of a stranger, particularly if the point sticks into the floor and the knife remains upright. To avoid risking the consequences, a dropped knife should be spun three times over one's head.

Spinning a knife with a white handle allows curious people to find out whether their future partner will be dark or fair: the person in question will be dark if the knife comes to rest with its blade towards whoever has spun it, but fair if the haft points towards the enquirer. Another superstition advises against pregnant women being allowed to use knives (they should have their food cut up for them), and an old proverb warns cooks of the dangers of stirring the pot with a knife: 'Stir with a knife, stir up strife.' It is also unlucky to sharpen a knife after sunset, and knives and forks should be put away

if a thunderstorm breaks out as they will attract LIGHTNING.

Knives made of iron will ward off witches and prevent the DEVIL getting into the house if they are hidden beneath the windowsill. Similarly, according to Scottish tradition, concealing a knife beneath the pillow will prevent the FAIRIES carrying off a person while asleep. Seafarers have been known to thrust a knife into the mast of their ships in the belief that this will summon up a favourable wind or keep them from harm, but they are also wary of saying 'knife', one of the taboo words that must never be spoken on the high seas.

Finding a knife in the road, or anywhere else for that matter, is deemed most unlucky and on no account should it be picked up.

**knocking** It is not surprising that superstition should have its own explanations for the eerie knocking sounds often heard in old buildings that more rational modern minds might attribute to insects or changes in temperature. An old but still familiar tradition speaks of the three knocks of death that are heard to rap at the DOOR, at the WINDOW or at the head of the sickbed when the occupant is about to expire, and many people still become nervous when they hear the knocking noise emitted by the death watch beetle as it calls to its mate, claiming that this is a warning of the presence of death. A US tradition recorded in Virginia places an ominous significance upon no one answering the door after a caller has rapped on it, and concludes that this is yet another omen of imminent demise.

**knot** Superstition places great emphasis on the magical power of knots, which is acknowledged in many different cultures. Many people, including gamblers (see GAMBLING) and SAILORS, have been known to tie knots in their clothing for luck, though there are other occasions when it is thought most unlucky to allow knots to remain tied. It is said, for instance, that all knots in nightgowns, bedclothes and so forth must be loosened when a woman gives birth (*see* CHILD-BIRTH), and similarly that they must be untied when someone is dying lest they prolong the death struggle. It is also thought unlucky to allow knots in shrouds or in a dead person's SHOELACES to remain tied as these will prevent the deceased from getting to Heaven and may lead to the materialisation of their despairing GHOST.

To get a glimpse of a future lover, all a person has to do is arrange to sleep in a different county and tie nine knots in his or her left GARTER while reciting the following, or a variation of it:

This knot I knit,
This knot I tie,
To see my love as he goes by,
In his apparel and array,
As he walks in every day.

To test whether a love affair will prosper, the lover must tie some lengths of GRASS together and then think of his or her partner for a time: if the grass remains knotted the affair will last, but if the knot comes undone they will soon part. In former times, frustrated rivals were known to attempt to deprive newly-weds of the pleasures of sexual union by tying knots in pieces of string while reciting curses on the marriage bed. To protect himself against such curses, the bridegroom was advised to go up the aisle with one shoelace untied.

Tying knots in HANDKERCHIEFS is an old ruse meant to help a person remember something: in fact, the theory goes that the intricacy of the knots will beguile the DEVIL or any other evil influence bent on distracting the person from what he is trying to remember. Another ancient British custom involves two people tugging at a piece of THREAD with a knot tied in it: whoever gets the knot when the thread breaks will have a wish granted.

In folk medicine, knots may be tied and then allowed to touch WARTS and other sites of disease before being ritually burned, buried or otherwise disposed of in the belief that this will cause the ailment itself to disappear.

*See also* APRON.

# L

**ladder** The taboo against walking under ladders is one of the most widely known and frequently observed of all surviving superstitions, encountered in many Christian and non-Christian countries even today. Many people who reject some of the more archaic superstitions will still cross the road or choose another route if a ladder propped against a wall blocks their path (though they may protest that they are simply nervous of something being dropped on them).

The reasoning behind the superstition, which is probably obscure to the majority of people who none the less observe it, is that a ladder leaned against a wall completes a triangle with the wall and the ground. The triangle is said to be the sign of the Holy Trinity, so anyone who walks straight through it is showing disrespect for God and possibly sympathy with the DEVIL. Alternatively, a ladder offers a means of ascent to Heaven for the recently deceased, in which case great care must be taken not to obstruct or offend any spirits mounting it. The usual punishment for such recklessness is said to be a bout of misfortune, though more specifically in the case of unmarried persons it may entail postponement of marriage hopes for another year. In the Netherlands and formerly in parts of the British Isles retribution went further and the person concerned was fated to be hanged – a conclusion that probably dates from times when, if a proper scaffold was not available, condemned felons were often executed on impromptu gallows comprising a ladder leaned against a tree.

In cases where there is no alternative to walking under a ladder superstition does, however, offer a safeguard, advising that crossing the FINGERS and keeping them crossed until a DOG is sighted will afford the transgressor some protection. Similarly, SPITTING on one's SHOE and allowing the spittle to dry may negate any ill effects. One Scottish superstition suggests that if there is no alternative to walking under a ladder, breaking the taboo may have a beneficial effect: anyone who makes a wish as they pass underneath may well have it granted.

Those who work on ladders are not immune to their dangers. In the USA it is said that anyone who climbs a ladder under which a black CAT has just walked will experience bad luck, while in many European countries it is unlucky to pass anything through the rungs of a ladder – as it also is at sea. If the ladder has an odd number of rungs it may actually bring the climber good luck, but if he or she should slip on a rung this is an omen of a financial setback. Even if the ladder is resting on the ground, bad luck is risked if any person treads between the rungs.

In many non-Christian countries the taboo against walking under ladders is simply one aspect of a wider superstition that applies to walking under a variety of objects. The idea behind this is that it is inadvisable to allow anything to be placed over one's head, as the head is the seat of the spirit and should never be overshadowed. In Japan, for instance, it is thought that anyone who walks under a telegraph wire will be possessed by devils.

**ladybird** The distinctive colouring of the ladybird (otherwise known as the ladybug, or by some as God Almighty's cow) has long made it a favourite among those INSECTS that are of interest to the superstitious. Associated with the Virgin Mary for obscure reasons, it is regarded as a harbinger of good fortune in many regions (the principle being the redder the insect the better the luck; *see* RED). Particularly blessed is any person on whom a ladybird lands, as long as it is not brushed off.

On no account should the creature be harmed: if a ladybird is accidentally killed its body should be buried and the ground over it stamped on three times, according to East Anglian superstition. In southern England, the number of black spots on a ladybird is supposed to reveal the number of happy months that lie ahead, making ladybirds with an abundance of spots particularly welcome. Hebridean folklore, however, has it that the five spots that distinguish ladybirds there are symbolic of the wounds of Christ, while the rural mythology of the West Country used to advise that the number of spots on the ladybirds indicated the number of shillings a bushel of wheat would fetch that season. In the USA a ladybird landing on a dress or some other item of CLOTHING promises that the owner will soon acquire a new garment of the same kind. Elsewhere a ladybird landing on the hand is a sign of good WEATHER to come.

Children throughout the UK are familiar with the rhyme:

Ladybird, ladybird, fly away home,
Your house is on fire and your children
are gone.

Chanting this couplet to a ladybird sitting on one's finger is sure to cause the ladybird (which is said to have the power of understanding human speech) to take to the air, and the flight path that the insect takes is claimed to indicate the direction from which one's future true love will come. A Scottish variation of the rhyme runs like this:

Lady, Lady Landers,
Lady, Lady Landers,
Take up your coats about your head,
And fly away to Flanders.

Alternatively, single girls may get advance news of their own impending nuptials if they follow the same procedure while chanting:

Bishop, Bishop Barnabee,
Tell me when my wedding shall be;
If it be tomorrow day,
Open your wings and fly away.
Fly to the east, fly to the west,
Fly to them that I love best.

People suffering from TOOTHACHE are recommended to collect the yellow liquid exuded by the insect when alarmed: rubbed on the teeth, this will assuredly lessen the pain.

**Lady Day** In the Christian calendar, the Feast of the Annunciation of Our Lady, observed on 25 March. An English superstition of considerable antiquity claims that Christ was crucified on this date, so if GOOD FRIDAY or EASTER Sunday fall on 25 March it is considered an augury of some national disaster, as made clear in an old rhyme:

If Our Lord falls in Our Lady's lap,
England will meet with a great mishap.

Two kings, Edward VII and George VI, died within a few months of such dates coinciding (in 1910 and 1952 respectively). Similar traditions are to be found in the folklore of several other Christian countries.

**Lady's trees** Sprigs of dried seaweed, which are said in some coastal regions to protect the house and its occupants from FIRE and other evils. The seaweed is usually placed over the hearth or upon the mantelpiece.

**lamb** As a Christian symbol of central importance, the lamb is generally associated with good magic, rather than evil. Witches are deemed unable to disguise themselves as lambs because of the latter's holy status (though they can materialise as SHEEP) and one old tradition has it that the outline of a lamb bearing a standard decorated with a blood-red cross (a lamb and flag) may be discerned against the sun from hilltops early on EASTER morning.

Particular attention is paid to the first lamb of spring, as various things may be gleaned from it. Farmers throughout Europe will congratulate themselves if the first lamb is BLACK, while the arrival of TWIN white lambs is doubly welcome as this also promises great good fortune. Bad luck, however, will attend anyone connected with a flock that has more than one black lamb in it, especially if twin black lambs are born. To avert this evil the animals must be slaughtered before they bleat for the first time. Ironically enough, if more lambs are born than usual this may also be a warning of bad times ahead: nature is preparing for the outbreak of WAR or some other calamity.

If the first lamb that a person sees in the spring is looking back at the observer, this is considered lucky as a year of meat dinners lies ahead. Any money in the pocket should be turned over at once to ensure twelve months of financial prosperity. If the lamb is black, some people will make a wish in the belief that it will surely be granted. Should the lamb be facing the opposite way, however, the observer must resign himself to a year of hardship and a diet of vegetables.

*See also* BLADE-BONE; SHEEP.

**lameness**  Various superstitions of ancient origin suggest that it is unlucky to meet a lame person or animal. Most specifically, it is claimed that it is deeply unfortunate for a FUNERAL procession to meet a lame DONKEY, a certain sign that the recently departed soul is bound for Hell.

**lamp**  The symbolic value of a lamp or lantern dispelling the darkness, where evil has its natural home, has not been lost on the superstitious, though most beliefs concerning such objects have fallen into disuse since the invention of electric lighting. It was once considered unlucky to go out at night without a lantern, as evil spirits would then be able to creep up upon their human victims unobserved. For much the same reason, it was once common for lamps to be left burning at the bedsides of the newborn and the dying. Tampering with someone's lantern while they slept was not recommended – extinguishing the light might also extinguish the sleeper's life. Similarly, in Massachusetts, it was said that holding a lamp over a sleeping person would threaten their life.

As in the case of CANDLES, rooms should not be illuminated by three lamps as this is a portent of imminent death – though some authorities claim, conversely, that this is a sign that a marriage will soon take place. One rural English superstition warns farmers never to place a lantern on the table as this will cause their COWS to abort.

**lapwing**  The eerie, high-pitched cry of the lapwing or peewit has inspired various superstitions in the regions where they are commonly seen, and they are generally considered an unlucky bird. The Welsh and Scots claim that their call consists of the words 'Bewitched! Bewitched!'; when the Scottish Covenanters were in hiding from English soldiers, lapwings are said to have betrayed their hiding-places to their pursuers. The Irish curse the bird for leaving them only its droppings while the Scottish get all the eggs, and the English nervously speculate that the birds are the incarnation of restless spirits. The mere sight of the bird is regretted by many people and in some areas it is thought extremely reckless to handle the dead body of a lapwing. The forked tail of the bird is said, in Swedish folklore, to be proof of the story that the very first lapwing was formerly a handmaid to the Virgin Mary until transformation into a bird as punishment for stealing a pair of Our Lady's scissors.

**lark**  Songbird whose musical talents have inspired a number of curious superstitions. Revered for the sweetness of its voice, the lark was formerly said to sing best if blinded with a red-hot needle. Humans could share in the lark's musical gifts by eating three larks' eggs before the church bells rang on Sunday, a procedure that was guaranteed to benefit the voice. Eating the lark itself did not necessarily help improve one's singing, but consuming a dish of crested larks was once recommended as a cure for colic.

Disturbing the well-being of a lark or its nest should not be undertaken lightly, however: inhabitants of the Shetland Islands believe that the three black spots under a lark's tongue are curses that will be directed at anyone who shows it malicious intent. German folklore cautions against pointing at a lark, as a pus-filled inflammation called a whitlow will appear on the outstretched finger.

In some parts of northern England and Scotland it is said that anyone who lies on their back in a field and listens carefully to the lark's song will eventually be able to make out the words, which are said to run as follows:

Up in the lift go we,
Tehee, tehee, tehee, tehee!
There's not a shoemaker on the earth
Can make a shoe to me, to me!
Why so, why so, why so?
Because my heel is as long as my toe.

Welsh superstition adds that larks singing joyfully high in the sky are a certain sign of fine WEATHER to come.

The lark is closely associated with the cause of lovers in many different cultures. One love spell suggests that concealing a lark's eye wrapped in wolfskin in the right pocket will make the wearer overwhelmingly attractive to the opposite sex. Likewise, surreptitiously slipped into someone else's drink a lark's eye will be sure to provoke feelings of love in anyone who drinks it.

In the field of folk medicine, a lark brought into the bedroom of a sick person will avert its gaze if the patient is fated to die, but will stare without flinching if the patient is going to recover.

**last** In some circles it is deemed unlucky to talk of the 'last' one of anything on the grounds that to do so is TEMPTING FATE. Thus FISHERMEN never talk of casting their last net for fear that they will never see the net again, and members of flying clubs talk of the 'last flight but one' when discussing what is actually the last flight of the day. MINERS and workers in similar hazardous industries sometimes arrange to avoid working the last shift before holidays or strikes on the grounds that ACCIDENTS are more likely to happen at that time, while ACTORS AND ACTRESSES customarily leave the last lines of a play unspoken until the first actual performance. Bad luck will also attend the spirit of the last person to be buried in a graveyard (see CHURCHYARD WATCHER).

In contrast, it is widely held to be lucky to take the last bite (or drink) of various foods. An unmarried woman who is invited to take the last piece of BREAD AND BUTTER from the plate will marry a rich man, though if she takes the last piece before it is offered she will never find a husband. In Oxfordshire it is said that the last nine drops poured from the teapot will soothe the pangs of unrequited love. Similarly, the dregs of wine drunk over the NEW YEAR festivities will bring good luck upon the drinker.

**laughter** A good laugh is said to be good for the health, but if excessive is thought to be injurious, especially in children. Thus one old Suffolk rhyme warns:

Laugh till you cry,
Sorrow till you die.

A sudden and uncharacteristic outburst of merriment in someone who is usually of a more morose nature is thought by many to be a bad omen, and may even suggest that the hour of that person's death is near. An old English saying has it that laughter before breakfast promises tears before bedtime; laughing before saying one's prayers in the morning, or after saying them at night, was similarly thought to be unlucky in less godless times.

**laundry**   *see* WASHING.

**laurel**   *see* BAY.

**lead**   Of all metals, lead is the most closely assocated with death. In former times COFFINS were often made of lead. Various ancient spells designed to deliver death curses against an enemy involved hiding a piece of lead bearing the victim's name somewhere in his home, or else burying it in the ground. To determine whether someone suffering from illness was under the influence of WITCHCRAFT, a little molten lead might be held over the patient and then dropped in water: if the lead congealed into a definite image then evil spirits were clearly at work. A little of the lead thus formed might then be given to the patient to wear over his heart in the belief that this would counter any spell. More cheerfully, in different circumstances observing the shapes formed by molten lead immersed in cold water may reveal some symbol, such as an anchor or book, that identifies the occupation of a future lover.

The link with witchcraft is reflected in the tradition that witches cannot be killed with lead bullets but are vulnerable only to bullets made of SILVER; according to the Scots, if a lead bullet is used it may even rebound and kill the person who has fired the shot. Conversely, the density of the metal made it the favoured material from which to make caskets to preserve important religious relics, the idea being that the lead would keep the relics safely sealed from any malevolent interference from the outside spirit world and prevent their dissipation into the air.

**leaf**   If TREES shed their leaves before the autumn this is widely considered a portent of a severe winter or some other disaster, probably in the shape of diseased cattle if ELMS or FRUIT TREES lose their leaves earlier than usual. If someone manages to catch a falling leaf before it reaches the ground, however, this will guarantee them a winter free of COLDS. A British variation of this well-known tradition runs that one happy day (or even a whole month) will follow for every leaf thus caught between Michaelmas (29 September) and HALLOWE'EN (31 October).

Dead leaves should not be brought into the house as they can bring ill luck in with them (though leaves that blow in of their own accord bring good luck). They are particularly unwelcome in churches as, according to one Welsh superstition, their presence threatens the life of any child who has recently been baptised there. Leaves that rustle suddenly or turn their lower sides over while still on the tree, meanwhile, are an omen of approaching RAIN.

Sleeping with a spring of HOLLY bearing nine leaflets under the pillow will, claims one superstition from northern England, conjure up dream visions of one's future partner. Lovers uncertain of their partner's interest are advised to mark a BAY leaf with the other's initials and wear it in their cap or SHOE for a day: if the initials are clearer to read at the end of that time, there is no cause to doubt the other's love.

*See also* ASH.

**leap year**   A leap year, with its extra added day, 29 February, is generally thought to be a propitious time for embarking on important new projects. Choosing 29 February itself as the starting date is particularly astute as the project is sure to prosper, and children conceived or born on that date are thought to enjoy special blessings. The best-known tradition connected with leap years is that this is the one time when girls can decently make marriage proposals. Men are warned that it is bad luck to turn such an offer down, though – according to the Scots – they will be immune from such ill fortune if the girl concerned has neglected to wear a scarlet flannel petticoat, which must be partly visible, under her dress.

*See also* CALENDAR.

**leather**   A superstition of ancient origin claims that those who wear leather will be protected from malevolent spirits. Caution should be taken, however, about bringing anything made from leather into the house at CHRISTMAS as this threatens ill luck, hence the reservations that many people once had if they received a gift of leather SHOES at this time. In the Highlands of Scotland it was once customary for a small piece of cow leather to be burned in a fire and then offered to every member of the household, and to any domestic animals, for them to smell. The belief was that this would preserve them from bad luck, disease and enchantment by FAIRIES or other supernatural spirits in the months ahead.

**Lee Penny**   A coin belonging to the Lockhart family of Lee that is reputed to have miraculous healing powers. A groat dating from the reign of Edward I, the Lee Penny incorporates a dark red pebble that is supposed to have been brought back from the Holy Land in the fourteenth century. Legend has it that, when dipped into drinking water, the coin has proved most effective in the treatment of various livestock diseases as well as against such human ills as rabies and haemorrhages. In 1645 the coin was credited with having curtailed an outbreak of the plague in Newcastle-upon-Tyne.

**leek**   Appropriately enough, as it is a national symbol of Wales, Welsh superstition sets great store by the magical properties of the leek. According to ancient tradition any warrior who smears himself with the juices of a leek (or alternatively with GARLIC) will be invulnerable to his enemies in battle.

**left side**   It is almost universally recognised that the left (Latin, *sinister*) side is associated with evil and ill luck. Soothsayers in the ancient world identified the left as the abode of evil (Christ Himself sat at God's right hand) and ever since then it has been linked with WITCHCRAFT, the DEVIL and malevolent spirits.

Various superstitions warn that it is bad luck if certain birds and animals cross one's path from the left-hand side, and witches and sorcerers often use their left hand more than the right in working their spells. In PALMISTRY it is the left hand that is examined for information about a person, as it is believed to show inherited characteristics, while the right hand reveals only what a person has made of himself or herself. The left hand should not be used in situations where its baleful influence might endanger the owner's luck: players are often careful to avoid picking up their CARDS with the left hand, and since Roman times people have been wary of entering a house with the left foot first. At confirmation in the Christian Church it is said that those blessed with the bishop's right hand will enjoy the full benefit of his favour, while those blessed with the left hand will experience only ill fortune.

Historically, left-handed people have always been regarded with mistrust, and in times gone by left-handedness was powerful evidence that someone might be a witch. It is said to be unlucky to meet a left-handed person on a Tuesday morning but lucky to encounter such a person on any other morning (*see* DAYS OF THE WEEK). Attempts to switch from the left hand to the right hand are not always successful and, according to US folklore, the person concerned runs the risk of developing a stutter.

*See also* RIGHT SIDE.

**lemon**   An English superstition dating from the mid-eighteenth century claims that the peel of a lemon can be employed to divine the outcome of a future love affair. If a woman takes the peel and keeps it hidden in her armpit for a day, then rubs the peel on the four posts of her bed, she will be rewarded – if the affair is to be consummated – by a vision of her lover bringing her two lemons. If he does not appear, the affair is doomed to failure.

**Lent**   The period of forty days before EASTER, which is a time of fasting and penitence throughout the Christian Church. Self-denial is the characteristic theme of most superstitious beliefs surrounding the season of Lent. Among the best-known of the Lent taboos are the traditions that penitents should refrain from wearing new CLOTHING during this period and that, in the words of the old rhyme,

If you marry in Lent,
You will live to repent.

**letter** A largely forgotten though once widely known English superstition of some antiquity holds that it is extremely unlucky to drop a letter on the ground before it has been sent. If this happens, the writer must expect any business mentioned in the letter to end in disappointment. If two letters cross in the post this is also unlucky as the two parties are fated to fall out with each other.

See also CHAIN LETTER; INK; LOVE LETTER; MAIL VAN.

**lettuce** Since Roman times the lettuce has been credited with a wide range of magical properties. Eaten in large quantities at Roman banquets because it was supposed to prevent DRUNKENNESS, and at WEDDING celebrations because it was believed to be an APHRODISIAC, it was subsequently used in various love potions in medieval times. A further superstition had it that young women who ate plenty of lettuce would have little trouble giving birth (see CHILDBIRTH), though an English variation warns that too many lettuces in a garden will prevent a woman having children at all. Wild lettuce is used to treat insomnia and HEADACHES, among other minor ailments.

**lice** A persistent nuisance even in modern civilised Western society, the louse has always inspired the most loathsome associations. Infestations of lice in medieval times were often blamed on WITCHCRAFT and several witches admitted, under pressure, that they had engineered the infestation of hitherto clean people who had incurred their displeasure. It is said that dreams of lice signify the onset of sickness in the family,

and that the sudden disappearance of lice from someone who has been infested (or conversely their sudden appearance on an uninfested person) is a sure sign that the person's death is nigh. If a nurse finds a single louse on her head she may be certain that her patient will die.

On a slightly more positive if distasteful note, consuming a spoonful of live head-lice was formerly warmly recommended in the north of England for the treatment of JAUNDICE; elsewhere they had to be eaten in BREAD AND BUTTER or boiled in MILK.

**life-token** A phial of URINE, a KNIFE, an item of CLOTHING or some other object associated with an absent member of the family that is carefully preserved in the family home so that it may be observed for clues about that person's fortunes. The theory ran that if the urine clouded, the knife tarnished or the clothes rotted this was a sure sign that the erstwhile owner was similarly in decline or even dead. In times when communication over long distances was more problematic than it is now, whole families would unquestioningly go into mourning if the condition of the life-token indicated that the absentee was no more.

**lightning** The age-old fear of thunder and lightning, once credited to the anger of the gods, is reflected in the body of superstitions designed to offer comfort to those seeking reassurance that they will be safe from it. The tradition that lightning never strikes twice in the same place is, unfortunately, demonstrably untrue (the Empire State Building was once recorded as having received sixty-eight lightning strikes in just three years) but remains a universally popular fallacy.

Opinions differ over which trees offer the safest shelter in a storm, with some recommending the OAK and others preferring the BEECH or WALNUT. A Sussex rhyme rejects all these in favour of the HAWTHORN:

Beware of the oak; it draws the stroke.
Avoid the ash; it courts the flash;

Creep under a thorn; it can save you from harm.

Wood taken from a tree that has been struck by lightning should never, US superstition dictates, be burned on a domestic hearth as this will draw lightning towards the house itself. Opening DOORS and WINDOWS in a thunderstorm so that any lightning bolt that does enter the house will be able to escape again is advised in many areas, as is the putting away or covering up of MIRRORS and metal objects like SCISSORS which are said to attract the strike. Keeping ACORNS or plants such as ELDER, HAZEL, Christmas HOLLY and HOUSELEEK in the house is also supposed to deflect lightning.

If further reassurance is required, tying a snakeskin around the head will provide added protection, as will keeping a fire going in the grate, wearing natural silk and sleeping on a feather mattress. Keeping one's distance from the family DOG is also a good idea, as dog's tails are alleged by some to attract lightning.

In times gone by it was considered foolhardy to look directly at a lightning flash as this was reputed to make people mad. Neither is it advisable to draw someone else's attention to lightning, as this will draw the bolt, and the old custom of counting the seconds between the flash and the thunder to determine how many miles away the storm is should also be discouraged, according to some. Any fires started by lightning can be extinguished by pouring cow's MILK over the flames.

Christian mythology claims that it was the Virgin Mary who created lightning as a means of warning against Satan's thunder, allowing men on Earth just enough time to cross themselves for safety's sake. In gratitude to the Virgin, some people click their tongues three times whenever the lightning flashes.

Lastly, it is said that close inspection of any site where lightning has struck may be rewarded by the discovery of 'Devil's pebbles' or 'lightning stones', fragments in the shape of hatchets or arrowheads that have their own magical properties. Placed in an open WOUND they will, according to the folklore of Alsace, bestow great strength upon the injured party, who will be able to strike his enemies dead by simply threatening them with the words: 'May lightning crush you'.

See also STORM; THUNDER.

**lilac**  With its soporific perfume, lilac (especially white lilac) is considered an unlucky plant in certain parts of the British Isles. It is among the least welcome flowers for HOSPITAL patients, though some people say that lilac blossoms with five petals will bring luck to those who find them.

**lily**  The lily is associated with the Virgin Mary and has always represented the qualities of purity and innocence. It is therefore considered unwise in many countries to spoil the blooms in any way; one superstition warns that any man who does this will be punished by the discovery that virgins within his own family have been similarly defiled. The lily (sometimes with stamen and pistils removed) has long been thought a suitable flower for the decoration of churches, and these religious connotations have promoted its reputation as a protection against the forces of evil. Lilies may be employed in spells designed to counter WITCHCRAFT and will deter GHOSTS from entering the house if planted in the garden outside. More mischievously, lilies mixed with the sap of a BAY tree and left to rot in manure will produce WORMS that can be slipped into an enemy's pocket to rob him of sleep. A girl surreptitiously fed powdered yellow lily betrays the loss of her VIRGINITY if she does not immediately feel the urge to urinate.

The use of lilies at FUNERALS, symbolising the restored innocence of the soul at death, has led to a more profound linking with the afterlife. As a consequence many people refuse to allow lilies into the house (although they are often seen at WEDDINGS as a symbol of purity). Dreaming of lilies may be thought ominous but is in fact supposed to signify good fortune. In parts of Europe the notion that lilies symbolise innocence and death is represented in the tradition that lilies will spring from the grave of any felon who has been executed for a crime he did not commit.

In folk medicine, lilies are used for the treatment of BOILS, whitlows on fingers and toes, and various other growths.

**lily of the valley** Garden and woodland flower, which despite its attractive appearance is generally considered unlucky. The first lilies of the valley are said to have sprouted from the blood that spilled from the wounds that St Leonard suffered when vanquishing a dragon, though the alternative name of Our Lady's Tears, used in parts of France and Britain, suggests that they sprang up where the Virgin Mary's tears fell on the ground. Planting a bed of these plants, which the Irish claim are used as ladders by the FAIRIES, is thought to be unwise: a West Country tradition warns that any gardener who does so will be struck dead within the year. More positively, the plant may be administered as medicine to alleviate the pain of GOUT, to ease painful EYES, to restore speech, to assist in the treatment of heart disease and to aid the memory.

**linden** Deciduous tree, also known as the lime, that in ancient times was dedicated to the goddess Venus. The fact that the linden is reputed, in German folklore at least, to guard local communities from evil accounts for its popularity as a name for modern housing developments.

**lion** As the 'king of the animals', the lion is said to be virtually fearless; as a result, most traditions surrounding it reflect its strength and regal bearing (feeding a little lion heart to a child, for instance, will make it grow up healthy and courageous). Only when faced with a gamecock (*see* COCK), which refuses to acknowledge the lion's rank, will the animal betray anything like trepidation. Superstition claims that a lion will never kill a fellow king and the lions formerly kept in captivity at the Tower of London were said to be mysteriously attuned to the well-being of the English sovereign: if one of them died then an ailing monarch's days were surely numbered. Any warrior going into battle dressed in a lion's skin could congratulate himself on the certain knowledge that no harm could befall him.

Lionesses are said to breed every seventh year, an event that is marked by a larger number of stillbirths among other species, including humans. Other superstitions state that lions sleep with their eyes open and that lion cubs are born dead and remain so until their parents breathe life into them.

**lips** A superstition common to both sides of the Atlantic dictates that itching lips are a sure sign that the owner of them will shortly receive a KISS.

**lizard** The lizard has always been regarded in a somewhat dubious light, reflected in the range of both positive and negative superstitions that have accumulated around it. In medieval England many people feared lizards, thinking they were venomous (though another belief had it that lizards would warn sleeping humans of the approach of poisonous SNAKES). Accordingly they became linked with the mythology of witches, as ingredients, FAMILIARS and even as the progeny produced by couplings between witches and the DEVIL. A lasting relic of this mistrust is to be found in two surviving pan-European traditions: it is an ill omen if a lizard crosses the road in front of any traveller, and it is most unlucky for a bride to see a lizard on her way to church, for her marriage will not be happy. In contrast, a woman who allows a lizard to run over her hand will enjoy increased skill with her needle.

Lizards are reputed to go blind during their long winter hibernation but to recover their sight on looking into the rising SUN in the spring. The fact that lizards can regrow their tails has always inspired superstitious awe, and Italian tradition places special store by a lizard that has two tails. The tails themselves are widely considered lucky TALISMANS, and the tails of green lizards are occasionally worn in the right SHOE to promote happiness and prosperity. German folklore dictates that no one should kill a lizard, since it was one of these creatures which licked up Christ's blood when on the cross.

Sleeping in a field with one's mouth open is considered an open invitation for a lizard to crawl inside. However, no lizard will act in this way if it is first licked all over, according to the Irish. A person who can bring himself to do so will be rewarded with a TONGUE that has remarkable powers of healing, particularly of BURNS. Other beliefs around the world variously credit lizard medicines with the power to treat syphilis, impotence, WARTS and skin diseases, among other complaints.

**Lockerbie Penny** A small SILVER disc that was once highly regarded, in the Lockerbie region of what is now Dumfries and Galloway in Scotland, for its apparent efficacy in treating cattle diseases. Dipped in the animals' drinking water, the Lockerbie Penny, of obscure origin, was credited with countless cures by local farmers and was still in regular use up to the middle of the nineteenth century.

**lodestone** A rock that is naturally rich in magnetite and thus has strong magnetic properties. In Cornwall, where lodestones have frequently been found, such rocks carried about the person are credited with the power to cure SCIATICA.

**Logan stone** A large stone that is so balanced that it may actually be rocked to and fro. Superstition inevitably places some importance on these rare natural phenomena, several examples of which are to be found in Cornwall in particular. Such is the latent power of these stones that they are reputed to be favourite meeting-places for covens, and it is said that merely touching one of them nine times at midnight is enough to transform a person into a witch. If children who suffer from rickets are rocked at midnight on the Logan stone at Nancledra, St Ives, in Cornwall it is said they will be cured (though the treatment will not work if they were born out of wedlock).

**longevity** Various procedures, some simple and others more complicated, have been advanced throughout history for the prolongation of life. Perhaps the simplest of all is the time-honoured European notion that anyone who drinks a lot of soup can expect to live into their old age.

*See also* AGE.

**looking back** The tradition that looking back at something can be perilous is very ancient. Well-known examples include the biblical story of Lot's wife, who was turned to SALT after she defied God's order not to look back as she left the sinful city, and the Greek legend of Orpheus, who lost his lover Eurydice for ever after looking back at her on leaving the infernal regions. The BIBLE itself counsels the ploughman from looking back at the furrow he has cut, warning that he will be disbarred from Heaven, and even today the notion survives in the widely honoured tradition that the groom must not look over his shoulder for his bride as she enters the church at the beginning of their WEDDING ceremony.

**looking glass** *see* MIRROR.

**looking under the bed** The irrational fear of something hideous lurking under the BED when one retires for the night may be scorned by many people, but rural superstition readily forgives such weakness and advises that no one should be ashamed of a quick glance under the bed as this may well warn off the DEVIL and his minions.

**love** Countless superstitions, spells and proverbs cater for the multifarious needs of the lovelorn. The bulk of them are designed either to help identify the one 'true love' whom everyone is presumed to seek, or else to persuade a reluctant partner of another's desirability.

In order to glean information about – and perhaps even a vision of – a future partner, various authorities recommend a range of possible courses. These vary from throwing the peel of an APPLE over one's shoulder, to see what initial may be discerned from the shape it assumes on the floor, to chanting various CHARMS on going to bed and sleeping with certain flowers, pieces of WEDDING CAKE or a MIRROR beneath the pillow. Other procedures will reveal the direction from which the lover will come and even his trade or profession.

Measures that may be taken in an attempt to win over a particular person by magic vary from stealing his hatband and wearing it as a GARTER, feeding him or her certain foods or potions noted for their APHRODISIAC properties, and casting a spell over a HAIR surreptitiously taken from the other's head (samples of blood or nail-parings may also be used; see FINGERNAILS) to employing the magic of KNOTS and enlisting the help of certain saints or demons. Alternatively, simply reciting the name of the loved one over and over in the form of ancient charms may have the desired effect.

Once focused on one particular potential lover, his or her fidelity may be checked by such means as plucking the petals off a DAISY while intoning 'He loves me, he loves me not.'

Having secured the partner of one's choice, affianced parties are advised to avoid various actions that might magically endanger the smooth progress of the affair. These include being photographed together at any time before the WEDDING (a piece of recklessness that is bound to bring about an estrangement), kissing when one partner is seated, exchanging gifts of SHOES (which encourages the recipient to 'walk out'), and, in the case of girls, taking the last piece of BREAD AND BUTTER from a plate unless it is specifically offered.

*See also* ENGAGEMENT; HALLOWE'EN; LOVE LETTER; ST VALENTINE'S DAY; SEX.

**love letter** The emotional importance attached to love letters means that the writing and receiving of them is surrounded by a wealth of superstition. The best day for writing love letters is Friday, as this day belongs to Venus, the Goddess of Love. They should always be written in INK, rather than pencil, and they should never be posted on Sundays or on 25 December, 29 February or 1 September. Finding that one's hand trembles while writing a love letter is an encouraging sign that the intended recipient is equally besotted, while accidentally blotting the ink on the paper is actually a good omen, signifying that the other party has the writer in his or her thoughts.

On receiving a love letter attention should be paid to the condition of the envelope. If the flap has come open or the stamp is not of the correct value these are unmistakeable signs that all is not well. To test the other's fidelity the recipient of a love letter may set fire to it: if the letter burns with a bright, tall flame there is no cause for concern, but if it gutters and burns blue the affair is doomed. This procedure does, however, carry some risk as burning love letters invites bad luck; such letters, if they must be destroyed at all, are much better torn up than burned. No one should ever propose by letter, as this bodes extremely ill for the chances of a happy marriage resulting.

**Lucifer** *see* DEVIL.

**luck** The role of luck, that indefinable governing factor in virtually every field of human activity, is recognised and respected in every culture throughout the world. Inevitably, many superstitions are concerned with the preservation and improvement of one's luck; many taboos, from walking under LADDERS to putting up UMBRELLAS indoors, are observed simply because to ignore them threatens a decline in one's luck.

Many people believe themselves naturally lucky or fated to misfortune, or at least admit to believing in lucky or unlucky streaks in which fate seems either for or against them. In either case they may place great store by certain 'lucky' CHARMS, AMULETS and TALISMANS personal to themselves, ranging from the ubiquitous HORSESHOE, RABBIT's foot and four-leafed CLOVER to treasured items of CLOTHING and ritualistic actions (such as always getting out of bed on a particular side or TOUCHING WOOD when ill fortune has been risked). Superstition claims that black CATS and certain other animals can confer excellent luck in given circumstances, while others, such as single MAGPIES, take luck away. There are also 'lucky' or 'unlucky' buildings, ships, roads, plays, alignments of the stars and times in the cycle of the MOON. Other traditions include lucky or unlucky NUMBERS (the best known of which is THIRTEEN), COLOURS, GEMSTONES and dates in the CALENDAR.

Many people who would not otherwise think themselves of a superstitious nature automatically wish someone luck when undertaking a challenge, be it a driving test, a sporting contest or a business deal, but there are circumstances when this is seen as TEMPTING FATE. ACTORS AND ACTRESSES in particular are nervous of anyone wishing them luck just before they go on stage, and FISHERMEN and gamblers (*see* GAMBLING) have also been known to protest against anyone expressing similar sentiments.

Psychologists have often noted the irony that in a hi-tech age, in which rationality is the ruling credo throughout the civilised world, society should commonly place such reliance upon the random and largely uncontrollable actions of fate. The wisest observers, however, see this as entirely healthy, an acknowledgement of unknown possibilities and influences that can only whet the human appetite to know more about the way in which their own minds – and the universe – work. Scientific exploration of the concept of luck seems to suggest a psychological process at work: 'lucky' people are generally more confident when facing challenges, while those who complain of being fated to failure are by nature less sure of their abilities, and thus more likely to be disappointed.

**luck flower**  An unidentified blue flower, sometimes confused with CHICORY, which is held to have various magical powers in German folklore. Any person carrying a luck flower will be able to gain entrance into a secret subterranean world, where he may find great stores of gold and jewels. If he neglects to take the flower out with him, however, he runs the risk of being maimed or killed as the rocks of the exit close on him.

**luck penny**  A single COIN or small sum of cash that is returned to a purchaser by the vendor in the belief that it will give the buyer good luck with his purchase. The custom of handing over 'luck money' was once commonplace, particularly on the sale of livestock and crops – though records exist of the same practice in all manner of other BUSINESS transactions. Butchers in former times often expected to be returned a shilling on buying a COW for slaughter, the ritual being widely known as 'tipping the cow's horn with silver'.

**lucky bird**  *see* NEW YEAR.

**lucky bone**  A small T-shaped bone from the head of a SHEEP that is reputed to bring good luck to anyone who customarily carries it about their person. Of magical significance as far back as the Druids, such lucky bone amulets are said to provide protection against evil spirits and generally to promote the luck of CHILD-REN, FISHERMEN or anyone else who keeps one.

**lucky tip**  *see* CALF.

**lychgate** The fact that the original purpose of the lychgate of a church was to provide a temporary resting-place for a COFFIN before it was carried into the churchyard means that lychgates are generally considered unlucky. It used to be thought particularly ill-omened for a WEDDING procession to pass through a lychgate: it meant the marriage would fail, or that one of the happy couple would be dead within a year. Some churches have two gates, one reserved for funerals and the other for weddings, though most newly-weds now pass through the one lychgate without any qualms and in most cases without suffering any apparent ill effects.

# M

**mackerel** According to an old English superstition this fish should not be eaten 'until Balaam's ass speaks in church'. This is a reference to the lesson telling the story of Balaam's ass, from the biblical Book of Numbers, which is read in churches each year.

**madness** The superstitious have tradditionally regarded mad people with awe, sometimes avoiding them altogether and sometimes welcoming their appearance on the grounds that the simple-minded are in some mysterious way harbingers of good luck. It is said that the mad are chosen by God and enjoy the special favour of Heaven. Accordingly, it is thought particularly lucky throughout Europe to live in the same house as someone who is mad and historically the mad have often been well cared for by their local community.

Meeting such a person in the street is itself a lucky event, particularly in the folklore of FISHERMEN, who interpret such an encounter as confirmation that the day's catch will be a good one. The spit of a simpleton is said to have special healing powers (*see* SPITTING) and such persons are often reputed to be able to see into the future. In many areas there was once a strong taboo against allowing a mad person to move out of their home district, because it meant that someone else in the area would become retarded in their stead. The Japanese warn that anyone who has their HAIR set alight is almost certain to go insane, while inhabitants of Lincolnshire have traditionally avoided naming their children Agnes, as they contend that anyone with that name will go mad.

Cures for madness include an Irish recipe which involves the consumption of honey, MILK and SALT before sunrise, and a more challenging European antidote for rabies, which dictates that anyone bitten by a rabid dog should be fed the burned and powdered liver of the dog concerned in BREAD AND BUTTER.

**magpie** The magpie is widely thought to be unlucky and has evil associations in many cultures. According to the biblical story of Noah it was the one bird that refused to enter the ark, preferring instead to perch on the roof, while another Christian tradition blames the bird for refusing to wear full mourning at Christ's crucifixion. The bird's piebald colouring suggests its perverse nature, which combines the white of the blameless DOVE and the jet-black of the RAVEN, both of which left the ark before the other animals and were thus left unbaptised by the waters of the Flood.

Popular superstition holds that it is most unlucky to see a single magpie, but less alarming to encounter a pair of them. Particular dread is associated with seeing a lone magpie when setting out on a journey (particularly if it is to church), and the sight of one of the birds circling a house and croaking is thought to be a portent of death. A lone magpie flying away from the SUN is especially ominous, though the threat is removed if the observer quickly hurls something after it with the words 'Bad luck to the bird that flies widdershins.' Other protective measures that may be taken on seeing a lone magpie include bowing to it and wishing it good morning, taking off one's HAT to it or immediately making the sign of the CROSS. In Yorkshire the procedure is to cross the thumbs and call out:

I cross the magpie,
The magpie crosses me,
Bad luck to the magpie,
Good luck to me.'

Braver souls may spit three times over the right shoulder (or once in the general direction of the bird; see SPITTING) and intone 'Devil, Devil, I defy thee.'

One West Country precaution is always to carry an ONION in the pocket, as this will counter the bird's baleful influence. In Wales it is said that anyone working in the fields will come to a bad end if a magpie hovers above him, and that in all probability he will be decapitated. Coming across a larger group of magpies busy chattering away to each other is also an ill omen, for the birds are probably plotting some evil or other.

Several interpretations may be placed on the sight of a number of magpies, of which the following is the best known:

One for sorrow, two for mirth,
Three for a wedding, and four for a birth.
Five for silver, six for gold,
Seven for a story never to be told.

A fuller version recorded in Lancashire in the mid-nineteenth century runs:

One for anger, two for mirth,
Three for a wedding, four for a birth,
Five for rich, six for poor,
Seven for a bitch, eight for a whore,
Nine for a burying, ten for a dance,
Eleven for England, twelve for France.

Scottish superstition claims that each magpie holds a drop of the DEVIL's blood under its tongue and offers its own regional version of the same rhyme:

One means anger, two brings mirth.
Three a wedding, four a birth.
Five is Heaven, six is Hell.
But seven's the very Devil's ain sell.

On a more positive note, a single magpie perching on a rooftop is said to be an encouraging sign that the building will never fall down, while a magpie chattering noisily in a tree close to a house is giving notice of the arrival of a stranger. To understand what the bird may be saying, one course of action is to scratch the bird's TONGUE and pour into the scratch a drop of human blood, which will enable the bird to speak.

Finally, in contrast to the mixed reputation the bird enjoys in Europe, the Chinese actually consider the magpie a harbinger of good luck and warn that dire misfortune will befall anyone who kills it (a belief that is shared throughout Europe). Whoever is reckless enough to destroy a magpie is earnestly advised to resist the temptation to eat the bird's brain, which can cause madness.

**maiden's garland** A garland of white paper or linen, often embellished with streamers and a single white GLOVE, which was formerly carried at the FUNERALS of unmarried women of blameless reputation. Such garlands were hung on display in the church for many months or even years after the funeral, and superstition had it that they should be allowed to fall gradually to pieces and then be buried in the graveyard; to remove them any earlier was held to be very unlucky.

**mail van** A superstition clearly of twentieth-century origin has it that the humble mail van is itself a magical object, a notion no doubt inspired by the emotional significance that may be attached to the personal messages and business correspondence that the vehicle conveys. The mere sight of a mail van is said to be lucky, though a Welsh variant states that it is unlucky to see the back of the vehicle. Touching the crown on the side of a British mail van is said to ensure that a person's wish will come true, providing that person then observes the ritual of TOUCHING WOOD; whoever touches the crown second will get a kiss, while the third will suffer a disappointment.

*See also* CHAIN LETTER; LETTER; LOVE LETTER.

**make-up** Superstition warns that care should be taken not to spill face powder: to do so means that the person concerned will shortly quarrel with a friend. In the theatre (*see* ACTORS AND ACTRESSES), it is said to be unlucky to put on one's stage make-up while looking over someone's shoulder into their MIRROR, and also that it is unlucky to tidy a make-up box or to use new make-up on an opening night. If an actress spills her face powder she may dance on it in order to preserve her fortune.

**male fern** A variety of FERN, reputed to have various magical properties. Also called Lucky Hands in the English Midlands, the male fern can be used as an ingredient in a range of spells, charms and cures. Most effective of all these is the procedure by which a root of male fern is dug up on MIDSUMMER'S EVE, stripped down to five unfurled fronds (which look rather like fingers) and then smoked until hard over a bonfire. This 'lucky hand' is said to offer complete protection against any threat of evil or WITCHCRAFT.

**mandrake** The distinctive root of the mandrake, which to many eyes resembles a human figure, was one of the most valued ingredients of medieval medicine and has been credited by the superstitious with all manner of magical properties. The somewhat grotesque root of this member of the potato family was used in many witches' brews and was alleged to have various soporific, APHRODISIAC and purgative powers (the root does, in fact, contain an alkaloid that can suppress pain and promote sleep).

The Egyptians called the mandrake the Phallus of the Field, while the Arabs identified the plant as the Devil's Testicles – both clear evidence that it has long been recognised as a potent influence on sexual drive and appetite; the English later nicknamed the plant the 'love apple'. In the BIBLE, Jacob's two wives – one barren and the other too old to conceive – both become pregnant after acquiring some mandrakes. The mandrake may also be used in spells and potions to increase one's wealth by magic, to fix broken bones, to ease the pain of TOOTHACHE or RHEUMATISM, as an anaesthetic before operations, to cure depression, to enable the dying to recover, to prevent fits and even to give up smoking. Overdoses of mandrake will, however, drive the patient insane.

In witchcraft, a mandrake root dug up, watered with human blood and embellished with berries for eyes and mouth is said to acquire the power of speech and will reveal the future, open locks and locate gold. Mere ownership of a mandrake root was, in consequence, enough evidence to have a suspect condemned to death as a witch in former times.

Care must be taken in pulling up the root of the mandrake: anyone who attempts to do so with their own hands will shortly be struck down dead, or never be able to have children. The conventional method for gathering the roots, therefore, is to get a dog to dig them up. As the root leaves the soil it is said to utter a terrible shriek, which is itself enough to kill or drive any living thing mad. Adding to the rather sinister image of the plant is the ancient European belief that the mandrake only grows naturally under a GALLOWS, springing from the semen falling from the decomposing bodies of executed felons.

**maple** A superstition common to both sides of the Atlantic dictates that the maple tree, though not noted for hardiness or longevity itself, will bestow the blessings of long life upon any child passed through its branches.

**marigold** The golden flower of the marigold, allegedly so named because the Virgin Mary wore one on her breast, has been credited with various properties over the years. Some say that the flower can be used as an APHRODISIAC (hence the alternative names husbandman's dial and summer's bride) and it is sometimes included in WEDDING bouquets because it represents fidelity and endurance in love. Others claim that the yellow petals will ward off witchcraft, while dreaming of marigolds signifies approaching riches.

Should the marigolds fail to open before seven o'clock in the morning this is a sure sign that RAIN is on the way, according to the Welsh. A note of caution about the plant is sounded by one West Country superstition, which claims that anyone who picks marigolds – or even looks at them – runs the risk of developing a weakness for strong drink, and the plants themselves are sometimes known by the alternative name 'drunkards'. Elsewhere in Europe, though, the marigold is variously associated not with love and drink but with unrequited love, sorrow, pain and anger.

The flower is alleged to be effective in easing the pain of wasp and bee stings when rubbed on the skin, and powdered marigold was formerly used to ease the ague. Inhaling the scent of the marigold or taking a little distilled water of the flowers is reputed to cure HEADACHES and depression.

**marriage**   *see* BRIDESMAID; ENGAGEMENT; HONEYMOON; WEDDING; WEDDING CAKE; WEDDING DRESS; WEDDING RING.

**martin**   The martin is traditionally a lucky bird that will bring good fortune to any household where it makes its nest. Said to be, in company with the SWALLOW, God's 'bow and arrow', the martin should never be harmed and its young and eggs should be respected; if they are not, dire misfortune will follow. According to West Country superstition the martin is actually wife to the swallow, while an ancient Sussex rhyme runs:

The martin and the swallow
Are God Almighty's shirt and collar.

**mascot**   An emblematic design or object that is taken to represent the luck of a particular ship, team, regiment and so forth. Motorists often prize the mascots that adorn their bonnets, ships' crews show the profoundest respect for FIGUREHEADS and ships' cats, and military regiments throughout the world proudly parade mascots such as goats and dogs on ceremonial occasions. In the last case, their totemic role links them with the standards that for centuries were carried by armies into battle – objects that had a very clear purpose as rallying points and could allegedly provide added magical protection in times of crisis. In all cases mascots are considered repositories of luck, which may be kissed or touched for psychological reassurance. The loss of a mascot may be considered very serious and thereby actually trigger a decline in the fortunes of those who value it.

**May blossom**   *see* HAWTHORN.

**Mayday**   The first day of May, formerly the Roman Feast of Floralia and later the Celtic Beltane FIRE festival, is widely considered one of the most magical days of the year and is associated with a host of superstitious beliefs, many of which concern the business of prediction and divination – especially the obtaining of information about future partners.

In years gone by, the date was marked by large processions of people making their way in the early hours to nearby woods, drinking and blowing horns as they went. These huge street parties still take place in some villages and towns throughout Europe and include dancing round maypoles, music and other forms of riotous entertainment with their roots in ancient fertility rites. Decorations of green foliage and garlands of flowers are carried in honour of the continual rebirth of nature, again a symbol of fertility. Symbolic battles were once staged to represent the struggle between winter and summer; summer always won and took the place of glory (now occupied by the May Queen, a girl chosen for her wholesome beauty). The aim of all these elaborate festivities was to ensure the good luck of the coming season's harvest and to protect the welfare of both livestock and their human owners.

The Mayday festival, with its origins in paganism, was temporarily abandoned in England in the mid-seventeenth century after the Puritans banned it and burned all the maypoles. However, the popularity of the event ensured its revival a few years later.

Unmarried boys and girls may gaze into wells at noon on Mayday and discern in them the face of their future partners; if they see nothing at all they are fated to remain single, and if they see only themselves in a COFFIN they are doomed to die within the next twelve months). To conjure up an apparition of a future lover, a girl has only to toss a ball of yarn into an old cellar or barn and then rewind it while intoning:

I wind, I wind, my true love to find,
The colour of his hair, the clothes he'll wear,
The day he is married to me.

Before the yarn has been quite wound up the lover in question will materialise to assist her.

Singeing cattle with a lighted straw will grant them protection against evil over the coming year, and for the same reason cows should also be bled on this day. Boiling cuttings taken from herbs on the first day of May together with a few HAIRS from a cow's tail ensures that the BUTTER will be safe from interference by witches throughout the coming year. If it rains on Mayday a farmer must expect to lose half the milk yield of his herd.

An old Irish tradition, meanwhile, advises against selling or giving away fire, SALT or WATER on Mayday as this will bring ill luck on the house.

*See also* DEW; WALPURGIS NIGHT.

**meadowsweet**   The heavy scent of meadowsweet, reputed to have the power of inducing sleep from which a person cannot be roused, means that the plant is regarded with some mistrust by the superstitious. Many people are there-fore reluctant to let flowering meadowsweet into the home, though records from past centuries suggest that there was a time when the plant was welcomed as a decoration at summer feasts and that its perfume was believed to be conducive to a cheerful atmosphere. In ancient times, meadowsweet was, with water-mint and VERVAIN, one of the three most highly valued herbs of the Druids.

**measles**   Highly contagious viral disease, which is usually contracted in childhood but may also strike adults. A widely known folk cure of considerable antiquity suggests that it may be cured by the simple expedient of plucking a few strands of HAIR from the neck of the afflicted person, putting them between two slices of BREAD AND BUTTER, and feeding them to the first strange DOG that comes along. In this way the disease will be transferred to the dog and the person will enjoy a speedy recovery. Alternatively, authorities in Cornwall recommend cutting off the left ear of a CAT and allowing three drops of the blood to fall into a wineglass filled with water, which must then be drunk.

**measuring**   The simple, but deeply symbolic, act of measuring something or someone is not without its significance to the superstitious. Just as it is unlucky to weigh BABIES, which is deemed to be questioning God's bounty, so it is unwise to measure a child for CLOTHING before it has reached the age of six, as this runs the risk of it being fated to want clothing throughout its life. A tradition from the north of England, meanwhile, advises against using the same piece of string to measure two people's arms, as this also risks bad luck.

On a more optimistic note, measuring the head with a length of red wool was once considered an effective cure for HEADACHES and RHEUMATISM, a procedure known in Wales as 'measuring the yarn'.

**meat**   Cooks are advised to make a careful note of what happens to a joint of meat as they cook it. If the piece of meat shrinks in cooking then the family must expect to endure hardship and bad luck, but if it swells prosperous times are in store.

**medicine** Superstition provides a wealth of magical cures, potions and remedies, but if a patient must have recourse to conventional medicine the empty bottle must never be sold; if it is, the vendor will very soon have need of another prescription. Of the countless concoctions suggested as effective by folk tradition, the most notable include a relatively simple recipe including branches of RUE, nine JUNIPER berries, a WALNUT, a dried fig and some SALT: properly prepared while the sun is at the zenith and taken on a regular basis, this medicine is reputed to cure virtually any ill.
*See also* DOCTOR; HOSPITAL; ILLNESS.

**menstruation** Women who are menstruating have always been regarded with some misgiving by the superstitious. In various primitive societies women were considered natural, if unwitting, harbingers of evil and were deemed to be doubly dangerous when having their period; they were consequently disbarred from many important ritual events or completely isolated from normal human contact at this time. Other precautions over the centuries have included elaborate measures taken to prevent the feet of a menstruating woman from resting on the earth, which would pollute it, and careful avoidance of eye contact, as the briefest glance of such a female was reputed to be lethal. Back in Roman times, menstruating women were said to cause fruit to fall from trees, to make seeds infertile, to kill swarms of bees and to cause plants to wither and die; their mere look blunted SWORDS and dulled MIRRORS. Menstrual blood in particular has always been viewed as a dangerous substance, which in some cases has been interpreted as a sacrifice to the MOON.
Various taboos limit the involvement of a menstruating woman in everyday domestic affairs in rural European areas even today. It is said that she should never attempt to make mayonnaise or jam, as the eggs will curdle and the jam will not set. Neither should she be allowed to participate in baking BREAD, as this will prevent the dough from rising, nor be permitted to handle meat, milk or cows or to approach hams hanging to mature. In parts of Africa menstruating women are prohibited from any role whatever in the preparation of meals for fear that the food will in some way be contaminated and those who eat it will fall ill. The presence of a menstruating woman will also prejudice the luck of hunting parties.

**merrythought** *see* WISHBONE.

**meteorite** A rock that falls to Earth from space, often appearing briefly in the night sky in the form of a shooting star. Most meteorites are burned up on entering the Earth's atmosphere, but some actually reach the ground and these remnants have, inevitably, inspired superstitious awe over the centuries (the black stone worshipped by Moslems at the shrine of the Ka'aba is thought to be a meteorite).
In primitive times it was widely believed that meteorites were some form of message from the gods and were variously interpreted as signs of coming war, famine or other calamities. In more recent eras, however, they have come to be celebrated almost everywhere as omens of good fortune. Many people claim that wishes may be made on sighting shooting stars; in Wales at least, it is actually risking ill fortune for a whole year if one fails to do so. Some add that the wish must have been completely made before the star has vanished. In the USA, superstition advises that the observer should repeat the single word 'Money' over and over again until the meteorite has disappeared in order to enjoy an improvement in his or her financial prospects.
One rather quaint interpretation of shooting stars, recorded in Yorkshire,

holds that shooting stars are souls falling to Earth in order to bring life to newborn children.

*See also* COMET.

**Midsummer's Eve** The last night before the summer solstice, 21 June. Identified in the Christian calendar as St John's Eve, Midsummer's Eve is one of the most magical times in the year, marking the moment when the SUN's power gradually starts to diminish. In order to bolster the strength of the sun, in pagan times huge bonfires were lit on Midsummer's Eve in the hope that this would keep evil spirits at bay just a little longer. Leaping through the flames was said to promote by magic the welfare of the CROPS and to purify the souls of those participating in the ceremony. Burning torches were sometimes carried through the fields to ward off evil, or else burning straw cartwheels were rolled downhill in imitation of the sun on its course through the Heavens. Herds of cattle might be driven through the smoke of these fires to purge them of any diseases they might be carrying. Modern-day Druids still attend ritual ceremonies at Stonehenge to mark this auspicious date in the year.

Because Midsummer marks the decline in the sun's power, it is a time when the forces of darkness are believed to be especially active (*see* WITCHCRAFT). Witches favour Midsummer's Eve as a date for the holding of covens and are said to break open hens' EGGS to divine what the future holds in store. It is also on this evening that anyone who sits patiently in a church porch may eventually be rewarded by seeing the apparitions of all those souls who are fated to die in the parish over the next twelve months. Nervous people are advised to keep their distance from WALNUT trees on this date, as these are said to be meeting-places for demons and other spirits bent on a night of revelry and mischief-making. Inhabitants of Cornwall claim that this is also a time when SNAKES gather in huge writhing masses. Children born on Mid-

summer's Eve, furthermore, will have the power of the EVIL EYE.

Midsummer's Eve is the traditional time for the gathering of ST JOHN's WORT, which is much valued for its efficacy in treating nervous disorders and is also put up over doorways (as is fennel) to prevent the passage of malevolent spirits. Any woman who is unable to conceive is advised to pick a sprig of St John's wort from her garden on Midsummer's Eve in order to become fertile, though this will only work if she is entirely naked at the time. A rosebud (*see* ROSE) picked on Midsummer Day and carefully wrapped in white paper will stay fresh until CHRISTMAS DAY if a girl's lover is true to her; if the rose withers she should find herself a new partner. One option is to wear the rose to church – the man who takes it from her is destined to be the girl's husband.

In order to conjure up a vision of the man a girl is to marry one procedure is to prepare a meal of bread, cheese and wine on Midsummer's Eve and to leave the door open: the man concerned will enter, bow and raise a glass to his future wife. To dream of a future lover, girls should gather YARROW from the grave of a young man and place it under their pillow on this night.

If it rains on Midsummer's Eve there will be a poor harvest of NUTS later in the year.

*See also* FERN; HAZEL; NEED-FIRE.

**milk** Perhaps the most familiar European tradition concerning milk is that spilling it will bring seven days' ill fortune. The reasoning behind this is that the FAIRIES and other mischievous sprites will be attracted to any household where they can find milk on the floor. An elaboration of this superstition, dating from the days when milk was boiled over open fires, advises that it is most unlucky for milk to boil over so that some of it falls on to the coals. The COW that gave the milk will consequently produce a much smaller yield and may even sicken and die unless some SALT is immediately scattered over the flames. Similar results will ensue if anyone inadvertently puts their foot in a bucket of milk.

Milk should never be given away or sold on MAYDAY, but a little of it may be poured over the doorstep to preserve the luck of the house. When a cow gives milk for the first time a little of it may be kept aside in a bronze basin to ensure the animal's continued productiveness; three drops from each udder may be passed through a RING when a cow is milked for the first time after calving in order to ward off infection and to cleanse the milk itself. If the cow should later be sold, a few HAIRS may be taken from its tail in the belief that this will guarantee it proves a good milker under its new owner. Indian superstition, meanwhile, claims that it is lucky to see some milk immediately on waking.

The dangers posed by witches (*see* WITCHCRAFT), who may try to gain power over a cow by casting spells over its milk, may be averted by adding a small amount of SALT to any milk sold, while rubbing a cow's udders with 'passion grass' will prevent the animal being milked by any witch disguised as a snake or other creature. More difficult to guard against is the witch's trick of placing a pail in the fireplace and 'milking' the pot hook, thus magically stealing a neighbour's milk.

To cure WHOOPING COUGH, the sufferer should drink milk from a dish from which a FOX has lapped, or else be offered some mare's milk to drink. Other minor medical ailments may prove susceptible to applications of milk from human mothers, as this is also said to have special healing powers.

*See also* BEASTINS; BUTTER; GLOW-WORM; LIGHTNING.

**Milky Way** *see* STARS.

**miller** A curious superstition recorded throughout the British Isles holds that a miller has the power to cure WHOOPING COUGH. The procedure is to hold the afflicted child over the hopper when the mill is working and intone: 'In the name of the Father, Son, and Holy Ghost, grind away this disease.'

**mince pie** According to the mythology of the CHRISTMAS season, every mince pie that a person eats during the twelve days of the festive period will ensure for them one happy month in the year ahead. One variation claims that each of the twelve mince pies must be eaten in a different house, while others have it that one mince pie (and only one) must be eaten on each one of the twelve days and that the pies must be eaten in silence. There is also a suggestion that it is actually unlucky to consume a mince pie at any time outside the twelve days of Christmas.

Some people add that a wish may be made when the first mince pie is eaten and, further, that it is bad luck to refuse a mince pie when it is offered, as this constitutes a denial of the good things in life. If one of the currants sticks to the lid of the mince pie when it is opened this constitutes a prophecy that the person concerned is destined to have a lover (more than one lover if more than one currant sticks). Mince pies are lucky foods, but they must never be cut, which entails cutting one's own luck too.

One theory about mince pies is that they acquired their reputation as a luck-giving food because they were originally oblong in shape and thus reminiscent of the manger in which the infant Christ was laid. None the less, the superstitions surrounding the humble mince pie infuriated the Puritans and at one time it was thought disgraceful for a clergyman to be seen eating one.

**miner** In common with other people engaged in dangerous occupations miners are renowned for their stock of time-honoured superstitions, many of which are still observed. Like FISHERMEN, who are traditionally highly sensitive to ominous signs as they make their way to the harbour, many miners will show extreme reluctance to go underground in certain circumstances. These include catching sight of a DOVE or a ROBIN flying around a pithead (a prophecy of imminent disaster below), encountering a woman, a RABBIT or a cross-eyed man (*see* EVIL EYE) on the way to the pit, having to turn back home for something once one has started out and dreaming the previous night about broken SHOES. The sight of flowering BEANS may also be unwelcome, as accidents are said to be more frequent when these plants are in bloom. In the USA, meanwhile, the sight of RATS deserting a mine is said to presage some catastrophe.

Once underground, miners can be very nervous of marking anything with a CROSS, which may provoke interference by pagan spirits, and will also object to the presence of a CAT – which must be killed immediately – or the sound of a person WHISTLING. Should any of these taboos be broken, a miner may touch IRON in the hope that this will avert disaster. On re-emerging from the pit, some miners will avoid WASHING their backs, as this is supposed to lead to a weak spine and may also cause the roof of a mine to collapse.

Miners working underground throughout Europe have always been wary of meeting DWARFS, the magical masters of all subterranean excavations. Rock falls and other setbacks are often atttributed to the dwarfs, who are presumed to have been angered in some way. However it is said that kindly disposed dwarfs, in return for offerings of food, warn human miners of danger by making tapping sounds and may also help in their digging. Numerous reports have been made of the sound of the dwarfs' picks at work, and some miners have even recorded eye-witness accounts of these diminutive fellow workers.

*See also* COAL.

**mirror** The tradition that a person will suffer seven years' bad luck if he or she breaks a mirror ranks among the most widespread and persistent of all superstitions. Mirrors have always been regarded as magical objects. Before they were conceived of, many myths surrounded the reflections that men and women saw in pools and lakes. The theory developed that what a person saw was not a mere reflection but a visual representation of the soul, which was thus temporarily divorced from the body. Such reflections could be asked questions about the future, and if they trembled or broke up the prognosis was generally considered bad. In some remote parts of the world it is still maintained that if any 'harm' befalls a reflection its owner too will come to grief.

With the invention of mirrors came the new practice of catoptromancy or 'scrying', the art of looking into mirrors and divining information about certain matters. 'Scryers' were much sought after in Elizabethan and Jacobean times, and a relic of the practice survives in the crystal ball gazers of fairgrounds and holiday resorts. Dr John Dee, whose interests spanned science, mathematics, astrology and magic, was perhaps the most famous of these diviners and it was claimed that he uncovered the existence of the Gunpowder Plot of 1605 by scrying. One of the most common applications of such mirror divination was the seeking out of witches. Those fearful of WITCHCRAFT also purchased small 'witch-balls' of reflective glass, which were reputed to ward off sorcerers, and mirrors were credited with the power to deflect the influence of the EVIL EYE, a notion that led to a fad for wearing hats decorated with small mirrors. Witches themselves are said to favour mirrors framed on just three sides, as these enable them to see over immense distances.

Belief in the mystical power of mirrors has survived into modern times, not just in the taboo against their breakage. Some mothers harbour a prejudice against allowing their BABIES to see their own reflection before they are a year old, for fear that the shock will retard their growth or that they will be doomed to suffer EPILEPSY, develop cross EYES or a stutter or even be fated to an early death. Brides are commonly warned not to look at their reflection when trying on their complete WEDDING outfit (particularly if they are wearing a veil) as this will endanger the happy outcome of the marriage plans, though conversely it is lucky for newly-weds to examine their reflection in a mirror side by side once they are safely united.

Many people (notably ACTORS AND ACTRESSES) admit to being wary of looking into a mirror over someone else's shoulder; this threatens the luck of the person 'overlooked' or signifies a quarrel between the two parties. In the theatre, performers are similarly reluctant to see a real mirror anywhere on stage. No one, incidentally, should look into a mirror by candlelight, which is thought to be unlucky; neither should they look into one for too long, for the DEVIL's face will surely appear in the glass in response to such vanity. It is also unlucky for a CAT to be allowed to see its reflection in a mirror.

If someone in a household is ill mirrors may be covered up to prevent the invalid seeing his or her reflection, the theory being that in a weakened state the patient may be unable to re-establish contact with the soul after it has been temporarily separated from the body and trapped in the glass. If the patient dies, it is doubly important that the mirrors be covered or turned to the wall – failure to do so not only risks the well-being of the deceased's spirit but also threatens the welfare of anyone who then looks into the glass, as their own soul may be snatched by that of the dead patient to provide company on the journey to the hereafter. Some people will also turn the mirrors to the wall or cover them with a sheet during thunderstorms, for fear that they attract LIGHTNING. The chilling tradition that a VAMPIRE, having no soul, has no reflection is well known from twentieth-century cinema; if a normal person looks into a mirror and finds no reflection this is a sign that the soul has already departed and is thus an omen that he or she is about to die.

More cheerful is the tradition that a girl wishing to know how many years will pass before she is married may consult her mirror. She must go outside on the night of a full MOON and stand on a stone that she has not stood on before while holding a mirror, with the moon behind her: besides the moon's reflection she may see smaller moons, and the number of these corresponds to the number of years she must wait.

Bearing in mind the magical nature of mirrors, it is not so surprising that their breakage should be attended by such dire consequences. These apply even if a mirror breaks by itself, in which case the death of a close friend or a loved one must be expected. Should the unthinkable happen, however, all is not lost, according to one relatively little-known English superstition: if the pieces of the broken mirror are buried in sacred ground or thrown into a swift-flowing stream or river one's luck will remain intact. In the USA, where superstition is less sensitive about the breaking of mirrors generally, misfortune may be averted by taking a five-dollar bill out of one's pocket and at the same time making the sign of the cross.

*See also* HALLOWE'EN.

**miscarriage** The loss of a foetus before birth, accidentally as the result of natural processes or else by an abortion procured through conventional medical intervention or less conventional, and often highly dangerous, artificial means. Hedged in by the threat of social disgrace and physical danger, the whole subject of miscarriage and abortion was for centuries obscured by religious prejudice and inadequate medical knowledge and was a natural breeding ground for all manner of superstitious belief. Many of the spells associated with witches all over the world were specifically intended to terminate PREGNANCY, usually through the action of various potions whose effect was generally to make the pregnant woman so ill that a miscarriage became inevitable (an approach that all too often also placed the life of the patient herself in grave danger). Among the natural substances employed were the poisonous pennyroyal, rye ergot, and oil of tansy.

See also CHILDBIRTH.

**mistletoe** An evergreen, parasitical plant which was revered for its magical properties by the Druids and has retained to this day certain mystical associations (it is also thought to have been the Golden Bough of the classical legend of Aeneas). The Druids held that mistletoe – preferably growing on an OAK – had to be cut with a golden sickle during the summer or winter solstice. On no account was it to be allowed to fall on the ground, which robbed it of its magical powers; instead it was caught in the lap of their robes while two white bulls were sacrificed. Norse mythology also placed special importance upon the mistletoe, the plant with which the evil Loki killed the Sun God, and throughout Scandinavia enemies meeting beneath a bush of mistletoe were supposed to lay down their weapons as the plant was also the plant of peace.

Allegedly the wood of which Christ's CROSS was made and also the 'burning bush' of the story of Moses, the mistletoe is ironically unwelcome in churches because of its pagan history and will be carefully removed if accidentally included in decorative greenery. Despite this it used to be carried in solemn procession to the altar at York Minster in medieval times, and was allowed to remain there throughout the CHRISTMAS season as a symbol of the general pardon that was then in force. The plant, which flowers in the winter, has none the less come to be identified particularly with the Christmas festivities; in the English Midlands at least it is said to be unlucky to cut mistletoe at any other time in the year.

English people have kissed beneath boughs of mistletoe since Saxon times, a man having the right to demand a kiss from any woman who passes (either inadvertently or on purpose) beneath a bough of mistletoe hung from the ceiling. Until relatively recently, the men plucked a berry with each kiss and no more kisses could be claimed after the last berry was gone. This superstition derives from the days of the Druids, when the plant was considered to have strong sexual potency – though another suggestion has it that the practice originated in a curse placed on the mistletoe as a punishment by the pagan gods, so that it would always have to look on while pretty young girls were kissed beneath its leaves.

Any girl who refuses a kiss demanded in this fashion risks dying unmarried, according to a US variation, while any single girl unfortunate enough to remain unkissed even after standing beneath the mistletoe must reconcile herself to another year without a husband. A girl who marries without ever having been kissed under the mistletoe is doomed to remain childless. A girl who is fortunate enough to be kissed under the mistletoe by no fewer than seven men will marry one of them within the year. Perhaps not unlinked is the now rarely revived custom of hanging a sprig of mistletoe over the doorway of a newly married couple to ensure their happiness, or else outside their bedroom to keep nightmares at bay.

Once Christmas is over some people insist on burning the mistletoe, maintaining that if it is not burned on TWELFTH NIGHT the couples who kissed beneath it are fated to quarrel before the year is over. Others, however, claim that there is some virtue in keeping the bough carefully in place until the following Yuletide before it is ceremonially burned. Keeping the cut bough through the year is said to preserve its luck-giving qualities, and farmers formerly fed the first cow to calve after the New Year a sprig of the plant in the belief that this would promote the welfare of the whole herd over the coming twelve months. A little mistletoe hung over a CRADLE, meanwhile, is supposed to ward off FAIRIES and to prevent the child being replaced by a changeling.

Also known by the name all-heal, the plant is credited with various healing powers. It is beneficial, usually in the form of a tea, in the treatment of EPILEPSY, heart disease, nervous ailments, snakebite (*see* SNAKE), TOOTHACHE and St Vitus's Dance. The plant does in fact contain the drug guipsene, which can indeed be used to help sufferers of hypertension and nervous disorders. Mistletoe is also said to have the power to mend quarrels, to ward off LIGHTNING and to promote fertility. Not surprisingly, in view of the plant's varied properties and magical associations, anyone who is reckless enough to take the whole bush or actually cuts down a mistletoe-bearing tree is warned to expect a particularly grisly end.

**mole** This small, burrowing, nearly blind mammal, rarely seen above ground, has inevitably acquired its own mythology. Some people claim it is lucky to see a mole, while others rather fancifully believe that moles only emerge from their tunnels at night in order to listen to the angels singing. The sudden appearance of molehills in a garden that was previously free of them is open to more than one interpretation. This either constitutes a prediction that someone will soon be moving elsewhere or, more ominously, is a portent of illness or death (intensified if the molehills surround the house, according to the Scottish). If the animals dig close to a bathroom or kitchen the life threatened is taken to be that of the woman of the house. US tradition, meanwhile, predicts that bad weather is in the offing if there are more molehills than usual.

Among the cruellest folk remedies is one recommended for those suffering from TOOTHACHE, RHEUMATISM, CRAMP

and other ailments. This involves cutting the paws from a living mole and carrying them about the person (if the problem is in the arms the front paws of the mole must be carried, and vice versa if the problem is in the legs). Sleeping with the affected part wrapped in moleskin – or else in the two halves of a mole's body – may also prove beneficial. Hands that have been used to strangle a mole are said to have the power to give relief to anyone suffering from pains in the chest. People troubled with WARTS might try bathing them in the still-warm blood of a freshly killed mole, while blood taken from a mole's nose and swallowed on a lump of sugar will cure fits and the skinned and powdered body of a male mole, consumed with gin, will ward off FEVER. Owners of moleskin purses, meanwhile, will run out of small change. HORSE thieves will be interested to know that rubbing a black horse with water in which a mole has been boiled will apparently cause the horse to turn white.

**moles** The position of moles on the human body has a particular significance according to superstitious people, who on the whole regard them as lucky (hence the now defunct fashion for wearing beauty spots in strategic places). Technically known as 'moleosophy', the science of divination by examining a person's moles assigns specific traits of character and patterns of fortune to moles on virtually any part of the anatomy. These may signify good or bad luck, interpretations varying from one region to another, but most authorities agree that those found on the LEFT SIDE of the body tend to denote misfortune while those on the RIGHT SIDE promise good things. One notable exception concerns girls with moles on the left breast: they may be assured of enjoying their choice of lovers, whereas those with moles on the right breast will bring poverty down on both themselves and their partners. Circular moles signify good character, while angular ones warn of a less likeable personality and oblong moles indicate wealth. Light-coloured moles are luckier than those of a darker hue.

Commonly agreed conclusions about character that may be drawn from the position of moles include:

toe: appreciation of art and beauty.
foot: melancholy.
ankle: ambition and quick-wittedness.
calf: resourcefulness and optimism.
knee: extravagance.
thigh: poor health, poverty and sorrow.
genitals: lust.
buttocks: lacking ambition.
hip: contentment and intelligence.
stomach: strength and love of life.
breast: laziness and argumentativeness.
centre of chest: friendliness.
shoulder: fortitude.
back: caution and timidity.
arm: happiness and industry.
elbow: talent and love of travel.
wrist: dependability and intelligence.
hand: happiness, self-reliance and children.
finger: anxiety.
neck: generosity, love and luck.
back of neck: death by hanging.

An abundance of moles on the lower arms indicates a troubled middle age with more prosperous years to follow. A traditional English rhyme offers a concise summary of the main points:

A mole on the arm
Can do you no harm.
A mole on your lip
You're witty and flip.
A mole on your neck
Brings money by the peck.
A mole on your back
Brings money by the sack.
A mole on your ear
Brings money year by year.

Moles on the face may be regarded as cosmetically unwelcome, but say a lot about a person and his or her future fortunes. A mole on the cheek denotes a quiet and thoughtful or lucky personality, while one on the chin indicates generosity and trustworthiness and the likelihood of considerable wealth. A mole on the nose indicates a love of travel or success in business, while one on the lip confirms that a person is a good eater or eloquent talker. A girl with a mole on the right eyebrow may expect to marry at an early age, and furthermore the match will prove a good one. A mole on the ear is lucky, but one on the lower jaw prophesies only ill fortune. A mole on the right temple bespeaks a life of good luck and achievement, while one on the left temple denotes either bad luck or increased powers of comprehension; a mole in the middle of the forehead warns of a cruel nature and possibly loose morals and an inclination to MURDER (though it may also signify wealth). A somewhat malignant Scottish tradition has it that a 'mole above the breath' (in other words, above the mouth) is evidence that the person concerned is a witch. Hairs that grow out of facial moles are especially lucky and should not be removed.

*See also* BIRTHMARK; WART.

**molucca bean** A kind of bean or nut, sometimes worn as an AMULET in the Western Isles of Scotland. Such beans are occasionally found on the shoreline, having been washed across the Atlantic from the West Indies by the Gulf Stream. White beans in particular are supposed to have some power against witches and other evils when worn about the neck. When witchcraft is threatened the beans turn black, warning of misfortune or death. They are particularly credited with assisting women in CHILDBIRTH and with preventing death by DROWNING, and to this day they are sold in certain shops 'for luck'.

**Monday** *see* DAYS OF THE WEEK.

**money** The universal desire to accumulate wealth is reflected in the number and variety of superstitions that have attached themselves to the day-to-day running of BUSINESS affairs and other speculative enterprises, ranging from rituals to be observed when setting out for a business appointment to the gambler kissing his cards for luck (*see* GAMBLING).

Keeping a tiny money SPIDER in the pocket will ensure a constant supply of cash, and many people place great faith in holed COINS on the grounds that these are very lucky and liable to attract other coins (a measure that will be doubly effective if the coin concerned is carefully spat upon each new MOON; *see* SPITTING). Other tips for the superstitious include always keeping one's money in just one pocket, and carefully pocketing the first money made each day to guarantee further profit. Cash boxes and purses should never be left completely empty, as this allows the DEVIL to get in and to prevent any more money coming in. Those reduced to wearing threadbare clothes are warned against repairing their garments without taking them off, which in some mysterious way will also forestall any improvement in their finances.

If a person drops a coin on the floor it is best to persuade a friend to pick it up, which will cause more money to materialise – failing this, it should only be picked up after it has first been carefully trodden on. Curiously, it is sometimes considered unlucky to find money lying on the ground, though in some areas the money may be gathered in without harm if it is spat upon or is found to be resting 'heads' up.

*See also* TWO-DOLLAR BILL.

**monkey puzzle tree** With its distinctive convoluted branches, the monkey puzzle is generally considered an unlucky tree. One superstition recorded in Scotland warns against speaking anywhere in its vicinity for fear of the consequences. In eastern England the monkey puzzle was sometimes planted at the edge of graveyards in the belief that its sparse foliage deprived the DEVIL of a hiding-place from which he might observe FUNERALS taking place.

**months of the year** Each month, linked as it is to the lunar cycle, has its own magical significance and character. Some months are luckier than others, and most people pay lip service at least to the notion that when they are born dictates to some extent their personality and their particular strengths and weaknesses (*see also* ASTROLOGY; GEMSTONES; ZODIAC). Observing the state of the WEATHER at a particular time of year can also provide some idea of what is to follow.

Key months in the CALENDAR are credited by superstition with specific qualities. January, for instance, is thought to be especially unlucky for rulers and a time for revolutions and assassinations. In England it is said that mild weather in January means that it will remain cold all the way through to the summer, with inevitable consequences for harvests later in the year. A wet March, meanwhile, will cause further damage to crops, though conversely a March that is dry and cold is a prophecy of an excellent harvest later on.

May, though it marks the beginning of the warmer months, is widely considered to be the unluckiest month, a bad time for WEDDINGS or for embarking on new projects of any kind. The proverb 'Marry in May and you'll rue the day' is possibly a relic of the fact that in agricultural communities everybody's presence was required in the fields at this time of year to sow seed and plant crops, and no one could be excused merely to get married; it was also, rather ominously, a time for honouring the dead back in Roman times. May is, though, a good time to announce an ENGAGEMENT.

BABIES born in May will not thrive or will turn out rebellious, while CATS born during the month will prove poor mice-catchers and will tend to chase snakes and worms instead; 'May kittens' are also reputed to suck the breath of young children, and in times gone by many people drowned them rather than risk the ill luck they threatened. Illnesses contracted during May are likely to prove fatal, and this is also a time when witches and other evil-doers are particularly noted for their activity. Decorating the house with bunches of May flowers and greenery will, however, provide a degree of protection against witchcraft.

An old English proverb further advises 'Ne'er cast a clout till May be out', suggesting that it is unwise to wear fewer clothes because the weather is warm in May because it may easily turn cold without warning and threaten one's health. It is also inadvisable to wash blankets in May, according to one old West Country saying:

Wash a blanket in May,
Wash a loved one away.

Among the other months, it is said that early frosts that appear before 11 November (St Martin's Day), are a sign that the coming winter will be wet rather than cold.

See also DAYS OF THE WEEK.

**moon** As might be expected, the moon occupies a prominent place in the superstitions of the entire Western world. While the SUN represents the life essence and the more positive aspects of existence, the moon, ruler of the TIDES and other elemental forces, is generally taken to symbolise darker, more mysterious and often negative influences. The reverence that ancient moon worshippers felt for the moon is reflected in the mixed feelings that most people still have for the Earth's nearest neighbour in space, even in an age when science has revealed much about the moon's real nature.

Perhaps the oldest and widest known of the superstitions connected with the moon is that those who gaze too long at the full moon risk becoming 'lunatic', that is, mad, and will henceforth be subject to attacks of insanity whenever the moon is full. The moon's disorientating influence is also to be seen in the erratic behaviour of animals at certain times in the lunar cycle and may be linked, according to many authorities, with the human female MENSTRUATION cycle.

Primitive awe of the moon and its strange wonders has never quite died away and it continues to be treated by the more superstitious with the utmost respect. In various ancient cultures, for instance, young girls in particular were warned against sleeping in the moonlight, lest they become 'moonstruck' and beget monsters, and even today children may be instructed to chant 'I see the moon and the moon sees me, God bless the moon and God bless me' to ward off ill luck should moonlight come into their room. To be on the safe side, many adults will greet the new moon with a respectful bow or curtsey (in which case they believe they will be granted a wish). Witches and other sorcerers, meanwhile, have long been credited with the power to 'draw down the moon', attracting its malevolent power to use for their own nefarious ends.

Many ancient CALENDARS depended on the lunar phases, and there have been many attempts to determine from the moon's cycle the optimum times to begin various enterprises. Broadly speaking, the waxing of a new moon is a time when lovers may divine what the future has in store for them, when new projects may be safely begun and when journeys may be best undertaken. Farmers – despite any real evidence to support them – will choose if possible to do their planting and sowing when the moon is waxing (though such plants as runner beans, which grow anti-clockwise, are sown on the wane) and this is also the best time for WEDDINGS, CHILDBIRTH and convalescence. Livestock slaughtered when the moon is waxing will give better meat.

Bowing to the new moon and turning over any SILVER coins in one's pocket will guarantee a doubling in the amount by the end of the next cycle. If in company, the first person to see the new moon should KISS one of his or her companions without delay: they may then expect a gift in the near future. It is important, however, that the new moon should not be seen for the first time through GLASS (SPECTACLES excepted) or through the branches of a TREE, as this is a bad omen (similarly if it is first seen to the LEFT SIDE of the observer). Ideally it should be sighted in the open air via a glance over the right shoulder (in which case a wish may be made).

It is highly inadvisable to be caught POINTING at a new moon, as this offends 'the man in the moon' (an obscure mythical figure allegedly banished to the moon for gathering sticks on the Sabbath) and is an invitation to dire misfortune; if done nine times the person concerned will be barred from entry into Heaven. Moreover, no one should consent to surgery when the moon is full, and any death that occurs during the new moon will be followed by three further mortalities. There is general agreement, however, that no person can actually die while the moon is rising.

Lovers are advised that the first new moon of the year, if approached in the right way, may reward them with visions of future partners. Generally speaking, the moon must be addressed with respect and the following rhyme (or a variation of it) recited:

All hail to thee, moon, all hail to thee,
I prithee kind moon, reveal to me,
Him/Her who is my life partner to be.

If all goes well, the lover will see his or her future partner in their dreams – or may even wake to find a single HAIR from the other's head tucked in between their big toe and its neighbour. The number of moons a lover sees when gazing at the moon through a new silk HANDKERCHIEF or when examining their reflection in water or in a MIRROR indicates how many years (or months) must pass before his or her marriage.

A waning moon exerts a generally baneful influence and is a particularly bad time for births and weddings. Anything cut in this period will not grow again, including the HAIR and FINGERNAILS, though it is apparently a good time to move house, let blood, pick fruit, cut down trees and stuff feather mattresses. Worst of all is the period between cycles,

when there is no moon at all: children born during this time will come to nothing, as an ancient English proverb warns – 'No moon, no man'.

The period immediately following a new moon is the most significant. One ancient English tradition advises on the character of each of the ten days immediately following:

Day One: Ideal for births and new projects, but bad for those who fall ill.

Day Two: Ideal for business matters, sea voyages and sowing seeds.

Day Three: An inauspicious day for most undertakings.

Day Four: Ideal for construction projects and for the birth of politicians.

Day Five: Ideal for conception and the model for the month's weather.

Day Six: Ideal for hunting and fishing.

Day Seven: The most propitious day for new lovers to meet.

Day Eight: The worst day to fall ill, as the illness may prove fatal.

Day Nine: A day to avoid moonlight on the face, lest insanity follow.

Day Ten: A day for the birth of restless souls.

Should two new lunar months fall within the same calendar month, extremely bad WEATHER is sure to follow and may extend to flooding and other natural catastrophes. If this happens in May it will rain 'for a year and a day'. Other weather predictions connected with the lunar cycle include the notion that new moons that fall at the weekend will be followed by bad luck and foul weather. If the 'horns' of the new moon point upwards, good weather is in the offing; if they point down, it will be wet. A halo around the moon at any time in the cycle is a warning of rain to come. A full moon that falls on Christmas Day, meanwhile, is lamented by farmers as a prophecy of a poor harvest in the year ahead.

In folk medicine, a superstition from the north of England recommends blowing on one's WARTS in the light of the full moon to cure them, while many regions boast the tradition of 'washing' hands affected by warts in a shiny metal basinful of moon's rays while reciting:

I wash my hands in this thy dish,
O man in the moon, do grant my wish,
And come and take this away.

*See also* ECLIPSE.

**moonwort** A diminutive variety of FERN, which is supposed to have a range of magical powers. It has the curious property of being able to open locks and loosen nails and other fastenings made of IRON. This is said to make it a great favourite of housebreakers, who have only to insert a leaf of the plant into a lock to overcome the obstacle. Woodpeckers are said to be privy to the secret of the moonwort and will similarly apply its leaves to remove old nails or other iron obstructions when building their nests; they are also said to rub their beaks on the plant, thus acquiring the strength to pierce iron. Rural tradition alleges that horses which step on moonwort will immediately cast their iron shoes.

**mop** In a time-honoured superstition shared by SAILORS of many nationalities, it is an omen of great misfortune if a mop or bucket is accidentally lost overboard. Going about the seemingly straightforward business of mopping a floor in the home is also not without its hazards: mop across the cracks in the floorboards rather than in line with them and the person concerned is fated to be unhappy in love – or else will end up married to a drunkard.

**mosquito** Contrary to what might be expected of an insect that is both a nuisance and in some cases a carrier of life-threatening disease, the mosquito is generally considered a harbinger of good luck. Mosquitos may even be welcomed in the bedroom of a sick person on the grounds that, as they fly out again, they will take the illness with them. They may also be used as indicators of the WEATHER: if they fly close to the ground, RAIN is coming, but if they fly high in the air the

weather will be fine. Mosquito bites may be treated, it is said, by applying butter, GARLIC, lemon peel, oil, onion or vinegar and then blowing on them.

**moth** Like the BUTTERFLY, the moth – particularly if WHITE in colour and discovered flying at night – is said to be a reincarnation of a lost soul and is thus treated with some mistrust by the superstitious, who are wary of this link with the dead and are careful not to harm the insect. In some parts of England, however, it was once customary for children to hunt down any white moths they saw and to kill them while accusing them of stealing the miller's wheat (hence their dusty white appearance). The appearance of a black moth in the house is particularly to be dreaded as a portent of the death of one of the occupants within a year (or even within a month). More cheerfully, many people welcome the appearance of moths in their vicinity as it promises the arrival of an important LETTER.

**mother-die** One of a number of plants which, if picked by a child, will result in the death of one its parents. In the north of England the red campion is identified as a 'mother-die' flower – though some claim that the child's mother will die if the white-flowered campion is picked, but it is the father who will perish if the red one is selected. In the West Country children may show caution in picking death-come-quickly, a local name for herb robert. Similar traditions have attached over the years to HEMLOCK, wild PARSLEY, MEADOWSWEET, hogweed and rose bay willow herb, all known in various localities by the name 'mother-die'.

**mother-in-law** Comedians may have much to say on the subject of mothers-in-law, but European superstition generally maintains a tactful silence. American Indians, however, venture to warn young men from looking into the eyes of their mother-in-law, as this will cause them to go blind. Scottish superstition, moreover, advises young women that they will experience a much happier married life if they marry men whose mothers are already dead.

**mother-of-pearl** Prized for its shiny appearance, mother-of-pearl is widely considered lucky to own, hence the popularity of various nick-nacks incorporating it that are commonly found in seaside resorts and gift shops.

**motor-racing** The perilous nature of modern motor-racing has ensured that it has developed with the full range of superstitions that are common to most dangerous sports. Drivers boast the usual battery of AMULETS, pre-race rituals, lucky clothing and MASCOTS, and stories abound of fatal accidents that followed a driver's negligence in observing well-established taboos of his or others' devising. Superstitions peculiar to motor sport include the notion that it is unlucky to get into a car on the side where the exhaust pipe is mounted (assuming the car has only one of these) and also that it unlucky to walk in front of the car more than once in the period before the race starts. Drivers may also show reluctance to allow themselves to be photographed (*see* PHOTOGRAPH) before a race begins, and may refuse to sign autographs for fans until after the event is over.

*See also* CAR.

**mountaineering** A superstition of Alpine origin recommends that climbers facing challenging routes will fare much better if they arrange to have the tongue of an EAGLE sewn into their coat collar.

**mourning** It is perhaps not surprising that anything connected with FUNERALS and DEATH should be regarded as unlucky, and this applies also to clothes and other funeral paraphernalia. In particular, it is thought unlucky for lovers to meet for the first time while wearing funeral apparel, for their affair is fated to end unhappily. It is also unlucky to keep any black-edged writing paper or black crêpe left over after a funeral as it will bring bad luck to the house.

**mouse** Mice, though timid and not loathed with the same ferocity as RATS, are none the less viewed with considerable suspicion by the superstitious, some of whom have claimed that the species was an invention of Satan himself. Their appearance in houses previously free of them is regarded with foreboding and is a warning of an imminent death in the family (as is their sudden disappearance from a house for no apparent reason). Doubts about their significance are not eased by the widely held tradition that they are in fact the souls of MURDER victims, returned to the world, or else the souls of the sleeping which have temporarily left the body.

Discovering damage done by mice to clothing is itself an unlucky act, redolent of further evil to come, and the sound of a mouse squeaking near the bed of a sick person may be interpreted as a black sign for the patient's recovery. Anyone who has a mouse run over them is sure to die soon, and the sight of a WHITE mouse crossing the floor is also a portent of death. Many travellers dislike meeting mice when on a journey for fear of the bad luck they bring, and FISHERMEN will not suffer the word 'mouse' to be uttered while at sea. In Scotland one measure that may be taken to clear a house of mice is to capture one of their number and to roast it slowly before the fire, suspended by the tail: the other mice will apparently take the hint and vacate the premises. White mice are said to be a favourite disguise of witches' imps; none the less they are considered lucky in Germany, where few people will kill a mouse for fear of provoking bad fortune.

Folk medicine has several uses for the mouse. A meal of roasted, boiled, stewed, baked or fried mouse – or a drink made with powdered mouse – is especially recommended for the treatment of WHOOPING COUGH, SMALLPOX, COUGHS and COLDS, FEVER or MEASLES and it will also cure children of BEDWETTING. Dropping mouse blood on a WART will cause it to disappear, while stroking the cheek with a dead mouse will, it is claimed, relieve the pain of TOOTHACHE. Swilling the mouth with mouse ashes mixed with honey is highly recommended to sweeten foul-smelling breath.

*See also* SHREW.

**moustache**   *see* BEARD; HAIR.

**mugwort**   Herb that is reputed to have considerable power as a defence against WITCHCRAFT, poisons, spells and various illnesses. If placed carefully in the SHOE, it will also prevent tiredness on long journeys (a notion that was commonplace among travellers up until the seventeenth century). It is said to be particularly efficacious in preventing disease in women, and was formerly much respected as a means of treating CONSUMPTION. Any person who digs up a mugwort plant on MIDSUMMER'S EVE, meanwhile, will find a small coal hidden in the soil; this has its own special magic properties, being able to protect its owner from BURNS, the plague, carbuncles and FEVER, and also from being struck by LIGHTNING.

**mullein**   A type of herbaceous plant, including Aaron's rod, which may be used to test a partner's loyalty. Lovers anxious to establish their partner's fidelity should locate a mullein plant growing near the latter's house and bend the stalk in that direction; if the plant dies they have cause to doubt the other's faithfulness, but if it returns to an upright position their fears are groundless.

**murder**   The deliberate taking of another person's life is the most heinous of all crimes and inevitably the focus of an extensive body of superstition in all cultures. Not surprisingly, most superstitions agree that it is unlucky to witness a murder or to discover the body of a murder victim.

Various places around the world boast patches of ground that are perpetually stained with blood or are otherwise barren because a murder took place there. Well-known examples include Holyroodhouse in Scotland, scene of the murder of Mary Queen of Scots' secretary David Rizzio in 1566, where all attempts to remove a stain on the floor (reputed to be his blood) have been in vain. Another Scottish example is Glamis Castle, where a stain left by King Duncan's blood after his murder at the hands of Macbeth had eventually to be covered over by laying a completely new floor. Far more numerous are those patches of ground where nothing will grow, allegedly because of a murder or an unjust execution that occurred there (*see* BARREN GROUND). Somewhat confusingly, though, in some regions small plots of earth where the grass grows unusually green and thick are identified as places where murder victims have lain.

In former times it was widely believed that the body of a murder victim would bleed if brought into the presence of (or touched by) the murderer, thus revealing his identity. Another well-known tradition claims that the eyeballs of the deceased person carry the image of the murderer in them even after death. In cases where the murderer has remained unidentified, suspicion has all too readily been laid on alleged witches and sorcerers, whose preferred methods of murder are reputed to be poison and spells.

German tradition holds that the soul of a deceased murderer is condemned to roam the Earth until the natural lifespan his or her victim would have enjoyed in other circumstances has expired. The souls of murder victims are supposedly reincarnated as mice and may only be released from Earth when the killer is found and put to death. To prevent their souls walking abroad, one simple measure is to remove the person's SHOES and to bury them without delay, ideally between the high and low water marks.

**mushroom** Different cultures suggest a variety of ways of telling whether a mushroom is edible or not. Some of these are more reliable than others, and the danger involved in such selection is reflected in the awe with which primitive man, at least, approached fungi. The Hebrews considered mushrooms holy and only priests were allowed to eat them, while the hallucinogenic properties of some varieties were ritually employed by certain holy men and warriors preparing for battle. The white-spotted scarlet mushroom known as fly agaric, pressed for its juices and mixed with milk or curds, is reputed to have been the food on which the gods of ancient Greece feasted in their home on Mount Olympus.

A superstition common to many societies is that mushrooms are the offspring of LIGHTNING sent from the Heavens. Another tradition credits them with various APHRODISIAC properties. To be on the safe side, according to one Essex tradition, mushrooms should only be picked at the time of a full MOON. Other superstitions include the odd Irish contention that a mushroom will grow no more once it has been looked at – so it might as well be picked.

**music** Musicians and music lovers boast a body of superstitions peculiar to themselves. Musicians, in parallel with sports players and ACTORS AND ACTRESSES, often show a weakness for 'lucky' items of clothing, batons, instruments and pre-performance rituals of their own devising. To take just two examples, conductor Leonard Bernstein always took care to wear the same pair of cufflinks (a present from Sergei Koussevitsky) at his concerts, while in a different sphere rock singer Axl Rose, of the US band Guns 'N' Roses, refuses to play in towns whose name begins with the letter M in the conviction that this letter is unlucky.

Many performers, and listeners, have their own 'lucky' tunes; the ill-fated Judy Garland, for instance, was reputed to include her song 'Over the Rainbow' in every performance she gave not so much because audiences loved it, but because she thought it brought her luck. The composer Gustav Mahler was another who betrayed superstitious preoccupations back in 1907, when he gave his ninth symphony the title Das Lied von der Erde rather than simply calling it by its number. The reason was that several famous composers, including Beethoven, Schubert and Bruckner, had all died after composing their ninth symphony.

One taboo shared by orchestras everywhere concerns taking up a piece of music at the same place where it has been left off if there has been a lengthy delay; many musicians will insist on playing a few notes at least of another work before resuming the original piece. Other traditions include the widely shared idea that 'musical' insects, such as crickets and grasshoppers, are very lucky. Of the instruments themselves, those with slightly dubious reputations include the violin, the bagpipes and the drum, all of which are said to be favourite instruments of the DEVIL.

As regards the music itself, the unluckiest piece of all (excepting the witches' song in Shakespeare's play Macbeth) is probably the song 'I Dreamt I Dwelt in Marble Halls', which has acquired an evil reputation through the many strokes of ill fate that have befallen its performers and indeed the theatres in which it has been sung. The only circumstance in which it may be safely delivered is in its proper place within The Bohemian Girl, the opera from which it comes. Other 'unlucky' works include Tosti's 'Goodbye', Tchaikovsky's Pathétique symphony, the Halévy opera Charles VI, the Barcarolle from Offenbach's The Tales of Hoffmann and the children's song 'Three Blind Mice'. Paganini and Tartini are considered 'unlucky' composers.

In contrast, the latent power that is supposedly released when music is played loud and fast is evidenced by the long-established notion that playing such music to accompany a wild dance by a person who has been bitten by a tarantula spider will generally effect a cure. More recent 'proofs' of the ameliorating effects of music include the quasi-scientific theory that playing music to plants encourages their growth.

*See also* BELL; SINGING; WHISTLE.

**muskrat** North American rodent, not dissimilar to the beaver, which is associated with a handful of North American Indian superstitions. The Indians believe that the construction of the muskrat's home can reveal much about the coming season's WEATHER. If the muskrat builds its home well clear of the water, heavy rains are due, but if it constructs a house with thin walls the winter will be mild. In folk medicine, it is alleged that a muskrat pelt pressed against the chest will relieve ASTHMA.

**myrtle** This evergreen shrub or tree is generally considered to be lucky, having associations with love, marriage and fertility. Planting a myrtle on both sides of the front door will, according to the Welsh, promote the peace and happiness of the household – though the plant should be carefully looked after, for if it withers and dies through neglect or is actually dug up only misfortune will follow. In several European countries myrtle blooming abundantly in the garden is interpreted as a sign of a coming WEDDING in the household, and brides formerly carried myrtle bouquets.

The plant will prosper best if put in the ground by a woman, who must take care to spread her skirt over the plant and look as proud as she can while performing the task; in Germany, however, authorities warn that any girl who plants myrtle while engaged to be married will suffer the wedding being called off (the same authorities advise that a bride decked out with myrtle will avoid becoming pregnant on her wedding night). Young girls who drink myrtle tea will enjoy greater BEAUTY – in which case they might have need of an old English superstition that employs myrtle as a means to discover the identity of a future husband. This advises girls to lay a sprig of myrtle against the words of the marriage service in their prayer book and then to sleep with the book under their pillow: if the myrtle has disappeared in the morning, their lover is destined to marry them.

# N

**nail** Being made of IRON, nails are reputed to have numerous magical powers, notably as a means of protection against evil and in the treatment of various medical ailments. Hammering iron nails into the wall or lintels of a house (usually the kitchen lintel) will keep evil spirits and disease at bay, a precaution that is particularly effective if the nails are rusty or have been taken from an old COFFIN and are arranged in the pattern of a CROSS. It is lucky to find a nail lying in the road, especially if it is an old one, and carrying such a nail about the person will ward off the EVIL EYE.

One way to test for WITCHCRAFT involves driving an iron nail into the footprint of the suspected person: if the allegation is accurate, the person concerned will shortly reappear in order to remove the nail, thus revealing their guilt. Nails used to fasten HORSESHOES are reputed to be doubly effective against witchcraft. Driving nails into a TREE, meanwhile, will ensure that it grows as it should, while removing every nail or tack in the floor before laying a new carpet will help to preserve the household's luck.

In folk medicine, driving a nail into the ground where an epileptic has suffered a fit will cure that person of their ailment (*see* EPILEPSY). Various other physical problems, such as TOOTHACHE and FEVER, may be similarly cured by bringing a nail into contact with the affected part and then hammering the nail into the ground (the affliction may then transfer to the first person to walk over the nail). A more elaborate cure for fever involves going to a CROSSROADS at midnight, turning round three times when the church clock strikes, driving a tenpenny nail into the ground and then retreating, facing the clock, until it finishes striking. An Irish treatment for HEADACHES recommends driving nails into an old SKULL. Should one suffer an injury from a nail, the nail itself should be hammered into an OAK tree to ward off infection.

*See also* FINGERNAIL.

**names** Choosing names for the newborn is not to be taken lightly, for every name has its own magical properties and meaning and becomes far more than a means of identification. The latent power of names is reflected in the widely held belief that simply chanting the name of a spirit or demon over and over again is enough to cause it to manifest itself, and furthermore in the notion that sorcerers may harness the magic of names in their evil-working spells.

As well as paying heed to the meanings allotted to names, parents should also bear in mind a number of well-established principles laid down by superstition. Perhaps the most familiar of these is that it is extremely unlucky, as well as insensitive, to name a baby after an older sibling who has already died. This is regarded as TEMPTING FATE and tantamount to sentencing the newborn child to the same end. Neither should a baby share its new name with any family pet, which spells doom for both parties. Naming children after the parents is also hazardous, as this may lead to the children dying first. It is, however, lucky to name a child after some great or successful person, which will allow the child to share in that person's luck.

Another strategy, popular in more religious times, involves opening the BIBLE at random and reading until the first name is reached. Choosing the name of a saint or of a Christian martyr is alleged to guarantee the infant the protection of that holy person, though some authorities baulk at this, claiming that the saint will take the child to Heaven if it shares the same name.

Specific names that should be carefully considered before being chosen include Agnes: anyone of this name is fated to become insane, according to one rather obscure English tradition. Conversely, the name George is said to be lucky as no one called George has, so superstition claims, ever met his death by hanging (though history refutes this). Choosing names whose initials spell a word, incidentally, is also reputed to be lucky. The number of letters in a name is also important: those with seven letters are doubly fortunate (*see* NUMBERS), while names with THIRTEEN letters will attract bad luck.

Once a name has been decided upon, superstition warns the parents to keep it to themselves and the immediate family until the CHRISTENING, lest some malevolent spirit should use the name in a spell and exert a harmful influence over the child. In times gone by, some fathers kept the final choice even from their wives until everyone was gathered at the font. Similarly, many people in rural areas once preferred to be known by nicknames rather than their real ones, for fear that witches and sorcerers would learn their identity and use their names in spells.

In most cases, first names are for life (it is in fact most unlucky to change one's name after being christened) – but women at least have a chance to change their maiden names on getting married. Superstition advises that any woman about to marry should take care not to use her new name before the WEDDING actually takes place: uttering it or even writing it down to see what it looks like is enough to cause the wedding plans to fall apart. Once the marriage has taken place it is conversely unlucky for anyone to address the new bride by her old name, even innocently (though some women in contemporary society choose to brave this taboo by keeping their maiden name for professional reasons and may refuse to adopt their husband's name even in private life).

Many an English bride is familiar with the notion that it is unlucky to marry a man whose surname shares the same first letter as her maiden name, though the origins of this idea remain obscure. The superstition is most usually heard in the form of a cautionary rhyme:

Change the name and not the letter,
Change for the worse and not for the
  better.

Cheshire superstition claims that any woman who marries into another family of the same surname as her own, though there is no blood link, will be blessed with special powers of healing – as is also the case if a woman has two husbands of the same surname. Such women are credited with the power to cure WHOOPING COUGH and other ailments by the simple expedient of feeding the sufferer a little BREAD AND BUTTER (though this will only work as long as the patient accepts the food without saying 'thank you'). Married couples who have the names Joseph and Mary are also considered lucky, for obvious reasons, and these too are credited with the power to cure whooping cough in the same way.

The same seriousness applies to the naming of animals and even to various inanimate objects. One regional tradition, recorded in the English Midlands, dictates that COWS, for instance, should not be named until their first calf has been safely delivered, in order to safeguard their welfare. The names of SHIPS are also magical and SAILORS will express grave reservations if a ship is renamed by new owners, often citing examples of vessels lost at sea after their names have been changed. Ships whose names end in an 'a' are considered particularly unlucky (a notion much fuelled by the sinking of the *Lusitania* in 1915).

*See also* CHRISTENING.

**napkin** Folding one's napkin at the end of a meal may seem a natural enough thing to do, but superstition advises that to do so when visiting a house for the first time means that the visitor is fated never to dine there again. If staying for longer than one meal, the visitor is, however, at liberty to fold the napkin as neatly as he wishes without any risk of offending superstition.

**narcissus** Spring flower named after the Greek legend of Narcissus, who became obsessed with his own reflection in a pool, fell in, was drowned and then reappeared as this flower. Its powerful perfume was reputed in ancient times to induce HEADACHES, MADNESS and DEATH. Later generations, however, found that the plant had its uses in folk medicine, employing the bulb as an antiseptic dressing for WOUNDS and mixing it with honey as a painkiller.

**navel** Superstition offers its own explanation of how the first navel, actually marking the site where a person's UMBILICAL CORD was attached, came about. According to the Turks the DEVIL spat at the first human being he saw, but Allah quickly ripped out the affected flesh to leave the scar still visible today, replicated on all human torsos.

**neck** An aching neck is, according to Dutch superstition, a warning that the person concerned is fated to die by hanging. Cures for stiff necks include wrapping around the affected part an unwashed SOCK, a towel holding warm BAY leaves or COTTON dripping with olive oil in which a poppy head has been soaked.

*See also* MOLES.

**need-fire** The sacred fire around which many of the traditions associated with the ancient ceremonies of MIDSUMMER'S EVE and other festivals revolved. The need-fire was usually ignited by friction and was then carried into neighbouring homes to rekindle the fire in the domestic hearth, which would then be kept continually alight until the time of the next festival. It was important that the man who ignited the fire was innocent of any crime, and he was prohibited from carrying anything made of metal on him when going about this sacred duty.

Symbolising renewal and the never-ending cycle of the seasons, the need-fire was revered in many ancient European cultures and various rituals surrounded its honouring on auspicious dates in the pre-Christian calendar. Worshippers jumped through the flames in order to get the full benefit of their purifying properties, and livestock was driven through the still-warm embers for similar reasons. Such fires would also be lit at other times of the year when livestock were afflicted by disease or the locality was troubled by plague or some other calamity. Though forbidden by the Church back in the eighth century, the practice is still occasionally reported in the twentieth.

**needle** The humble needle is connected with a whole host of superstitions. It is said to be inviting bad luck not to pick up a dropped needle, though German authorities warn that it is bad luck to find a dropped needle in the street if it still has a length of black thread attached to it. If a pregnant woman finds a needle, this is a sure sign that she will give birth to a girl (if she finds a PIN she will have a boy). It is also unlucky to say the word 'needle' first thing in the morning. Caution should also be taken when lending a needle to a friend: to protect the friendship, the owner should first prick themselves with the needle. Witches are said to prize needles that have been used to sew FUNERAL shrouds as they are useful in casting spells of the darker variety.

If a needle breaks into two while being used this is thought to guarantee good luck for the wearer of the garment being worked upon, while if the needle breaks into three pieces an offer of marriage can be expected. Much the same tradition applies to the needles in modern sewing-machines: if these break the operator can look forward to a piece of good news, specifically a legacy. It is, however, a bad omen for a seamstress to break her needle when working on a WEDDING DRESS, which will endanger the happiness of the marriage – one counter-measure that may be taken if she actually pricks herself is to leave a tiny smear of blood on the dress itself.

A macabre love charm common to both sides of the Atlantic advises a girl to stab a corpse with her needle, then to cover the needle in soil taken from a grave and to wrap it in a length of winding-sheet: this will guarantee her success with the partner of her choice. Alternatively, in order to fetch an absent lover back she must prick the ring finger of her left hand with her needle, write her initials and those of her beloved in her blood, draw three circles around them and then bury the needle: the lover in question will make an appearance within three days. Another procedure by which a girl may gain influence over her lover is to pierce a CANDLE with seven needles and then let it burn completely down while reciting prayers to the Virgin Mary. This will ensure that the partner in question falls helplessly in love with her; it also has the useful side-effect of making him catastrophically impotent with other women.

**nest** The fact that BIRDS often pick up strands of human HAIR in making their nests has the unfortunate result of causing severe HEADACHES to afflict the erstwhile owner of the hair. An Austrian version of this superstition claims that the person from whom the hair came will break out in spots.

**net** A FISHERMAN's nets are obviously of paramount importance and are tradi-tionally treated with considerable respect, being periodically blessed and regularly attended to. Some fishermen will place a few small COINS in one of the knots in their nets, or else in one of the corks, to placate Neptune in return for the bounty he allows them. Other fishermen avoid putting out their nets on All Saints' Day, believing that the only things they will catch on that inauspicious date will be CORPSES.

**nettle** Stinging weed, reputed to have the power to ward off LIGHTNING and to bring courage to those in danger. Another superstition advises that if anyone suffering from a FEVER (or a friend standing in) pulls a nettle up by its roots, while intoning their name and those of their parents, they will imme-diately be cured. Nettle tea is credited with the power to purify the BLOOD. Consuming nettle seeds will negate the effects of various poisons and stings and will also heal damage done by the bite of a mad DOG.

A somewhat drastic remedy for a nose-bleed (see BLOOD; NOSE) involves pack-ing the nostril with stinging nettles (a less excruciating procedure involves placing a bruised dead-nettle on the back of the neck). Sufferers from RHEUMATISM, meanwhile, have been known to thrash the affected limb with stinging nettles in the belief that this will ease the problem, and people who are losing their HAIR may try brushing it the wrong way using a comb coated in nettle juice. The most efficacious nettles, incidentally, are said to be those that grow in patches where sun-light never falls.

The relieving of nettle stings by rub-bing the site with a DOCK leaf is among the best known of all folk remedies. In some areas those who have been stung may recite 'In dock out nettle' or a varia-tion while applying the soothing leaf. A Lincolnshire tradition adds that nettles only grow where human URINE has spill-ed on the ground.

*See also* PARSLEY.

**new moon**  *see* MOON.

**New Year**  The beginning of a new year is widely celebrated as a time of great magical significance, and every society has its own rituals associated with the event. Perhaps the best known of all the New Year superstitions in the Western world is the business of 'first footing'. Apparently a Scottish invention, the 'first footer' is the first man to cross the threshold after the hour of midnight has struck: if he is dark-haired and carries with him such propitious objects as a piece of COAL, BREAD, SALT and MONEY, the good luck of the household is guaranteed for the whole year ahead. If, however, the first footer is blond or red-headed, bad luck will befall the house; if the first footer is female this is even worse, as she ushers in only the direst misfortune.

In an ideal world the first footer will be a stranger to all present and on no account must he be cross-eyed (*see* EVIL EYE) or flat-footed or have EYEBROWS that meet in the middle. Once let into the house, he may then be shown out again by the back door, thus symbolically letting the old year out. In the event that no suitable first footer presents himself, the owner of a house should carry a piece of coal into his own home early on New Year's Day. Historical variations include regional traditions that have the person concerned entering the house on Christmas Day (in which case, in Yorkshire at least, he was referred to as the 'Lucky Bird').

Other New Year superstitions depend on the notion that whatever happens at this particular time sets the pattern for the rest of the year. It is unlucky, therefore, to see the New Year in with no food or drink in the cupboards – they will remain bare over the ensuing twelve months. The same applies to money. Some people similarly contend that the fire should not be allowed to go out during this first night of the year, lest the hearth remain cold permanently. Likewise, it is important that before anything is allowed out of the house (even the ashes from the fire or the dust from the floor) something must be brought in – indeed, in many areas people will show reluctance to throw away anything at all during New Year's Day for fear of throwing their luck away with it.

Rising early is a good idea, and to ensure a busy and profitable year at work (*see* BUSINESS) all those in employment should do something during New Year that reflects their work in some way, even if they take New Year's Day itself off (it is, incidentally, very unlucky to do any serious work on this day). Wearing something new on New Year's Day, meanwhile, promotes the chances of receiving further new CLOTHING in the year ahead. By much the same token, New Year is a bad time to pay money or to make loans, lend precious belongings or break anything. Ideally, any outstanding debts should be settled by New Year's Eve to ensure that further debts are not incurred in the year to come. WASHING clothes on New Year's Day is inadvisable, for one of the family will themselves be 'washed away' in the months ahead.

The practice of 'ringing in' the New Year on church bells dates back centuries and is echoed in the wild shouting, singing and other noise-making that takes place at midnight. This is more than just high spirits: the noise is supposed to drive away demons and other evil spirits and get the New Year off to a good start. Partygoers, meanwhile, are advised that they should avoid speaking ill of the dying year until it is actually over in order to preserve their luck, and that to give their own fortune a boost they should consume the very last drops of any bottle that has been opened. If the party drink runs out, they may also like to know of the superstition which claims that WELL water turns to wine on New Year's Eve.

Attention should be paid to the WEATHER during the early hours of New Year's Day. If the WIND blows from the north, bad weather is in store; if it comes from the south, fine weather and prosperous times lie ahead; if it blows from the east, famine or some other calamity is on the way; if it blows from the west, the year will witness plentiful supplies of MILK and FISH but will also see the death of a very distinguished personage. If there is no wind at all, a joyful and prosperous year may be expected by all.

Lastly, BABIES born on New Year's Day will grow up with luck always on their side.

**nightingale**  Famed as one of the most sweet-voiced of all birds, the nightingale is associated with several long-established traditions. An English superstition dating back at least to the Middle Ages maintains that if the nightingale sings before the CUCKOO is first heard it is a portent of success in love. It is also said that anyone who dines on nightingale tongues will enjoy greatly improved vocal skills and, further, that consuming the bird's flesh will help to overcome sleepiness.

**nightjar**  Superstition regards the nightjar, with its nocturnal habits and eerie cry, with a jaundiced eye. Called the lychfowl or corpsefowl in parts of central and northern England, and the whippoorwill in the USA, the nightjar is supposed by some to be the reincarnation of a child's soul that has died unbaptised. It is generally considered unlucky to hear the cry of the nightjar after dark as this is a premonition of death, and worse still if the bird alights on a house, for someone within is thus fated shortly to die. More optimistic, though, is the US tradition that anyone hearing the bird's first call in the spring may make a wish, which will almost certainly come true.

In ancient times it was alleged that the nightjar had the habit of drinking milk from the udders of GOATS, with the consequence that the unfortunate goat went blind. In the West Country it is further claimed that the nightjar is a favourite disguise of witches and can only be killed by shooting with a SILVER bullet.

**nightmare**  Superstition maintains that nightmares are sent by the DEVIL and his minions to trouble the dreams of sleepers. Such demons steal into bedrooms in the dead of night, often taking the form of spectral HORSES (hence 'nightmare').

Superstition offers various remedies for those unfortunate enough to be plagued by nightmares. These include pinning one's SOCKS in the shape of a CROSS to the end of the bed or else placing a KNIFE or some other metal object nearby, on the grounds that the latent magic of IRON or steel will see off malevolent spirits. Carefully placing one's SHOES under the bed so that the toes point outwards is also said to be effective. Other precautions include sleeping with the hands crossed on the breast and fixing little straw CROSSES to the four corners of the bed. Any lingering ill effects resulting from nightmares may be dismissed by SPITTING three times on waking up.

**nightshade**  The poisonous nature of the various nightshade plants is reflected in the superstitions concerning them. Alleged to be a favourite ingredient of witches' spells, deadly nightshade was, in former times, consumed in small quantities by those wishing to see into the future; too large a dose, of course, could induce MADNESS and even prove fatal. It was also said to be an ingredient in the mysterious FLYING OINTMENT with which witches smeared their bodies in order to acquire the power of flight. Sprigs of woody nightshade festooned about the person or around the home will, however, keep evil spirits away and may also be used to protect livestock from the threat of WITCHCRAFT and disease.

**nipple**  According to one central European superstition, certain information about a man may be obtained by careful observation of his nipples. If they are pink he has never fathered a child, but if they are brown he has already sired offspring.

**north**  Superstition assigns various qualities to the directions of the compass, particularly to the north. Perhaps because the north is, in the northern hemisphere at least, associated with cold weather, it is considered the least inviting of the four directions. The north side of churches is the least favoured for BURIAL, being cast in shadow much of the time; some churches reserve the luckier south door for the entrance of brides and others, while the north – or 'Devil's' – door is reserved for letting demons out during CHRISTENING services. In some circumstances, however, the north is lucky. All travellers should take at least a few steps in a northerly direction before setting off on a journey, and unmarried girls are advised that failure to glance north when leaving the house in the morning risks the punishment of never finding a husband.

**nose**  According to the pseudo-science of PHYSIOGNOMY, the business of deducing traits of character from the physical appearance, the shape of the nose reveals something of a person's hidden qualities. The French advise that a short nose is indicative of a lazy nature. A long nose, conversely, suggests a proud and courageous nature. A pointed nose signifies a tempestuous character and a good memory, while a fat nose bespeaks loyalty and honesty. Those with turned-up noses are said to be daring and lustful. Men with large noses are reputed to be endowed with large sexual organs, and the same applies to women with long thin noses. Any child who has a nose with a blue vein running down it is fated to die young, according to US superstition, and a similar vein running across the nose is also a portent of death (though European tradition claims this simply means that the person concerned will never marry).

Whatever the shape of the nose, it is linked with the magic of the BREATH and there is evidence that in primitive times some peoples actually worshipped the nose as a symbol of the life-force. To guard against evil spirits gaining access to the body via the nose it was sometimes pierced with an AMULET or RING to bar entry.

An itching nose is a sign that the person concerned may shortly expect a LETTER or will become embroiled in an argument or fight. Other interpretations suggest that he or she will soon be meeting a new lover, receiving a KISS, getting cursed, becoming angry, shaking hands with a fool or colliding with a gatepost. A Canadian rhyme lists the portents of an itching nose thus:

You'll be mad,
See a stranger,
Kiss a fool,
Or be in danger.

Nosebleeds are on the whole unlucky omens unless just one drop of blood falls from the left nostril, which is taken to signify the imminent arrival of a large sum of money. Blood from the right nostril is ominous as it predicts the death of a member of the family. A nose that bleeds when someone of the opposite sex is present may be taken as proof of love.

*See also* BLOOD; COLD; SNEEZE.

**nosebleed**  *see* BLOOD; NOSE.

**numbers**  Certain numbers, particularly single figures, have always been considered to have magical significance. In ancient times, the science of numerology allowed for divination of the future through the use of numbers. Ever since then people have put great faith in 'lucky' numbers, while avoiding contact with those that are thought ill-omened – particularly, of course, the number THIRTEEN. Countless spells dictate that certain actions or words must be repeated a given number of times, often three, seven or nine. Numbers have their own sexes, even numbers being 'male' and odd ones being 'female' (odd numbers are luckier).

The number one is generally thought lucky, being associated with God and with the SUN. Children born on the first day of the month are considered blessed with good luck, and one is among the most popular house numbers.

The number two is also lucky, representing the concept of balance and harmony – though it is less so for women.

The number three is reputed to have special powers, largely because of the Christian concept of the Trinity. The fact that in ancient Greece the prophetess Pythia stood on a three-legged stool may account for the fact that this number often features in rituals connected with the business of divination. Many people talk of being 'third time lucky', believing that the third attempt at something is more likely to succeed than the first two attempts. More pessimistically, it is widely held that ACCIDENTS (and FU-NERALS) always happen in threes. Authorities suggest that where the number three has connotations of bad luck this is in recollection of the biblical story of Peter denying Christ three times.

The number four has no particular significance in the Western world, but is regarded as unlucky in the Far East where it represents death. It is otherwise interpreted as symbolising the material foundation of the world, as well as the seasons and the four directions of the compass.

The number five is another magical number used in many spells and charms. The ancient Greeks avoided speaking their word for 'five' as they feared its influence, and it is said to have been sacred to the Mayan civilisation. Christ suffered five wounds, and the number features in various ways in Christian churches. It is also said to symbolise the five senses, fire, love and marriage.

The number six has a mixed reputation and represents creation. In Judaeo-Christian symbolism, it is associated with the six-pointed star of David. People born on the sixth day of the month will enjoy prophetic gifts.

The number seven is associated with the supernatural and will bring success to any project connected with it. God created the world in seven days, man lives through seven 'ages' and in ancient times there were thought to be seven planets. The seventh son of a seventh son is said to have the gift of second sight and will make a good doctor, having special powers of healing. If the date of a person's birth is divisible by seven, he or she will enjoy good luck throughout life. The myth of the 'seven-year itch', said to tempt adults who have been in the same relationship for that length of time to form new partnerships, is probably derived from the ancient notion that major changes in a person's life occur after every seven (or nine) years. This idea is welcomed by some parents, who console themselves that badly behaved children will change their ways once they reach the age of seven.

The number eight has few magical associations, though it represents the material aspects of existence.

The number nine, being the number of months between conception and birth in humans and also the multiple of three by three, is thought to be very lucky and features in many magical spells, especially in those concerned with healing. To this day, doctors of conventional medicine will ask patients to intone 'ninety-nine' in throat examinations.

The number ten is generally beneficent, being the number of the biblical Commandments.

The number eleven has unlucky connotations.

The number twelve is lucky due to its religious significance, being the number of Christ's disciples.

With the notable exception of thirteen, numbers over twelve are less significant. Some people, however, maintain that forty is a 'dangerous age', when husbands are vulnerable to the temptation of turning their lives upside down at the onset of middle age. The number 666, meanwhile, is traditionally considered to be the most evil of all numbers, being the 'number of the Beast' – the DEVIL's number.

Specific traditions involving numbers include the Jewish superstition that adding up the numerical value of the letters in a husband and wife's names (by equating each letter with its position in the alphabet) will reveal which of them will die first: if the total makes an even number it will be the husband, if odd, the wife. According to numerologists past and present, much the same process may be undertaken to reveal the essential traits of a person's true character. The numbers relating to the letters in a person's names are added up and these are then added together until a single number is left which has certain pre-ordained attributes. In brief, people whose names produce the number one in this way have dominating and ambitious personalities; two denotes a kinder and gentler character; three signifies high intelligence and an artistic temperament; four suggests dependability, if a lack of originality; five indicates intelligence, impatience, sociability and sexuality; six bespeaks a nature in harmony with itself; seven is the number of the intellectual; eight denotes the powerful and wealthy; and nine suggests idealism and high achievement.

Counting is itself a magical act that can be turned to one's advantage. If afflicted by WARTS, for instance, simply counting them and telling the number to a stranger will cause them to disappear. In other circumstances, though, the act of counting is unlucky: counting up one's money, one's cattle, one's children, the number of fish one has caught or other blessings and belongings is considered a questioning of God's bounty and may be punished by misfortune. Finally, many localities boast ancient STONE circles and accompanying legends to the effect that it is impossible to count the individual stones and to reach the same number twice. In some cases it is said that anyone who none the less attempts the task will be struck dead or taken ill before the task is completed.

**nun**  *see* CLERGY.

**nurse**  *see* APRON; DOCTOR; HOSPITAL.

**nut**  Traditional symbols of life and fruitfulness, nuts are therefore emblems of good luck. One common superstition has it that it is very lucky to find two kernels in the same nutshell; if this happens, one of the nuts should be eaten and the other given to a friend or tossed over the left shoulder while a wish is made. Such a 'double' nut may also be carried in the pocket to guard against TOOTHACHE and to ward off WITCHCRAFT.

A good harvest of nuts is interpreted in many areas as a prediction that unusually large numbers of BABIES are on their way in the locality. One suggested explanation for this notion is that wives in past centuries were able to excuse themselves from their husbands for hours at a time on the pretext of gathering nuts, thus having the opportunity to meet their lovers and run the risk of becoming pregnant. No one, incidentally, should go nutgathering on 14 September, as this is the date that the DEVIL goes out in search of nuts (authorities in Sussex extend this to nut-gathering on any Sunday).

The concept of the nut as a symbol of fruitfulness undoubtedly lay behind the now defunct custom by which bags of hazelnuts were presented to brides by elderly married relatives with children as the happy couple left the church. This custom dated back to the Romans and was done in the belief that it would promote the fertility of the newly-weds (the tossing of RICE eventually replaced the tradition).

Nuts may be employed in the engrossing business of divining the future course of a love affair. A nut should be named after each partner and then placed in the fire or on the bars of the grate. Various deductions may logically be made from what happens to each nut: ideally, they will stay close together as they burn with a bright and cheerful flame. In some regions the nuts are placed in the flames while the person utters the words:

If he/she loves me, pop and fly,
If he/she hates me, lie and die.

Conclusions are made accordingly. The practice is particularly identified with HALLOWE'EN.

*See also* ACORN; ALMOND; HAZEL; NUTMEG; WALNUT.

**nutmeg**   Superstition claims that this spice has various luck-giving properties. Sprinkling a little on a competition entry or on one's lottery numbers, for instance, is sure to promote one's chances of winning. Dreaming of nutmeg, meanwhile, constitutes notice of changes in the dreamer's waking life. Nutmeg also has its uses in folk medicine: if carried about the person, it will ward off RHEUMATISM and BOILS, improve the eyesight (*see* EYE) and eradicate unwanted freckles. Caution should be taken by the single girl, however: if she should carry nutmeg about on her person she will be fated to marry an old man.

**oak** Of all trees, the oak is the one with the most powerful and sacred reputation. Venerated by various pre-Christian cultures, including those of the Druids and the Vikings, the oak retains much of its mystique in modern times and the emblem, though essentially a pagan symbol, is found even in churches. The fact that the oak tends to be struck by LIGHTNING as much as, if not more often than, other trees has promoted its association with supernatural powers and made it sacred to the thunder-wielding Norse god Thor. A southern English rhyme sensibly warns:

Beware the oak,
It draws the stroke.

Elsewhere, somewhat perversely, the tree is actually recommended as a suitable shelter in the event of a thunderstorm. Keeping boughs of oak (particularly if taken from a tree that has been struck by a lightning bolt), or a few ACORNS, in the house is reputed to protect the home from lightning. Standing beneath an oak, or wearing oak leaves, is further said to furnish protection from evil spirits and from WITCHCRAFT.

In Cornwall, superstition advises that hammering a NAIL into an oak tree will relieve the pain of TOOTHACHE, while in Wales rubbing sores with a piece of oak bark on Midsummer Day will help them to heal. Embracing an oak tree, meanwhile, is enough to cure hernias and to promote the fertility of couples unable to have children. Oak trees planted at CROSSROADS are considered to have the most effective healing powers.

In some areas memories survive of particular oaks that were once used for the solemnisation of marriages in pagan times, and even after this custom was prohibited newly-weds often danced round these trees to promote their luck. Other places still boast 'gospel oaks', where Rogation processions, marking the Sundays before Ascension Day, once paused for readings from the gospels. The oak acquired a reputation as a royal tree in the seventeenth century after the future Charles II hid in one to escape his Parliamentarian pursuers after the battle of Worcester. In honour of this event, loyal subjects took to wearing oak leaves to proclaim their Royalist sympathies on what became Royal Oak Day after the restoration of the monarchy in 1660. Anyone failing to comply was beaten with stinging NETTLES.

In past centuries it was thought to be reckless in the extreme to cut down an oak tree, especially if it bore the sacred MISTLETOE. Many people believed that if an oak was felled its screams would be heard up to a mile away. Back in more brutal times, in pagan Germany, any man who harmed an oak was punished by having his navel hacked out and nailed to the tree; he was then forced to walk round and round the trunk, with the result that his intestines were slowly pulled from his body.

Like the acorn, the oak-apple too has magical significance. It is considered very unlucky to find a WORM in an oak-apple: one portends poverty and two an imminent illness. If a fly is found inside, WAR will break out in the coming year; if a

SPIDER is concealed within, a time of pestilence is nigh.

The choice of clusters of oak leaves as a military decoration hails back to ancient Rome, when soldiers who had performed some act of bravery or selflessness were honoured with the presentation of an oak leaf crown.

**oats** In Scotland, where oats have long enjoyed a central place in the national diet, at HALLOWE'EN a girl may use them to divine information about her future married life. If she pulls an oat stalk from the sheaf, the number of grains attached to the stalk indicate the number of children she may expect – but if the top grain is missing she is destined to lose her VIRGINITY before she is married.

**oil** A superstition dating back to ancient Greece claims, probably in reflection of the value of lamp oil, that it is most unlucky to spill any – a crime that will be punished by the loss of all one's wealth. OLIVE oil, meanwhile, has been widely credited with various medicinal properties. Taking olive oil nine mornings in succession, for instance, will promote virility and cure DRUNKENNESS. Another tradition claims that floating a drop of oil on some water is a good way of detecting the presence of any evil spirit: if the droplet splits up, demons are abroad.

**olive** The long-lived olive tree, common around the Mediterranean, has been associated with peace, prosperity, beauty and other positive qualities since classical times. In keeping with this beneficent reputation, the olive is still supposed to offer protection against WITCHCRAFT, LIGHTNING and other evils.

*See also* OIL.

**onion** The onion, with its pungent smell, eye-watering properties and strong taste, is the object of a host of widely held superstitious beliefs, not least in the lore of love. Placing an onion under the pillow is recommended for those who wish to see their future partners in their dreams. To decide between potential lovers, the person concerned should inscribe their names on two onions and leave them in a warm place: the first to sprout carries the name of the more promising prospect. Other magical properties of the onion include the power to ward off SNAKES and witches, who will be repulsed by the smell.

In medicinal lore, it is said that carrying an onion is excellent for the health, particularly for the avoidance of COLDS. Likewise, hanging an onion up in a room – was once commonly done in times of plague – will help to maintain a generally healthy atmosphere (scientists concede that this is basically true as a cut or peeled onion will attract germs to itself and thus away from any human occupants). Leaving a cut onion about the house, however, has its drawbacks, because it will engender quarrels between the various occupants.

Other applications for onions include the treatment of dog bites, hangovers, insomnia, earache (*see* DEAFNESS), CHILBLAINS, TOOTHACHE and FEVER. In some parts of the southern USA, meanwhile, it is maintained that rubbing the scalp with onion will cure BALDNESS. In days gone by, when schoolboys were subject to regular beatings, a popular superstition had it that rubbing oneself with onion juice before being caned would prevent the pain being felt. If onion was rubbed on the cane itself, it would break at the first blow and might even cause the pain to be felt by the person delivering the punishment.

When onions seem to have a thicker skin than usual this is a sure sign that a severe winter is on the way.

**onyx** BLACK gemstone, linked by superstitious people with the darker forces in nature. The stone is associated with WITCHCRAFT and sorcery and features in various malevolent and death-dealing spells. Owners of onyx will find themselves prone to NIGHTMARES and plagued by worry in their waking hours.

Some authorities express particular unease at the idea of pregnant women wearing onyx, though conversely there are those who claim that onyx brings lovers closer together and promotes a cheerful frame of mind. An Indian superstition, meanwhile, advises that possession of onyx magically restores a person's immune system.

**opal** Among the various BIRTHSTONES, opal is considered perhaps the most unlucky. It brings luck to those born in October, but is otherwise dangerous to own. It is particularly important that ENGAGEMENT rings do not incorporate opal, as this threatens an early widowhood. Tradition has it that opal should be worn with DIAMONDS to negate its baleful influence, but also that the opal will lose its shine if its owner dies. Properties of the opal include the power to improve eyesight (*see* EYES) and the gift of INVISIBILITY; if worn by blondes, opals will help the HAIR to keep its colour much longer. It is also said that opals will turn pale if brought into the presence of poison. Rare black opals are considered rather more lucky than the more common and ominous blue-green variety.

**orange** The orange has long been prized for its power to promote fertility and love, traditions that sprang up originally in the warm climates in which oranges naturally flourish but have since been adopted anywhere that the tree has been transplanted. Superstition advises that lovers who exchange gifts of oranges will be drawn even closer together. If a young man seeks to win a girl's love, he should prick an orange all over and then sleep with it tucked firmly into his armpit. The following day he must offer the orange to the girl of his choice, and if she eats it she is sure to feel passionately about him. Similarly, brides are warmly encouraged to carry orange blossom at their WEDDINGS as this will guarantee good luck, especially in regard to having children.

**orchid** Venerated by plant-growers for its exquisite beauty, the orchid is of interest to non-gardeners as an APHRODISIAC. This tradition has its roots in classical folklore. In ancient times women wishing to excite the sexual ardour of their lovers would surreptitiously offer them drinks of GOAT's milk combined with the larger of an orchid's two tubers. If they wished to take the edge off their lover's sexual appetites they did exactly the same, only this time using the smaller tuber. By the same token, men who ate the large tubers of orchids were expected to sire male children, while women who ate the smaller tubers were more likely to give birth to girls.

**orpine** Purple-flowered plant, sometimes known as live-long or midsummer men, which is reputed to have the power to safeguard the luck of the household. Hung up in houses on MIDSUMMER'S EVE, it is thought to ward off LIGHTNING and to keep disease from the house as long as it remains green. Lovers may also use orpine for the purposes of divination. They should take a stalk of orpine on Midsummer's Eve and fix it firmly upright somewhere in the house before going to bed. In the morning, if the stalk bends to the right a lover is faithful, but if it bends to the left then he or she is untrue. Alternatively, two stalks can be set up, one for each of the two lovers. If in the morning these 'midsummer men' have bent towards one another, the affair will go from strength to strength; if, however, one of the stalks has withered, one of the partners will soon die.

**oven** According to a superstition of Jewish origin, it is unlucky to leave an oven completely empty at any time since the cook may then find that he or she has no food to cook in it in the future. Leaving a baking tray or some other kitchen utensil in the oven is, however, sufficient to prevent any such ill luck.
*See also* COOKING.

**overlooking** *see* EVIL EYE.

**owl** Being essentially a nocturnal bird, the owl is regarded with mistrust by the superstitious. To see an owl or to hear it hooting is unlucky (especially in daylight), as is looking into an owl's nest, which will result in the person concerned suffering from melancholy for the rest of his or her days. Should an owl be heard to hoot near the home, one remedy is to toss some SALT into the fire to negate the threatened ill fortune. If this happens when someone in the house is ill, some authorities suggest that efforts should be made to kill the owl and then to place the body on the patient's chest. In France, owls hooting within the hearing of a pregnant woman mean that the baby will be a girl. In Welsh folklore, meanwhile, an owl hooting among houses reveals the fact that an unmarried girl nearby is about to lose her VIRGINITY.

Sightings of owls are usually considered omens of death or of other serious misfortune. If an owl appears when a child is born or if it settles on the roof of a house this is particularly to be lamented, threatening ill luck. In the Shetlands, farmers believe that their COWS will give bloodied milk and then die if an owl brushes against them.

Despite their rather gloomy reputation, owls do have their uses as safeguards against evil. In times gone by it was common practice to nail the bodies of dead owls on barn doors to protect livestock and to fend off the damaging influence of thunderstorms (*see* STORM), while warriors carrying an owl's heart were assured of renewed courage in battle. Feeding a drunkard owl EGGS will cure the weakness for alcohol. If consumed in the form of a soup they will ward off fits (*see* EPILEPSY), cure WHOOPING COUGH and restore grey HAIR to its original colour. Eating charred and powdered

owls' eggs will also help those with weak eyesight (*see* EYES). A paste of salted and baked owl, combined with boar's grease, was formerly recommended as an ointment for the treatment of GOUT. In Germany, those suffering from the bite of a mad DOG are advised to keep the heart and right foot of an owl in their left armpit to prevent the onset of rabies.

**ox** Most superstitions concerning oxen duplicate those associated with COWS and BULLS. One tradition linked specifically to the ox, however, is the contention recorded in eastern parts of England that eating the animal's spinal cord can make a person go deaf.

**oyster** The notion that oysters have strong APHRODISIAC properties is among the best known of all superstitions concerning food. The idea – possibly inspired by a fancied resemblance between the appearance of an oyster and the female genitals – dates back to the Romans, who feasted on oysters at orgies. Almost as well known is the theory that one should only eat oysters in months that have the letter 'r' in them (this idea confines their consumption to the months of September to April, those of the English oyster season – though oysters are now often imported from abroad all year round). Other traditions include the idea that oysters 'wax and wane' with the MOON and the belief, originating in Yorkshire, that dropping into the ear saliva that has been kept in an oyster shell buried in manure for two days will cure DEAFNESS. In the USA it is supposed to be lucky to carry an oyster shell about one's person, and English tradition claims that eating an oyster on 5 August (St James's Day) guarantees that the person concerned will never be without food.

# P

**palm** As an important Christian symbol, the palm tree has long had significance for the superstitious. In early Christian times palms were carried as a symbol of martyrdom, and palm fronds are still carried during Palm Sunday services to commemorate Christ's entry into Jerusalem. In past centuries, in countries where palms did not grow people often substituted sprigs of HAZEL, WILLOW and other native plants. It is said to be most unlucky to allow palms or their alternatives into the house before Palm Sunday itself, but once in the house they will protect the occupants from evil over the coming year. The WEATHER on Palm Sunday itself should be carefully noted: if it is fine, a good harvest will surely follow later in the year.

**palmistry** Since ancient times it has been believed that a person's character and destiny may be divined by examination of the palms of their hands. Every aspect of the palm – its shape, its colour and the lines upon it – are studied by those who claim proficiency in these matters.

In terms of shape, a long HAND indicates a meticulous and thoughtful personality, while a small hand denotes impetuosity and intuitiveness and a big hand a cautious character. Narrow palms suggest selfishness, while those with wide palms are sociable and gentle. The shape of the FINGERS is also relevant, long thin ones denoting an artistic temperament and crooked ones suggesting untrustworthiness. Smooth fingers indicate alert minds, while individuals with somewhat pointed fingers have strong sensual appetites.

The shape of the fingertips is important too. If they are conical the owner has an intellectual frame of mind, but if they are broad at the tip then the person concerned is energetic and loves to be constantly busy and on the move. Those with flattened fingertips are given to hard work and have conventional tastes and a realistic outlook on the world.

The shape of the THUMB is crucial. The lower half relates to a person's reasoning ability, while the upper half concerns willpower. A short thumb indicates an inhibited and weak character, but a long one suggests high achievement and confidence. Straight thumbs are a sign of independence of spirit and sincerity; while curved thumbs reveal impulsiveness and generosity.

Most information, however, is obtained by 'reading' the lines on a palm. Broadly speaking, the left hand is supposed to reveal inherited character while the right hand reflects acquired characteristics. The most important line of all is the life line on the left palm, which traces the edge of the Mount of Venus, around the base of the thumb, and ends at the wrist. The length of this line is said to correspond directly to a person's lifespan, and a short life line may suggest lengthy periods of ill health (though not necessarily an early death). This line also reveals much about a person's vitality and sexual drive: the deeper and more curved the line the stronger the constitution and the person's love of life. Authorities on palmistry insist that life lines will alter as a person's circumstances change in response, for instance, to successful medical treatment.

The head line runs more or less across the centre of the palm and refers to a person's mental faculties. The most logical and practical individuals will have fairly straight head lines, while artistic types will have head lines with a pronounced curve. If the head line actually touches the life line this is a sign of a sensitive personality. If it ends in a fork, the person concerned has strong powers of expression.

The heart line runs above and almost parallel to the head line and concerns a person's emotional being. A curved line suggests a warm and friendly character, while a straight line bespeaks a cold and reserved individual.

The line of fate runs vertically down the left palm. In the rare case of a long and unbroken line of fate, this suggests that a person is exceptionally lucky in all his or her dealings. If the line peters out below the middle finger this indicates a prudent personality given to hard work and saving money. If it ends under the first finger the owner is ambitious, if below the fourth finger he or she yearns for fame in the arts.

The marriage line (or lines) is a short line at the very edge of the palm. If deep and straight the individual will have a happy married life; small lines extending upwards from this indicate the number of children that he or she will have. Other lines may be read to reveal information about the success a person may expect in life and to glean further details of their health as well as analyses of their passions, future travels and healing powers.

The fact that some medical authorities have claimed that it is possible to detect signs of ILLNESS in the hands long before actual symptoms emerge suggests that there may be at least some scientific basis for palmistry.

**palpitations** An involuntary fluttering sensation of the heart, the eye or the muscles, which is said by some to be an omen. Palpitations on the right side of the body signify good luck, but if they are felt on the left side of the body misfortune is in store.

**pancake** Traditionally cooked on Shrove Tuesday ('Pancake Day') in Christian countries throughout the Western world, pancakes are generally considered lucky, possibly because they may contain a variety of lucky ingredients such as herbs. Eating a pancake on Shrove Tuesday, the last day before LENT, will ensure a person's luck in the coming twelve months and prevent them running out of money or food. The pancake must be eaten before eight o'clock in the evening, however, or bad luck will follow. Some people may offer a pancake to a COCK in the hope that he will turn it down and leave it to the HENS, in which case good luck will ensue; if he eats it himself, though, this will usher in misfortune. One tradition claims that the number of hens who join the cock in eating a pancake signifies the number of years a girl must wait before she is married. The tradition of tossing pancakes, incidentally, is said to have been derived either from the barbaric sport of throwing fighting cocks at each other on Shrove Tuesday or else from the age-old custom of turning PROSTITUTES out of their lodgings on this holy date.

**pansy** Brightly coloured ornamental flower, which is widely grown in gardens. Gardeners are warned that picking a pansy when the weather is fine will bring on a rainstorm.

**paper bag** A superstition of obscure but probably relatively recent origins advises that it is unlucky to burst a paper bag indoors.

**parsley** Like most other herbs, parsley is credited with a variety of magical properties. Ancient superstition links parsley with the DEVIL (perhaps a relic of the Roman custom of planting parsley on graves), and it is said that only wicked people can grow good parsley. Furthermore, the seeds must be sown nine times before they will come up because the Devil claims the first eight sowings; while the long period of germination is attributed to the fact that the seeds go to Hell and back before sprouting. Parsley must never be planted by a stranger and it is always best for the seed to be sown by a woman, as this will encourage its growth. A garden where parsley flourishes is therefore believed by some to belong to a household where the woman rules the roost. A note of caution is, however, sounded by the tradition that a young woman who sows parsley seed will soon fall pregnant. Eating parsley or placing some in the reproductive tract will, though, prevent or end pregnancy, and nursing mothers should not eat it lest their milk dry up. Once successfully grown, parsley should never be given away to a friend or replanted elsewhere, as this invites bad luck and possibly even death: to be on the safe side it should always be grown from seed.

Parsley was once considered an antidote to poison and adding a sprig to garnish a dish, as done by cooks to this very day, was originally intended as a gesture of good faith. Care should be taken in bringing parsley into contact with GLASS, however, as this may mysteriously weaken the glass and cause it to shatter. In medicinal lore, parsley seeds sprinkled on the head will cure BALDNESS and, if consumed before a bout of drinking, will enable a person to resist the effects of DRUNKENNESS a little longer. Chewing parsley will relieve RHEUMATISM and a little parsley fed to livestock will cure disease. Carrying a little dried parsley, meanwhile, will fend off the unpleasant symptoms of nausea.

By old English tradition, curious children are sometimes informed that baby girls are found in parsley beds, while baby boys are born under GOOSEBERRY bushes or else in beds of NETTLES. Really insistent children are further enlightened with the information that the doctor digs up the new babies with a golden spade.

**parting** Various superstitions surround the simple act of saying goodbye to someone. These include never saying the word 'goodbye' more than once, which threatens a rift in the relationship, never saying goodbye over a GATE or STILE and never watching someone out of sight as this means the two parties will never meet again (see TRAVEL). Such traditions are strongest among the spouses of FISHERMEN, pilots and other people engaged in potentially hazardous activities, although lovers are often similarly sensitive to the dangers involved.

**pasque flower** The purple-flowered anemone, which is widely grown for its attractive bloom. A southern English tradition of considerable antiquity claims that pasque flowers only grow where Saxon blood has been spilt, though in the Midlands they are known as Dane's flower and are reputed to grow where invading Danish warriors fell. Dye from pasque flowers was once used to decorate Easter eggs.

**passing bell**   see BELL.

**pavement** Ever since proper pavements were laid in towns and villages boys and girls (and even adults) have played the game of avoiding stepping on the cracks between them for fear of some dreadful fate befalling them. Over the years supposed punishments for such carelessness have ranged from giving birth to black babies to being eaten by bears round the next corner.

**pea** The pea is a harbinger of good luck and may also be used for the purposes of love divination. Finding a peapod with just one pea inside is very lucky. It is similarly fortunate to find a pod with nine peas inside, in which case the pod may be thrown over the right shoulder while a wish is made. Such a pod may also be used to glean information about a future partner. If a girl places the pod over her door, the first unmarried man to enter is destined to become her husband (a variation advises that the man who enters merely shares the same name as the husband-to-be). A pod containing nine peas may also be employed to cure WARTS, being rubbed on the warts and then tossed away with the words 'Wart, wart, dry away.'

**peach**  Chinese superstition gives the peach an exalted place, interpreting the fruit as a symbol of long life and immortality and crediting it with the power to ward off evil spirits. In the Western world, the peach tree is said to give warning of cattle epidemics by shedding its leaves early.

**peacock**  Though revered by Hindus as a sacred bird, the peacock is widely regarded as unlucky in Western tradition. In India it is believed that it will eat SNAKES and this idea at least has been absorbed in other cultures, one English superstition from Tudor times (when the peacock was considered a 'royal' bird) claiming that its cry scares off venomous animals.

The splendour of the peacock's feathers meant that it was depicted in art as a symbol of Heaven, but the 'eyes' on its tail have inspired more ominous associations. One legend claims that the eyes belong to the seven deadly sins, plucked out as a punishment by God. The seven deadly sins are, therefore, thought to lurk in the vicinity of the peacock, trying to get their eyes back, and the bird itself is consequently a harbinger of intense bad fortune. Another tradition links the eyes to the classical story of the giant Argus, who had a hundred eyes.

Peacock feathers should on no account be allowed indoors or worn as decoration, and ACTORS AND ACTRESSES are among those who express real fear about their presence and are likely to talk apprehensively of the EVIL EYE. Another suggested derivation of this taboo links it with the tradition that peacocks were kept in the temples of ancient Greece, where removal of their tail feathers was a crime punishable by death.

Other superstitions concerning the bird include the notion that, though proud of their plumage, peacocks are ashamed of their feet. Peacocks are also said to foretell the coming of RAIN, as a traditional rhyme indicates:

When the peacock loudly calls
Then look out for rain and squalls.

**pearl**  The link between pearls and the SEA means that the stone has a somewhat dubious reputation among the superstitious. Giving a BABY the gift of a pearl – the BIRTHSTONE for June – is said to guarantee the infant a long life, but to others pearls symbolise tears and are therefore unlucky, especially if worn by brides. Pearls are, however, supposed to have certain APHRODISIAC properties, and sleeping with a pearl beneath the pillow is reputed to help childless couples conceive. Medicinally speaking, wearing a pearl will cure MADNESS and prove beneficial in the treatment of JAUNDICE and snake and insect bites. A superstition with its tongue perhaps in its cheek adds that pearls will also cure depression in women.

**peewit**  *see* LAPWING.

**pendulum**  A weighted line that may be used for the purposes of dowsing or divination. The movements observed when gently swinging a gold RING on the end of a string or length of hair may be interpreted in different ways according to context. In an age when clocks and watches were a luxury, it was commonly said that a person could find out what time it was by letting a pendulum swing against the sides of a glass or goblet containing a little water: the number of times it struck the sides would give the hour of the day. Other applications over the years have included the settling of various questions, among them the identity of future spouses.

The best-known use of the pendulum today is the swinging of a WEDDING RING over the belly of a pregnant woman to determine the sex of her unborn child.

If the ring, which should be suspended by a strand of the woman's own hair, spins in a clockwise direction a boy may be expected; if in an anti-clockwise direction (or up and down rather than in a circle) it will be a girl. In answering other questions it is usual for a ring spinning in an anti-clockwise direction to be interpreted as a discouraging sign.

**penny** The humble penny has always been considered lucky. Many people are familiar with the tradition of carrying a penny about the person for luck, while others will toss one overboard on setting out to SEA in the belief that this will appease the marine gods and guarantee them a safe passage.

See also COIN; LUCKY PENNY; MONEY.

**peony** English superstition claims that the peony, named after Paeon, the Greek God of Healing, should be valued for its protective properties. SAILORS are advised that by burning a peony they can cause STORMS to subside, while the sick are recommended to wear a necklace made from peony roots to relieve such ailments as EPILEPSY and CRAMP. In children it is said to encourage the development of healthy TEETH.

**pepper** Though less important in terms of superstition than SALT, pepper none the less has its mystical significance. Supposedly an APHRODISIAC, it should not be eaten by anyone suffering from FEVER as it will only cause the problem to intensify. A US tradition holds that applying cotton wool dipped in black pepper to the ear will cure earache (see DEAFNESS) and, further, that eating whole chilli peppers will see off a COLD. Finally, sprinkling a little pepper on the chair of a guest will ensure that he or she does not overstay their welcome.

**periwinkle** Evergreen plant with a blue flower which has a somewhat dark reputation, being traditionally linked with WITCHCRAFT and death. The Italians used to adorn dead BABIES with garlands of periwinkle, and in former times here-tics burned at the stake were given periwinkle crowns. Maintaining the link with death, a Welsh tradition warns that anyone who picks a periwinkle from a grave will suffer for a whole year from NIGHTMARES about the dead person buried there. In Germany, the periwinkle is considered the flower of immortality. A more cheerful English superstition advises that if a man and a woman eat the leaves of a periwinkle together they will fall passionately in love.

In folk medicine, periwinkle leaves may be chewed to treat haemorrhages and TOOTHACHE. The plant may also be used in treatments for diabetes, and scientists have verified that it is in fact rich in valuable alkaloids.

**petticoat** A long-standing tradition has it that a girl whose petticoats show beneath her dress is loved more by her father than by her mother. Sleeping with one of her petticoats under the pillow will ensure that a girl enjoys dreams about her future husband. In the USA this might be attempted while reciting the following lines:

This Friday night while going to bed,
I put my petticoat under my head,
To dream of the living and not of the
    dead,
To dream of the man I am to wed,
The colour of his eyes, the colour of his
    hair,
The colour of the clothes he is to wear,
And the night the wedding is to be.

According to the Portuguese, meanwhile, a woman who fears she is threatened by the EVIL EYE can escape harm by wearing seven petticoats at once.

See also UNDERWEAR.

**petting stone**    see BARRING THE WAY.

**photograph** The art of photography may be a relatively new phenomenon, but it has none the less inspired certain superstitious beliefs that are now well entrenched. Perhaps the most familiar is the belief among many people in technologically undeveloped parts of the world that it is extremely bad luck to allow someone to take their photograph (a taboo that previously applied to hand-drawn portraits also). The reasoning is that the image of a person contains something of their life-force, so anyone who obtains a photographic likeness also acquires a degree of influence over their soul.

Other superstitions include the more or less redundant notion that engaged couples should decline to have their photograph taken together, as this threatens their chances of eventually being married. It has also been suggested that it is reckless to be photographed with an animal, which may be a witch in disguise. Neither should people be grouped in threes for a photograph, as the middle one is thereby placed under sentence of death. Sport players, furthermore, have been known to refuse to have their team photograph taken until after the match in the belief that otherwise they will prejudice their luck on the field. In the Netherlands, motorists fix photographs of their lovers on the dashboard of their cars to protect them from accidents. Many people who otherwise see no magic in the science of photography will baulk at the prospect of destroying a photograph of someone who is still alive.

To deliver a curse against someone, the simplest procedure is to turn a photograph of them to the wall or turn it upside down (or, even better, to do both).

**phrenology** The pseudo-science of 'reading' a person's character by examination of the shape of their head and by paying particular attention to any bumps felt on the SKULL. An invention of nineteenth-century occultists, though in many respects a refinement of the age-old practice of PHYSIOGNOMY, phrenology divides the head into areas relevant to different spheres of human activity. The neck relates to matters of love, the upper part of the back of the head to pride, the top of the head to the conscience, the frontal central area to the impulses of generosity and kindness, and so forth.

**physiognomy** The time-honoured practice of deducing a person's character from their facial appearance. Chaucer adopted the art of physiognomy in delineating the characters in *The Canterbury Tales*, and behaviourists today assert that in everyday life people make important conclusions about their fellow human beings purely on the basis of what they look like – though many authorities are nervous of suggesting that there really are identifiable 'types' as this is far from 'politically correct'. Specific conclusions advanced by converts to physiognomy include the assumptions that happy people have round faces, that intellectuals have triangular faces and that the physically active have square faces. Every feature has its significance, including lines or wrinkles.

*See also* BEARD; CHEEK; EAR; EYE; EYEBROW; LIPS; MOLE; NOSE; TEETH.

**picture** A widely held superstition warns that a picture falling off a wall for no apparent reason is an extremely bad omen, probably signifying the imminent death of someone in the household (though a variation claims that the GLASS covering the picture must be broken for the omen to apply). This tradition was originally confined to portraits and meant the death of the person depicted: like PHOTOGRAPHS, portraits are alleged to capture something of the life-essence of the subject and so the fortunes of the two parties are magically linked.

Other superstitions concerning pictures include a taboo in the theatre against hanging pictures over dressing room doorways and a more general prejudice against placing them over beds.

**pie** A rather curious Irish superstition claims that it is unlucky to see a single pie on its own. It is, however, lucky to see two of them.

**piebald** *see* HORSE.

pig

**pig** The superstitions of many cultures grant the pig an elevated status as a special animal with various occult associations. Pigs were sacrificed to the gods of ancient Greece, were once worshipped in Crete and Egypt and have been credited by the Chinese (who think the pig lucky) with psychic powers, while the Jews and the Arabs refuse to eat its meat on the grounds that the animal is 'unclean'. In the British Isles rural superstition claims that the DEVIL often takes the form of a pig, and there are many legends of 'demon pigs' that terrorised whole localities. A variety of demon pig, the 'yird swine' or earth pig, was reputed to scavenge in graveyards for newly buried bodies. The Isle of Man, meanwhile, boasts its own stories of 'fairy pigs'.

A pig crossing one's path is generally regarded as unlucky, particularly so in the case of WEDDING parties, though it is conversely fortunate if a sow with a litter of young comes along. The runt of a litter is said to be protected by St Anthony, and some farmers are therefore reluctant to slaughter what is sometimes called the 'pantony pig'. Pig farmers are also careful not to hit their pigs with sticks of ELDER, reputed to cause immediate death.

Observation of a pig's behaviour can be informative about coming events. If a pig runs about with straw in its mouth, a storm should be expected. If it utters a high-pitched whine or suddenly dies, this is an omen that some person's life too is coming to an end. According to the Irish, it is unlucky for pigs to enter a house as this threatens hardship, though it is a good omen to drive pigs indoors on MAYDAY morning.

Saying the word 'pig' is discouraged among FISHERMEN at sea because it will cost them a good catch, and likewise they will refuse to allow ham or pork or anything to do with pigs on board their vessels. By the same token, many seafarers will be reluctant to set sail if they happen upon a BLACK pig on their way to the harbour. In coastal parts of Scotland the bad luck threatened when someone utters the word 'pig' may be negated by at once touching IRON and intoning the phrase: 'Cauld airn'.

When pigs are slaughtered for food it is always best to kill them when the MOON is waxing, which means that the meat will swell in the pot rather than shrink. Eating pigs' brains is ill advised because it will cause the person concerned to spill all his or her secrets, and the bite of a pig is said to cause CANCER. Pork soup, however, has various medicinal properties, and washing WARTS with pig's blood or rubbing them with BACON will make them disappear. According to the Irish, children suffering from mumps and other ailments should rub their heads on a pig's back so that the disease will be transferred to the animal.

*See also* BOAR.

**pigeon** Like DOVES, pigeons have a fairly ominous reputation among the superstitious. Should a WHITE pigeon settle on a rooftop this is taken as a sure sign of the imminent death of someone within, though the settling of pigeons of other colours on a rooftop is to be welcomed as they bring good luck. The appearance of any pigeon, white or otherwise, inside a house is to be regretted, while a pigeon perching on a table is doubly unfortunate as it is an omen of imminent sickness in the house. Feeding pigeons is said to guarantee the making of new friendships, and the sight of twelve pigeons passing overhead is reputed to constitute a promise of coming wealth. Pigeons flying in circles over water, meanwhile, may be interpreted as a sign of approaching RAIN.

Piercing a pigeon's heart with PINS is supposed to be effective in persuading a lover to return home, while burning one in a fire will ward off WITCHCRAFT. In former times pressing one half of a freshly killed pigeon's body against the soles of the feet was reputed to draw off FEVER. As is the case with doves, any pillow or mattress containing pigeon feathers should be removed from the bed of a dying person, as no one can die peacefully while lying on such feathers.

**pimple** A widespread British superstition has it that the appearance of a pimple on the TONGUE is a sure indication that the person concerned is given to telling lies.

**pin** Though a humble enough domestic item, the pin is associated with a range of superstitious beliefs. It is lucky to find a pin on the floor: it should always be picked up, as an old rhyme insists:

See a pin and let it lie,
Sure to rue it by and by.

A variation on this tradition adds that it is good luck if the pin points away from the person who finds it and bad luck if it points in the opposite direction, in which case it should be left well alone. A pregnant woman who finds a pin will give birth to a boy (*see* PREGNANCY).

Some people claim that it is bad luck to lend pins (particularly if the other party is a suspected witch) unless the lender has first stuck him or herself with it. Pins used to secure clothes worn at a FUNERAL, meanwhile, should never be used again, for fear of the misfortune they will bring. Similarly, WEDDING DRESSES should be carefully checked for any forgotten pins, as these will bring bad luck to the bride if not removed before she walks up the aisle on her wedding day. However, the pins may be carefully set aside by the dressmaker as they are thought to be lucky and will also promote the wedding chances of anyone to whom they then pass.

Bent pins are supposed to be very lucky if thrown into WISHING WELLS and they will also protect houses from WITCHCRAFT. Some SAILORS will, however, express reluctance to see pins on board their vessels, as they are said to be the weapons of witches. Another use for pins concerns lost belongings: the solution is to take a pin and stick it into a cushion with the words, 'I pin you my Devil' – the lost article will soon be found. Lastly, crossing WARTS with a pin

and then burying the pin in the ground will cause them to disappear.
*See also* CANDLE.

**pinch** Giving someone a pinch for luck is an old tradition particularly associated with seafaring communities. In former times, families of SAILORS newly returned from long voyages used to give the man concerned a good pinch to confirm that he really was there in the flesh and that it was not his GHOST standing on the threshold.

**pine** *see* FIR.

**pipe smoking** A superstition specific to pipe smoking warns that a pipe should never be lit from a burning lamp or CANDLE, which, according to the French, will provoke a wife to argumentativeness and possibly even infidelity. Blowing smoke rings is, however, a good omen said to promote the luck of both the smoker and those in the immediate vicinity. Among American Indians, smoking a pipe of peace is an important social ritual and no one must refuse to take a puff if the pipe is offered to them. The ceremony must be done in total silence – if anyone speaks, the pipe must be dropped at once. Disaster will befall anyone who attempts to smoke from it again.
*See also* CIGAR; CIGARETTE.

**pips** *see* FRUIT TREES

**plantain** Sometimes called ribwort, this plant is valued in folk medicine for its healing properties. It is said that drinking tea made from plantain leaves will cure MEASLES. Another use of plantain involves wrapping two bare spikes of the plant in a DOCK leaf or otherwise secreting them under a stone and leaving them overnight: if they have blossomed in the morning, this is a sign that a love affair will prosper.

**plants** Superstition credits plants of virtually all kinds with a myriad of magical properties, proclaiming their usefulness in healing and divination as well as in protecting and promoting luck and guarding against evil in various disguises. Many plants – particularly herbs – have their own specific powers and characteristics, but a few superstitions apply to all. These include the notion that, as is the case with bees, plants kept in the house should be meticulously informed of important events within the family, especially deaths. If a plant is not kept up to date on such matters it will wither and die, and some people insist that to be on the safe side treasured plants should be decorated with a small piece of black cloth to ensure that they feel fully involved in the mourning process.

In recent times this tradition has come into focus once again, with gardeners and scientists debating the desirability of talking to one's plants as a matter of course to encourage their growth. Some experiments do indeed seem to suggest that a plant will grow more healthily if talked to on a regular basis.

Plants that are widely renowned for their magical properties include BEANS; BROOM; CLOVER; DAISY; DANDELION; FOXGLOVE; GARLIC; HENBANE; MANDRAKE; NIGHTSHADE; POPPY; ROSE; ST JOHN'S WORT and YARROW.
*See also* FLOWERS; TREES.

**plate**   As is the case with other everyday kitchen utensils, plates have a magical significance. It is reckless in the extreme to eat from a plate stacked on top of another, or to place a plate upside down on the TABLE: both actions are a portent of imminent death. Neither should a diner turn a plate on the table after it has been placed in front of him, as this too invites bad luck. Breaking a plate is triply unfortunate, as breakages always occur in threes (*see* NUMBERS) and two more are therefore likely to get broken in the near future. If a bride breaks a plate at her wedding reception she is doomed to an unhappy married life. It is, however, lucky to eat from a cracked plate.

If someone in the family has just died, a plate should be put out for the deceased at the first meal after the funeral so that the dead person's GHOST may fortify itself for the journey to the hereafter.
*See also* DISH.

**playing cards**   *see* CARDS.

**plough**   The great importance of the plough in rural communities in former times meant that the superstitious insisted on various rituals and precautions regarding its safe-keeping. Blessing a plough in church was once a common practice designed to promote the year's crops and is still carried on in some agricultural areas, a distant relic of pagan practices. According to another ancient tradition, ploughs also had to be carefully put away in the winter – if they were left out in the fields, a farmer's land would be invaded by WOLVES.

When actually in use, no plough should be stepped over lest the ground tilled with it becomes infertile; neither should anyone cross the path of the horses or tractor pulling it. In Scotland, it is said that good luck will come to any person who sees the first plough of the season coming towards them, but conversely that they will suffer misfortune if they see it when it is going away from them. Records exist of witches ritually putting together miniature ploughs pulled by teams of TOADS so as to render an enemy's land barren and to claim the ground for the DEVIL.

**plover**   The plover is, in English superstition at least, an unlucky bird. Hearing its first call in spring may have dire consequences if a person does not have any money about them at the time: it signifies that they will remain hard up until the following spring. Seven plovers (*see* NUMBERS) seen in flight together is also unlucky.
*See also* GOLDEN PLOVER.

**plum**   If a plum tree produces blossom in December someone in the owner's family is doomed to die shortly, according to a Welsh superstition.

**pointing** Most people are familiar with the notion that pointing is rude, but some claim that it is actually dangerous, an idea which is probably the origin of the modern social taboo. Pointing at someone or something is supposed to concentrate bad luck in that direction by drawing the attention of evil spirits. It is therefore particularly unlucky to point at other people, SHIPS or anything else that may be considered prone to sudden and complete catastrophe. In some fishing communities, for instance, pointing is absolutely forbidden unless done with the whole hand rather than a single finger (*see* FISHERMEN). Pointing at the sky, the MOON, a RAINBOW or some other 'heavenly' phenomenon is similarly frowned upon as it risks incurring the wrath of the gods.

**poker** Being connected with the hearth and thus with the magic of FIRE, the humble poker is the subject of various popular superstitious beliefs. For centuries past, people lighting fires have leaned the poker upright against the bars of the grate, thereby forming a CROSS that bestows its blessings on the hearth and encourages a reluctant fire to blaze. Witches are supposedly drawn to the CHIMNEY as a means of introducing their evil influence into a house, but the sign of the cross will prevent them interfering with a fire or otherwise with the welfare of the occupants (*see* WITCHCRAFT). It has been suggested that this superstition is not so fanciful as it might first appear: if the poker is first heated before being placed against the grate it may indeed draw a helpful draught down the chimney and so help a fire to catch hold.

Other superstitions warn that it is unlucky to lay a poker on a TABLE and that it is ill advised to keep both poker and tongs on the same side of the fireplace. If this is done, an argument will break out between the master and the mistress of the house.

**politician** The popular concept of the average politician suggests a hard-headed individual with little time for superstition, but the high-profile, high-risk nature of the job means that he or she may be more prone to such apparently illogical thinking than might be assumed. Politicians admit to honouring as many lucky mascots, rituals and taboos as other mortals, and in some cases these notions have actually influenced their decision-making faculties in a significant way.

History is full of instances of national leaders who, after consulting personal astrologers and other 'experts', would not decide important issues at inauspicious times. Relatively modern examples include the Irish statesman Charles Stewart Parnell, who had a deep mistrust for the colour GREEN; Canadian Prime Minister William Lyon Mackenzie King, who liked to make major decisions when the two hands of a clock came together; Adolf Hitler, who interested himself in astrology and timed many military offensives to start on the seventh day of the month (which he believed to be the most auspicious date); and US President Ronald Reagan, who is said to have bowed to his wife's pressure when the stars were unfavourable about certain undertakings. The fact that Reagan, who was elected in 1980, survived his presidency (though he only narrowly avoided being assassinated) dented a cherished US superstition that grew out of the curious historical fact that every previous president elected at twenty-nine-year intervals since 1840 had died in office.

**poltergeist** *see* GHOST.

**poodle** German superstition reserves a special place for the poodle, claiming that black poodles will lurk in the vicinity of the graves of disgraced members of the CLERGY as evidence of their failure to live up to their calling during their lifetime. The reason why, of all DOGS, the black poodle should be sensitive to such characters is lost in the mists of time.

**poplar** Like the ASPEN, the poplar is renowned for its trembling leaves and shares the same reputation as a tree with special powers for healing FEVER and similar ailments. Witches may also use poplar leaves in the preparation of FLYING OINTMENT. Traditional theories to account for the shivering of the leaves variously attribute it to the fact that wood from the tree was used to make Christ's cross, that Christ prayed under a poplar in the Garden of Gethsemane and that the poplar was the only tree that refused to mourn at the Crucifixion.

**poppy**  As a reminder of the dead of two world wars and other conflicts, the blood-red poppy – which flourishes on the battlefields of Flanders – is now regarded primarily as a symbol of remembrance. This idea had its roots in the old notion that the plant sprang up from the blood of dead warriors (hence its colour).

On account of its narcotic powers, however, the poppy originally had various other magical associations dating back to classical legend. The flower has long been associated with fertility, and farmers in the ancient world maintained that corn would not grow unless there were a few poppies among it. English tradition, however, insists that the poppy is an unlucky plant and in parts of the Midlands there are those who claim that it should never be brought indoors because it will cause illness. Simply picking a poppy may trigger a thunderstorm. Looking into the heart of the plant is reputed to be enough to rob a person of their sight, and the poppy's scent is supposed to bring on HEADACHES. If pressed against the EAR, a poppy will allegedly cause earache (*see* DEAFNESS).

More positively, if contradictorily, poppies made into a poultice are alleged to relieve the pain of TOOTHACHE, earache and other ailments, and in former times they were an ingredient in potions intended to cure insomnia. Given their hallucinogenic properties, poppies have long been prized for divining the future. It is also possible for lovers to use them to confirm a partner's interest: if a poppy petal snaps with a distinct noise when pressed between the fingers, the other party's love is genuine. For those bewitched into love, spells involving poppies are said to offer an antidote.

**porpoise**  Like the DOLPHIN, the porpoise is generally considered a harbinger of good luck by the world's SEAFARERS and should never be harmed. As well as warding off SHARKS, they are said to have some influence on the WINDS, calming stormy seas; if they play around a boat when the sea is calm, however, they may whip up a gale (though others claim this is simply another good omen). In predicting the WEATHER, the sight of porpoises swimming north is said to indicate fine days ahead, but if they swim south foul weather is in store.

**portrait**  *see* PHOTOGRAPH; PICTURE.

**potato**  Since its introduction into Europe in the sixteenth century, the potato has inspired a variety of superstitions. In the early days it was much prized as an APHRODISIAC, credited with the power to cure impotence. Much later, having lost this reputation as a food of love, the potato developed a new and widespread reputation as a cure for RHEUMATISM, being carried in the trouser pockets of sufferers far and wide; as the potato (which according to some has to be stolen) slowly shrivels and hardens it is said to absorb the poisons that cause the problem in the first place. The fact that the drug atropine, which is reputed to cure rheumatism, can be found in small quantities in potato 'eyes' suggests that this notion may not be entirely without cause.

Other superstitions include the idea that potatoes are best planted on GOOD FRIDAY in order to be immune to interference from the DEVIL (though some authorities claim exactly the opposite), and the quaint custom that allows anyone eating a new potato for the first time in the season to make a wish. To make sure harvested potatoes keep well, every member of the family should share in eating the first few that are prepared. US superstition adds that if a cook allows a pan of potatoes to boil dry there will be a rainstorm.

**pots and pans**  Like other everyday kitchen utensils, a cook's pots and pans have considerable relevance to the superstitious. To prevent the DEVIL fouling up the cooking by gaining influence over such utensils it is important to treat them with care. When a pot was first hung up above a hearth, it was once usual to toss seven grains of SALT into the fire to drive away evil spirits. It was also considered unwise to allow the chains from which a pot hung to sway, because it caused the Virgin Mary to weep. Should an earthenware pot be broken while a cook is thinking about a lover, the number of pieces into which the pot breaks are said to indicate how many years they will enjoy a happy relationship. When cooking meat, if the joint shrinks in the pot this is an omen of bad times ahead. If, however, the meat swells the household may expect prosperous days in the future.

Perhaps the best-known superstition relating to saucepans is the notion that if a single woman wipes the bottom of a pan with a piece of BREAD she is destined never to be married. A rather more complex tradition, however, concerns using a saucepan to divine what fate lies in store for the soul of a recently deceased friend or relative. The procedure dictated by superstition is to place a black CAT in a copper saucepan for twenty-four hours. If the cat is still alive at the end of that time the soul of the person concerned is safely in Heaven, or else in purgatory – but if the cat is dead, the soul has descended to the fires of Hell.

To be on the safe side, metal pot hooks should be thrown out of the window during a thunderstorm in case they attract LIGHTNING.

**pouring**  The act of pouring out gravy, sauce, wine or some other liquid foodstuff may seem innocent enough, but superstition reveals a hidden risk. It is very important that the hand should not be turned backwards over the wrist in the act of pouring, because it endangers a person's luck and may lead to an argument.

*See also* WAITING ON TABLE.

**powder of sympathy**  *see* WOUND.

**pram**  As with CRADLES, babies' prams are subject to certain superstitious beliefs and taboos. The most generally observed of these is the notion that it is TEMPTING FATE to buy a pram before a baby is actually born, a taboo that almost certainly developed out of the similar prohibition against purchasing a cradle too soon. Other superstitions include the idea that to push an empty pram, or one containing someone else's baby, is to risk becoming pregnant oneself.

**prayers**  Normally associated with conventional religious worship, the saying of prayers has in fact been a feature of pagan rituals since primitive times. Prayer of various kinds, both Christian and pagan, was involved in the treatment of animals, folk medicine and other forms of magic as far back as the Anglo-Saxons. The incantations essential to many spells and love CHARMS are presumably derived from such traditions, and any chance of success they had was probably improved by the power of suggestion.

Reversing Christian symbols is a common feature of black magic rituals around the world, and the reciting of the Lord's Prayer backwards is one of the central elements in the black mass. Saying the Lord's Prayer backwards may, however, also be used against WITCHCRAFT, specifically in the rituals surrounding the burning of a witch bottle (a bottle containing samples of hair, blood, nail parings and so forth from the supposed victim of witchcraft). This ceremony is said to cause a spell to be lifted, and will culminate in the witch's death if the bottle bursts. Similarly, curses may be delivered by being spoken backwards.

The theory that witches spoke backwards when casting their spells inspired the idea that anyone who betrayed some hesitation or reluctance in saying their prayers the normal way should be suspected of witchcraft. During investigations alleged witches were sometimes ordered to recite prayers, and failure to do so without making a mistake was taken as strong evidence of guilt. Should a member of the CLERGY make a mistake when saying prayers in church a death in the parish will surely follow (though some authorities claim that he must make three mistakes before such consequences become inevitable).

Those who say their prayers in the traditional way before going to bed are advised that it is thought to be unlucky to say them while kneeling at the end of the bed and far preferable to kneel at the side.

**precociousness**  A child who shows early intellectual promise may delight his or her parents and teachers, but may be looked upon with doubt by the superstitious. A widespread tradition warns that precocious CHILDREN are doomed to premature death, which is presumably why they are trying to reach a level of sophistication and learning beyond their years. This is why some people will lament the sight of a BABY that is fully alert to everything going on and the child will be deemed 'too wise to live'.

**pregnancy**  The time between conception and the birth of a BABY is inevitably fraught and has inspired countless superstitions and taboos that purport to enlist the reassurance of magic in the business of a safe confinement and delivery. Pregnant women and their unborn children are considered especially vulnerable to the threat of evil. Among the dangers against which superstition warns are allowing a RAT or WEASEL to leap over a pregnant woman's belly, thus causing a BIRTHMARK; permitting a mother-to-be to look at a CORPSE, which will give her child a pale complexion; letting her knit or spin, which dooms her child to death

by hanging; failing to prevent her from stepping over a grave, thus sentencing the baby to a premature death; and shocks of all descriptions (a pregnant woman frightened by a bird, for instance, may bear a child with a wing in place of one of its arms).

If a pregnant woman gazes at the MOON her child will be born with mental problems. According to Scandinavian superstition, if she steps over a CAT her baby will be born a hermaphrodite. If she meets a HARE or, according to another Scandinavian tradition, drinks out of a cracked cup her child will suffer from a HARE-LIP. It is also risky, according to one old English superstition, to talk openly about a baby before the birth as this invites the interference of FAIRIES, who may seek to harm the unborn child or to steal it; to counter this danger some women refer to the foetus as the 'pot lid' or use some other substitute word to avoid arousing the fairies' interest.

Superstition attaches considerable import to the cravings which some mothers develop during pregnancy. One old tradition has it that unless the craving is satisfied the image of the thing longed for, whether it be an apricot, a slice of liver or an OYSTER, will be forever imprinted on some part of the child's body in the form of a BIRTHMARK.

To influence the sex of the unborn child the expectant mother is advised to dress in BLUE if she wants a boy and in pink if she wants a girl. In the USA it is said that a baby that delivers kicks on the right-hand side of the womb is a boy, while one that kicks on the left-hand side is a girl. To ensure that the baby is healthy it is best to conceive at midday, when the sun is at its highest, and to promote its intelligence a pregnant woman should do as much reading as she can over the nine months. She should resist any temptation to steal or her child too will grow up to be a THIEF.

Close contact with pregnant women increases other women's chances (or risks) of conceiving. Variations on this theme include taking care not to sit on a chair that a pregnant woman has recently vacated and never trying on her coat. It is also traditional in Scotland to bar a pregnant woman from the room of a woman who is in labour, as this is thought to be unlucky. As with MENSTRUATION, pregnant women are forbidden in many cultures to prepare food or to help with livestock on the grounds that their touch contaminates. There is also a prejudice against pregnant women taking oaths of any kind; for this reason they are sometimes turned down as prospective GODPARENTS, superstition claiming that the child concerned may die if this custom is not followed.

Male partners are not entirely ignored in the superstitions that surround the business of pregnancy. Indeed, in some societies it is the male who behaves like the one who is having the child, suffering all the pangs and aches of pregnancy in the woman's stead. He may even take to his bed and be treated by others to all intents and purposes as the expectant partner (a tradition known as 'couvade'). This curious notion derives either from the prejudice that men, being allegedly stronger and more intelligent than females, are better able to defend the unborn child's interests, or else from the idea that such actions will confuse any malevolent spirits. Even in modern Western society, tales abound of husbands and other partners experiencing 'sympathy pains' in the form of stomach upsets or cramps when their children are born.

Couples who are experiencing difficulty in conceiving a child may like to sleep with a PEARL beneath the pillow, or try the US remedy which suggests that tossing black-eyed peas across a road close to their home will successfully promote their chances of having a baby.

*See also* BLADE-BONE; CHILDBIRTH; MISCARRIAGE; PENDULUM.

**priest**  *see* CLERGY.

**primrose**  English superstition dictates that, when picked for the first time in spring, primroses should never be brought into the house in anything but bunches of at least thirteen flowers. If this is ignored, bad luck will follow – specifically, the ruining of that season's EGG yield. If only one primrose is brought inside, only one egg will hatch from each clutch; worse still, this may also presage the death of a member of the family. Much the same tradition has been extended to various other spring flowers, including the DAFFODIL. In Wales, it is said to be bad luck if primroses flower out of season.

In folk medicine, primroses may be used as a safeguard against evil spirits and also to cure insomnia, among various other ailments.

**prostitute**  Superstition claims that it is lucky to meet a prostitute in the street, especially early in the morning, in which case the rest of the day's BUSINESS will turn out well. Prostitutes are, however, less welcome on board SHIPS, where their presence is said to provoke STORMS.

*See also* PANCAKE.

**pumpkin**  Revered by the Chinese above all other plants, the pumpkin is widely respected as an emblem of fertility, presumably because of its generous size. Associated throughout the Western world primarily with the celebration of HALLOWE'EN, pumpkins hollowed out and carved into grotesque faces and then illuminated from within by a CANDLE are reputed to scare away the evil spirits that roam abroad on this particular night. In keeping with this reputation, pumpkins are best planted on GOOD FRIDAY. Once growing, they should never be pointed at, which will cause them to rot. Pumpkin seeds may be consumed to quieten an excessively passionate nature and, if mixed into a paste with oil and rubbed on the skin, will eradicate freckles.

**purse**  Superstition has several pieces of advice to ensure that a purse (or wallet or handbag) is never empty. As well as keeping various good luck charms in it, the owner should make doubly sure that his or her purse is never totally empty since even one small COIN will attract others. Anyone who gives a purse as a present should slip a coin into it to get the new owner off to a good start; a length of string secreted in it will apparently have the same effect.

# R

**rabbit** Like HARES, which share many of the same traditions, rabbits are closely associated with WITCHCRAFT and have a mixed reputation among the superstitious. This link with the powers of darkness may date back to pagan times, when rabbits' tendency to play in the moonlight led to them being identified with the MOON god. Witches are said to favour rabbits as one of their disguises, and their FAMILIARS may also appear in such a form. Various parts of the rabbit's body feature in mischief-making spells and potions, and many cultures assign certain supernatural qualities to this animal.

On a lighter note, the rabbit's reputation for fecundity means it has become one of the symbols of EASTER (the mythical Easter Bunny of US superstition is said to deliver chocolate Easter eggs), and in the right circumstances seeing a rabbit can have beneficial consequences. If a rabbit crosses in front of someone, for instance, this is said to be fortunate, though only bad luck will ensue if a rabbit passes behind a person's back. More pessimistic is the notion common among MINERS that it is unlucky to see a rabbit on the way to work because it may presage some disaster, and the general belief that misfortune will follow any DREAM in which rabbits appear.

Farmers have been known to express unease if rabbits approach too close to their livestock, but may show reluctance to shoot BLACK rabbits in particular on the grounds that they may be the reincarnated souls of their ancestors. WHITE rabbits are especially loathed by some people, who claim that a death will occur in a household if such a creature is seen in the immediate vicinity – though it is lucky to say 'white rabbits' before anything else on the first day of the month or on the first day of a new MOON. A rabbit running down a street, moreover, constitutes a warning that one of the houses in the neighbourhood will shortly catch FIRE, and SAILORS include 'rabbit' among the taboo words that must never be uttered while at sea.

Carrying around a rabbit's foot (*see* AMULET), on the other hand, is supposed to guarantee exceptional good luck, and such macabre mascots are among the most popular of all lucky charms, being carried by people all over the world. Ideally made from the 'lucky' left hind leg of a rabbit killed by a cross-eyed man in the light of a full moon, these are often hung on babies' CRADLES. Similarly, brushing a baby, a FRUIT TREE or some other valued object with a rabbit's foot is said to keep it from harm. In rural areas many poachers carry rabbit's feet in the belief that this will ensure they are not caught, and in the theatre ACTORS AND ACTRESSES often boast lucky rabbit's feet that they usually keep in their MAKE-UP boxes. Women should think twice, though, before carrying a rabbit's foot about their person, as this is said to increase their chances of having a large family. On no account should such charms be mislaid, which will prove disastrous to the erstwhile owner's fortune.

It has been suggested that the reason rabbits are supposed to be harbingers of good luck derives from the fact that young rabbits are born with their eyes open, and can thereby ward off evil. Or perhaps it is simply that the rabbit's powers of procreation link it with the idea of fruitfulness and success in all one's ventures.

The rabbit has several uses in folk medicine. These include wearing rabbit-skin SOCKS to guard against pleurisy and feeding rabbit's brains to an irritable child, a procedure reputed in Dorset to lead to an immediate improvement in the child's behaviour.

**railway** Superstition usually regards technology with awe and mistrust, and is not slow to devise new taboos and tips in response. In the case of railways the most widespread superstition, dating back to the early years of the twentieth century at least, claims that it is unlucky if a train passes over a BRIDGE while a person is walking beneath; if this happens, the fingers should be firmly crossed. It is also unlucky to talk while walking under a railway bridge. This idea appears to have its origins in the tradition that witches and other evil spirits inhabit bridges and arches of other kinds.

In the days before the introduction of diesel and electric trains, some people claimed that it was lucky to stand in the clouds of steam that billowed from loco-motives passing under bridges. It was also widely believed that encouraging a child to breathe air through the open window of a train while it travelled through a tunnel would alleviate WHOOPING COUGH.

**rain** Predicting the onset of rain has always been a prime preoccupation among those who work on the land, and superstition is rich with portents con-cerning changes in the WEATHER. Many of these depend upon close observation of bird and animal behaviour (for instance, a CAT rubbing behind its ear when washing means it will rain, as do SPIDERS seeking shelter), though others suggest that aching limbs or painful CORNS are equally reliable indicators of

imminent downpours – a notion that has in fact been backed by modern science, which has linked changes in atmospheric pressure with such symptoms. If a piece of BREAD AND BUTTER falls face down on the floor when accidentally dropped, or SOOT comes down the chimney, or SALT sticks together in lumps, or the BREAD goes soft, these too are portents of wet weather.

The most famous superstition con-cerning rain is the tradition that if it rains on St Swithin's Day (15 July) it will rain for another forty days in succession. This belief dates back to an attempt that was made to move the remains of St Swithin to a more prestigious location in Win-chester Cathedral on 15 July 871. Heavy rain that lasted forty days prevented the work being completed, and was taken as a sign of the saint's disapproval of the pro-posed move. The plan was eventually abandoned, leaving the saint in the humble spot in the open graveyard that he had chosen for himself on his deathbed – until, that is, the year 963, when he was moved regardless of his own wishes. The tradition is referred to in rhyme:

St Swithin's Day, if thou be fair,
For forty days 'twill rain nae mair;
St Swithin's Day, if thou bring rain,
For forty days it will remain.

Weather forecasters admit that mid-July often sees a fundamental change in weather patterns, but deny that it is pos-sible to discern distinct annual forty-day droughts or downpours following this particular date.

Meanwhile, rain on St Paul's Day (25 January) signifies poor supplies of corn, while rain at EASTER indicates that grass later in the year will be lush, but there will be little hay. If it rains on St Peter's Day (29 June) the saints are deemed to be send-ing water for the APPLE orchards, and it is predicted that the apple crop will be a good one. If it rains around St Mary Magdalen's Day (22 July), this is said to be because the saint is washing her handker-chief ready to weep on St James's Day (25 July).

Superstition offers numerous suggestions for those wishing to try their hand at rain-making. The simplest of these procedures vary from burning FERNS or HEATHER to dipping a CROSS or other religious relic in holy water (formerly, in various parts of Europe, statues of the saints were often dipped in lakes and rivers in times of drought). Another solution is to step on a beetle or ant or to get a German band to play in the open – an idea that dates from the Edwardian era when such bands often visited England.

If it rains too much, one English remedy suggests that persuading a first-born child to undress and then stand on his head in the rain will cause it to cease. Another measure involves chanting the well-known rhyme, or a variation of it:

Rain, rain go away,
Come again another day.

Other miscellaneous superstitions concerning rain include the notion that it is unlucky if it rains during a WEDDING, but lucky if it rains during a FUNERAL, as this constitutes evidence that the deceased has gone to Heaven.

In folk medicine, rainwater is supposed to be excellent for the HAIR and treatment of EYE problems. In times gone by, people often collected rainwater that fell on ASCENSION DAY in the belief that, so long as it had not come into contact with rooftops, trees or the ground, it had special healing properties. The Welsh, meanwhile, claim that a BABY bathed in rainwater will learn to talk much sooner than other infants of the same age, and also that MONEY washed in rainwater will never be stolen.

A bizarre German superstition insists that couples who make love when it is raining will conceive girls (whereas those who indulge in sex when it is fine will have boys).

*See also* UMBRELLA.

**rainbow** The mysterious nature of the rainbow, which seems to link the Heavens with the Earth, means that it is a phenomenon that inspires dread in superstitious people of many cultures – though many think a rainbow lucky and will make a wish on seeing one. Christian mythology claims that the rainbow is God's promise that He will never again flood the Earth, as happened in the story of Noah's ark. Some people, however, show reluctance to accept this idea that the rainbow is a positive reassurance that no harm will befall those living beneath its span. Instead, they interpret its appearance as an omen of death, an idea that is perhaps a folk memory of the celestial bridge of Norse origins over which the dead (particularly children) get to Heaven. In the Shetland Islands, for instance, the sight of a rainbow arching over a house is taken as a portent of imminent death, and elsewhere various superstitions are concerned with negating the evil influence of rainbows.

In some areas the superstitious will chant rhymes to make a rainbow disappear, while in others they will lay down two sticks or straws in the form of a CROSS to 'cross out' the rainbow. It is also considered reckless to be caught POINTING at a rainbow, which will cause the rain to start again or may invite even worse luck. Rather more positive, though, is the popular tradition that a crock of gold may be found at the end of the rainbow – if only that spot can be located.

Other superstitions about rainbows include the contention that they suck water from rivers and lakes to feed the clouds, the SAILORS' theory that a rainbow can swallow up a whole vessel, and the warning that WATER that has been touched by a rainbow becomes poisoned. Miniature rainbows spotted in oily patches on the ground inspire similarly mixed feelings: some people recommend avoiding them, saying that it is bad luck to step over them, while others suggest holding a foot over the rainbow pattern and intoning:

Rainbow, rainbow, bring me luck.
If you don't, I'll break you up.

The appearance of a rainbow allows a certain amount of information to be gleaned about the WEATHER to come. As with red skies, a rainbow in the morning signifies wet weather on the way, while one in the afternoon or evening suggests that the following day will be fine. In the British Isles at least, science supports the notion that a rainbow in the west (the direction in which British weather systems usually develop) means it will rain, while one in the east indicates that the wet weather is over.

**rake**  Gardening lore advises that, should a rake fall down on the ground with its tines pointing to the sky, RAIN is sure to arrive the following day.

**rat**  These creatures are almost universally loathed and feared, and almost all the superstitions concerning them point to their association with death and disaster. Rats are said to have a sixth sense when it comes to predicting death, and various traditions credit them with knowing when a calamity of some kind is nigh. According to one shared by SEAFARERS worldwide, rats will always desert a sinking SHIP – even though it may appear at the time to be entirely sound and in no danger (accordingly, it is actually lucky if rats are seen boarding a new vessel). It is no surprise, then, to learn that it is deemed most unlucky even to mention the word 'rat' on board ship.

On land, it is claimed that rats will vacate a house that is in imminent risk of collapse or will similarly leave the property if one of the occupants is close to death. The same consequence must be expected if rats gnaw at a person's clothing or damage the bedroom furniture. A sudden invasion of rats for no apparent reason, meanwhile, may be interpreted as a prediction that the residents will soon be on the move (though a variation from Scotland signifies that someone in the house will shortly come into money). Infestations of rats may be ended by various magical means, several of which depend upon writing a curse on a piece of paper and then leaving it where the rats will find it. The Irish in particular boast a long tradition of rat-cursing poetry. Alternatively, sitting beside a rat-hole and politely requesting the occupants to move on, without resorting to actual curses, is sometimes reputed to have the desired effect. The idea that rats are peculiarly susceptible to the charms of MUSIC is reflected in the legend of the Pied Piper of Hamelin; rat-charmers still working in remote areas in the current century have been known to lure rats from their hiding-places by whistling or singing.

Other superstitions concerning rats include the notion that an explosion in their numbers constitutes a suitably macabre warning that WAR is about to break out, and the belief that a concoction of dried rat's tail may be used to treat a bad COLD. Lastly, parents anxious that a child should develop strong biting TEETH are advised to leave one of the infant's lost milk teeth by a rat-hole and to request the resident rat to accept it in exchange for a really good new one.

**raven**  Like other BLACK birds, the raven (an attendant upon the gods of both ancient Greece and Scandinavia) is widely considered a creature of ill omen and is feared for its apparent ability to foresee death. It is particularly disliked in the vicinity of the sick, as the call of this 'messenger of death' – sometimes heard as the words 'corpse, corpse' – is an omen that the patient will not recover. In times gone by, it was suggested that the bird was a favourite disguise of the DEVIL and also that it carried disease around the countryside on its wings. Scientists suggest that this association with death may have some root in the bird's extremely sensitive powers of smell, which will draw it to decaying flesh even some distance away. Another explanation harks back to the eleventh-century Norman invaders of England who carried the raven as an emblem on their banners, thus linking the bird in the minds of the English with the ravages of war.

In other circumstances, though, the raven is less ominous and the Welsh suggest that if a blind person shows kindness to a raven the bird will repay this by helping them to regain their sight (a tradition presumably derived from the allegation that ravens pluck out the EYES of their prey and thus enjoy excellent vision themselves). The Welsh also welcome the sight of a raven perching on a rooftop, which presages good luck to everyone within. In the West Country ravens are saluted by the raising of the hat, and anyone who robs a raven's nest will be punished through the death of a BABY in his or her home village. Similarly the Cornish warn against harming a raven, explaining that the bird may be the reincarnation of King Arthur himself.

The royal connection is expanded in London, where it is said that the British monarchy and the United Kingdom itself will last only so long as there are ravens at the Tower of London. This well-known superstition is thought to have evolved from the story of Bran the Blessed, a mythical figure in the Welsh *Mabinogion*, whose head was buried on Tower Hill facing France to ward off any invasion of England (the name Bran means 'raven'). Anyone who kills one of the ravens which live at the Tower is fated soon to die.

A relatively obscure tradition allows a person to glean information about the future by counting ravens. If one raven is seen, sadness is in store; if two are spotted, happy days lie ahead; if three ravens are counted, there will be a marriage; and if four ravens appear, there will be a birth. A variation, however, claims that it is only lucky if one raven is seen, and unfortunate to see any more.

In folk medicine, a soup made from ravens is recommended for the treatment of GOUT. Raven's EGGS, meanwhile, may be used to dye the HAIR black – with the warning that they should only be applied to the hair while the mouth is full of oil, or the teeth will go black as well.

In the business of WEATHER prediction, ravens flying towards the SUN are a sign of fine weather on the way, but if they are preening themselves while on the wing this is a sure portent of RAIN. Should they fly recklessly at one another, this may be taken as an omen of WAR.

**razor**  Superstition dictates that razors, in common with KNIVES, are unsuitable presents to give to one's friends, as the gift of any blade risks severing the friendship. Similarly, it is thought unlucky on both sides of the Atlantic to find a razor.

*See also* BEARD.

**recognition**  According to an ominous English superstition it is supposed to be unlucky to mistake a total stranger for someone else. The consequence of such an error is the imminent death of the person the stranger was mistaken for.

**red**  As the colour of blood, and therefore of passion and vitality, red is reputed to have strong supernatural properties and is particularly valued as a defence against WITCHCRAFT and evil spirits. Because of this, red is sometimes selected as a propitious colour to wear at important ceremonies and religious rituals around the world. Lengths of red THREAD feature in a variety of spells, being tied around limbs affected by RHEUMATISM, around the neck to staunch nosebleeds (*see* BLOOD; NOSE) and to cure WHOOPING COUGH, and otherwise employed to treat a range of ailments. Tying a loop of red thread about an animal's horn or tail will protect it from witches and from the threat of the EVIL EYE, and pre-pubescent girls may be given red RIBBONS to wear in their hair as a form of protection against misfortune. By the same token, red ribbons are sometimes tied to PRAMS or to the interior of new CARS.

Red cars are reputed to be involved in fewer ACCIDENTS than vehicles of other colours, and card players will sometimes insist upon marking down their scores in red for luck (*see* GAMBLING). Red is, however, an unlucky colour to use when writing a LOVE LETTER, and red flowers such as ROSES and POPPIES may also be considered harbingers of ill fortune, especially if they shed their petals on the ground, like blood. There is also a long-standing prejudice against giving bunches of red and white FLOWERS TO HOSPITAL patients as these represent death (though red flowers alone are fine, because they symbolise healthy red blood).

Many people consider meeting a red-headed man or woman unlucky, especially at NEW YEAR, presumably on the grounds that such individuals are widely thought to be hot-tempered and untrustworthy. Red-haired children, meanwhile, are reputedly born to unfaithful mothers.

*See also* WEATHER.

**red hot poker** Ornamental garden flower with livid red and yellow blooms, which may be regarded unfavourably if it should flower twice in the same season. Such an occurrence is widely thought to presage the death of someone in the gardener's family.

**reed** The water-loving reed should never, according to one old English superstition, be grown in gardens or near houses. Failure to observe this taboo, it is alleged, will result in the death of someone in the household.

**rheumatism** Superstition offers a range of magical cures and treatments for this condition, ranging from the possibly helpful to the alarmingly bizarre. The simpler solutions include carrying a lucky RABBIT'S foot, a piece of ROWAN or a POTATO in the trouser pocket, putting slivers of green pepper under the fingernails and tying a length of RED thread around the affected part. More dubious measures include persuading BEES to sting the patient in the area of the rheumatic joint, crawling under an ARCH of BRAMBLE and, according to Welsh tradition, stripping the sufferer naked and repeatedly burying him vertically in the churchyard for two hours at a time until the problem has disappeared. Some jewellers also sell special RINGS and bracelets made of copper that are supposed to have the power to dispel the pain of rheumatism. If all these cures fail the patient may consult a mother who has undergone a breech delivery, as such women are reputed to have special healing influences in these cases.

**ribbon** Wearing lengths of ribbon or thread is widely recommended by superstition as a protective measure against various kinds of evil and also as a treatment for certain ailments. Headbands, especially RED ones, promote the happiness of the wearer and, if borrowed from someone in love, have the useful side-effect of alleviating migraine HEADACHES. Other medicinal applications usually involve tying a ribbon or piece of thread around the affected body part. A ribbon worn round the neck will therefore ease a sore throat and a GARTER secured around the calf will prevent CRAMP. In the East, however, folklore casts a less convinced eye over the wearing of ribbons in general and warns that anyone who wears a coloured ribbon around their head at night will attract the EVIL EYE.

**rice** The throwing of rice at WEDDING ceremonies throughout the Western world is a reference to its time-honoured status as a symbol of fertility, and in essence constitutes the wish of the guests that the new marriage be blessed by the birth of children in due course. Before rice was introduced, newly-weds were customarily presented with bags of NUTS as they left the church, and now rice, in its turn, has largely given way to paper CONFETTI. Other superstitions relating to rice around the world include the Arabic notion that every grain of rice is a drop of sweat from the brow of Mohammed, and the Japanese custom of honouring rice with plays and prayers to propitiate the gods who control the coming harvest.

**right side** The right side is generally the 'lucky' side in world superstition. Just as the LEFT SIDE is associated with the

DEVIL and ill fortune, so the right is the side of God and good luck. Numerous superstitions concerning ANIMALS dictate that if the creature concerned approaches from the right good luck will ensue, while misfortune will follow if the creature appears on the left. Thus the SUN, symbol of life and good, moves through the heavens sunwise (that is, towards the right), and various taboos insist that when getting out of bed, entering a house or starting out on a myriad of other projects it is the right foot that must go first. Simply making a sharp turn to the right is thought to be a lucky move that will enlist the support and protection of benevolent guardian spirits.

See also SUNWISE TURN; WIDDER-SHINS.

**ring**  Symbolising a number of things, according to their design and composition, rings are widely credited with supernatural powers. These include various healing properties and the ability to act as LIFE-TOKENS, conveying through the maintenance of their lustre or any deterioration in their condition the fortunes of the absent owner.

Rings bearing inscriptions, which might range from certain magic words to the names of the Holy Family or the three Magi, are supposed to be effective against the EVIL EYE and were once said to ward off the plague. If made of metal that is in some way 'holy', a ring will have extra powers of healing. Edward the Confessor owned a ring (now preserved in Westminster Abbey in London) that was reputed to have the power to heal CRAMP, and many subsequent English monarchs obliged in bestowing their blessing upon so-called 'cramp rings' that would then be given out to sufferers. It was also once quite commonplace to take the first five silver COINS offered at Communion and to melt them down, while saying prayers, to form rings for this purpose.

In cases where neither the monarch nor the Church could help, healing rings were sometimes made from coins or various other small silver objects donated by five unmarried members of the opposite sex; these were regarded as equally beneficial. Superstition has it that some of the best cramp rings are those made from the melted down handles and other metal fittings of old COFFINS. Even in modern times rings and bracelets, usually made of copper, are advertised by jewellers for their efficacy in healing the ravages of RHEUMATISM. Such is the magic of rings that one West Country superstition claims that simply running the ring finger of the left hand along a WOUND will heal it.

Swearing oaths on rings is a practice dating from at least Anglo-Saxon times and is reflected in the giving and receiving of WEDDING RINGS during modern marriage services. The idea underlying this custom is the fact that a ring, being a circle with neither beginning nor end, represents the three concepts of eternity, unity and perfection.

See also DEAD HAND; ENGAGEMENT; PENDULUM.

**ringing in the ears**  see EAR.

**ringworm**  According to Scottish tradition, ringworm can be cleared up by rubbing ASHES over the affected area of skin three mornings in a row before breakfast and intoning the following rhyme:

> Ringworm, ringworm red,
> Never mayest thou either spread or speed;
> But aye grow less and less,
> And die away among the ash.

**robin**  The robin ranks among the most sacred of all garden birds and enjoys the special protection of superstition, though not all the traditions surrounding it are beneficent. A time-honoured saying dictates that the robin and the WREN are God's 'cock and hen' and thus enjoy divine favour. According to the Welsh, the bird acquired its distinctive red breast when it was singed while carrying drops of water to souls tormented in the fires of Hell, though others suggest it scorched itself when extinguishing the burning feathers of the wren after it had fetched fire from Hell as a gift for mankind. Another widely heard superstition, however, accredits the bird's red breast to the legend that it was splashed with Christ's blood or else was pricked when it attempted to pull the thorns from His brow. As a consequence of this kindly act it is supposed to be extremely unlucky to kill a robin, to cage it or to destroy its EGGS.

Anyone who breaks the taboo against killing robins will find that they suffer an immediate and lasting decline in their fortunes. Specific punishments include the hand that did the awful deed developing an uncontrollable shake or else being afflicted by a painful growth that prevents the person concerned going about their usual work. The guilty party may also find that his or her cows will only give red-stained milk.

Causing a robin a non-fatal injury will be punished by the individual responsible suffering a parallel hurt – such as a broken leg if the robin has had its leg broken. Breaking a robin's eggs will lead to the destruction of one or more of the perpetrator's most treasured possessions or, in the case of a child, will – according to the folklore of Dorset – lead to the youngster concerned growing up with crooked little fingers. More drastically, some claim that the hand that actually robbed or broke the eggs will drop off, while in Germany the culprit's house will be struck by LIGHTNING. Such is the dread of harming robins that even CATS are said to refrain from attacking them.

Among the more ominous superstitions attached to the bird is the widespread belief that if a robin flies into a house or sings close to it someone within will die shortly afterwards. The same conclusion may be drawn if a robin taps at the bedroom WINDOW of anyone who is sick, and some people are reluctant to send sick friends and relatives get-well cards that bear pictures of robins (they may also avoid Christmas cards depicting the bird). If a robin flies into a church, the life of one

of the parishioners is deemed to be drawing to a close, and should one appear near a mine shaft this is a portent of disaster below (*see* MINERS). This association with death is extended by the age-old tradition that the robin, like the wren, will not suffer a corpse to remain unburied but will cover the body with leaves (a superstition kept alive through the fairytale *Babes in the Wood*).

A more cheerful tradition holds that a person can make a wish when they see their first robin of the year, but they must take care to complete their wish before the bird flies away. Failure to do this means a whole year of bad luck.

In terms of WEATHER prediction, spotting a robin deep within a hedge or tree suggests that rain is in the offing, but if it is seen in the open the weather will be fine. A rhyme from Sussex summarises this tradition:

If the robin sings in the bush,
Then the weather will be coarse;
But if the robin sings on the barn,
Then the weather will be warm.

**rolling-pin** According to English superstition GLASS rolling-pins are lucky, particularly if given as presents at WEDDINGS and similar celebrations.

**rook** In common with other BLACK birds rooks are widely associated with death, but are otherwise unusual in being regarded by landowners throughout the British Isles and elsewhere in Europe as harbingers of good luck. The appearance of rooks round a particular house or village is usually greeted with dismay and interpreted as a death omen, but well-established rookeries near homes are considered lucky. The sudden disappearance of rooks from a rookery is therefore regarded as a bad sign, suggesting a coming calamity. Many people claim that if rooks nest close to human habitation the occupant may rest assured of financial prosperity and general good luck. In Shropshire and some other areas householders treat these birds as others treat

BEES. They will inform any resident rooks of a death in the family, and will reassure them that only the landowner will be allowed to shoot them – this is to encourage them to stay where they are. Similarly, finding a broken rook's nest in January is lucky, signifying a happy year ahead. In former times, anyone who killed a rook or drove it from the neighbourhood and thus threatened a landowner's luck was subject to harsh punishment.

Various other superstitions concerning rooks include the notion that the birds have a sixth sense when it comes to predicting when a tree is about to fall down, and will accordingly move their nests before the event takes place. Furthermore, rooks will refrain from building nests on ASCENSION DAY, and anyone who fails to put on new CLOTHING on EASTER Day will become the target of their droppings.

Where WEATHER is concerned, it is said that if the rooks build their nests high in the trees a fine summer is in the offing, but if they nest lower down the weather will be wet and cold. Rooks that feed in the street or perch close together on fences or walls with their heads turned into the wind are a sure sign that a STORM is imminent, as is the sight of rooks swooping recklessly downwards in flight.

**rooster**   *see* COCK.

**rope**   The use of rope by hangmen in centuries past has endowed it with supernatural powers. Lengths of HANGMAN'S ROPE were credited with all manner of magical properties, including the power to cure various ailments and the general improvement of a person's luck. Using a length of ordinary hemp rope as a belt to keep up one's trousers, meanwhile, is said to cure lumbago. More in keeping with the idea of the rope as a means of execution is the widespread taboo against saying the word 'rope' when on board SHIP or in the theatre (*see* ACTORS AND ACTRESSES).

A curious superstition that was formerly observed by Scottish FISHERMEN involved the passing of a boat through a 'rope circle'. If it was thought that a boat's fortunes had been blighted by some malevolent force, the vessel was sailed through a large loop of rope passed right under the keel to free it of the evil influence.

**rose**   The rose is perhaps the most significant of all flowers in terms of the superstitions attached to it. It is the flower of love, and in Victorian times specific interpretations were placed by lovers upon gifts of roses of certain colours – red symbolising passion and white pure love, for instance. This association with lovers and with the communication of secret passions also made the rose the emblem of discretion and silence. Its image therefore is often found set into the ceilings of council chambers and other meeting-places as a reminder that what is discussed there should remain private or *'sub rosa'* – 'under the rose'.

The red rose is said to have got its colour either from the spilt blood of Christ, Venus or Adonis or, according to Islam, from the sweat of Mohammed's brow. In ancient Roman times, roses were traditionally planted at gravesides in the belief that they had the power to protect the dead from evil. Over the centuries white roses, symbolic of innocence, have often been planted at the graves of virgins, while red roses have been planted on the graves of lovers or of philanthropists renowned for the love they showed their fellow men.

This association with death probably lies at the root of the body of generally pessimistic traditions now linked to the flower. Superstition warns that if a rose drops its petals while someone is holding it this is an omen that the person is soon to die. Roses that bloom out of season, meanwhile, are also disliked, as they are supposed to presage misfortune in the year to come. Dreaming of roses may be interpreted as a prediction of success in love, but if they are white misfortune lies in store. The wild dog-rose is also reputed to be unlucky. It is thought to be unwise to make any plans in its vicinity, as its influence will blight the proposed undertaking.

On a more cheerful note, girls may use roses to identify their husband-to-be by wrapping a rose in white paper on MID-SUMMER'S EVE and keeping it until CHRISTMAS. Then it is unwrapped and, if still fresh, worn by the girl on her dress: the first man to admire the rose or remove it is destined to marry her. To determine how sincerely one is loved, a person has only to snap the stem of a rose – the louder the noise produced, the stronger the passion.

The rose has various uses in folk medicine. In England in the eighteenth century it was alleged that it could promote fertility, and women who wanted to bear children wore red roses in small bags round their necks. The gall of the rose (an abnormal growth caused by insects, fungi, bacteria or injury) is supposed to be an effective cure for WHOOPING COUGH and TOOTHACHE if worn around the neck, and will combat insomnia if placed beneath the sufferer's pillow.

**rosemary** Like many other herbs, rosemary is widely respected for a variety of alleged supernatural properties. Sacred to remembrance and friendship, at FU-NERALS a sprig of rosemary was formerly tossed on to the COFFIN by each of the mourners as a sign that they would not quickly forget the deceased person. It was also drunk in wine by newly-weds at their WEDDING breakfast celebrations as a symbol of lasting fidelity in love. Rosemary is further said to ward off the EVIL EYE, to cure MADNESS, to guard against nausea and NIGHTMARES and to prevent STORMS. It may also be carried about the person or pinned up by the front door to keep witches and disease away. It is, moreover, a crucial ingredient in many love charms and in spells intended to reveal the future; sleeping with a sixpence

and a sprig of rosemary under the pillow on HALLOWE'EN, for instance, will draw forth visions of a future partner in one's dreams. Wearing a sprig of rosemary in the buttonhole, meanwhile, is reputed to aid the memory and will also promote the wearer's luck in all his or her undertakings.

It is said that rosemary will only grow in households where a woman holds sway; also that the plant grows upwards for thirty-three years until it reaches Christ's height at the time that he was crucified, after which it grows outwards only. Another ancient tradition claims that, in common with the Glastonbury Thorn, rosemary flowers at midnight on Old Christmas Eve (*see* HAWTHORN).

Other miscellaneous traditions associated with rosemary include the notion that a little rosemary added to a barrel of beer will rob it of its intoxicating properties, and the idea that spoons made of rosemary wood add taste to even the most unpalatable dishes, as well as negating the effects of poison. Similarly, COMBS made of rosemary wood are reputed by the French to combat dizziness, while other authorities claim that applications of lotion containing rosemary will restore thinning HAIR.

**rough music** Known by various colourful local names, including 'riding the stang' and 'low-belling', this superstitious custom has featured in various guises in numerous cultures and is clearly of very ancient origins. The thinking behind the tradition is that any social or moral offence – typically adultery or the breaking of some other sexual taboo – that is allowed to go unpunished, even though not strictly against the law, will result in local crops and livestock being visited by various ills. Typically, the transgressors were visited by a mob of unruly locals banging pots and pans and generally making as much noise as possible in order to drive away the demons responsible for the offence, and sometimes even the perpetrators themselves.

Occasionally effigies of the guilty parties were drawn through the streets in donkey carts or publicly burned.

The victims of such rowdy demonstrations of public disapproval rarely regained their reputations in the community, and, even if not actually driven out, it was usual for them to leave the area before any more threatening action was taken. Instances of 'rough music' being practised in the British Isles continued to be recorded on a regular basis until the late nineteenth century, and isolated recurrences of the old custom have been recorded in rural areas even in modern times.

**rowan** The rowan or mountain ash was sacred to the Druids and continues to be respected for its protective properties. Planting rowan trees in the garden is highly recommended as a defence against WITCHCRAFT, while nailing rowan branches over the doorway to cowsheds and houses is likewise reputed to stop evil spirits entering. In many English counties these branches were formerly gathered on 3 May (Holy Rood Day or Rowan-tree Day) and then left in place for a whole year before being renewed. To be absolutely sure of keeping cattle free from the influence of witches a rowan twig could be tied to their tails with a length of RED thread. In the case of horses, it is advisable for the rider to carry a whip made of rowan or to wear a few sprigs of rowan in his or her hat. Carrying rowan about the person and attaching a small piece to the bedhead will further protect a human from interference by witches and has the added benefit of preventing RHEUMATISM. Touching a witch with a rowan stick, meanwhile, is said to result in the witch being immediately dragged off to Hell by the DEVIL himself.

Rowan trees are often found in graveyards because they are said to prevent the slumber of the dead from being disturbed. Other uses of the rowan which took advantage of its protective reputation include fashioning its wood into divining rods, water-wheels, farm tools and crossbeams in houses.

**royalty** Superstition, in remembrance of the days when kings and queens claimed semi-divine status, attaches special importance to members of a royal family, sometimes crediting the individuals with special healing powers (*see* CRAMP; KING'S TOUCH) or otherwise connecting the death of ruling monarchs with various supernatural happenings. The appearance of METEORITES or other celestial phenomena may be interpreted as a prophecy that a king or queen is about to die, and extraordinary behaviour among BIRDS and ANIMALS may also be read in a similar way. Another tradition involves the 'royal storm' – a period of foul weather that is always said to accompany the passing of a ruling monarch. Among other superstitions said to forecast the death of the king or queen is the ominous failure of the ASH to produce any of its customary winged seeds (as is reputed to have happened throughout England shortly before the execution of Charles I in 1649).

**ruby** The BIRTHSTONE for the month of July, the ruby is said to be one of the luckier gems. Those fortunate enough to own a ruby may wear it in the happy knowledge that it will safeguard them from evil of all kinds and prevent them from having impure thoughts. The association between the ruby and blood is reflected by the tradition that the stone will change colour according to the state of health enjoyed by the wearer.

**rue** Herb that is widely regarded as representing sorrow and repentance. In times gone by it was customary for someone who felt he had been wronged to throw a handful of rue in his enemy's face and to curse them with the words 'May you rue this day' or something similar (hence the phrase 'rue the day', meaning to regret some past action). In contrast, rue is said to bring luck to anyone who wears a sprig in their buttonhole and is also credited with certain healing properties, being particularly valued in treating EYE problems and as an antidote for poison (including SNAKE venom and the bite of rabid DOGS). It is also reputed to counter vertigo and EPILEPSY, to act as a painkiller if consumed with a fig, a NUT, some SALT and nine JUNIPER berries, and to work as a deterrent against witches and the EVIL EYE. During plague epidemics in the sixteenth and seventeenth centuries rue was often sprinkled on the floor in the belief that it would combat infection, and judges carried posies of rue to prevent them catching gaol-fever from the criminals brought before them.

Slipping some rue into one's SOCKS will promote a person's happiness, but sprigs of rue must never be given away as good luck will go with them. The plant itself will grow best if it has been stolen, and should ideally be damaged in some way. Lastly, rue has a particular significance in Moslem countries, where it is said to have been the only herb blessed by Mohammed.

**rush** Tall, moisture-loving plant that is reputed to have various luck-giving properties, especially if it has a GREEN head. The Irish claim that the rush was cursed by St Patrick, but still favour them for making protective CROSSES to put up over doors of houses and cowsheds. In folk medicine, a tradition from the West Country recommends drawing a peeled rush gently over the lips to heal mouth ULCERS, while a remedy recorded in Cheshire advises that a similar procedure will cure WARTS. In Devon it is said that picking three rushes from a stream, passing them through a child's mouth one by one and then throwing them back in the stream will cure the infant of thrush.

**rust** The association of rust with that most magical of metals, IRON, means that rust has some significance among superstitious people. Rust is, a little surprisingly, not necessarily a bad thing, as rusty KEYS, KNIVES and so forth are often said to have greater supernatural power in this condition. The Welsh claim that the discovery of such rusty items means that an unidentified party is saving up money for the person concerned.

# S

**sage**  Like many other herbs, sage is prized as a lucky plant with various beneficial medicinal properties. Legend has it that it was introduced to the British Isles by the Romans, who dropped bits of it while marching along the roads they constructed (said to be the reason why the plant is often spotted growing on grass verges). Credited with promoting wisdom and improving the memory, sage is said to flourish in gardens where a woman holds sway and also responds well when tended by someone who is very wise. It is important, however, that sage is picked before it can bloom, as flowering sage brings bad luck to the household. Hanging a sprig of sage in the kitchen will enable the occupants of the house to know how a missing member of the family is faring when away from home: if the sage wilts and perishes, the person concerned is in trouble of some kind.

For the purposes of love divination, a girl is advised to pick twelve sage leaves at midday on 25 April (St Mark's Day) or at midnight on MIDSUMMER'S EVE, plucking one leaf at each stroke of the clock. The first unmarried man she sees after doing this is destined to become her husband.

In folk medicine, eating sage on seven (or nine) mornings in succession before breakfast will cure the ague, according to one ancient Sussex belief. It may also be used in treatments for sore throats and weak EYES, in healing WOUNDS, in promoting fertility and in facilitating CHILD-BIRTH. In the days before the introduction of toothpaste, many people rubbed their TEETH with a sage leaf to keep them clean.

An old proverb heard in various forms in different countries suggests that eating sage in May, when the plant is deemed to be at its most potent, may have benefits for those seeking to extend their lifespan:

He that would live for aye,
Must eat sage in May.

**sailors**  Because of the perilous nature of their work seafarers around the world are among the most superstitious groups of individuals, and many of these beliefs still persist long after the demise of the age of sailing SHIPS. The sea has always inspired the deepest respect from those who spend time upon it, and most sailors' superstitions reflect the need for reassurance on the subjects of shipwreck and DROWNING.

Some precautions to ensure a safe voyage may be taken even before a sailor leaves home. These include wearing EAR-RINGS made of GOLD and the careful preservation of a CAUL, both of which are supposed to be powerful charms against the threat of drowning. Adorning the body with tattoos is also popular, as this is said to ward off evil spirits and also to prevent seafarers contracting any sexually transmitted disease. In the days when flogging was a frequent punishment, many sailors had tattoos depicting the Crucifixion put on their backs in the belief that this would cause sentences imposed to be lighter and, furthermore, that the lash itself would flinch at striking the image of Christ. Touching a wife's or lover's genitals 'for luck' is also alleged to promote a sailor's chances of survival. If, however, he wakes to find his earthenware basin turned upside down he may interpret this as a very bad sign and refuse to go down to his ship that day.

Sailors may show sensitivity in meeting certain people or animals on their way to the harbour to join their vessel. It is, for example, thought unlucky for a sailor to encounter a member of the CLERGY, anybody who is cross-eyed (*see* EVIL EYE) or someone who has red HAIR, as well as various birds and animals. It is also unlucky if a voyage is scheduled to begin on a Friday or on certain specific dates in the calendar, namely 2 February (Candlemas Day), the first Monday in April (said to have been Cain's birthday) and 31 December (when Judas committed suicide).

On safely reaching the ship many sailors will be careful to board with the right foot rather than the left in order to avoid the bad fortune that might be thus invoked. They will not be reassured, either, if well-wishers watch the ship until it is completely out of sight and point after it, thus threatening the evil eye, but they may be heartened if the same friends and relatives hurl old SHOES after the vessel for luck.

Sailors may express reservations if they find CORPSES, women or representatives of the cloth on board during a voyage, and they may also be prejudiced against anything BLACK in colour (Welsh crews also dislike transporting spinning wheels for some obscure reason). In the case of corpses, these must either be given a burial at sea at the first available opportunity or else carried 'athwart' the planks and never parallel with the bow and the stern. On reaching port the body must leave the ship before any living person. Conversely, the birth of a child on board a ship is almost universally greeted as a stroke of the greatest good fortune for ship and crew alike.

Disaster will be confidently predicted if certain animals – or even traces of them – are found on board a vessel. These include DOGS, HARES, HORSES and PIGS. It is taboo even to mention such animals by name, as it is also forbidden to make references to clergymen. Conversely it is thought to be an ill omen if RATS suddenly vacate a ship, which is seen as a sure sign that the vessel will sink. The luckiest of all animals to have on board is a CAT and many ships' companies cherish their 'ship's cat', which may often be made the vessel's MASCOT (though some US crews dislike having cats aboard). Most dangerous of all creatures to have in the vicinity of a ship is the ALBATROSS, which – like some other seabirds – is reputed to be the soul of a drowned sailor; the bird brings good luck if left unharmed, but if killed it will bring dire misfortune upon the vessel and its crew. Sailors will also show a certain nervousness if their ship is tailed by SHARKS, as these creatures are supposed to have a sixth sense concerning the approach of death.

Other portents of possible disaster include losing a mop and bucket over the side, tearing the ship's colours and absentmindedly passing something through the rungs of a LADDER. It is also unlucky to play CARDS at sea, to do any SEWING, to throw SALT overboard and to indulge in WHISTLING, unless the ship is becalmed and there is a deliberate wish to 'whistle up' strong winds.

Various superstitions reassure seafarers that there are ways in which they can influence the WEATHER in their favour while at sea. Apart from the risky remedy of whistling to raise a wind when lying becalmed, sailors may scratch the foremast with the fingernail, in which case a helpful breeze will soon spring up. Alternatively, the wind may respond if asked politely to oblige, or else burning an old BRUSH may have the desired effect. When the wind does come, a dead KINGFISHER nailed to the mast will prove useful in indicating the quarter from which the wind is blowing. Cutting the hair at sea or trimming the nails is unwise, as this will blow up a gale. Tossing a COIN into choppy water, however, may cause the waves to subside.

Among the oddest rituals observed at sea is the ceremony of 'crossing the line', in which those who are crossing the Equator for the first time are publicly humiliated in various ways in a kind of initiation ceremony. This custom derives from a more sinister primitive tradition that involved sailors sacrificing one of the crew to propitiate the gods of the deep.

Not unnaturally, sailors may feel extra anxiety when sailing through areas where many other ships have been lost. Perhaps the sight that fills seafarers with the most dread is the appearance of a 'ghost ship' of the *Flying Dutchman* variety; if this heaves into view, shipwreck is deemed certain. Should the worst actually happen, a French tradition rather ghoulishly advises that the sweetheart of a sailor lost at sea will be made aware of the awful truth by the sound of dripping water beside her bed.

Other miscellaneous superstitions commonly believed among seafarers include the notion that it is unlucky to sail in a boat painted GREEN, that it is inviting bad fortune to borrow something from or lend something to another boat, and that changing the NAME of a vessel is unlucky. Naval salutes, meanwhile, are never fired in even numbers, apparently for luck.

Sailors themselves are sometimes seen as harbingers of good luck. A well-known superstition (more often encountered away from the coast, where sailors in uniform are a rarer sight) claims that good luck will befall anyone who touches a sailor's collar, especially if they manage to do so without the sailor's knowledge.

*See also* FIGUREHEAD; FISHERMEN; GLASS; SEA; SEVEN WHISTLERS; SHIP.

**saining** Age-old superstition, recorded in various parts of the British Isles, involving a ritual ceremony by which a newborn BABY or recently deceased body is offered special supernatural protection. The more or less defunct practice of saining requires the whirling of lighted CANDLES in a SUNWISE direction around the bed in which the baby or body lies. A variation involves the midwife circling the bed nine times while reading from the BIBLE.

**St Agnes's Eve** In the Church calendar, 20 January, which is said to be an auspicious time for divining what the future might have in store. According to some, the day must be spent in fasting and complete silence and culminates in the preparation of a DUMB CAKE. If the whole procedure is correctly carried out the person concerned may be rewarded with a vision of their future partner or partners. Alternatively, the curious party may stick their sleeve with PINS in order to see their partner in their dreams or may simply restrict their intake to stale BREAD and PARSLEY tea and go to bed with a prayer to St Agnes to be shown a future partner.

**St Catherine's Day** In the Church calendar, 25 November, which is said to be a day when women may appeal to St Catherine, the patron saint of spinsters, for supernatural aid in the business of finding a husband. Prayers to the saint may vary in wording but all have the same intent, most succinctly summarised in a prayer recorded at Milton Abbey in Dorset in 1865, in which the woman concerned prays for 'a husband, St Catherine; a handsome one, St Catherine; a rich one, St Catherine; a nice one, St Catherine; and soon, St Catherine!'

**St Christopher** The patron saint of travellers, whose image is widely carried by motorists and others in the belief that this will keep them safe on their journey. The tradition was originally inspired by St Christopher's request of God that wherever his body went no evil or disease would be able to follow. His image was therefore frequently to be seen at entrances to churches and on public thoroughfares in medieval times, and in time came to be adopted by travellers everywhere. His image now most often appears on silver fobs attached to drivers' keyrings. Some modern academics, however, question whether the saint ever existed.

**St Elmo's Fire** Electrical phenomenon, which causes the masts and rigging of a SHIP to glow eerily in thundery weather and which is sometimes also seen around AIRCRAFT during storms. Not unnaturally such lights, which crackle with a noise as of burning twigs, have inspired awe in travellers at sea over the centuries. Seafarers agree that, if confined to the tops of masts, St Elmo's Fire is generally a good omen because it means that a storm is past its worst. If it comes down to the deck, however, it is more ominous, and if it surrounds the head of one of the crew this is a sure portent of the unfortunate man's death. St Elmo, incidentally, is the patron saint of Mediterranean seamen and is often identified with St Erasmus, who died on board ship during a storm at sea but is said to have returned to the vessel in the form of a shining light to guide the vessel through the waves.

**St John's wort** Yellow-flowered wild plant, which is reputed to have various healing and protective properties and is the flower most closely linked with the festivals marking MIDSUMMER'S EVE. Named after St John the Baptist, at whose festivals the flower was once ceremonially burned, St John's wort is supposed to keep evil spirits and witches from approaching and was formerly often kept indoors for exactly this purpose. The red spots that may sometimes be discerned on its leaves are said to represent the blood spilled when St John the Baptist was beheaded and are alleged to appear on 27 August, the anniversary of the saint's death.

Women experiencing difficulty in becoming pregnant are promised by superstition that they will overcome the problem if they take off all their clothes and venture into their gardens during the hours of darkness on Midsummer's Eve and there pick a St John's wort. Midsummer's Eve is also the best time to gather St John's wort for use in treating people suffering from nervous disorders such as depression and insanity. Sleeping with a St John's wort under the pillow, meanwhile, will vouchsafe the sleeper visions of a future marriage partner.

Some regional superstitions warn that it is dangerous to step on a St John's wort. A fairy horse may rear up under the person's feet and carry them off on a wild ride that will last all night before the hapless rider is unceremoniously dumped in some far-off spot.

**St Mark's Day** In the Church calendar, 25 April, which is thought to be an ideal time to attempt to learn what the future has in store. For the purposes of love divination, a girl should pluck twelve leaves of SAGE as the clock strikes noon that day, in order to be rewarded either with a vision of her future husband or by his appearance in the flesh. Alternatively, she may set an extra place at the supper table and wait for a future lover to materialise to join them. A more ominous superstition claims that a person knows they are about to die if they discover a footprint that matches their own in the ASHES of the fire that burned on St Mark's Eve. Equally morbid is the tradition that anyone who waits in a church porch at midnight on St Mark's Eve will see the shades of all those who are destined to die in the parish over the next twelve months pass by into the church.

**St Martin's Day** In the Church calendar, 11 November, which is regarded as one of the more ominous days of the year. The Irish place some importance on the day, insisting that it is unlucky for millers to grind corn or for women to do any spinning on this date. Another, somewhat grisly, Irish tradition requires that St Martin's Eve should be marked by the sacrifice of a COCK, its blood being sprinkled over the threshold and into the four corners of the house. Should a cock be impossible to obtain, the ritual may be carried out by spilling blood from a deliberately cut finger. In former times it was usual for millers to kill a cock in a similar way and to sprinkle its blood on the machinery on this date in a ritual called 'blooding the mill'. The miller was then believed to be safe from accidents in the year ahead.

**St Paul's Day**   In the Church calendar, 25 January, on which date certain predictions may be made about the harvest later in the year. If there is RAIN on St Paul's Day, a poor harvest must be expected.

**St Swithin's Day**   *see* RAIN.

**St Valentine's Day**   In the Church calendar, 14 February, which is widely recognised as a day for the exchanging of cards, red ROSES and other gifts between lovers. Cards are by convention left unsigned, and much of the day is spent by recipients in delicious speculation about their identity (originally the cards were designed and illustrated by the senders themselves).

St Valentine's Day is, it is alleged, a good time to try to divine future partners. One tradition has it that if a girl leaves her house early in the morning that day and the first person she meets is a man, then she will be married within three months (quite possibly to that particular man). Her chances of meeting the love of her life may be enhanced if she wears a yellow crocus in her buttonhole, and further information may be gleaned about a future spouse by noting which species of bird she sees first. The following list suggests the interpretations to be made according to the bird first spotted:

Blackbird: a clergyman.
Bluebird: a happy man or a poor man.
Crossbill: a quarrelsome man.
Dove: a good man.
Goldfinch: a rich man.
Robin: a sailor.
Sparrow: a farmer.
Woodpecker: nobody.

Less romantic is the tradition recorded in parts of eastern England that St Valentine's Day is an auspicious occasion for the preparation of EELS for the purposes of magic.

St Valentine was a Christian martyr who was executed under the Roman Emperor Claudius II around AD 269, apparently for opposing a ban on the marriage of young men of soldiering age. Perhaps not insignificantly, 14 February was also the date when ancient Greeks honoured the gods of women and marriage. According to medieval folklore, 14 February also marks the first day of the mating season among birds.

**saliva**   *see* SPITTING.

**salmon**   According to Scottish superstition, the salmon is an unlucky FISH in many circumstances. It is thought particularly unlucky for FISHERMEN to find a salmon in their first haul of the day, and many of them regard 'salmon' as a taboo word that should never be uttered while at sea.

**salt**   Vital to the maintenance of life and, to the primitive eye, apparently magical in its properties of food preservation and evaporation, salt has been highly valued for centuries. Roman soldiers and workers were often paid a *salarium* (from which we get our word 'salary') in the form of salt. Some superstitions connected with the substance may indeed date back earlier, to pre-classical times, when salt was frequently used in sacrifices to placate the gods, to ratify important agreements and to solemnify other social transactions. The Aztecs boasted a Salt Goddess, while Christian religion referred to its mystical nature in the story of Lot's wife and her transformation into a pillar of salt after she turned to look back at the evil city of Sodom (which was itself swept away by the heavily salinated Dead Sea). Salt has also been used in some of the major Christian religious ceremonies, including baptism and exorcism.

The most commonly observed superstition concerning salt in modern times is the assumption that evil spirits are roused when salt is accidentally spilt – in some areas it is said that a tear will be shed for every grain thus scattered. This notion undoubtedly has its origins in the high value that was once placed on salt, though some authorities also link it to the legend that Judas overturned the salt cellar at the Last Supper. The tossing of a pinch of the spilt salt over the left shoulder is regarded as an antidote to any ill luck risked, in the belief that it will drive away the DEVIL before he can whisper in the ear of the person concerned (variations in this tradition add that a CROSS should then be traced in the salt that is left on the table). Similarly, a pinch of salt thrown after a gipsy is believed to nullify any curse he or she may have just pronounced. Throwing salt after someone who has just visited the house, meanwhile, is said to ensure that they do not return for a long time.

Other less well-known traditions are based on the luck-giving powers of the substance. FISHERMEN, though they regard the word 'salt' as one of the taboo words never to be spoken when at sea, have been known to sprinkle their NETS with a little salt, while boatbuilders traditionally spill salt between the planks of a craft under construction in the expectation that this will safeguard the crew on their voyages. The burning of salt on seven consecutive mornings is reputed to ensure an absent lover's return, and brides sometimes sprinkle salt in their pocket for luck (just as SAILORS do). Salt is also carried over the threshold in many British homes as part of the NEW YEAR celebrations because it brings the promise of prosperity (a clear reference to the earlier financial value of salt). Once inside the house salt should never be lent out again, particularly on New Year's Day, as this constitutes giving away one's good luck. Salt should, in any case, never be borrowed – if it is, the borrower should take care to offer money for it and never to return it, as though it has become his or her own property in the usual way.

Salt is reputed to have considerable power as a protective against evil influences. A little salt held in the palm of a woman giving birth is said to be of great benefit to mother and child (*see* CHILD-BIRTH), and newborn children were once presented with gifts of salt or bathed in salty water to ward off the threat of WITCHCRAFT. If witchcraft is suspected, throwing a handful of salt in the fire for nine mornings in succession may break the spell. Dairymaids in former times often sprinkled a pinch of salt in their pails and in the butter churns to prevent interference by witches. A saucer of salt, sometimes mixed with SOIL, is sometimes laid on the chest of a dead man, ostensibly to prevent the body swelling but more probably to scare away any evil spirits.

In everyday use at the table salt should never be openly offered to another diner, as evidenced by the traditional saying 'Help me to salt, help me to sorrow.' Care should also be taken not to break the salt cellar, as this threatens a broken friendship. According to the Germans, a girl who neglects to put the salt on the table in the first place is revealing the fact that she is no longer a virgin. Too much salt in the food, incidentally, is sometimes interpreted as a sign that the cook is in love.

**sapphire** The BIRTHSTONE for September, which is reputed to promote love and happiness in those who possess one. According to Buddhist tradition, the sapphire has special powers to induce trances.

**sardonyx** The BIRTHSTONE for August, which is said to promote marital happiness. In classical times it was also reputed to have the power to make lawyers more eloquent.

**Satan** *see* DEVIL.

**Saturday** *see* DAYS OF THE WEEK.

**saucepan** *see* POT.

**scarlet fever** Folk medicine boasts several magical cures for scarlet fever. One of the most widely repeated is the rather obscure Irish remedy that involves taking a HAIR from the patient and feeding it to a DONKEY.

**school** Many schools may lay claim to superstitions unique to themselves, evolved by generations of classmates over many years, but other traditions are shared more widely. Among those that are more widely recognised are the notions that it is unlucky to drop textbooks on the way to school because the pupil concerned will make mistakes throughout the day ahead, and that staring at a teacher's back for too long will result in a child being singled out to answer questions (a reference to the time-honoured belief that teachers have eyes in the back of their heads). In schools where corporal punishment is sanctioned, pupils may adhere to the age-old idea that rubbing the skin with the juice of an ONION prevents the pain of a beating being felt.

**sciatica** A painful form of neuralgia, for the cure of which superstition offers several suggestions. In Cornwall, it is said that carrying the knucklebone of a SHEEP about the person will cause the problem to disappear, while elsewhere much the same is said about carrying a small POTATO or a piece of LODESTONE.

**scissors** Being made of metal and having the power to cut, scissors are regarded as potent objects in superstition. They must be handled with care as their misuse risks one's luck, which can be 'cut' all too easily. It is therefore very unfortunate to drop a pair of scissors, and even worse if they then stick into the floor because this constitutes a DEATH omen (though regional variations suggest an imminent WEDDING if both points stick in the floor and a funeral only if one point pierces the floor). Neither should the person who dropped a pair of scissors attempt to retrieve them. He or she should ask a friend to pick them up, or, failing this, the scissors should be trodden on before being touched. To be on the safe side the scissors should then be warmed between the hands before being used again. Scissors that come apart while held in the hands are also a portent of bad luck in store.

As is the case with KNIVES and other sharp objects, scissors should never be given as presents unless the recipient hands over a coin or two in exchange as though buying them in the usual way; failure to do so may lead to the friendship between the two parties being severed. Scissors may, however, act as a deterrent against witches (*see* WITCHCRAFT) and in former times they were sometimes placed under the doormat to prevent any malevolent spirit coming into the house (usually in the opened position so that the blades formed a CROSS).

A curious superstition of African origin claims that scissors should not be opened and closed during the celebration of a wedding, as this will result in the groom becoming impotent.

**scrofula**   *see* KING'S TOUCH.

**scrying**   *see* MIRROR.

**scythe** The traditional depiction of death mowing down the living with his scythe has inspired various ominous superstitions connected with both this implement and the smaller one-handed sickle. The Roman god Saturn, the ruler of death, was conventionally depicted holding a sickle. The Druids, meanwhile, insisted that MISTLETOE be cut with a golden sickle if it was to retain its magical properties. Both the scythe and the sickle thrive on blood and will only give good service if they draw blood from the person who wields them when first used. It is thought to be very unlucky to find a scythe in a field; if this happens, the unfortunate person should beat a hasty retreat after first making the sign of the CROSS. Other traditions connected with these two implements include keeping a scythe in the thatch of a house to prevent the dwelling being struck by LIGHTNING, placing two scythes in a cross at the foot of a CRADLE to protect a newborn child, and leaving a rusting scythe on top of a haystack to guard against the hay catching fire.

**sea** The sea has always inspired feelings of awe and dread and in ancient times was considered the source of all evil. The Great Beast in the Book of Revelation is described as rising up from the sea, and the lingering doubts that man harbours about the world's oceans are reflected in the countless taboos and superstitions relating to the business of travelling over its surface (*see* FIGUREHEAD; FISHERMEN; SAILORS; SHIP). The creatures which inhabit the sea and the birds that fly above it are often regarded with suspicion, though sightings of even such ominous animals as the ALBATROSS and SHARK are not necessarily unlucky in all circumstances. The sea itself has its beneficial aspects too: taking a spoonful of seawater every morning, for instance, is said to increase a person's chances of living to a great age, according to the Welsh.

Many seafarers personalise the inherent malevolence of the sea in the mythical figure of Davy Jones, who whips up storms and causes shipwrecks almost at whim (sailors and a good many landlubbers still talk of drowned seamen sleeping in 'Davy Jones's Locker'). It has been suggested that 'Davy Jones', who was first heard of in the eighteenth century, was introduced through the combination of the West Indian 'duppy' (meaning 'devil') and the English surname Jones, which may itself have been a derivation of Jonah, the name of the luckless biblical seafarer.

*See also* DROWNING; SEAGULL; TIDES; WAVE.

**sea-anemone** *see* HERRING.

**seagull** Generally regarded as being unlucky birds, seagulls are widely associated with death among coastal communities. Superstition has it that a seagull is the reincarnation of a dead FISHERMAN or SAILOR, usually one who has died by DROWNING. It is therefore held in many

regions to be unlucky to kill a seagull. Other superstitions extending this link with death include the notion that a seagull that flies in a straight line is following the path of a CORPSE on the seabed, and the fear that a seagull hitting the window of a house warns of death or some other calamity being about to befall a member of the household out at sea. Likewise, three gulls flying over someone may be interpreted as an omen of death. It is also unlucky to catch a seagull in fishing nets and to hear their call (because they are said to cry just before some accident takes place). In the West Country, meanwhile, superstition cautions against feeding seagulls and particularly against looking them in the EYE; if this last taboo is broken the gull will return at a later date, should the person concerned get into difficulty in the water, to peck their eyes.

Lastly, it is said that when seagulls are seen far inland this is a sign of bad weather at sea, as summarised in a Scottish rhyme:

Seagull, seagull, sit on the sand;
It's never good weather when you're on the land.
*See also* ALBATROSS; STORMY PETREL.

**seaweed** Superstition credits seaweed with various supernatural properties, including the power to predict the WEATHER. According to widely followed tradition, a piece of seaweed kept beside the front door will shrivel up when warm weather is expected but will become moist when showers are on the way. It is also said that seaweed kept in the house may act as a deterrent to witches and other evil spirits (*see* WITCHCRAFT) and will also guard against the building catching FIRE. A superstition recorded in Wiltshire, meanwhile, claims that a person will never be without friends so long as he or she keeps a little seaweed.

**seven** *see* NUMBERS.

**Seven Whistlers** A flight of seven spectral birds, whose appearance is much dreaded by SAILORS, FISHERMEN and MINERS in particular. Usually encountered at night, the Seven Whistlers utter eerie high-pitched calls and are said to be an omen of death or some other disaster. According to some witnesses, the birds are actually six in number and they fly in constant search of the seventh: when the seventh bird finally joins them the world will end. Another tradition concerning the birds claims that they are the spirits of drowned seafarers, or else the souls of unbaptised BABIES, though the less superstitious sometimes identify them as flights of CURLEWS or PLOVERS or other birds with distinctive whistling calls.

*See also* GABRIEL'S HOUNDS.

**sewing** The business of sewing is hedged in by a variety of superstitions of considerable antiquity. Among the best known are the claims that it is unlucky for anyone to sew a garment while still wearing it, and that an argument will shortly break out if the THREAD gets knotted while it is being sewn. On the other hand, a tradition recorded in Mediterranean countries has it that it is lucky to tangle the thread, as this promises good health and prosperous times ahead. Sewing clothing on a Friday is not a good idea, as the clothes will attract LICE.

A curious superstition is associated with the making of patchwork quilts. If a woman manages to complete a whole quilt without help from anyone else she may congratulate herself on her achievement but may be sobered to learn that this means she will never get married. According to West Country tradition there will be no marriage in a house for as long as there is an unfinished bedspread in it.

*See also* THIMBLE.

**sex** Men and women have always regarded sex as in part a magical or supernatural activity, and the act of sexual union has thus acquired a mythology of its own over the centuries. In primitive times the phallus, for instance, was worshipped in many cultures as a symbol of life and was widely employed as a charm

(*see* AMULET) against evil. In some early societies it was held that the world itself had been created through sexual activity between the gods, and the orgasm was viewed as a moment of mystical communication with the world beyond. Subsequently sex became a central feature of various religions and also of much black magic practice, with witches traditionally attending covens naked and frequently indulging in sexual intercourse – sometimes, it was alleged, with the DEVIL himself. Similarly the body fluids released during sex were reputed to have immense potential in spells and potions. Extreme forms of this belief in the power of sex have included reported cases of sorcerers having sex with corpses prior to attempting to bring them back to life.

Certain foods have always been thought to promote sexual desire (*see* APHRODISIAC) and superstition is replete with recommendations designed to enhance fertility or conversely to avoid PREGNANCY. Much can be told about a person's sexuality by their appearance. Accordingly, men with large hands and feet are supposed to have large sexual organs, as are women with wide mouths. Hairy men, meanwhile, are reputed to have more sexual drive than others, as are men from hot Mediterranean countries.

Among other superstitions that continue to linger into modern times are the notions that a girl who stands up while having sex cannot get pregnant; that too much masturbation makes a man blind; that repeated sex weakens the heart; that blondes and redheads are more sexually liberated than brunettes; that getting married confers protection against venereal disease; and that having sex with a woman while she is having her period will result in a man going bald. In parts of the Far East it is maintained by some that having anal intercourse will cure any sexually transmitted disease.

Hopes that the whole subject of sex was finally shedding its shady taboo nature in the wake of the liberated 1960s were firmly put in their place in the early

1980s, when the emergence of the AIDS epidemic was welcomed by many people as a divine punishment for those who engaged in homosexual practices.

*See also* LOVE; PROSTITUTE; VIRGINITY.

**shadow** According to a number of varied superstitions recorded around the world, a person's shadow is mystically linked to their real being and any injury suffered by a shadow may have serious consequences for its owner. In times gone by it has been claimed that the shadow, like the reflection, actually constitutes a person's soul (the reason why, according to one well-known tradition, a person who has sold his soul to the DEVIL will cast no shadow). Thus, harm suffered by a shadow will result in harm coming to the person who casts it, and particular care should be taken to guard against witches or other malevolent forces attempting to steal one's shadow. This idea undoubtedly lies at the root of the legends of mythical heroes killing their enemies by stabbing their shadows, and of the still prevalent belief that it is unlucky to allow another person to tread on one's shadow, a hostile act that may be interpreted as a great insult in some countries. In China, mourners at a FUNERAL may keep their distance from the COFFIN for fear that their shadow will fall on it and thus be buried with the deceased.

One last superstition relating to shadows is the custom of examining the shape of the shadows cast by a group of people as they sit by the fire at CHRISTMAS or NEW YEAR. If anyone's shadow appears to lack a head, the chances are that the person concerned will be dead before another twelve months have passed.

**shaking hands** *see* HAND.

**shark** With their uncanny ability to detect prey from great distances and their reputation for attacking the victims of shipwrecks and swimmers, sharks are feared and loathed by seafarers around the globe. Superstitions associated with them include the notion that if they tail a vessel someone aboard is close to death, especially if the sharks are three in number. The sight of PORPOISES near a ship may, however, offer some reassurance since these are reputed to ward off sharks.

**sheep** The central economic importance of sheep in many cultures means that there are numerous superstitions intended to safeguard their well-being, particularly from the threat of WITCHCRAFT and disease. Driving sheep under an ARCH of ROWAN is thought to be one of the best ways to provide such protection. A shepherd, meanwhile, should never count the number of sheep in his flock, as this means a WOLF will count them at the same time.

Sheep are generally thought to be lucky animals, largely because of their association with the Good Shepherd. This association is remembered by the animals at midnight on Christmas Eve, when they are reputed to bow to the east in remembrance of the Nativity. Timehonoured tradition also holds that shepherds buried with a tuft of wool will be excused from appearing before God so as to avoid being parted from their flocks. It is considered very lucky for a traveller to encounter a flock of sheep while on the road, especially so if he makes his way through them in order to overtake them. Carrying a LUCKY BONE taken from the head of a sheep is also said to promote a person's luck. Sticking a sheep's heart with PINS and roasting it at midnight with all the doors and windows open, meanwhile, will break any spell that might have been cast. Other superstitions claim that sheep that sit quietly on the grass are a sign of fine weather to come, while sheep that walk about bleating are a portent of rainstorms.

In folk medicine, various parts of the sheep's carcass are credited with magical properties. Wearing a charm made from a sheep's patella will cure CRAMP, while carrying the knucklebone will ward off RHEUMATISM and SCIATICA. Consuming a little sheep DUNG in water will relieve both JAUNDICE and WHOOPING COUGH. If this latter remedy is too daunting, it may suffice for a child with whooping cough to be breathed on by a sheep (*see* BREATH) and then rolled in the grass on which the sheep has recently been lying. In former times, people with consumption were often similarly encouraged to walk through a flock of sheep, on the grounds that this could only improve their condition. Other ailments will be cured by sleeping among sheep, by cleaning out their pens or, in the case of ADDER bites, by wrapping the patient in a fresh sheepskin. Placing a sheep's lung at the feet of someone suffering from pneumonia will draw the disease away from the patient. Least attractive of all is the treatment for ague, which requires the sufferer to swallow a live sheep tick every morning nine mornings in a row.

*See also* BLADE-BONE; LAMB.

**shepherd's-purse** White-flowered plant with triangular seed pods, which may be used for the purposes of divination. It is said in Yorkshire that if a person opens a seed pod and finds that the seeds within are yellow he or she may expect great riches, but if they are green poverty beckons.

**ship** In keeping with the superstitious ways of SAILORS, FISHERMEN and other seafarers throughout history, ships themselves are subject to a host of folk beliefs and taboos. In particular, the rituals connected with the launching of a new vessel are profoundly important to those who are to sail in her. In ancient times it was believed that bad luck would befall any boat that was not launched with appropriate blood sacrifices, sometimes human, in a ceremony that was deemed to bring the ship 'to life' and to propitiate the gods of the deep. Applications of this idea included the barbaric Viking practice of crushing prisoners beneath the keels of longships when they were first launched.

In time blood was replaced by red wine and this in turn by champagne, bottles of which are broken against the bows with due ceremony even today (it is, incidentally, a bad omen if the bottle does not break first time). Similarly, ships are still decked out with flags as a matter of course in continuation of the ancient practice of decorating boats with flowers to win the favour of the deities of the ocean.

Boatbuilders may place a silver COIN under the mast for luck, and the sailors themselves may nail a HORSESHOE to the mast for the same reason. Few ships carry FIGUREHEADS nowadays; in former centuries it was thought crucial for all large vessels to protect their luck in such a way. Alternatively, large EYES were painted on the bows to scare away hostile spirits. To safeguard a ship's luck still further superstition advises the cherishing of a ship's CAT, preferably BLACK – but cautions that having two cats on board will not double the luck but rather will create a risk of grave misfortune.

Other miscellaneous superstitions connected with ships include the fear that anyone who is caught POINTING at one inflicts the curse of the EVIL EYE upon it, the notion that carrying BALLAST that is wholly white is inviting disaster, the tradition that it is unlucky to board a boat on anything but the right-hand side, and that changing a ship's NAME is sure to cause it to come to grief. It is also unlucky to choose a ship's name before the vessel has been safely launched.

*See also* SEA.

**shirt** Because the shirt is worn next to the skin it is thought to reflect in various ways the fortunes of the person who wears it. To divine the health of a small infant, for instance, a parent should toss its shirt into a fountain: if the shirt sinks the child's health is at risk, but if it floats all is well. By extension of this idea, a worried father might allow his offspring to wear his own shirts – by doing so they will gain a little of their father's strength. By the same token, however, care should be taken in borrowing other people's shirts as their sins are said to be borrowed with them.

In times gone by it was believed that a shirt, or its forerunner the smock, could be used by a woman for divination. The procedure was to hang a shirt, newly washed in a running stream, inside out before the fire on HALLOWE'EN and to wait for the husband-to-be or his apparition to appear to turn it right side out.

Putting a shirt on back to front by mistake is said to be a portent of good luck, but buttoning it up wrongly or getting it on inside out is an omen of misfortune.

*See also* CLOTHING.

**shivering**  Superstition places a very gloomy interpretation on someone who shivers suddenly and without apparent cause. It is commonly held around the world that this is the effect of 'someone walking over my grave' – that is, someone has just walked over the patch of ground where the person concerned is destined to be buried. Alternatively, a sudden bout of shivering may be due to the proximity of death. Shivering on getting up in the morning is also a bad sign, said to signify that bad luck will haunt that person for the rest of the day. Shivering on getting into bed, however, is more encouraging and holds the promise of pleasant dreams ahead.

**shoe**  Of all items of CLOTHING, shoes are perhaps the most significant in terms of the wealth of superstitions associated with them. Old shoes are widely supposed to be lucky, hence the time-honoured customs of hurling old boots after departing SHIPS in order to guarantee the fortune of the crew and attaching old shoes to the rear bumper of the car in which newly-weds drive away on their WEDDING day. This linking of shoes with wedding ceremonies goes back to biblical times and is of obscure origin, though it has been suggested that throwing a shoe after the groom was formerly meant as a reminder that he had taken over responsibility for his bride from her family. Most modern interpretations of the ritual, however, suppose that the shoes or boots (which ideally should belong to a left foot) will promote the happy couple's luck in general or, more specifically, will ensure their fertility.

Less well-known superstitions relating to shoes include the now defunct idea that burning an old shoe indoors will drive contagion from the house, and that this is also a wise precaution to take before setting out on any journey. If an old shoe is burned on CHRISTMAS Eve, it is said by authorities in Devon that the person concerned will not go short of shoes in the year ahead.

For the purposes of love divination, placing the shoes in the shape of a letter T beside the bed on MIDSUMMER'S EVE and reciting the rhyme,

Hoping this night my true love to see,
I place my shoes in the form of a T

may be sufficient to give the sleeper visions of a partner-to-be. Putting one's shoes under the bed with the soles turned upwards, meanwhile, is said in parts of southern England to be a cure for CRAMP, while leaving them by the bedroom door so that one shoe is coming into and the other going out of the room will confuse the demons that cause NIGHTMARES. If one's sleep is disturbed by a DOG barking one remedy is to turn one's left shoe upside down, at which the noise will cease.

Superstitions conflict concerning gifts of new shoes, some claiming that such presents are harmful to the luck of the recipient, while others see only good luck in the act. A third variation advises that gifts of new shoes are perfectly acceptable, provided that the recipient gives a small COIN in return. All agree, though, that it is inviting bad luck to give shoes as presents at Christmas. Should a person never give someone else a pair of new shoes as a present, however, they are doomed to go barefoot after they die, according to another tradition.

Shoes should never be placed upon a TABLE because this is symbolic of death by hanging (condemned prisoners were usually hanged while still wearing their shoes). At the very least this risks an argument breaking out in the household. ACTORS AND ACTRESSES in particular are wary of putting their shoes on the table in their dressing rooms, for fear that this will blight their luck on and off the stage.

When putting shoes on it is a bad omen to try to put one on the wrong foot, and in any case unwise to put the left shoe on first (though some people claim it is the right foot that is unlucky). One superstition has it that a person who makes a habit of always putting the left shoe on first will never suffer TOOTHACHE. It is also unlucky, as well as perilous, to walk with just one shoe on. An old and rather mischievous English superstition claims that if a new pair of shoes squeaks when worn it betrays the fact that the shoes have not been paid for. By the same token, superstition warns that people with expensive-looking shoes that never seem to get dirty or worn are probably cheats and thieves. The Japanese, incidentally, think it unlucky to put on a new pair of sandals before five o'clock in the afternoon.

Much may be told about a person's prospects by the way in which his or her shoes (or SOCKS) wear out. If the toe goes first they are doomed to a life of hardship and poverty. If the heel wears out first, though, riches and success lie in store. An old Suffolk rhyme sums it up thus:

Tip at the toe, live to see woe,
Wear at the side, live to be a bride,
Wear at the ball, live to spend all,
Wear at the heel, live to save a deal.

*See also* BOOT; FEET; SHOELACE; SLIPPER.

**shoelace**  Just as SHOES are a focus of superstitious speculation, so too are shoelaces. Very familiar is the tradition that if a shoelace comes undone someone is talking about the person concerned. If the left lace comes untied bad things are being said, but if it is the right one only good things are being said. In the USA this superstition is expressed in the rhyme:

'Tis a sure sign and true,
At that very moment
Your true love thinks of you.

It is also widely acknowledged that it is a bad omen for a shoelace to break, but that it is good luck to find a KNOT in one's laces. A more obscure tradition warns that it is unlucky to mix the colours of one's shoelaces. If one shoe is tied with a brown lace and the other with a black lace this is particularly unlucky, brown representing the earth of the grave and black representing death.

**shooting**  Like FISHERMEN, hunters with guns share a number of time-honoured traditions. These include the superstitions that a bad day's shooting will be had if the hunter misses with his first shot and that getting a virgin girl to jump over the barrel of a gun will improve one's chances of success (as will rubbing the barrel with VERVAIN). Firing a shot in the air at midnight when seeing the NEW YEAR in is recommended as another way to ensure that a marksman gets his eye in over the coming twelve months. Meeting a member of the CLERGY or a pregnant woman on the way to a shoot is, however, fatal to one's chances of hitting anything and may even presage a shooting ACCIDENT. Mixing gunshot with lard and feeding it to someone who feels sick will settle their stomach and cure them of their nausea.

**shooting star**  *see* METEORITE.

**shrew**  In ancient times the shrew was widely regarded as an unlucky creature and it retains such associations to this day. Reputed by the Romans to have a venomous bite, the shrew was subsequently believed to have the power of casting the EVIL EYE and became to many people the personification of hatred and bitterness. Anyone setting out on a journey who encounters a shrew is therefore advised to return home, though conversely it is also said that shrews will die instantly if they attempt to cross a path used by men. Allowing a shrew to run over a person or animal will result in a marked decline in the latter's health, typically leading to pain in the joints and lameness. To counter such ill effects a sufferer must be passed through an ARCH of BRAMBLE, or else a shrew must be trapped alive in a hole in an ASH and left there to die. Such 'shrew ashes' then acquire their own magical properties, and their leaves and twigs can be used to ease any shrew-related injuries. Applying a dead shrew to the site of a shrew bite is supposed to cause the injury to heal quickly, and carrying one about in the pocket is also said to ward off RHEUMATISM.

**Shrove Tuesday**   *see* PANCAKE.

**sickle**   *see* SCYTHE.

**sieve and shears**   Traditional CHARM that was formerly employed in the detection of thieves or other guilty persons. Otherwise known as 'turning the riddle', the procedure involved piercing a sieve with a pair of opened shears and then, with the shears held in the air by the handles, reciting the names of suspects: the name that was being spoken when the sieve 'turned' or dropped off the points of the shears was the name of the guilty party. This procedure, which was still being used in nineteenth-century England, did not have any standing in legal terms but was sufficiently well thought of among rural communities for anyone found guilty in this way to find further life impossible in the locality. The practice may have had its origins in the magic that was associated with the sieve in classical times, when it was venerated for the way it seemed to imitate the falling of rain from the Heavens. Much later, witches were reputed to use sieves as vehicles on which to fly to the clouds or over water.

**silver**   Superstition holds silver to be one of the most potent of all precious metals, particularly associated with the MOON. This link means that silver has many uses in WITCHCRAFT and other occult practices. Among the many properties assigned to it is the notion, much popularised by the cinema, that only a silver bullet will kill a VAMPIRE. In fact such a bullet is also said to have the power to destroy a wide range of supernatural creatures, including witches, werewolves and various demons. Silver works because it cannot be deflected by magical means, being invulnerable to all enchantment; this also means that it has little power as a TALISMAN in itself, though it will increase the magical potential of a design or object that already has some mystical significance.

Silver is generally lucky and in the past many people carefully set aside 'lucky' sixpences or other silver COINS to be used in Christmas puddings or simply to ensure continued prosperity. Turning over any silver coins in the pocket on first sighting a new MOON is widely recognised as a sure way to attract more money. Boatbuilders like to place a silver coin under the mast of a vessel they are constructing in order to ensure its luck, and in former times householders often buried silver coins under the threshold for similar reasons. As well as wearing 'something old, something new, something borrowed and something blue', even today some brides will go through their marriage service (*see* WEDDING DRESS) with a silver sixpence in their left shoe for luck.

Anyone who encounters a gipsy and fancies they would like to make use of their services in divining the future must first 'cross their palm' with silver, a custom that was recorded before the birth of Christ and is still pursued today, only the amount of silver differing. Other miscellaneous traditions relating to silver include the superstition that if a piece of silver jewellery becomes tarnished this is a sure omen that its owner is about to die.

**sin-eating**   The practice of magically transferring the sins of a dead person to one still living, so that the deceased's soul might have an easier journey to the afterlife. This curious archaic custom was once found in various forms in many societies, both Christian and pagan. In the British Isles, where the practice was still prevalent in the seventeenth century and was occasionally revived as late as the nineteenth, the usual procedure involved eating foods that had been brought into close contact with the dead person. Typically the food would be placed on the breast of the dead person or passed over the corpse to the sin-eater, who would normally have been specially hired for the purpose and received a small payment for his services. In other cases food that had been placed on or near a corpse was surreptitiously fed to a beggar or to some other person unaware of the situation, so that they absorbed the dead person's sins unknowingly.

As the hired sin-eater gradually disappeared in common practice, so mourners gathered instead to drink a symbolic glass of wine in the presence of the dead person, the bottle and glasses being placed on the COFFIN. To decline a glass offered in these circumstances would be deeply resented.

**singing**   Although it might appear a harmless enough activity, singing is not without its dangers according to a number of superstitions. Singing in the bath, for instance, is supposed to be unlucky in the morning, as emphasised by the old saw 'Sing before breakfast and cry before night' (it is, though, quite safe to indulge in a bathtime singalong at other times of day). This idea apparently originated in the classical notion that a person should not celebrate the day's achievements in song before the day's business has begun. Singing while eating a meal should also be avoided, as in the English proverb 'Sing at the table, die in the workhouse.' It is also considered unlucky to sing while making BREAD or while playing CARDS.

*See also* MUSIC.

**skin**   Superstition offers a variety of courses for those who are concerned with taking care of their skin. To ensure a good complexion drink cold COFFEE (a German treatment), never wear furs on a Friday, or else smear a baby's first wet nappy all over one's face. A problem with the skin is interpreted by many as a positive sign, indicating that some inner malady is forcing its way out of the body. Among suggested treatments for skin problems are rubbing spit over the affected area (*see* SPITTING) or allowing a FROG to sit upon it; rolling on the grass early on St John's Day or doing the same thing naked in a field of OATS; and eating a LIZARD. Remedies for children range from paring the FINGERNAILS or smearing them with lard to making them wear a hat made of CABBAGE leaves or taking them to see a grey DONKEY on eight days in succession.

*See also* DEW.

**skull**   Since the skull houses the brain, superstition has identified it as the seat of the soul and has accordingly credited it with certain potent magical qualities, particularly in the realm of folk medicine. Consuming powdered human skull in one's food is reputed by some authorities to cure EPILEPSY, while driving a NAIL into a human skull is said to relieve HEADACHES (as is taking a little of the moss that grows on a dead person's skull as snuff). Holding a tooth taken from the skull of a hanged man against a living person's teeth or gums, meanwhile, is said to cure TOOTHACHE (according to some versions of this superstition the patient must 'bite' the tooth out of the skull with his or her own teeth).

Drinking wine or other strong liquor from the skull of one's enemies was formerly believed to endow the drinker with the courage of his vanquished foe, and was an accepted tradition at Viking feasts. Burying the skulls of dead people and animals was also once a widely accepted precaution when laying the foundations of buildings of various kinds. Witches and sorcerers also viewed the skull as a focus of supernatural power, and a skull is often depicted among the various essential accoutrements of their art.

Oaths taken on skulls are considered especially binding, and according to the Irish anyone who breaks such a vow will be punished by death. Such ideas should not be taken lightly, for various locations throughout the British Isles boast 'screaming skulls' that are notorious for disrupting the lives of those who dare to disturb them from their resting places. These include the famous skull of Bettiscombe Manor in Dorset, said to have belonged to a negro servant who died of CONSUMPTION in the seventeenth century, and that of Ann Griffith at Burton Agnes Hall in Yorkshire. Not only will these skulls utter piercing and unearthly shrieks if moved, but they may also roll back to their original position of their own volition.

*See also* PHRENOLOGY.

**sleep** Perhaps the most frequently observed superstition relating to sleep is the prejudice that many people exhibit about which way their BED is facing. The most popular preference is for beds positioned on a north–south axis, rather then east–west, and it is said that couples who lie like this will have male children. Many people favour sleeping with the head north of the feet, drawing an obscure connection with the lines of the Earth's magnetic forces. Others, however, insist that the head should lie to the south of the feet: strangely enough, scientists have evidence to the effect that those who lie like this generally enjoy sounder sleep. Sleeping with one's head lying towards the north is said to lessen one's chances of living to a ripe old age, while sleeping with the head to the east promotes one's chances of worldly wealth and to the west the likelihood of TRAVEL. Sleeping with one's head towards the local church, however, may over-ride the need to observe the points of the compass altogether, according to yet another tradition.

If correctly positioning the bed does not provide a person with a good night's sleep, other measures may be worth considering. Among these are smoking a pipe of red tobacco, powdered TOAD and honey, a concoction said to bring on sleepiness, and checking that no one has hung a BLACKBIRD's right wing in the house, as this is reputed to rob anyone in the vicinity of their sleep. Those troubled by sleepwalking, meanwhile, should arrange to be baptised again, since this may be a consequence of the original ceremony not having been carried out in the proper manner. The notion that it is unwise to wake a sleepwalker suddenly is also rooted in superstition, the original idea being that the soul leaves the body during sleep and that if a sleeper is woken up too abruptly the soul will not have time to get back again.

Other miscellaneous superstitions include the German notion that a girl who falls asleep at work will marry a widower and the ancient idea that an ailing elderly person should persuade a younger person to sleep in the same bed – in this way they will share the benefits of the younger one's vitality. It is also said that FLOWERS should be removed from bedrooms at night because they steal the oxygen otherwise available to sleepers (a theory particularly associated with HOSPITALS). Lastly, time-honoured tradition has it that the first of a couple of newly-weds to fall asleep on their wedding night will be the first to die.

*See also* DREAM; NIGHTMARE.

**slipper** A superstition peculiar to slippers among the different types of SHOES is that it is unwise to leave them crossing one another when they are taken off. This is apparently an open invitation to bad luck.

**smallpox** Although smallpox has been officially stamped out around the world as a result of repeated immunisation programmes, superstition still harbours a few precautions that may be taken should the disease ever return. These include feeding the patient a roasted, fried, boiled or baked MOUSE; opening the windows of a patient's room at dusk, so that GNATS may bite the patient and thus draw the poisons out of his or her body; and taking a bun (without paying for it or expressing thanks) from the shop of a woman who did not change her NAME when she got married.

**smoking** *see* CIGAR; CIGARETTE; PIPE SMOKING.

**snail** Few superstitions relating to snails have survived to modern times, but in years gone by they were associated with a range of beliefs relevant to the gleaning of information about future lovers and with a number of medicinal uses. It is generally held that it is unlucky for snails to come into the house, but great good luck will be enjoyed by anyone who manages to seize a snail by the horns and toss it over their left shoulder. It is said that when catching snails the person concerned will stand a better chance if they wear their jacket inside out.

Snails may also be used for the purposes of love divination. Anyone anxious to discover the initials of their true love should place a snail in a flat dish (or in the ASHES on the hearth) on HALLOWE'EN and leave it there overnight. In the morning he or she will be able to read the all-important initials in the trail of slime that the snail has left behind.

According to a superstition recorded in Devon, snails are a means of forecasting the WEATHER as enshrined in the following rhyme:

When black snails cross your path
Black clouds much moisture hath.

Elsewhere, though, it is thought to be a bad omen if a BLACK snail crosses a person's path, and in Cornwall at least MINERS will seek to appease the creature by offering it a little of their dinner.

In folk medicine, feeding children drinks in which a few snails have been boiled is said to cure them of COUGHS. To cure WHOOPING COUGH, one gipsy remedy dictates that a snail should be allowed to crawl over some brown sugar until the sugar is nicely coated in slime, after which the sugar should be fed to the patient. Snail slime consumed with milk and other ingredients will also cure constipation. Rubbing a live black snail on one's WARTS, meanwhile, and then impaling the creature on a thorn is said to be an effective, if cruel, treatment. On the same lines, doctors in seventeenth-century England recommended pricking a snail and pouring its juices into the EAR to treat poor hearing (*see* DEAFNESS). Snail soup is said to be good for people with breathing problems and snails may also be swallowed raw to relieve bronchitis. Snails have also been widely used over the centuries as an ingredient in poultices and in dressings for the EYES.

**snake** Superstition has always regarded snakes with fear and respect, crediting them with various supernatural powers. Snake cults have thrived in many different parts of the world and snakes occupy a prominent, if not always healthy, position in many of the world's religions, including Christianity. Christian snake-handling sects exist in the modern USA, practitioners believing that their faith protects them from a venomous snake's bite. The idea of the snake being in some way protective is shared by many traditions; tattoos, for instance, often take the form of a snake pattern, and hanging a snakeskin from the rafters will protect a house from FIRE. Killing the first snake that a person sees in the year will, meanwhile, guarantee them victory over any foes over the next twelve months. Snakes are also widely interpreted as a phallic symbol and are therefore strongly associated with various forms of SEX magic.

Superstition has cherished a number of misconceptions about snakes. These include the widespread beliefs that all snakes hypnotise their prey; that they inject their venom via their forked tongue; that they can all spit their venom and that, according to US tradition, 'hoop snakes' can roll in the form of a hoop at their enemies by seizing their tail in their own mouth. Another popular idea has it that snakes cannot die until the SUN goes down.

Seeing a snake crossing one's path is unlucky, as are dreams about snakes; a pregnant woman who is frightened by a snake may give birth to a child with a constricted neck (though it is also said that snakes will never bite pregnant women). Tying a snakeskin around the waist of a woman in labour will ease childbirth, while carrying a snakeskin is generally supposed to be beneficial to health, effective against HEADACHES and in extracting THORNS from the skin. In the USA it is said that women in labour who are fed a drink made from the powdered rattle of a rattlesnake will have an easier time. Carrying a snake's tooth will ward off FEVER, and one may be carried for luck in GAMBLING. Other uses of snakes in folk medicine include an old English treatment for swollen necks, which requires a live snake to be drawn across the affected part three times and then buried alive in a bottle.

Superstition recommends a host of animal and plant preparations for the treatment of snakebite. Among the more bizarre is one which claims that rubbing crocodile blood into the bite will negate the effects of the poison. Another course is to tie the dead body of a snake around the wound. To avoid getting bitten by a snake in the first place the simplest course is to wear an EMERALD.

*See also* ADDER; ADDER STONE.

**sneezing** Superstition claims that when a person sneezes they are temporarily deprived of their soul, which will only return to the body when someone says, 'Bless you.' Many people believe inaccurately that the practice of saying 'Bless you' dates only from the Great Plague of the seventeenth century, when blessing someone who had just sneezed had serious intent since sneezing was one of the supposed early symptoms of the dread disease. In fact, records exist of similar traditions as far back as the ancient Greeks.

An old rhyme suggests varying interpretations for sneezes on different days of the week:

Sneeze on a Monday, sneeze for danger;
Sneeze on a Tuesday, kiss a stranger;
Sneeze on a Wednesday, sneeze for a letter;
Sneeze on a Thursday, something better;
Sneeze on a Friday, sneeze for sorrow;
Sneeze on a Saturday, see your sweetheart tomorrow;
Sneeze on a Sunday, your safety seek,
The Devil will have you the whole of the week.

Sneezing before one has put on one's SHOES is reputed to be a bad omen, though some claim that a sneeze early in the morning promises the appearance of a LETTER or present later on. Sneezing just once or three times in a row is unlucky, but two sneezes in quick succession are said to bestow good luck (a variation suggests one for a wish, two for a kiss, three for a letter and four for 'something better').

Care should be taken about the direction in which one sneezes: sneezing to the right is lucky but to the left is unlucky, particularly if one is at sea or in the vicinity of a grave, while sneezing straight ahead presages the arrival of good news. Two people sneezing simultaneously will result in both parties enjoying good luck. A tickling nose that refuses to culminate in a sneeze, meanwhile, may be interpreted as an indication that the person concerned is the object of another's secret longing.

Another tradition relates to the first sneeze of a BABY: this should be welcomed, because until it happens the child is held to be in the power of the FAIRIES. This first sneeze also indicates that the infant is mentally normal, as a long-held superstition has it that a fool cannot sneeze.

Other miscellaneous traditions include the notion prevalent in the USA that someone who sneezes while talking is undoubtedly telling the truth. Moreover, should a person sneeze at the TABLE this is a sure sign that they will make a new friend before sitting down to their next meal.

*See also* COLD.

**snowdrop**  A small white springtime flower, representative of purity and hope, which is among the first plants to bloom each year. It is supposed to be very unlucky to take snowdrops into the house, being an omen that a member of the household will die before the following spring (though in some areas it is only unlucky if a single snowdrop is brought in and all right to bring in a whole handful). It is thought that this tradition evolved through the plant's association with winter, the time of year when historically there were the most deaths, and also because the bloom itself has the appearance of a corpse in a white shroud.

**soap**  In common with other domestic items, soap has its own mythology. Somewhat contrary to the modern practice of packaging soaps and other toiletries as presents, it is traditionally thought unlucky to lend or give soap as it will 'wash the friendship away'. Should a bar of soap break up in one's hands this is another sign of a broken friendship. Scottish superstition, meanwhile, claims that it is unlucky for a bar of soap to slip from the fingers while one is WASHING one's hands: this may even be interpreted as an omen of death. Lastly, in the theatre some ACTORS AND ACTRESSES always take their soap with them when they leave a theatre – to leave it behind means they will never work there again.

**soccer**  *see* FOOTBALL.

**sock**  Just as the SHOES are a focus for various superstitions, so too are the socks (or in former times, the stockings). Most people agree that the right shoe should go on first but that the left sock should be first to go on, a contradiction of the usual prejudice against the LEFT SIDE. It is also lucky to find that one has put a sock on inside out or to discover that one has put on an unmatching pair (in which case the wearer should leave them as they are to enjoy the full benefit). Should the wearer thrust his toes into the heel of the sock when putting it on, it signifies the imminent arrival of an important LETTER.

Once on, socks that descend to the ankle for no apparent reason are a sign that a lover is thinking of the person concerned. At the end of day, those who are prone to NIGHTMARES should pin their socks in a CROSS to the end of the bed to get an undisturbed night's rest. According to another old superstition, sleeping with a (left) sock or stocking around the neck will cure a sore throat and will also give a sleeper dreams of future marriage partners.

*See also* UNDERWEAR.

**soil**  Primitive man put great store in the magical properties of soil, from which crops and trees sprang. Over the centuries many people have buried themselves in earth for hours at a time in the belief that they would benefit from these properties, which were reputed to heal such conditions as CANCER, RHEUMATISM and even injuries suffered from LIGHTNING. Soil in churchyards and at the point where three parishes meet was alleged to be the most potent in such remedies. It was further claimed that both CHILDBIRTH and DEATH were made easier by laying the person concerned on the floor so that they had contact with the soil. Rubbing soil on to the skin will also cure RINGWORM and the stitch, among various other ailments.

According to time-honoured English superstition, any single female who digs a hole in the earth at midday on Midsummer's Day and puts her ear to it will hear what the occupation of her future husband is.

**soot**  Because of its connection with FIRE, soot is a magical substance associated with various superstitions. Most of these relate to soot falling from the CHIMNEY, an event that is usually welcomed as a promise that one of the household will soon come into some money (though some pessimists interpret it as a sign of bad WEATHER in the offing or even that any sick person in the house is close to death). Soot that falls on the fire grate, says one old English superstition, is an omen that a stranger will soon arrive. Soot that comes down a chimney during a WEDDING breakfast, however, is said to presage misfortune for the happy couple, according to one Scottish tradition.

**soul cake**  A small round flattened loaf of the sort that was formerly baked in many parts of England for good luck on 2 November, All Souls' Day. Children were given soul cakes as a special treat, though many people kept their cake carefully by, often for many years, in order to preserve the luck it brought them.

**sowing**  *see* CROPS.

**sow thistle**  Prickly-leaved plant that is supposed to have various magical properties. Reputed to ward off witches, the sow thistle will increase the stamina of anyone who runs with a sprig of it in their buttonhole, though it will sap the strength of anyone who runs alongside and transfer it to the wearer. Medicinal uses include boiling the plant in water and applying the resulting concoction to the EYES to benefit weak vision. Witches, meanwhile, are reputed to make themselves invisible (*see* INVISIBILITY) by smearing on their bodies an ointment made from sow thistle and TOAD spittle.

**spade**  As the main implement of the gravedigger, the spade inevitably has somewhat gloomy associations. It is almost universally unlucky to carry a spade into the house on one's shoulder, and it is also deemed unwise to wave a spade at someone to attract their attention because this threatens them with death. The only remedy here is for the potential victim to throw some SOIL in the direction of the waver.

**sparrow**  The sparrow is regarded with some distaste in European superstition and is one of the birds supposed to embody the souls of the dead. This attitude probably derives from the biblical tradition that sparrows first betrayed the whereabouts of Christ in the Garden of Gethsemane, and subsequently with the words 'He lives, he lives!' alerted the Roman soldiers at the Crucifixion to the fact that Christ was not yet dead and thus to the need to apply further torture. In punishment it is said that God bound the sparrow's feet together with invisible twine, causing the bird to hop rather than walk. It is unlucky for a sparrow to fly into the house and equally unwise to keep one in a cage (though in some parts of the British Isles the welfare of sparrows is directly linked to the welfare of the household). The idea of sparrows bringing bad luck is extended by a superstition from Kent, which claims that anyone who catches a sparrow must kill it or run the risk of losing both parents. Killing a sparrow, however, will also result in the death of the TREE in which it has made its home. The song of the sparrow is said to herald the onset of RAIN.

**spectacles**  A widespread superstition of long standing suggests that some people harbour considerable prejudice against those who wear spectacles, fearing that they bring bad luck. In years gone by, it was customary for those who mistrusted people in spectacles to spit as they passed in order to protect their fortune.

**speech**  *see* CONVERSATION.

**speedwell**  A blue-flowered plant which should never be picked, according to widespread English tradition. The superstition runs that anyone who does so will have their EYES pecked out by birds (hence the flower's alternative name of 'bird's eye').

**spider**  Superstition generally regards spiders as lucky, though many people regard them with loathing and even fear. In legend, spiders are said to have saved the lives of the infant Christ, Mohammed and Frederick the Great, in Christ's case by spinning a web at the entrance of the cave in which the Holy Family was hiding from Herod's soldiers, thus making it appear that no one had passed by recently.

Tradition insists that it is most unwise to kill a spider, as one ancient rhyme makes clear:

If that you would live and thrive
Let the spider run alive.

This notion probably dates from medieval times, when spiders in the home helped to keep down the numbers of flies and thus reduced the risk of disease. Killing a spider will, superstition adds, only cause it to RAIN or, according to the Scots, result in crockery BREAKAGES before the day is over.

Although the idea of a spider dropping on to one's face from the ceiling may be viewed with horror by arachnophobes, it is supposed to be very lucky. Similarly, if a spider is seen running over a person's garments this constitutes a promise of a set of new clothes (as does the sight of a spider actually spinning a web). If kept in the pocket or in a purse, the tiny red MONEY spider, meanwhile, will similarly attract money to the person concerned.

Folk medicine has many uses for the spider. Eating a live spider in a pat of BUTTER is highly recommended for anyone fearing an attack of JAUNDICE, while a spider eaten in an apple or in jam or treacle will ward off FEVER. Various other remedies for a range of ailments such as ague involve suspending one or more live spiders in a small bag around the neck until they are all dead. Spiders' webs also have their uses in medicine, being rolled up into pills and then swallowed to alleviate fever, ASTHMA and WHOOPING COUGH (see COBWEB).

**spitting** In common with other bodily fluids, saliva is widely thought to have supernatural properties and so the act of spitting has considerable magical significance. Since ancient times it has been believed that in spitting a person expresses a little of the essence of their soul, which thus becomes a sacrifice to the gods and is guaranteed to attract divine favour. Most people are familiar with the practice of spitting for luck, and people will spit on playing cards, gambling slips, letters, exam papers, footballs, fishing nets and sometimes on their own palms when shaking hands to seal a business deal. Spitting on the fists before a fight is another ancient idea, thought to harden the skin in preparation for the coming conflict (hence the reason why boxers often do it; see BOXING) and many manual workers will spit on their hands before undertaking a task not so much to improve their grip as to make the work easier by magical means. Spitting while taking an oath, meanwhile, is supposed by many people to be as binding as swearing an oath on a BIBLE – hence the children's practice of spitting on their finger and then intoning:

Finger wet, finger dry,
Cut my throat if I tell a lie.

Spittle is credited with the power to ward off evil demons, and some people will spit to protect their luck on seeing a cross-eyed person, a MAGPIE or someone or something else suspected of having the power of the EVIL EYE. To keep witches from using cut FINGERNAILS or HAIR trimmings in their spells, the safest course is to spit on them before disposal. Parents, meanwhile, should spit on their newborn children for luck and also whenever someone compliments their offspring, in order to protect the infants from misfortune. Other precautions that may be taken while going about one's business include spitting on fields before reaping a crop, spitting on new clothes before putting them on, spitting on money received as handsel (see BUSINESS), spitting on the right SHOE before setting out on a journey or entering a dangerous place and, if at sea, spitting with the WIND to prevent a storm developing.

Spit is also alleged to have certain curative properties (Christ Himself healed a blind man with saliva) and many people will automatically spit on INSECT bites to get relief. Smearing spittle on WARTS, RINGWORM, BIRTHMARKS and other skin blemishes is said to be an effective treatment, especially if the spittle is that of someone who is fasting. Less well known is the idea that spitting on a finger will help to restore a foot that has gone to sleep. Human saliva is also said to be poisonous to SNAKES.

**splinter** Superstition offers help to anyone who is experiencing difficulty removing a splinter. If the usual measures fail, one course is to recite the following prayer:

Our Lord was the first man
That ever thorn pricked upon:
It never blistered, nor never belted,
And I pray God that nor may this.

The splinter will then emerge without further trouble and the wound will not turn septic. In the unlikely event of this prayer not working, a coating of RABBIT fat or a URINE compress should do just as well.

Not everyone, however, will be anxious to rid themselves of a splinter quite so quickly. Gamblers have been known to leave any splinter they get in their left foot for a period of seven days, in the belief that they will then enjoy a winning streak that will last for the next seven Sundays.

**spoon** Like other items of CUTLERY, spoons are associated with a variety of superstitious beliefs. Just as dropping a spoon on the floor is held to be a sign that a BABY or child is about to call at the house, so dropping a large spoon on the table is said to give warning of the imminent arrival of a large group of visitors. Should the bowl of a dropped spoon lie uppermost a welcome surprise is in the offing, but if it lies bowl downwards someone is due for a disappointment. Extending the connection between babies and spoons is the Scottish tradition that particular significance may be placed upon the hand with which a baby first

picks up a spoon. If it is the right hand the child may expect a bright and happy future, but bad luck will permanently attend one who uses the left hand (*see* LEFT SIDE; RIGHT SIDE).

Other miscellaneous superstitions concerning spoons include the notion that it is unlucky to stir food with the left hand and also unlucky for anyone to pour from a spoon 'back-handed'. More optimistic is the idea that the discovery of two spoons on the same saucer indicates a WEDDING in the family – or that someone is about to give birth to TWINS. The Welsh, of course, have a long tradition of lovers presenting each other with wooden spoons, the carving of which communicates various coded messages from one to the other, while brides much further afield are often given wooden spoons for luck. In other circumstances, however, receiving the 'wooden spoon' is a metaphor for coming last in a competition, often of a sporting nature.

**sport** *see* ANGLING; BASEBALL; BOXING; CRICKET; FOOTBALL; HORSE-RACING; MOTOR-RACING; TENNIS.

**sprain** According to folk medicine there are a number of possible treatments for sprains. These range from wrapping the affected joint in an EEL skin to tying a piece of string from a flour sack round it, smearing the area with an ointment of bran, olive or juniper OIL and vinegar, and, in the case of twisted ankles, bathing the ankle in the WATER flowing through a millwheel. Most drastic of all is the employment of a 'stamp-stainer', a local expert in such matters who will stamp on the injury with his bare feet in order to hasten recovery. Such stamp-stainers were once much respected in northern parts of England, where it was said that after a first initial spasm of agony the treatment involved no pain. Once the stamping was complete, the injured area was wrapped in an eel skin.

**spring cleaning** Superstition warns the houseproud that it is unlucky to spring clean a house after the month of May. This tradition has its roots in the Jewish custom of having the house clean and tidy in time for the Feast of the Passover.

**springwort** An unidentifiable herb, which is said to have powerful magical properties. In medieval times the springwort was among the most prized of all plants, bestowing upon anyone who found it the gift of INVISIBILITY, the ability to find treasure and to open locked doors, extra fertility and great strength. Also said to attract LIGHTNING, it is coated with DEW all the year round and is particularly attractive to woodpeckers, which rub their beaks on it.

**squirrel** According to a widespread European superstition it is very unlucky to kill a squirrel. This belief is thought to have originated in the legend that the squirrel hid its eyes with its tail when it saw Adam and Eve eating the forbidden fruit in the Garden of Eden, and thus acquired the bushy tail it has today. Anyone who kills a squirrel will lose all their skill at hunting.

**stag** The stag was sacred in the mythology of various ancient religions, and several superstitions associated with it recall the awe that the creature inspired in primitive man. During the witchcraft hysteria that swept Europe after the Middle Ages it was often alleged that the DEVIL appeared to his followers in the form of a great grey stag, and the idea remains that it is a bad omen for someone to encounter a stag. The antlers, which through their constant renewal represented the concept of rebirth and fertility to a number of ancient religions, may be ground down to make a powder that is supposed to enhance virility. By the same token, various ritual 'stag-dances' around the world are intended to increase the chances of a good harvest.

*See also* DEER.

**stag beetle** *see* BEETLE.

**stairs** The relatively straightforward business of going up or down stairs is surprisingly fraught with danger according to a number of superstitions. It is, for instance, very unlucky to meet anyone on a flight of stairs, or to go past them. Should this happen, as it inevitably does, the person concerned should cross their FINGERS to ward off ill luck. It has been suggested that this notion dates back to the days when people making their way up or down narrow, ill-lit stairs might find themselves especially vulnerable to attack from behind by any enemy they encountered.

Tripping while walking on a staircase is said to be lucky and possibly even an omen of a WEDDING if the person is going up; but unlucky, as well as dangerous, if he or she is going down at the time. It is also supposed by many to be unlucky to turn back when halfway up or down a staircase – to be absolutely safe the person concerned should continue to the end of the flight before going back, or else should sit down for a moment or two or whistle before returning in the same direction.

**stamp-stainer** *see* SPRAIN.

**star** Superstition has always accorded a special place to heavenly bodies, and some of these ancient beliefs are still observed today in one form or another. Events in the Heavens may be interpreted as warnings of earthly catastrophes; study of the alignments of the planets has long been undertaken in the 'science' of ASTROLOGY, with all that it portends for the everyday fortunes of individuals on Earth. In primitive times the stars were naturally enough supposed to be departed souls or the homes of the gods, but early Christians reinterpreted this belief and contended that they were simply rocks set there to deter people from trying to enter Heaven by artificial means.

Miscellaneous superstitions concerning stars that are still current today include the taboo against POINTING at them, on the grounds that this offends the gods and will result in the guilty party finding their finger permanently pointed, and the quaint notion that counting the stars (*see* NUMBERS) will lead to the person concerned getting white spots under their FINGERNAILS. Running somewhat counter to this last tradition is the belief, recorded in Wales and other places, that a person who counts nine (or ninety-nine) stars on nine nights in succession will be granted a wish.

A person will also be granted a secret wish if it is made on the first star seen after dark and while reciting the following lines:

Star light, star bright,
First star I see tonight,
I wish I may, I wish I might,
Have the wish I wish tonight.

The galaxy known as the Milky Way is traditionally supposed to be a celestial road along which departing souls make their way to Heaven.

*See also* COMET; METEORITE; MOON; SUN.

**stealing**   *see* THIEF.

**steeplejack**   A superstition apparently unique to steeplejacks is that tying a KNOT in their braces will prevent them having an accident.

**stile**   Various traditions are associated with stiles throughout the British Isles, where many are of considerable antiquity. These include the notions that anyone who goes through a GATE when there is a stile close at hand will be widowed before they die; that sharing a KISS on a stile in the dark will bring good luck; and that it is unlucky for two people to cross a stile simultaneously. Hammering a NAIL into a stile is said to be a sure cure for the ague. Lastly, in a superstition shared by some coastal communities it is very unlucky to set a stile in a footpath that leads to the SEA, as ill fortune will befall all those who use it.

**stillbirth**   *see* MISCARRIAGE.

**stocking**   *see* SOCK; UNDERWEAR.

**stone**   In ancient times large stones were often the focus of religious rituals and beliefs, and impressive stone circles survive as material evidence of man's early veneration of them. Long-held superstitions about stones of all kinds claim that they actually 'grow' out of the earth and possess innate magical powers. Many people therefore carefully preserve 'lucky' stones with holes through them, and similar stones may be offered to women in labour in the conviction that they will ease the process of CHILDBIRTH. Stones that are placed in ancient circles are said to promote fertility in both sexes and generally to bestow good luck (though some circles share the superstition that calamity will befall anyone who attempts to count them). Finally, anyone who is in desperate straits has only to toss a stone into a churchyard to gain some form of supernatural assistance.

*See also* BIRTHSTONE; GEMSTONE; HOLED STONES.

**stonecrop**   Flowering plant, which often grows amongst rocks or on walls and is supposed to have various magical properties. It is said to ward off witches and to protect a house from FIRE and LIGHTNING. In folk medicine, preparations including extracts of stonecrop are reputed to be effective against such complaints as ULCERS, piles, EYE problems, scrofula and ague.

**stork**   It is widely acknowledged that the stork is a lucky bird, particularly associated with CHILDBIRTH and the young. In biblical tradition the stork flew around Christ's cross to express its sympathy, while the Romans held the bird sacred to Venus. Since ancient times it has been considered most unlucky to kill a stork and a good omen if storks build their nest on one's rooftop (not least because they will protect the house from the threat of FIRE). The mere sight of two storks is said to be enough to cause girls to become pregnant, and modern nursery superstition frequently depicts the stork carrying babies to their mothers direct from God (the alternative source of babies as far as the very young are concerned being the GOOSEBERRY bush and the PARSLEY bed). Quite where this tradition came from is arguable, but storks are celebrated for the care with which they rear their young and also, so superstition claims, for their kindness to the old.

Other miscellaneous superstitions concerning storks include the notions that in the fullness of time they are transformed into men; that it is lucky to see them returning to their old nests each year; that the bird weep human tears if injured; that the male will kill his mate if she proves unfaithful; and that they will peck out the EYES of any humans who betray their marriage partners. Fine days are in store if the storks arrive late in the spring (see WEATHER) but RAIN will follow the appearance of a black stork and droughts will accompany a white stork.

In the folk medicine of lands where the stork is indigenous, various parts of the bird are said to have useful healing properties. Wrapping the sinews of a stork around feet stricken by GOUT will lead to a marked improvement in the condition of the person concerned, while Jewish tradition claims that the gall of a stork may be used in treating scorpion stings.

**storm** Thunderstorms have always aroused the deepest forebodings in man throughout the ages, and inevitably countless superstitions have evolved concerning both their causes and their consequences. Storms have been variously blamed upon the anger of the gods, upon witches, demons and other malevolent spirits, and also upon ordinary mortals who have broken some taboo or other. Actions that are said to provoke storms at SEA include cutting one's FINGERNAILS or one's HAIR while on board ship and WHISTLING. If a storm breaks out while a

person is being buried this is likely to be interpreted in parts of Scotland as a sign that the deceased sold his or her soul to the DEVIL and he has come to fetch his own.

The coming of a storm may be forecast in a number of ways, in particular by observing that the MARIGOLDS have not opened before seven o'clock in the morning and by noting that the CAT turns its back to the domestic FIRE. Particularly violent storms, or ones that arise out of season, are widely believed to be linked to important happenings in earthly affairs, often the imminent death of a reigning monarch or other prominent person. In former times, it was often claimed that if a storm blew up when the assizes were being held this was a sure sign that more prisoners than usual would be condemned to death.

To make a storm cease, one Austrian superstition suggests hurling a handful of meal out of the window will be enough to appease the spirits which caused it in the first place. Elsewhere in Europe it is said that ringing the church BELLS offers some protection against storm damage.

*See also* LIGHTNING.

**stormy petrel** Small seabird, particularly associated with stormy weather and therefore with something of an ominous reputation among the superstitious. These birds are most frequently observed when the seas are whipped up by rough winds (the reason being that they feed on material stirred up from the ocean bed), and seafarers have long since come to fear their appearance on the very real grounds that it presages bad weather. SAILORS variously identify the birds as the souls of drowned seamen or as the tortured souls of captains who behaved callously towards their crews.

**straw** Various supernatural properties are credited to straw in rural superstition. These include potency as a fertility symbol, in which context virgin girls sometimes secretly wear GARTERS of straw to increase their chances of becoming pregnant. Young women will sometimes look out for the first man they see in a straw HAT at the beginning of the summer in order to wish him good luck. To enjoy good luck themselves they may recite or sing the following lines:

Strawberry Man, Strawberry Man,
Bring me good luck,
Today or tomorrow,
To pick something up.

In former times it was believed that if a witch obtained possession of the bed-straw on which a person lay she could work spells to establish magical power over them. Spotting a domestic animal such as a DOG or a HEN with straw stuck to its tail may be interpreted as a sign that a stranger is about to arrive, possibly to stay. Other miscellaneous traditions include the notions that it is possible to cut the DEVIL in half with a straw and that decking a COW out with straw will pro-tect it from evil.

Meeting a cart or lorry loaded with straw is variously interpreted as lucky or unlucky from one region to another. Most, however, think it lucky and that the person concerned is entitled to make a wish as it goes by – unless, that is, it appears in the wake of a hay cart, in which case it is a portent of misfortune. It is definitely thought to be bad luck to find two straws lying on the ground in the form of a CROSS.

**string**   *see* THREAD.

**stumbling**   Superstition regards an accidental stumble as a most significant and generally unlucky act, though the interpretation depends largely on the cir-cumstances in which it happens. Taking a stumble as one sets out on a journey or when embarking on some undertaking is a very ill omen for one's future progress. History records many instances of kings and warriors rueing their luck after stum-bling before a battle, and of newly-weds who lived to regret stumbles they took on crossing the threshold (if a bride or groom stumbles at the altar this suggests that he or she is guilty of some uncon-fessed moral offence). Similarly bad luck will attend anyone who witnesses a HORSE stumbling on the road. Stumbling on STAIRS is lucky if it happens when the person concerned is going up but unlucky if he or she is heading down-wards at the time. Stumbling near a grave is most ominous of all, as it foretells the imminent death of the person concerned. ACTORS AND ACTRESSES who stumble on making their first entrance will express trepidation about the rest of the perform-ance, as such an accident is usually said to portend further lapses on stage.

**sty**   *see* EYE.

**suicide**   Those who take their own lives have always been regarded with dis-approval by most religions, and this is reflected in the superstitions concerning them. It is widely believed that the souls of suicides will know no rest and that they are condemned to roam the Earth for-ever, though often they are rather confus-ingly supposed to be restricted to the vicinity in which they died. To keep the GHOSTS of suicides from returning to their homes, many communities over the centuries have insisted that they are buried not in holy ground but at such locations as CROSSROADS, in which case their spirits will not know which way to go, or under running WATER; or else that they should be physically pinned down by driving a stake through their corpses. Others maintain that the bodies of sui-cides will be rejected by water and will not sink (though experience does not sup-port this idea). Other superstitions include the notion that any pregnant woman who is careless enough to walk over a suicide's grave will suffer a MIS-CARRIAGE.

**sun**   As the source of light and crucial to life on Earth, the sun was central to many early religions and still occupies an important place in the world's superstiti-ons. Perhaps the clearest link with primitive sun worship is in the bonfires that are still lit to celebrate such festivals as MIDSUMMER'S EVE. These conflagrations were originally intended to mimic the sun and thus to bring luck to local communities and to promote the fertility of their CROPS and livestock. Christianity has added its own sun myths, which include the quaint notion that the sun dances for joy early on EASTER morning, when the holy image of the LAMB and flag may also be discerned on its surface.

The sun is said to shine brightest on the righteous and will hide its face if some catastrophe is in store (*see* ECLIPSE). Brides who are married in bright sunshine are especially blessed and may look forward to a happy marital life, but anyone who feels the sun on their head while attending a FUNERAL is warned that they too will soon be mourned. It is widely held to be unlucky to be caught POINTING at the sun, which is interpreted by many as an insulting gesture and may be punished by the person concerned being instantly struck dead. Only the EAGLE can stare directly into the sun. One of the most curious traditions concerning the sun is the old idea that its rays will put a FIRE out; even in relatively modern times people have shielded the domestic fire from sunshine in the belief that the flames will otherwise be extinguished.

For those who want to predict the WEATHER in the months ahead, one course is to study the sun's rays reflected in a bucket of water on Easter Day. If the rays shine bright and clear in the water the season will be a fine one, but if they tremble and are unclear foul weather lies in store. There will also be many fires if the sun shines strongly on Christmas Day and a good APPLE crop if the sun shines through the apple trees then or on Easter Day. A rather obscure English tradition also holds that the sun always shines on Saturdays, even if only for a few seconds. Children born at sunrise will be clever and energetic, while those born when the sun goes down will be less intelligent and inclined to laziness.

*See also* SUNWISE TURN.

**Sunday**   *see* DAYS OF THE WEEK.

**sunwise turn**   The practice of turning the way of the SUN, in other words east to west in imitation of the direction that the sun takes through the Heavens, while performing some magical rite or spell. Turning the way of the sun is associated with 'good' magic, while turning in the opposite direction, anti-clockwise or WIDDERSHINS, is linked with more malevolent spell-making. Many ritual dances begin with a turn to the right, and processions as part of various ancient ceremonies such as beating the bounds – the custom of touring parish boundaries on Holy Thursday or Ascension Day – usually go off in a clockwise direction. Port is passed round the table 'sunwise' (in other words clockwise or to the left), while a superstition among cooks claims that pots on the stove should always be stirred clockwise to get the best results; places at the TABLE should also be laid in a sunwise direction.

In former times, FUNERAL and WEDDING processions often made three clockwise circuits of the churchyard to obtain magical protection, and blessings were gained for a loved one by circling the person sunwise while saying prayers. More superstitious FISHERMEN to this day will often take a sunwise course on leaving harbour, predicting disaster if they should inadvertently go in a widdershins direction.

**swallow**   Superstition throughout Europe accords the swallow a special place, mostly identifying it as a bird of blessing and a herald of the summer. Christians claim that the swallow won divine favour by calling out 'Dead! Dead!' to the Roman soldiers at the Crucifixion in an attempt to prevent them inflicting further torture upon Christ (a Swedish version of this story has the swallow circling the crucified Christ and calling out, 'Cheer up! Cheer up!'). As a result it is thought to be very unlucky to kill a swallow or to damage its nest (or even to be holding one in the hand as it dies). Punishment for such reckless acts ranges from prolonged rainstorms and bloodied milk to death or some other extreme misfortune.

Allowing a swallow to nest in the roof will guard a house from LIGHTNING, FIRE and other evils, but if it deserts this nest ill luck will befall the household. It is usually thought to be unlucky if a bird flies into the house; however an exception is made in the case of the swallow, which brings only joy with it (though some people draw the more conventional conclusion that this signifies a death).

Some societies do indeed associate the swallow with death. In Russia, dead children are reputed to take the form of swallows and in parts of eastern England groups of swallows that gather on church roofs are said to be plotting the deaths that will occur in the parish over the coming year. In Scotland, it is alleged that the swallow carries a drop of the DEVIL'S blood in its veins, while the Irish claim that if a swallow plucks out a certain HAIR from a human head the unfortunate victim is doomed to go to Hell. If a swallow alights on someone then all are agreed that the person concerned is fated to die shortly.

Where WEATHER is concerned, it is said that STORMS will accompany the arrival and departure of the swallows each season and also that the height at which they fly reveals much about imminent WEATHER patterns – as suggested by the West Country rhyme:

Swallows fly high, no rain in the sky;
Swallows fly low, 'tis likely to blow.

Other superstitions relating to swallows include the belief that they carry small sticks with them when they migrate so that they can snatch a quick rest on the waves; that they hibernate under water in a huge mass; that their red feathers recall the fact that they brought FIRE to mankind; and that they spend the winter in caves.

Authorities in folk medicine have claimed over the centuries that swallows carry inside their bodies small stones that have various magical properties, specifically a red stone with the power to cure mad people and a black one that promotes good luck. In addition, anyone who puts such a stone under their TONGUE will enjoy great eloquence. Special stones gathered by swallows from the seashore, meanwhile, are said to benefit damaged eyesight (see EYE).

To treat TOOTHACHE, one ancient remedy is to behead a swallow in the light of a full MOON and to hang the severed head up in a piece of linen. Other body parts may be used in the treatment of snakebites and rabies. Consuming burned and powdered swallow is also said to cure alcoholism, while preparations of oil from swallows will mend fractures and ease sprains. To cure EPILEPSY no fewer than a hundred swallows must be mixed with an ounce of castor oil and some white wine.

See also MARTIN.

**swan** According to the superstitions of many different countries, swans are generally unlucky birds. They were considered semi-divine creatures in classical mythology, and many existing superstitions are of considerable antiquity. These include the notion that a swan only sings for the first time when it is dying and the theory that it can only hatch its eggs during thunderstorms, when the shells are broken by the thunder.

Swans have been protected in England as a 'royal' bird since medieval times and no one may kill a swan without special dispensation from the Crown. To do so is in any case the height of folly according to superstition, and will be followed by the death of the guilty party (or else of someone else in the parish) within the year. In Scotland and Ireland this idea is strengthened by the supposition that swans are in fact the reincarnation of human souls (according to the Irish, the spirits of virtuous maidens). Scottish FISHERMEN regard the very sight of swans as unlucky, and many people north of the English border conclude from the appearance of three swans flying together that a national calamity is imminent.

Observing the behaviour of swans will reveal much about coming WEATHER. If the birds stretch their heads backwards over their wings during the daytime this is said to be a warning of foul weather in the offing, and if they take to the air WINDS should be expected – gale force conditions are in store if they fly directly into the wind. Heavy RAIN is due if swans start building a nest unusually high up.

**swastika** Universally reviled as the symbol of the German Nazis in the twentieth century, the swastika has in fact a much longer history as a magical emblem. In classical times the swastika represented the SUN and evoked good luck and well-being.

**swearing** Superstition has always warned that the use of what society regards as bad language is fraught with risk. Because swearing is blasphemous, 'taking the name of the Lord in vain', and is likely to rouse up evil spirits, many people feel uneasy when they hear such language being used and maintain that only bad luck will follow. Such attitudes are particularly strong among those who undertake hazardous work, such as FISHERMEN, who have been known to ban swearing on their boats. The fact that mere words are sufficient to induce some kind of magical reaction is borne out by the many superstitions that depend upon the reciting of certain rhymes or CHARMS, and by the notion that the simple utterance of a curse by a witch may be enough to blight another person's fortunes.

A curious superstition recorded in rural Germany claims that the MOUSE population will thrive in villages where the local populace are given to using strong language.

**sweater** As with other items of CLOTHING, the sweater boasts its own specific superstitions. In common with other garments, it is lucky to put a sweater on back to front by mistake (though it must be left like this to enjoy the full benefits). More uniquely, it is held that a person who puts their arms into a sweater before pulling it over their head will never die by DROWNING. Another superstition warns that a light-coloured sweater should never be repaired with dark-coloured THREAD, which is an open invitation to evil.

**sweeping**   *see* BRUSH.

**swift**   Unlike the MARTIN and SWALLOW, the swift is widely regarded as an unlucky bird and often as an agent of the DEVIL himself – though a somewhat contradictory old rhyme claims that

The swallow and the swift
Are God Almighty's gift.

Whatever the allegiance of the bird, swifts and their nests should never be harmed. Anyone foolish enough to kill one should beware, as the bird will have vengeance by way of deaths within the culprit's household or among his or her livestock. In eastern England it is said that swifts flying around church towers are lost souls, lamenting the crimes they committed when alive.

**sword**   In the days when swords were one of the principal weapons of soldiers in battle they were often regarded as magical objects, with their own mystical names, emotions and supernatural properties. An oath made on a sword was once considered to be as binding as one made on a BIBLE. Among the various superstitions that have survived are the notions that a sword that falls out of its scabbard is an omen of approaching DEATH and the tradition that a sword may be used in place of a wand in witchcraft. Skilled practitioners of magic might use swords as a defence against hostile spirits and also for scrying (*see* MIRROR) by looking into the brightly polished blade.

For the purposes of love divination, a man should walk three times round a church at the hour of midnight and then thrust a sword into the keyhole with the words, 'Here is the sword, but where is the sheath?' He will then be rewarded by the appearance of his future wife. Women may follow a similar procedure, using the words, 'Here is the sheath, but where is the sword?'

# T

**table** Various superstitions should be observed by diners as they sit at the table for a meal. To avoid the risk of bad luck no one should move from the seat allocated to them and care should be taken not to kick over one's chair when getting up, which indicates that one has been telling lies. Children, meanwhile, should be discouraged from going under the table as this threatens their imminent demise; if they do crawl under the table they should be sent back the same way in order to escape harm. Single girls in particular should not sit at the corner of a table, which means they will never be married, and girls engaged to be married should never talk to their partners while sitting on a table because this risks the ENGAGEMENT being called off (though some people say that girls who sit on tables are subconsciously expressing their desire for a mate). Should two people sit on a table together, meanwhile, there is sure to be a quarrel.

Other taboo activities at the table include SINGING, lying down on it (said to be an omen of DEATH) and placing one's SHOES or a pair of BELLOWS on top of it. British superstition warns that should a coffin shape be found at the centre of a tablecloth when it is unfolded this is a portent of death in the family (some people add that it is also unwise to leave a tablecloth on the table overnight). A guest eating his first meal in a house should not fold his napkin at the end of the meal, since this means that he will never eat there again.

Some people insist on always laying an extra place at the table, claiming somewhat chillingly that this is for the soul of a recently deceased member of the family or else for Christ when he appears at the Second Coming.

*See also* THIRTEEN; WAITING ON TABLE.

**talisman** A tangible object that is usually carried about the person to protect one's luck. In the opinion of various authorities a talisman differs from an AMULET, which provides continuous general all-round protection: a talisman, on the other hand, may be used to perform a specific task which is often an act of healing. Examples include pieces of jewellery bearing one's astrological sign or other magical planetary characters and the Jewish Star of David, which is also often worn in the form of jewellery. Talismans will often have been obtained from someone who claims to be able to invest such objects with magic potential.

**tattoo** *see* SAILORS.

**taxi** A superstition unique to drivers of taxi cabs is that it is lucky to have a registration number which includes the NUMBER seven (one of the luckiest of all numbers) or a multiple of seven. Even better is a number plate that has both a seven and a letter U, the letter most closely resembling a lucky HORSESHOE.

*See also* CAR.

**tea** The business of preparing a cup of tea is loaded with symbolic meaning for the superstitious people, particularly in connection with the love life of the tea-maker. A woman who puts in the milk before the sugar will never win a husband, while a woman who pours from a pot that another woman has already poured from may be disconcerted to learn that this means one of them will have a BABY – possibly even red-headed TWINS – before the year is out (or will otherwise experience bad luck). A woman who allows a man to pour her more than one cup of tea will prove defenceless before his charms and, according to another superstition, may end up becoming pregnant by him.

Tea that is made too strong indicates the development of a new friendship, while tea that is too weak suggests that an existing friendship is coming to an end. If a person forgets to put the tea into the water altogether, this is a singularly bad omen. Likewise, stirring tea in the pot is a dangerous habit that is likely to provoke trouble, especially if the liquid is stirred WIDDERSHINS (anti-clockwise); and absent-mindedly forgetting to replace the lid of a teapot is also to be avoided for reasons of avoiding quarrels (though this might also be interpreted as a portent of the arrival of a stranger). No one should ever stir someone else's tea for them, which also presages a quarrel, and care should be taken never to stir tea with anything but a SPOON. Spilling some of the tea leaves when putting them in the pot is, however, lucky.

Bubbles that float to the surface of a cup of tea are a sign that the drinker will soon be receiving a kiss or some money, while a tea leaf or stalk that rises to the surface indicates the imminent arrival of a visitor. If the tea leaf is hard a man must be expected; if soft, a woman is about to appear. In either case, the person concerned should place the tea leaf on the back of one of their hands and then bang it repeatedly with the other hand until the leaf falls off: the number of times the hand is hit before this happens is equivalent to the number of days before the stranger will arrive.

Many authorities claim that other future events may be forecast by careful examination of the shapes suggested by the tea leaves that remain after a nearly empty cup has been swirled round three times and then turned upside down to drain the last of the liquid. According to this, the art of tasseography, a good spread of tea leaves around the cup is ideal, the leaves nearer the bottom of the bowl relating to events that lie in the more distant future than those nearer the rim. Star shapes suggest success, circles or bottles represent failure, bridges and birds foretell a journey, a castle suggests good news, a church indicates a WEDDING, a dagger warns of danger, and a horseshoe promises good luck – among many other possible readings.

Finally, some thought should be given to the disposal of used tea leaves. According to one English superstition these should never be thrown away but should be banked up at the back of the FIRE to ward off the threat of poverty. In the English Midlands, meanwhile, it is said that tossing tea leaves on the ground in front of a house will ward off evil spirits.

**tears**  *see* CRYING.

**teeth**  Like most body parts, the teeth are associated with a wide variety of superstitious beliefs. The most familiar of all superstitions associated with teeth is the tradition of the 'tooth FAIRY', who will bring the gift of a COIN to any child who sleeps with a newly lost milk tooth under the pillow. Variations in this tradition add that a little SALT should also be left for the fairy and that if the tooth has not disappeared by midnight it will harm the child's luck (though nowadays the fairy generally leaves both the money and the tooth for the child to find in the morning).

The first molar to be lost should, according to another tradition, be sprinkled with salt and thrown on to the FIRE to chase away any evil spirits lurking in the child's body. If this is not done, the tooth may be eaten by a DOG and the child will get dog's teeth as a result – or the luckless individual will be doomed to search for the tooth in a bucket of blood in Hell when he or she dies. Burning lost teeth also has the advantage that they will not fall into the possession of witches, who may use them to acquire power over their erstwhile owner. Alternatively, leaving discarded milk teeth at the entrance to a MOUSE or RAT hole is a good way to ensure that the replacements are strong and sharp.

It is thought to be very unlucky for a BABY to be born with any teeth already through, and in some regions this is supposed to prophesy that it will grow up a murderer. If a child's first tooth comes through in the upper jaw this is also unlucky and may be interpreted as an omen that the infant will die in childhood. Children who teethe early are either highly intelligent, doomed to die early or are developing a little faster than normal because they have advance warning that their mother will soon be having another baby, as indicated by the proverb 'Soon teeth, soon toes'. By the same token, the number of teeth a child has at the age of one year is said to predict the number of brothers and sisters that are yet to be born. The process of teething can be painful, and superstition recommends the use of CORAL, cowrie shells, orris root and WOLF teeth as ideal teething AMULETS.

People with gaps between their front teeth are widely thought to be lucky and will enjoy great riches and travel widely (though the Scottish believe such people are prone to lechery). Many people also carry animals' teeth as a matter of course, believing that they are among the most beneficial lucky charms.

Counting one's own teeth is unlucky, and dreaming that one's teeth are falling out is said to portend the imminent death of a relative.

*See also* TOOTHACHE; VAMPIRE.

**telephone**   Though it is a relatively recent technological development, the telephone has already attracted to itself a few curious traditions. These include the superstitions that it is unlucky for a tele-phone to make intermittent ringing noises when no call is coming through – a possible death omen – or for a telephone to ring but not be answered. Many people claim to have had at some time or other clairvoyant knowledge of who is about to call, and why, before a telephone has even started to ring.

**tempting fate**   The fear that celebrating one's good fortune in some way invites the special attention of malevolent spirits, which is the motivating force behind a great many well-known taboos and superstitions. To be on the safe side, one should never sing too loudly the praises of children, livestock, a person's health or anything else that is held precious, as the presumption implicit in such boasting is that one is disregarding possible interference by supernatural forces. Many people will show distinct unease if someone directs lavish praise in their direction and may attempt to ward off evil by TOUCHING WOOD or IRON, making the sign of the CROSS, SPITTING and saying 'God bless', or taking some other precautionary measure recommended by long-standing tradition. Specific examples of actions to be avoided include never bringing a newly acquired CRADLE or PRAM into the house before an expected baby is safely delivered, never asking a FISHERMAN where he is going when he is about to set sail, never admitting to being very well if someone enquires after one's health and never wishing ACTORS AND ACTRESSES good luck when they are about to go on stage.

**tench**   Freshwater FISH known as the 'Doctor Fish' because of the supposed healing properties of its oily skin. Ailing fish of other species are alleged to rub themselves against the tench in order to benefit from these properties, and humans have also learned to use it in folk medicine. It was formerly said that wrapping the feet and the region of the heart in the bodies of tench for lengthy periods would cure JAUNDICE, providing that the discarded fish, having absorbed all the poisons from the patient, were then immediately buried in the ground.

**tennis**  Players observe the usual array of superstitious beliefs shared by most competitive sportsmen and women, but also boast a few specific traditions of their own. These include a taboo against serving with three balls held in the hand and another prejudice against serving with a ball for which a fault has just been called. Many players who are having a poor game will welcome the arrival of new balls as this may signal a change in their luck. Others habitually tap their feet with their racquets before each rally or spit on their hands (*see* SPITTING) as much for luck as for extra grip.

**thatch**  Many people express reservations about having a thatched roof because of the fire risk, but this danger does have one advantage. Those who believe that they have been subjected to WITCHCRAFT can steal a little of the thatch from the house of the suspected witch and then burn it on their fire to release themselves from her power.

**theatre**  *see* ACTORS AND ACTRESSES.

**thief**  Superstition offers a number of courses for those who wish to commit burglary without being discovered. Among these is the notion that a thief who carries the heart of a TOAD about his person will be immune from detection (carrying a piece of COAL may also help). A central European superstition, meanwhile, claims that if a thief commits an undetected burglary at CHRISTMAS he or she will be able to continue in such nefarious activities throughout the following year without the slightest danger of getting caught. To be absolutely sure of getting away without interference thieves should equip themselves with a HAND OF GLORY, which will ensure that the sleeping occupants of a house do not wake until the miscreants are long gone.

To get past locked doors, a thief should carry in a cut in his hand a sliver of VERVAIN, which will cause all doors to open at a touch. It is generally agreed that it is very unlucky to steal anything from a church, especially the CHALICE used in Holy Communion, or to steal a pack of CARDS.

Superstition also offers assistance to thief-takers, though. One procedure, according to the folklore of Devon, is to take six stalks of GRASS from the scene of the robbery and to present them to a witch, who will scratch each one with a pin. If the spell works, corresponding scratches will disfigure the face of the culprit. Hungarians believe that a thief can be punished by obtaining an item of his or her CLOTHING and giving it a good thrashing: the owner will suffer the full effects of the beating and it will be some time before they are sufficiently recovered to resume their life of crime.

*See also* SIEVE AND SHEARS.

**thimble**  Just as various superstitions are associated with the business of SEWING, so the humble thimble has its magical significance. Thimbles are often given 'for luck', but it is also supposed to be unlucky to be given three of them, which means that the recipient will never be married. According to US superstition, a seamstress who loses her thimble brings good fortune to the person on whose clothes she is currently working (unless they happen to be her own).

**third time lucky**  *see* NUMBERS.

**thirteen**  Of all the NUMBERS, thirteen is the most ill starred. The prejudice against the number thirteen is almost universal and many people (who may be identified technically as 'triskaidekaphobics') will go to considerable lengths to avoid any association with the number. As a result there are many streets throughout the Western world which have no house with this number, and many hotels which lack a room thirteen and even a thirteenth floor, going directly from twelve to fourteen. Witches' covens traditionally have thirteen members, and in tarot CARD decks the number thirteen is reserved for Death.

Most unlucky of all is the discovery that one has sat down to dinner at a table where thirteen people are present, a reference to the fact that there were thirteen people present at the Last Supper, where Judas Iscariot was the thirteenth. Superstition has it that the first person to rise (or otherwise the last person to be seated) will die within a year. The only remedy is for all to sit and stand together, or for one or more of the party to be seated at another table.

Equally ubiquitous is the fear that a Friday, itself an unlucky day (*see* DAYS OF THE WEEK), that falls on the thirteenth day of the month is a day when anything that can go wrong will go wrong. Even in modern technologically advanced society, BUSINESS will fall off whenever a 'Friday the thirteenth' comes round as important deals are delayed until a more propitious date. New undertakings of many other kinds, including WEDDINGS and other events of a personal nature, will also be postponed.

In reality, the prejudice against the number thirteen is of obscure origins, as evidence exists of it in Roman civilisation long before Christ and the Last Supper, which is none the less usually cited as the source of the superstition. Perhaps significantly, the number thirteen was to the ancient Egyptians the last step of the ladder via which the soul reached eternity, though other authorities have suggested Hindu origins.

**thorn** The role of the Crown of Thorns in Christian belief means that the thorn has a somewhat dark reputation, though not all superstitions connected with it are of a pessimistic nature. Boughs of thorn placed over barn doors, for instance, will ward off witches (though many people will baulk at cutting a thorn

bush in any way for fear of grave misfortune). German superstition, meanwhile, advises that a girl who finds a thorn in her clothes is destined to marry a widower. It is, however, unlucky to pick a thorn on old Christmas Eve (5 January) as this may lead to the person concerned being permanently cursed. Should a person scratch themselves on a thorn, one treatment dating back several centuries is to recite the following lines:

Christ was of a virgin born,
And he was pricked by a thorn,
And it never did bell or swell:
As I trust in Jesus, this one never will.

*See also* BLACKTHORN; HAWTHORN.

**thread** Superstition has a number of uses for thread (as it does for string), and some of these date back as far as the classical era, when lives were, according to myth, measured out as lengths of thread by the gods. Perhaps the best-known tradition is that it is lucky to find a loose piece of thread on one's CLOTHING. Anyone wishing to know the initial of the name of a future lover should let such a thread drop to the floor, when it will form the shape of the letter (a variation involves wetting the thread and wrapping it tightly round the finger before letting it drop). ACTORS AND ACTRESSES, meanwhile, will congratulate themselves on promoting their luck in relation to the current production if they should happen to pick up a piece of thread from their dressing room floor.

Several superstitions relate specifically to the tying of lengths of thread or string around a finger. These include the custom of tying a thread round the finger to remember something one must do; this is best done on a finger of the left hand, being the one that influences the memory. In other circumstances thread or string may be tied round the little finger to staunch a bleeding NOSE, or else wrapped three times round a finger and then slipped off and thrown on the ground to transfer WARTS to whoever picks the thread up.

**threshold**

As regards love divination, a girl should go to a barn or some other darkened place on HALLOWE'EN, or some other auspicious date in the calendar, toss a ball of thread or wool into the blackness and then slowly reel it in. When the thread snags on something she should call out, 'Who is holding my thread?' and an unseen voice will respond with the name of her future husband. The procedure only works, apparently, if the girl goes through the ritual alone at midnight and otherwise in complete silence. If there is no answer, there will be no husband.

In times gone by it was considered unlucky for a woman to leave any thread on her spinning wheel, as the DEVIL would cut it for her or interfere in some other way with her work. Thread or wool should never be wound after dark, as this will cause seafarers to lose their way at sea and will threaten their safety. Tying lengths of thread to cattle and other livestock is reputed to protect them from evil, and in much the same way threads have been tied to CORPSES, BABIES and to people suffering from a variety of ailments. It is even said that on occasion tying a thread to a faulty car engine has enabled it to start.

A cautionary note is sounded by the traditions that cutting a piece of thread or string for no particular reason is unwise because it risks a year of poverty, and that only the foolhardy burn string since this too invites bad luck.

*See also* KNOT.

**threshold**   *see* DOOR.

**thrush**   A quaint rural superstition has it that thrushes exchange their old legs for new ones when they reach the age of ten. Another suggests that such birds are also born deaf.

**thumb**   As with the FINGERS, information about a person's character may be gleaned by examination of their thumbs (*see* PALMISTRY). Superstitions concerning thumbs include the notion that an itching one is a sign that an unexpected visitor is about to arrive, and a tradition

that it is particularly unfortunate to stick the thumb with a NEEDLE or PIN, which threatens bad luck to the person concerned. Holding one's thumb tightly in one's fingers is variously said to ward off GHOSTS, prevent HICCOUGHS and provide protection against WITCHCRAFT.

*See also* HAND.

**thunder**   The sound of thunder has always inspired feelings of awe and even terror in man, who in times gone by interpreted it as the anger of the gods. The commonplace reaction of children and more timid adults of pulling the bedclothes over their head when thunder is heard at night is in fact a simplification of an old superstition, which dictates that no one will suffer harm during a thunderstorm if they pull their bed into the middle of the room, cover themselves with the sheets and recite a Paternoster. In contrast, travellers should welcome the sound of thunder in the distance as they set off as this bodes well for their journey, and anyone who hears thunder to the right of them may treat this as a good omen (though not if it is heard on the left).

Publicans have been known to blame thunder for beer going sour in the barrel and will sometimes place an IRON bar on the barrel to prevent this – though it is apparently the heat associated with some thunderstorms that causes this effect. The same principle applies to MILK.

The time of day that thunder is heard is significant in forecasting the WEATHER to follow, according to one old English rhyme:

Thunder in the morning,
All the day storming;
Thunder at night,
Is the sailor's delight.

According to a superstition recorded in Tudor England, it is said that wider conclusions may be drawn from the day upon which thunder is heard (*see* DAYS OF THE WEEK). Thunder on a Monday signifies the death of a woman; on Tuesday it is a promise of a good grain harvest; on Wednesday it means the death of a prostitute or is a warning of approaching violence; on Thursday it bespeaks a good harvest and plentiful supplies of livestock; on Friday it forecasts the death of a great man or the fighting of a battle; on Saturday it threatens an epidemic; and on Sunday it predicts the death of a leading intellectual, judge or author. Another British tradition claims that the sound of thunder between November and the end of the year heralds the imminent death of a prominent person in the area, while thunder that is heard on the first Sunday in the year is a warning of the death of someone in the royal family.

*See also* LIGHTNING; STORM.

**Thursday**   *see* DAYS OF THE WEEK.

**thyme**   A herb that is traditionally associated with death, and in particular with MURDER. The scent of thyme is said to linger in places where murders have been committed, and its flower is supposed to provide a resting-place for the souls of the dead. In extension of this connection with death, thyme was often brought into the house in parts of England when there was a CORPSE awaiting burial and not removed until the body was taken away (though thyme was never used to deck the bier as 'the dead have nothing to do with time'). Other superstitions relating to thyme include the notions that it bolsters courage and may be used in treating depression.

**tickling**   A superstition common to both sides of the Atlantic counsels against tickling the feet of BABIES before they have learned to talk. Breaking this taboo risks the child subsequently developing a stammer.

**tides**   Superstition accords some significance to the influence of the tides, dependent as they are upon the mysterious elemental forces of the MOON and the SEA. It is widely believed that DEATHS are more likely to occur when the tide is on the ebb, and that most BABIES are delivered when the tide comes in. By the same

token it is thought to be unlucky, among FISHERMEN at least, to embark on any new work, such as baiting fishing lines, while the tide is out. In the Orkneys, it is said that any WEDDING that is celebrated when the tide is on the ebb will not be blessed by children. A rising tide is a good time to kill PIGS, make BUTTER, boil WATER and stuff feather mattresses, while an ebb tide is the best time to have one's HAIR cut, to take a bath and to dress a WOUND. Children in coastal communities are sometimes warned against making faces when the tide turns, as they may find that they stay that way.

In folk medicine, it is claimed that WHOOPING COUGH may be cured by taking the patient down to the water's edge when the tide is on the turn and either wading in the water or actually drinking some of it so that the patient is then sick: the retreating waves will carry the disease away with them.

**toad**   One of the animals most closely associated with WITCHCRAFT, the toad has a mixed reputation among superstitious people. In some circumstances it is a lucky creature, whose appearance means the end of a drought and general good fortune, possibly in the form of unexpected wealth. It is thought to be particularly lucky if a toad crosses the path of a bride on her way to church (*see* WEDDING), as this means that the union will be both prosperous and happy. The link with witchcraft, however, means that many people regard the toad with foreboding and consider it a harbinger of bad luck – in pre-Christian times so much as looking at a toad was reputed to be fatal. Toads are among the most frequent of a witch's FAMILIARS and a standard ingredient of magic potions, probably inspired by the fact that they were formerly believed to have venomous properties (in fact, they can exude acids from glands in the skin if alarmed). If cattle fell ill the bite of toads was often considered the cause, and many people habitually spat or threw stones if they happened upon one of the creatures.

**toadstone**

It is, however, unlucky to kill a toad, as this will bring on rainstorms.

Other miscellaneous superstitions concerning toads include the curious notion that if a THIEF carries a dried toad's heart about the person he or she will never be caught, and the suggestion that a man who equips himself with a dried toad's TONGUE will enjoy success with the opposite sex. Toads are also said to detect distant THUNDER long before it is audible to humans and are believed to have got their beautiful eyes by exchanging them with the LARK.

In the seventeenth century people often carried dried or powdered toads about them, usually in a bag around the neck, as a supposed defence against the plague and other diseases. Rubbing a live toad on the skin, meanwhile, is said to cure CANCER of the breast, according to one superstition from eastern England, while wearing the legs ripped from a living toad is supposed to be effective against EPILEPSY and scrofula. Handling toads is discouraged by another well-known superstition, however, which warns that this will cause WARTS.

*See also* FROG; SOW THISTLE; TOAD-STONE.

**toadstone** A small stone, sometimes slightly resembling a TOAD, which is supposed to have certain magical properties. In times gone by it was said that a brown toadstone grew inside a toad's head, and if worn as jewellery it would change colour if poison was brought near it. It was also believed to protect HOUSES and SHIPS, and applying such a stone to a bite or sting was reputed to bring relief. To confirm whether a suspected toadstone has any magical powers the best course is to present it to a toad: if the toad tries to wrest it from the person concerned it does indeed have the properties hoped for. Many long-preserved toadstones have since been identified as fossilised fish teeth.

**toast** The drinking of toasts in order to promote someone's health and good fortune is an ancient tradition, originally intended as reassurance that drinks being offered to a guest are not poisoned. Superstitions connected with the custom include the notions that it is lucky to spill some of the drink when so doing but that it is extremely unfortunate to break the GLASS when making a toast, as this is an omen of DEATH. Clinking glasses before taking a drink, meanwhile, is said to scare off any malevolent spirits lurking in the vicinity. The word 'toast', incidentally, derives from Elizabethan times, when a bit of toast was slipped into the drink in the belief that this improved the taste.

**toe** *see* FEET.

**tomato** The tomato was once considered a 'scandalous' food and was widely believed to have considerable power as an APHRODISIAC. Alternatively known as the 'love apple', the tomato was actually prohibited in Puritan England in the seventeenth century and only came back into fashion some two hundred years later. In particular, single women were discouraged from eating tomatoes. Placing a big red tomato on the windowsill, meanwhile, is said to scare away evil spirits, and if placed over the hearth a tomato will promote the prosperity of the household.

**tongue** Various superstitions relate to the tongue, several of which concern the painful business of tongue-biting. Anyone who bites their tongue may be suspected of telling lies – though an Indian tradition suggests that this is a lucky accident as it foretells the arrival of some good news or a present of some kind. The appearance of white spots or ULCERS on the tongue will similarly be interpreted as a sign that the person concerned has been telling untruths. In other circumstances tongues can be lucky, though. Carrying the tip of a CALF's tongue about the person is said to guarantee a person good fortune, and if kept in the wallet or PURSE will ensure that the owner is never without money. A husband who obtains possession of the tip of a CAT's tongue will find that his wife is instantly cured of over-talkativeness, while the acquisition of a TOAD's tongue will confer sexual magnetism upon the lucky owner.

**toothache** Superstition can offer a variety of possible remedies for those who are driven to distraction by toothache, but who are too nervous of pain or cost to visit a dentist. The most familiar involves taking a few strands of HAIR and some nail trimmings (see FINGERNAIL) from the sufferer and nailing these to an OAK, when the pain is sure to fade away. Nibbling at the first FERN that appears in the spring may also bring relief, according to Cornish folklore, while another tradition recommends chewing on a piece of wood taken from a tree that has been struck by LIGHTNING. When it comes to extracting a tooth without enlisting the aid of a dentist perhaps the least painful method is to make a powder out of some dried WORMS during their mating season and to apply this to the tooth, which will, it is said, fall out at once of its own accord.

The wearing of special charms written on small pieces of paper is also reputed to help. These usually take the form of a dialogue between St Peter and Christ concerning the former's toothache, as in this example: 'Jesus came to Peter as he stood at the gate of Jerusalem, and said unto him, "What doest thou here?" Peter answered and said unto Jesus, "Lord, my teeth do ache." Jesus answered and said unto Peter, "That whosoever carry these words in memory with them, or near them, shall never have the teeth ache any more."'

To avoid getting toothache in the first place it might be worthwhile obtaining a tooth taken from a CORPSE and wearing this in a bag around the neck, or else carrying a WALNUT or the legs of a MOLE about the person, since all these precautions will prevent the problem. US superstition counsels particularly against eating anything when a funeral BELL is

tolling, and the Welsh claim that anyone who takes care to ensure that they always put their right SOCK and right trouser leg on first will never suffer from toothache (others insist that the left SHOE should go on first for this to work).

*See also* TEETH.

**topaz** A golden-coloured GEMSTONE, the BIRTHSTONE for November, which is widely held to be one of the luckier stones, suggesting good fortune in making money and winning friends. Representative of the SUN, topaz has the properties of making its wearer both courageous and wise. It will also counter MADNESS and bestow a degree of control over wild animals.

**tortoise** Largely because of its longevity, the tortoise is considered a lucky creature, associated with strength and immortality. Sacred to the Chinese, the tortoise also enjoys the protection of superstition in that it is said to be very unlucky to kill one. Wearing a tortoiseshell bracelet is said to provide a defence against evil, and tortoise oil is supposed to have some value as a painkiller. Finally, suspending a tortoise foot from the matching foot of a person suffering from GOUT is reputed to bring some relief.

*See also* TURTLE.

**touching the dead** *see* CORPSE; DEAD HAND.

**touching wood** The time-honoured tradition of touching wood (or IRON) to counter the threat of evil is known in many different cultures. This measure is most often taken when someone fears that something he (or someone else) has said may be interpreted as TEMPTING FATE. According to some authorities, underlying the tradition is the idea of making an appeal to the wooden CROSS on which Christ was crucified, though others suggest that the help of pagan 'wood spirits' is being invoked. Originally it was considered essential that the person actually touched a piece of wood, preferably that of a sacred tree such as the OAK or the ASH, but the superstition has gradually been modified so that many people now think it sufficient just to say the words 'touch wood' after expressing some hope about their future affairs.

**towel** Many domestic rituals are governed by widely observed superstitions of obscure origins. These include the curious notion that if two people dry their hands on the same towel they are sure to have a quarrel in the near future; if lovers, they will soon split up. A dropped towel, meanwhile, signifies the imminent arrival of a visitor (though the Scottish claim that such visitors may be turned away if one immediately steps backwards over the towel).

**travel** Most superstitions relating to travel date back to days when journeying far from home was a much more hazardous activity than it is now. A lot may be gleaned from observation of various birds and other animals when taking the first few steps of a journey: generally speaking, things that are noticed on the left-hand side bode ill for the journey ahead, while those on the right are more encouraging.

It is particularly crucial that no traveller turn back towards his home once he has started out: doing so will blight his entire journey. If there is no other choice, the traveller should delay restarting his or her journey until the next day; alternatively he can sit down and count to ten, or else stay to eat a meal, before resuming it.

Those seeing a traveller off, meanwhile, should refrain from watching until the person in question is quite out of sight, as this is most unlucky and might mean that the two parties never meet again (*see* PARTING). By the same token the traveller should avoid looking back as well (a reference to the biblical story of Lot's wife, who was turned to salt when she looked back at the city of Sodom).

*See also* CAR; FISHERMEN; SAILORS; SHIP.

**trees** Superstition has always reserved a special place for trees of virtually every variety, evoking the pagan religions in which every tree had its host spirit. The emblem of the tree was central to Norse mythology, and veneration of trees seems to have been among the very earliest forms of worship in human society. The felling of trees was once punishable by death and is restricted even today – it may provoke vehement protests from local communities.

The fact that people still place some magical significance in trees is reflected in such practices as TOUCHING WOOD when evil threatens and in the custom of planting a tree to mark the birth of a child. Certain trees, such as the YEW, are associated with death and are often planted in graveyards. Others, such as the ASH and OAK, are respected for their protective powers and may also be much valued for their use in various folk remedies, which usually require the patient to hammer NAILS into the trunk of a certain tree or else to enclose some of his or her HAIR or some other object in a hole bored into the wood.

*See also* APPLE; ASPEN; BAY; BEECH; BIRCH; BLACKTHORN; CHERRY; ELDER; ELM; FIR; HAWTHORN; HAZEL; LILAC; MAPLE; MYRTLE; OLIVE; PLUM; ROWAN; WALNUT; WILLOW.

**trunk** A curious Scottish superstition relating to trunks and chests insists that these should be not locked when the owner is away from home. Associated especially with fishing communities, the implication of locking the trunk of an absent FISHERMAN is presumably that he will never return to open it.

**Tuesday** *see* DAYS OF THE WEEK.

**turning back** *see* TRAVEL.

**turpentine** A superstition recorded on both sides of the Atlantic claims that it is unlucky to smell turpentine when there is no obvious source of the smell.

**turquoise** Greenish GEMSTONE, the BIRTHSTONE for December, which is supposed to have various occult powers. Because the colour of the turquoise may become gradually greener, thus losing much of its value, the stone is associated with the idea of corruption and decay and may be regarded as unlucky, often being used in the black arts of necromancy and alchemy. More positively, some say the turquoise symbolises unselfishness, prosperity and happiness, adding that wearing it also increases sexual passion. Changes in the colour of a turquoise may, it is alleged, warn of imminent danger for its owner.

**turtle** According to US superstition, FEVER may be assuaged by rubbing the patient with oil obtained from a turtle that has been killed while the MOON is on the wane. Another tradition from the same part of the world, meanwhile, has it that RHEUMATISM can be relieved by rubbing the affected parts with the yellow meat of a turtle.

*See also* TORTOISE.

**turtle-dove** *see* DOVE.

**Twelfth Night** The last day of the CHRISTMAS season, which falls on 6 January (Old Christmas Day). The date is usually noted as the time when all the Christmas decorations must come down. Superstition decrees that it is very unlucky to leave the decorations up another day – and conversely that it is also unlucky to anticipate the date by taking them down any earlier (as this symbolises throwing away prosperity and even the life of a family member). Interestingly enough, this date has changed over the centuries, as it was once considered acceptable to leave decorations up until CANDLEMAS, at the very end of January.

The method of disposal of the decorations is also laid down by superstition, which usually advises that evergreens should be burned and not just thrown out, which again would risk the death of someone in the family (though in some areas, somewhat confusingly, the opposite is said and superstition insists that the decorations should never be burned). In neither case should these evergreens be burned if they are still green.

An exception to this is the deliberate keeping back of a sprig of HOLLY, IVY, MISTLETOE or YEW to preserve until the following Christmas in the belief that this will safeguard the luck of the household over the intervening twelve months. In some parts of the British Isles tradition dictates that the Christmas decorations should be put aside until Shrove Tuesday, and then burned in the fire on which the PANCAKES are cooked. In times gone by, the ivy brought into the house was sometimes fed to cattle at Candlemas.

Another superstition that relates to Twelfth Night is the Faroese tradition that seals take human form on this date. In Wales and elsewhere it has long been considered lucky to mark the close of the Christmas festivities by killing a WREN and then parading its body in procession (for some obscure reason supposed to protect local seafarers from shipwreck; *see* SAILORS).

**twins** Superstition has always regarded twins with mistrust, believing them to be in some way closer to the spirit world than other children. In many primitive societies twins may be ostracised and everything they touch will be declared taboo to other children (in pagan times both the twins and their mother risked being put to death). Superstitious people will suggest various reasons why a woman gives birth to twins, often speculating that she has at some point during her PREGNANCY consumed a DOUBLE FRUIT. Twins will also result if husbands spill the PEPPER while their wives are pregnant, and women with a red line down the middle of their stomachs are said to be naturally prone to giving birth to more than one baby at a time. A rather pernicious tradition holds that a man may only father one child at once, and that therefore the second child is the result of the wife's infidelity or of the action of spirits.

It is widely believed that twins, particularly those who are identical, enjoy telepathic sympathy with one another, knowing when the other twin is in pain and so forth, and science seems to provide some evidence for this. According to one ancient tradition twins share a single soul: and if one dies and rigor mortis does not set in in the usual way this is a sign that the dead twin is waiting for its partner to join it in the afterlife. If the remaining twin survives the demise of its sibling it is supposed to acquire new vitality as well as supernatural healing powers, being able to cure thrush by breathing (*see* BREATH) into the patient's mouth (though only if the patient is of the opposite sex). As regards livestock, farmers are inclined to see the birth of twin calves as an unlucky event and may seek to sell one of them without delay.

*See also* BABY.

**two-dollar bill** US superstition regards the two-dollar bill as a singularly unlucky denomination inclined to bring bad luck to the holder, particularly if found in winnings from GAMBLING. The safest way of countering such bad luck is apparently to tear off one of the corners of the bill when it is received; when all four corners have been removed, the bill itself should be destroyed. This prejudice against the two-dollar bill may have developed through association with the two (or 'deuce') in a pack of playing CARDS, which is also said to be unlucky – 'deuce' being an old slang name for the DEVIL.

# U

**ulcer**  Superstition interprets the appearance of ulcers on the TONGUE as evidence that the person concerned has been telling lies. For some reason it is claimed that a cure for mouth ulcers will be effected by reading the eighth Psalm ('Out of the mouths of babes and sucklings hast thou ordained strength, because of thine enemies; that thou mightest still the enemy and the avenger') over the patient three times three days in succession. More drastic measures include persuading the patient to eat the tongue of a DOG.

**umbilical cord**  The crucial role of the umbilical cord in sustaining the life of a foetus is acknowledged by the respect that superstition demands should be paid to it once the BABY is safely delivered and the cord's function is at an end. On no account must the cord be burned, as the baby will thus be condemned to die in a FIRE. Neither should it be thrown into WATER, as death will come by DROWNING. Ideally it should be buried under a ROSE bush, so that the child grows up with a healthy 'rosy' complexion. Alternatively, burying it at the foot of a vine will ensure that the child grows up with a healthy zest for the good things in life. Some people, however, may opt to preserve the umbilical cord, in which case it may be dried and worn in a bag around the neck to ward off evil spirits. Pieces of this dried cord can then be cut off and dipped in water with a few strands of the child's HAIR to aid its recovery in times of illness.

As with other body parts, it is thought vital that an umbilical cord be kept out of the hands of witches and other hostile forces, as it may be used in spells to gain magical influence over the person concerned. Lastly, women are warned against sewing or knitting during PREGNANCY and also against stretching their arms above their head, as all these actions supposedly lead to their unborn child getting the umbilical cord twisted round its neck.

*See also* AFTERBIRTH; NAVEL.

**umbrella**  Superstition pays a surprising degree of interest to umbrellas, around which several curious beliefs persist. Opening an umbrella indoors is, of course, absolutely taboo, as this will bring bad luck both to the person concerned and possibly also to the rest of the household (though some claim that it is all right so long as the umbrella is not then raised over the head). This well-known tradition might have its roots in the use of umbrella-like sunshades in the Far East, where royalty alone had the right to use them (the umbrella only came to be widely adopted in England in the late eighteenth century). Alternatively, the connection between the original sunshades and the SUN evolved into the notion that it was unlucky to open an umbrella anywhere that the sun's rays did not fall, as this might offend the sun itself. It is also unwise to open an umbrella out of doors when the weather is fine because this is reputed to cause RAIN.

Other superstitions claim that umbrellas should never be laid on BEDS or TABLES and if dropped must be picked up by someone else (women who pick up their own umbrellas will never find husbands). Gifts of umbrellas are also thought to be unlucky and SAILORS have a prejudice against having them on board ship, especially if the umbrellas happen to be BLACK.

**underwear** Superstitions about underwear generally confine themselves to the wearing of such items by women, though one unisex tradition has it that anyone who is having an unlucky day may reverse their luck by turning their underwear inside out. When putting underwear on it is important not to do catches or buttons up incorrectly, as this will cast a shadow over one's fortunes for the rest of the day, regardless of the wearer's sex. It is also unlucky for a man or a woman to attempt to repair underwear while still wearing it, as is true of mending any other kind of garment.

Single girls should be wary of borrowing underwear off married women, as this means that they will be married themselves within the year. If, on the other hand, they actively wish to attract men, slipping a few leaves of VALERIAN into the underwear will make them irresistible to the opposite sex, according to the Welsh. Should a girl's underwear slip down for no apparent reason this is supposed to betray the fact that she is thinking about her lover; if a girl's nightdress rides up at night, meanwhile, this is a sure sign that her lover is thinking of her. When a girl finally gets to walk down the aisle as a bride, she can enhance her luck in married life by omitting to put on any underwear under her WEDDING DRESS, according to one tradition from the English Midlands. This superstition may derive from the old belief that a bride who wore nothing but her wedding dress when she got married was excused past debts, for which her new husband would otherwise have been liable in years gone by.

Women may lament the appearance of a hole or ladder in a pair of stockings, but the discovery of two at the same time is said to be a good omen and suggests that the person concerned will shortly be receiving an unexpected present. If newly washed stockings curl up when drying, meanwhile, this constitutes a prediction of happy times ahead, possibly in the form of a new love affair. Furthermore, a woman who has trouble doing up suspenders and has to refasten them three times may console herself that this guarantees her a good day ahead. Anyone who is suffering from a sore throat is advised that wrapping a stocking still warm from the leg of a new bride around the affected part will bring relief – though acquiring such a stocking in the first place may prove a challenge.

*See also* GARTER; PETTICOAT.

**unicorn** Mythical one-horned creature, which has featured in popular superstition since classical times. Variously identified as a magical HORSE, an antelope, the extinct giant aurochs (European bison) or a rhinoceros, the unicorn in fact came about through a mistranslation by the Greek translators of the Old Testament. The most widespread superstition concerning this fictitious creature is that it can only be captured by a virgin, who if seated beneath a tree can lure the beast into laying its head in her lap and going to sleep. In some versions of this legend the girl must also carry a MIRROR, and if she lies about her VIRGINITY the unicorn will kill her. The powdered horn of the unicorn is said to be a powerful APHRODISIAC and an antidote to poison.

**urine** In common with other bodily fluids, urine retains a supernatural link with the body and therefore has certain magical properties. Measures should be taken against witches obtaining a person's urine, which might be used in spells to threaten that person's welfare – SPITTING into one's urine or WASHING the hands in urine are accepted ways to ward off such interference, as is sprinkling the door-posts of one's home and every member of one's family with urine. If witchcraft is definitely suspected, remedies include baking some urine in a cake or boiling some NAILS in the urine of the victim: in either case the witch will quickly reveal herself, usually by being suddenly taken ill.

In times gone by, friends and relatives could follow the fortunes of a person away from home for a prolonged period by keeping a bottle of their urine and examining it from time to time for any changes. If the urine clouded or otherwise deteriorated this could be interpreted as a sign that the missing party was ill, in trouble or even dead.

Beneficial uses of urine include wiping the face with a BABY's first wet nappy to ensure a good complexion, pouring urine over bites from SNAKES or into the ear of someone with hearing problems to effect a cure (*see* DEAFNESS) and adding the urine of a patient suffering from FEVER to a few NETTLE leaves in order to make a prediction about the outcome of the illness. If the leaves stay green the patient will recover, but if they dry out the patient will die. Other superstitions concerning urine include the SAILORS' taboo against urinating against the WIND as this will stir up a storm; a general prejudice against two people urinating together, which means they will soon quarrel; and the German folk belief that a man will fall in love with any girl who urinates in his SHOE.

*See also* BEDWETTING.

# V

**Valentine's Day** *see* ST VALEN-
TINE'S DAY.

**valerian** Strongly perfumed plant,
also called allheal, that is prized both for
its healing properties and for its traditional association with matters of love.
Valerian is one of the plants that is
thought to have APHRODISIAC qualities
and its perfume was much admired in
medieval times, though tastes have
changed long since and the scent, which
reeks of tomcats, is usually avoided
today. British superstition maintains that
any girl who wears a sprig of valerian
will enjoy great popularity with the
other sex (*see also* UNDERWEAR). In folk
medicine, the plant is credited with
curing such ailments as COUGHS, sleep-
lessness and nervous complaints.

**vampire** Supernatural being that
feeds on the blood of the living and is
universally identified with evil. The
long-fanged vampire has a time-
honoured history in many of the world's
cultures and the idea of this merciless,
blood-sucking monster still captures the
imagination, as evidenced by the pleth-
ora of vampire movies in the modern
cinema. Vampires are variously thought
to be the reincarnated 'undead' corpses of
criminals or heretics, or simply the victims of another vampire's infectious bite.
Alternatively, one tradition from
southern Europe claims that BABIES who
are born with teeth are destined to
become vampires.

Superstition, aided and abetted by
*Dracula* author Bram Stoker, has furnished the vampire with an extraordinarily detailed body of curious traditions.
It is said that vampires cast no reflection (because the reflection embodies the
soul and the vampire has no soul); that
they have a strong aversion to the light
of the SUN, which may destroy them; and
that they may be obliged to return to
their COFFINS – lined with SOIL from
their birthplace – during the day. They
may also be credited with hypnotic
powers, with exerting a tremendous
sexual hold over women and with the
power of turning themselves into BATS
when going in search of prey. Transyl-
vania, the home of the semi-legendary
Hungarian ruler Vlad Dracula who was
renowned for his bloodthirsty ways, is
usually identified as the traditional haunt
of such beings.

Superstition holds that vampires,
being already dead, can only be destroyed
in certain ways. These include driving a
stake through their heart while they lie in
their coffins, shooting them with a SILVER
bullet and exposing them to sunlight.
They will also be driven off by the presence of GARLIC and by the sight of a cruci-
fix, or else by the sound of BELLS or the
presence of IRON. Attempts to track
down the vampire superstition to some
basis in reality have drawn links between
the creature's taste for blood and its
hatred of sunlight with the symptoms of
various obscure diseases that can inspire
such reactions. Psychologists, though,
prefer to assign the continuing evolution
of the vampire over the centuries to
repressed eroticism and sado-masochism
in society.

**vervain** Herb of the verbena family
that is credited with a variety of magical
properties, many of which were apparently recognised back in Roman times.
The plant is identified with the *sacra herba*
of Roman tradition, a herb that was used
in the course of various religious rites and
was also thought to promote fertility and
ward off evil. The ancient Persians and
the Druids venerated the plant for its
magical qualities and it continues to be of
importance to herbalists and witches
today, sometimes being dubbed the
'enchanter's plant'. As well as warding off
evil vervain may be used in various love
charms, to open locks by magic and as an
APHRODISIAC. Keeping vervain in the
house will ensure the prosperity of the
occupants, and children who carry a little
vervain about their person will grow up
both intelligent and friendly. Enemies
who share an infusion of vervain, meanwhile, will immediately forget their
quarrels and be reconciled. The plant
must be gathered with great care,
though, as its properties are lost unless it is
picked during certain phases of the MOON
and with the intonation of certain special
charms.

In folk medicine, vervain has a wide
range of uses. These include treating the
bites of SNAKES, CANCER, piles, scrofula,
EPILEPSY and the plague. For cancer, the
procedure is to split a vervain root in two,
suspend one half round the patient's neck
and smoke the other half over a fire, with
the result that any tumour will wither
away. Malevolent parties subsequently
wishing to harm someone who has cured
themselves in this way, however, have
only to soak the smoked root in some
water for the tumour to return.

*See also* SHOOTING.

**violet** Along with a number of other
garden flowers, violets should never be
brought into the house except in generous bunches as singly they threaten bad
luck. Violets that bloom out of season are
widely considered an ominous sign
which may signify the approaching death
of the person who owns the land on
which they grow, or the imminent
arrival of an epidemic. In contrast,
dreaming of violets is lucky and they may
be used in various love potions.

The violet is variously employed in
folk medicine to treat FEVERS, JAUNDICE,
pleurisy and a host of other ailments. In
order to predict the outcome of an illness,
the petals of a violet should be bruised and
the flower tied to the forefinger of the
patient: if the patient sleeps he or she will
recover, if not the illness will culminate in
death.

**virginity** The issue of maidenhood
was once crucial in the negotiations that
led up to marriage in a great many
societies, and largely in remembrance of
this prejudice the subect is still surrounded by myth and superstition. Chastity
was in former times considered a girl's
most prized treasure, reflected in the
special magical status accorded to virgins
in many cultures. Only virgins can
subdue UNICORNS, stare directly into the
SUN, walk through swarms of BEES without getting stung and restore the flame of
an extinguished CANDLE, for instance.
Clues that are supposed to indicate that a
girl has in fact lost her virginity, despite
all claims to the contrary, include the
development of large BREASTS and the
discovery that she has forgotten to put the
SALT cellar on the table. Another test is to
slip a little powdered COAL into a girl's
food: if she is still a virgin she will immediately express an overpowering desire to
urinate.

Ancient English custom decrees that it
is lucky for a newborn BABY to be held
for the first time by a virgin and that such
unblemished girls and boys have greater
powers of divination and healing – the
mere touch of a virgin is said by some to
make WARTS disappear and other minor
ailments clear up. Likewise, the grass
grows lushest on a virgin's grave and soil
and plants taken from it are supposed to
possess a number of magical properties.

Among more bizarre notions are the

**V sign**

central European tradition that a woman regains her virginity after giving birth to seven illegitimate children, and the rather more pernicious belief that a man may cure himself of a sexually transmitted disease by making love to a virgin.

*See also* SEX.

**V sign** Gesturing towards someone with the first and second FINGERS upright so as to form the shape of a V is an insult that has its roots in superstition. The two fingers upraised were originally meant to signify the horns of the DEVIL, so by 'flicking' a V sign at someone the person concerned is attempting to place his enemy under a curse. In former times making a V sign with the fingers pointing downwards was supposed to send the Devil back down to hell (Spanish Catholics formerly made this gesture as a matter of routine on getting up in the morning).

Winston Churchill's reinvention of the V sign during the Second World War, with the palm facing outwards, seems to have had nothing to do with the earlier tradition, being intended only to spell out the letter V as shorthand for 'Victory'. The two interpretations of the V sign now exist side by side, neither showing any sign of falling into disuse.

**vulture** Perhaps not surprisingly, in view of their diet of CORPSES, vultures are universally regarded as birds of ill omen. The ability of the vulture to predict death, even days in advance, is legendary and as a result their mere appearance is interpreted with alarm in many of the countries where they flourish. The contrasting belief that vultures are very good parents may owe something to a confusion between the similar Hebrew words for 'vulture' and 'compassion'.

# W

**waiting on table** Just as various superstitions relate to the business of preparing food, so too do those who actually serve it have their own rituals and taboos. It is, for instance, unlucky to serve gravy or anything else 'back-handed', and waiters everywhere may show due deference to the various superstitions that debar a person from picking up any items of CUTLERY they have accidentally been dropped. Superstitions unique to those who wait at table include the notions that it is unlucky if a diner insists on sitting in a different seat from the one to which he or she has been shown, and that it is an ill omen to have to serve a diner with only one arm. Somewhat against expectation, a waiter may lament a big tip early in a shift, as this too is supposed to be unlucky.

*See also* COOKING; POURING; TABLE.

**walking** Simply walking down a street may seem a safe enough exercise, but particular care should be taken in certain circumstances. The taboo against walking under LADDERS is one of the most widely observed of all superstitious practices, but it is by no means the only precaution to be borne in mind. If two friends walking together are parted by a child, a DOG or some other person or object their future friendship is in dire peril – though it will be saved if one of them has the presence of mind to mutter 'bread and butter'. In Scotland it was once held that if a PIG got in between two lovers as they walked together they would never be married, while elsewhere newly-weds parted by a dog, pig, HARE

or CAT will similarly never enjoy good luck (brides and grooms are therefore advised to stand as close as they can during the actual WEDDING ceremony to prevent any evil spirit coming between them).

Children, and indeed many adults, prefer not to walk on the cracks in PAVEMENTS in case ill luck should befall them, and walking backwards for any reason when going on an errand is to be avoided as this also invites misfortune (in the case of children, specifically the death of their mothers). Lastly, should a person stumble over a kerbstone they should always go back and walk over it again in order to negate any misfortune thus risked.

*See also* STUMBLING; WALKING STICK.

**walking stick** Superstition advises that the best walking sticks are those that fulfil certain conditions concerning their manufacture and the way in which they are looked after. Apparently, walking sticks are best cut from ELDER on All Souls' Day and should be hollowed out so that various magical objects can be placed inside the wood. These include seven leaves of VERVAIN and such less easily obtainable items as a powdered WOLF's eye, the tongue and heart of a DOG, three green LIZARDS and three SWALLOW's hearts. If a walking stick can be prepared in this way it is guaranteed never to break, however much weight is put upon it. GLASS walking sticks filled with various seeds or HAIR and other items are also thought to be lucky objects worth keeping in the house, though probably not a very practical aid to walking (*see* CHARM WAND). Ordinary wooden walking sticks will bring good luck to the house if hung up over a front or back door.

**walnut** Like most other trees the walnut is associated with a body of largely beneficial superstitions, ranging from ways to divine what the future holds in store to various folk remedies and protective measures to take against witches. The Romans stewed walnuts to promote fertility, and the tree continues to be widely linked with the business of love and romance. For the purposes of divination of future love affairs, one procedure is to walk three times round a walnut tree at midnight on HALLOWE'EN and then to look up into its branches and ask out loud for some nuts; if all is done correctly, the face of one's true love should appear. Falling asleep under a walnut tree may also grant the sleeper dreams of a future lover, but this is risky because the person concerned may fall into a sleep from which there is no awakening.

Witches are said to favour the shelter of walnut trees when meeting in foul weather, perhaps because the tree is reputed to ward off LIGHTNING, but if the nuts are placed beneath a witch's chair they will rob her of all power of movement. The nuts themselves are much improved if the tree is given a sound whipping. In Romania, meanwhile, a bride who is in no hurry to have children should secrete in her bosom, during her WEDDING, as many roasted walnuts as years she wishes to remain childless; after the ceremony is over she should bury the nuts. Actually consuming walnuts is recommended in the USA as a cure for sore throats and a means of restoring thinning HAIR.

It is said that if a walnut bears a heavy crop of nuts this is a warning that a severe winter lies ahead, but also that it will be followed by a good harvest of CORN the following season.

**Walpurgis Night** The evening of 30 April, traditionally supposed to be one of the two nights in the year given over to the forces of evil (the other being HALLOWE'EN). Among practitioners of WITCHCRAFT, this is thought to be one of the most auspicious times of the year for casting spells and holding sabbaths. Perhaps the most famous of these gatherings is the traditional meeting of German witches that is supposed to take place on the Brocken peak of the Harz Mountains every year.

**war** Fear of the outbreak of war has motivated many people over the centuries to try to identify from the world around them magical signs offering advance notice of such calamities. As a result, the imminence of war may be read into scores of odd events in the natural world. The appearance of anything unusual in the Heavens, particularly the arrival of a COMET or the witnessing of an ECLIPSE, is widely interpreted as an omen of war – traditions that are backed up by references to the comets that were seen before the Norman invasion of England in 1066 and subsequently before the First World War (*see also* AURORA BOREALIS). Similarly, the WEATHER is deemed to give certain clues about coming conflicts: in British superstition, for instance, it was formerly believed that if the SUN failed to shine at all on St Paul's Day (25 January) war was almost certainly in the offing.

Observation of animal behaviour is also relevant. If such birds as MARTINS and RAVENS fight among themselves many people conclude that a broader human conflict is imminent. The appearance of large numbers of VULTURES may also be considered ominous, and great dread may be occasioned among those witnessing a flypast by the SEVEN WHISTLERS. In the USA, it is said that war is usually anticipated by a huge increase in the numbers of locusts, ANTS and RATS.

A rather grisly portent of war concerns sudden fluctuations in the human birth rate. If many more boys are being born than girls this is a sign that nature is compensating in advance for the losses of men that will inevitably result from prolonged warfare. In the same way, the outwardly welcome sight of bumper crops and greater numbers of LAMBS may also be interpreted as nature bracing itself for devastation in the near future.

Other indications of the outbreak of war are more unmistakeable. In the USA, it is said that the GHOST of President Abraham Lincoln will be seen in the White House if war threatens, while in England danger to the nation may be revealed by reports of the beating of DRAKE'S DRUM. Other miscellaneous portents of war include children playing at soldiers in the street, dreams of blood, untypical idleness among bees and, in Sweden, the appearance of the hoopoe bird.

When it comes to the actual fighting, the combatants themselves have recourse to a body of superstitions that have been shared by fighting men for decades, if not centuries. Every army, navy and air force boasts its own FLAGS, MASCOTS, mottoes, tunes and myths, all designed to bolster the confidence of the individual fighter. None the less, in common with other people engaged in dangerous activities, everyone from generals to humble 'squaddies' cherishes lucky AMULETS and ritual ways of doing things in the belief that these will in some mysterious way grant them supernatural protection.

Each of the three services has its own cherished mythology. Soldiers, for instance, acknowledge that there is no escaping death if a bullet fired at a man 'has his number on it', a reflection perhaps of the fatalism necessary in the effective fighting man. Pilots who flew sorties during the Battle of Britain in 1940, meanwhile, deliberately left their beds unmade when setting out on a mission, believing that this would ensure their return. Sailors, of course, have probably the most superstitions to fall back on, but are just as capable of developing new myths to suit the times; during the First World War, for example, British seamen eagerly exchanged stories about ghostly lights that were said to lure German ships

on to the rocks of the coastline of southern England. Many superstitions, though, are common to all, ranging from never discussing what will happen after the war, on the grounds that this is simply TEMPTING FATE, to never volunteering for anything.

Just as war sees a huge escalation in interest in superstition and the protection it appears to offer among the armed forces themselves, so too will those on the home front take comfort in observing time-honoured taboos or in evolving new rituals and beliefs to protect both themselves and their loved ones and to further their own side's cause. Examples include the habit of workers in munitions factories during the Second World War of scrawling names and caricatures on bombs and shells in the vague belief that this would ensure that they reached their target.

See also ASTROLOGY; CIGARETTE; GREMLIN; POLITICIAN.

**wart** Superstition offers a host of alternative treatments for warts, which range from the barely plausible to the totally bizarre. Many of these remedies date from Tudor and Jacobean times, when the WITCHCRAFT mania reached its height in the British Isles and suspected witches were often inspected for warts and other 'marks of the DEVIL' (from which a sorcerer's imps drank blood) as evidence of their guilt. The need to eradicate such imperfections, innocent or not, became pressing for many people and superstition responded with suggestions relying partly on magic and partly on herbalistic theory.

Many of the more straightforward treatments depend on washing warts in various healing liquids, which include the WATER that collects in a stump, HOLY WATER and the blood of such animals as EELS, CATS, PIGS and MOLES. Encircling warts with a horse HAIR or a THREAD of silk might do the trick, as will blowing on them nine times in the light of a full MOON, SPITTING on them every morning or making faces at one's own reflection in the MIRROR at the hour of midnight for three nights in succession. Another superstition has it that if one can arrange to rub them surreptitiously against a known adulterer who has fathered a child out of wedlock, this too will cause the warts to disappear.

Many other treatments depend upon the notion that a person's warts may be magically transferred to another person or another living thing. Rubbing warts with the two halves of an APPLE and then burying the rejoined fruit is a relatively innocuous cure: as the apple rots, so the warts will diminish. Instead of an apple, some people recommend using an ELDER twig, a pod containing nine PEAS, grains of CORN, lard, a rasher of stolen BACON or a length of thread in which a knot has been tied for each wart. Working on the same principle, some authorities suggest pricking warts with a PIN and then sticking the pin into a TREE so that the warts disappear into the wood. It is also possible to 'sell' warts to a willing friend or to transfer them to a CORPSE when a FUNERAL passes, or to inflict them upon some enemy by rubbing them with a pebble or COIN and then seeing that this object comes into the possession of the foe.

More drastic measures to cure warts include wearing a live TOAD in a bag round the neck until the creature dies, or carrying a toad's leg about the person; suspending a freshly killed mole over the head for a few moments; and rubbing the warts with a live FROG or black SNAIL and then impaling the creature on a THORN.

Superstition suggests various precautions that may be taken to avoid getting warts in the first place. These include never handling toads, which are said to cause them, and, somewhat curiously, never washing one's hands in water in which EGGS have been boiled.

**washing** The washing of the human body has ritual implications in many of the world's religions and some significance among superstitious people generally. The notion that a good wash will purify a person of his or her sins is reflected in the various traditions that it is beneficial for the soul, as well as for the body, to wash before and after such important events as CHILDBIRTH, FUNERALS and the slaughtering of animals.

As part of the daily routine, people should take care about the disposal of the WATER in which they have washed, since a trace of their own soul goes into the water with the dirt – and thus a witch may use this water to gain magical influence over them. Other taboos include never flicking water from the hands when performing the morning ablutions (which signifies parting with one's share of luck for the day) and never sharing water with someone else – the parties concerned are sure to fall out unless the sign of the CROSS is first made over the bowl or one of the pair spits into the water (*see* SPITTING).

Welsh MINERS, meanwhile, have an aversion to washing their backs, believing that this will cause a roof collapse when they are next underground, while FISHERMEN are among those who refrain from washing while their luck is good for fear of washing away their fortune. It is also held to be very unlucky to wash the right hand of a BABY until it has reached the age of one, as this means that the child will never be rich. In the case of the sick, giving them a thorough wash and then throwing the water out of the house (or over a CAT) is said to take the disease away with it.

When it comes to washing CLOTHING, superstition dictates that there are various times when this should never be attempted or ill luck will ensue. On the whole it is best to do the family washing as early in the week as possible, ideally on Monday. A rhyme from the north of England draws conclusions about people who do their washing at other times:

They that wash on Monday, have the
    whole week to dry.
They that wash on Tuesday, are not so
    much arye.

They that wash on Wednesday,
will get their clothes so clean.
They that wash on Thursday, are not
so much to mean.
They that wash on Friday, wash for
their need.
But they that wash on Saturdays, are
dirty folks indeed!

Blankets should never be washed in the month of May, for fear that one of the family will also be 'washed away'. The same risk applies to washing clothes on New Year's Day and GOOD FRIDAY (the latter supposedly because Christ laid a curse on a washerwoman who taunted him as he made his way to the Crucifixion). Should anyone attempt to do the washing on Good Friday, the water may turn to blood and garments hung up on the line to dry may also be spotted with blood.

Other miscellaneous superstitions relating to washing clothes include the notions that bad luck will follow if too much water gets splashed around during the process, and that a single girl who soaks her own APRON while doing the washing is fated to marry a drunkard. Clothes washed for the first time when there is a new MOON will quickly wear out.

See also BATHING.

**washing up** The humdrum task of doing the washing up after a meal is, like other domestic rituals, not without its taboos. It is said to be particularly unlucky to break any piece of crockery while doing the washing up, as such BREAKAGES always happen in threes; to avoid further breakages two pieces of old china or glass should be deliberately smashed so as to protect more treasured items. A quaint rhyme heard on both sides of the Atlantic, meanwhile, advocates the sharing of responsibilities at the kitchen sink in the furtherance of a harmonious home life:

Wash and wipe together,
Live in peace together.

**wasp** A time-honoured superstition, recorded as early as the first century AD, has it that the first wasp of the season should always be killed. This is reputed to bring good luck to the person concerned and also to provide a degree of protection against one's enemies.

**wassailing** The custom of honouring one's crops or livestock during the CHRISTMAS season in the hope that this will promote the harvest in the coming year. This ancient rural tradition, sometimes carried out on Christmas Eve or at NEW YEAR or else on Twefth Night, can include the drinking of toasts to CORN, COWS and FRUIT TREES. Celebratory fires may be lit in the fields and cider drunk in barns or in the orchards while men armed with shotguns fire into the air or into the branches of the trees to scare away evil spirits. One old custom is to stick a plum pudding on a cow's horn and then to frighten the animal so that the pudding is tossed off: if the pudding falls forward this predicts a good harvest, but if it falls backwards the harvest will be poor. In parts of Scotland, in times gone by, the SEA was similarly honoured with greetings and with the pouring of a glass of ale into the waves in the hope that this would ensure a plentiful supply of fish.

See also APPLE.

**water** In keeping with the crucial role of water in the sustenance of life on Earth, superstition places great value on the healing, spiritually cleansing and other magical properties of water. Virtually every major religion in the world makes use of water in its most important rites and every society boasts its 'magic' springs, wells and lakes as well as mythical 'fountains of youth'.

Running water in any form is widely thought to be supernaturally potent. Many peopole believe it constitutes a magical barrier that no spirit can cross. Pursuing witches may therefore be evaded by jumping over streams or by crossing BRIDGES, and the bodies of SUICIDES, executed criminals and VAM-

PIRES have often been buried under running water to prevent their GHOSTS walking. Immersion in running water will cure WARTS, SCIATICA, thrush and a host of other ailments, and in some cases rubbing the patient with stones taken from the bed of a river or stream will suffice. Keeping a bowl of cold water under the bed, meanwhile, will prevent the sleeper from getting CRAMP.

Other superstitions concerning water claim that witches can cause rainstorms by dipping twigs in water and then shaking them in the air; that, according to the French and the Welsh, water kept in stone jugs turns to wine in the hour before midnight on Christmas Eve and on the eve of Easter; that water should never be thrown out of the house after dark as it wards off evil spirits; that boiled water should never be taken into a bedroom as it will adversely affect the occupants because the Devil dislikes it and will cause trouble; and that dreaming of water is unlucky.

Water companies should perhaps note that, according to Welsh folklore, it is unlucky to accept payment in return for water. Those who do so are fated to beg for just a few drops of it as they burn in the fires of Hell.

*See also* DEW; DROWNING; HOLY WATER; RAIN; SEA; TIDES; WASHING; WASHING UP; WAVE; WELL.

**wave** Seafarers around the globe associate waves with a variety of odd beliefs. One old idea has it that the souls of drowned men emerged from the oceans to ride the 'white horses' that appear on the crests of the waves at CHRISTMAS, EASTER and HALLOWE'EN. In Scotland, meanwhile, it is said that pouring water taken from the crests of nine waves over the head of a sufferer from CONSUMPTION will cure them, as long as they are then passed through a hole in a rock in a SUNWISE direction. Lastly, seamen and surfers alike claim that every ninth wave is bigger than those that precede it, despite a total lack of evidence to support this notion.

*See also* SEA; TIDES.

**waxwing** Songbird, whose appearance is regarded with misgiving in many European countries. The arrival of large numbers of waxwings is variously interpreted as an omen of WAR, famine, severe WEATHER or some other calamity. In parts of Switzerland, where the bird is reputed to appear every seven years, the bird is synonymous with death.

**weaning** *see* BABY.

**weasel** In many countries the weasel is considered a most ill-omened creature, with close links to WITCHCRAFT. Witches are said to favour the form of a weasel as one of their disguises and thus any encounter with the animal, either outside or inside the house, is said to bode ill, especially if it is WHITE in colour (according to some, the person concerned will face death before the year is over). Even the cry of a weasel is bad luck; and if the creature is seen running towards the left the outlook is doubly ominous and warns that one has enemies in one's own house. The only defence is to throw three small stones directly in front of oneself and then to make the sign of the CROSS seven times.

Other superstitions which involve weasels include the notion, recorded in Dorset, that it is impossible to catch one as it will turn into a FAIRY if approached, and the related idea that a human will never spy a weasel asleep. Another suggestion claims that weasels that have feasted on RUE can kill snakes. On the more beneficial side, treading on the tail taken from a young weasel is said to be a good way to stop a DOG from barking, and keeping one's money in a weasel-skin PURSE will ensure that the coins never run out. Anyone who eats a weasel's heart while it is still beating, moreover, will enjoy the gift of divination of the future for the space of a whole year.

**weather** According to superstition, there are countless ways in which the weather may be forecast. The ability to predict weather patterns is crucial to the livelihood and indeed the safety of SEA-FARERS, farmers and others, and many of the traditions relating to the weather are of considerable antiquity and common to many cultures.

A well-known guide to the next day's weather is the oft-heard rhyme:

Red sky at night, shepherds' delight.
Red sky in the morning, shepherds' warning.

This rhyme is fairly reliable for British weather systems, which generally approach from the west. A SUN setting in the west when there is little moisture in the air will cast a red glow on clouds departing to the east – however, a red sun rising in the east may suggest that weather that has already passed was dry but offers no such reassurance about the approaching clouds from the west upon which it also casts its red light.

A large body of weather forecasting lore depends upon close observation of animal behaviour, ranging from the height at which SWALLOWS fly to the way in which COWS in the fields huddle together or spread about. Signs that the weather is going to change for the worse include SEAGULLS flying inland, CATS sneezing or washing behind their ears, FISH taking bait more enthusiastically than usual, CUCKOOS calling, CROWS cawing, BEES remaining in their hives, DONKEYS braying and PIGEONS swooping over water. Indications that the weather will be fine include the appearance of BATS in the early evening, SPIDERS spinning their webs on the grass, ANTS clearing out their anthills and ROOKS building their nests high in trees.

In the USA, the sight of two new MOONS in one month or the appearance of a crescent moon 'on its back' is much dreaded because it signifies disastrous flooding. Another tradition, that it always pours on British bank holidays when most people particularly want it to be fine, is so well known that it just about qualifies as a superstition.

Long-term forecasts about whole seasons may also be made by reference to nature. The summer will be good if the OAK bears leaves before the ASH, while severe winters are presaged by thick skins on various fruits and vegetables, SQUIRRELS hoarding larger stores of nuts than usual and GEESE flying south as early as August, among other signs. In the British Isles it is said that a mild January warns of a wintry spring, while in the USA the groundhog, or woodchuck, gives its own opinion of coming spring weather when it emerges from its burrow on 2 February: if the creature can see its shadow the winter will last another six weeks, but if there is no shadow spring has already dawned.

The state of the weather at certain moments may have more than a purely physical influence on human affairs. Various superstitions suggest that a magical influence is also exerted, as evidenced by the belief that it is lucky for the sun to shine on a bride and also for the Heavens to open during a FUNERAL. This makes the ability to influence the weather doubly desirable and all kinds of actions may be taken in the hope that they will change meteorological patterns. These include the performing of ritual dances, tying KNOTS in lengths of string while muttering special incantations and at the most basic level the chanting of such charms as

Rain, rain, go away,
Come again another day.

*See also* DEW; FOG; RAIN; SEAWEED; STORM; SUN; THUNDER; WIND.

**wedding** Superstition has always placed the greatest importance on the ritual of marriage, and virtually every aspect of the ceremony, from the engagement to the HONEYMOON, is governed by a body of time-honoured traditions and taboos.

Making one's choice of partner is of course the first and most crucial stage of the whole business (*see* ENGAGEMENT; LOVE). Superstition supports social taboos against marrying blood relatives, though sometimes going beyond what is genetically inadvisable to include marriages between sets of brothers and sisters, for instance. In former times, if a man faced a choice between two sisters he was often put under pressure to marry the elder as to do otherwise was tantamount to an insult. Sisters, incidentally, should never marry on the same day or even in the same year, as this condemns both marriages to unhappiness, according to the Germans.

Choosing a date for the wedding is the first hurdle that a newly engaged couple must cross. This should not be lightly undertaken as certain months, and indeed days, are luckier than others for getting married. May is a month particularly to be avoided, as it has been associated with rites honouring the dead since Roman times. The periods of LENT and Advent are also deemed to be unlucky. June, however, is ideal, particularly if the wedding is timed to take place when the MOON is on the wane.

Various attempts have been made to summarise the advantages and disadvantages of certain months, of which the following English rhyme is but one example:

Married in January's hoar and rime,
Widowed you'll be before your prime.
Married in February's sleepy weather,
Life you'll tread in time together.
Married when March winds shrill and roar,
Your home will be on a distant shore.
Married beneath April's changing skies,
A chequered path before you lies.
Married when bees over May blossoms flit,
Strangers around your board will sit.
Married in the month of roses – June,
Life will be one long honeymoon.
Married in July with flowers ablaze,
Bittersweet memories on after days.
Married in August's heat and drowse,

Lover and friend in your chosen spouse.
Married in September's golden glow,
Smooth and serene your life will go.
Married when leaves in October thin,
Toil and hardship for you gain.
Married in veils of November mist,
Fortune your wedding ring has kissed.
Married in days of December cheer,
Love's star shines brighter from year to year.

Couples should avoid choosing to get married on a date that marks one of their birthdays. It is generally agreed that the ideal dates for weddings are as follows:

January: 2, 4, 11, 19 and 21.
February: 1, 3, 10, 19 and 21.
March: 3, 5, 13, 20 and 23.
April: 2, 4, 12, 20 and 22.
May: 2, 4 12, 20 and 23.
June: 1, 3, 11, 19 and 21.
July: 1, 3, 12, 19, 21 and 31.
August: 2, 11, 18, 20 and 30.
September: 1, 9, 16, 18 and 28.
October: 1, 8, 15, 17, 27 and 29.
November: 5, 11, 13, 22 and 25.
December: 1, 8, 10, 19, 23 and 29.

As to the day of the week, one ancient English rhyme runs:

Monday for wealth,
Tuesday for health,
Wednesday the best day of all;
Thursday for crosses,
Friday for losses,
Saturday for no luck at all.

Regarding the time of day, in practice few people get married after dark. This is just as well because to do so would be highly unlucky, foretelling a troubled married life, children who die prematurely and an early death for the 'happy' couple.

Once the date of the wedding has been decided it should not be changed as this is very bad luck. Neither should the happy couple attend church to hear their BANNS read – another bad omen. Choosing a venue for the wedding is less restricted by superstition, though it is said to be particularly lucky for a woman to be married in the same church in which she was christened. Brides should not be permitted to read the whole of the marriage service before the day appointed, as this means that the wedding will never take place.

The weeks or months between the engagement and the wedding are the time for making the many preparations that are usual for the big day. Superstition is full of suggestions about BRIDESMAIDS and the WEDDING DRESS. This is also the time for the making of that most essential item on the wedding breakfast menu, the WEDDING CAKE.

On the morning of the wedding itself, before leaving for the church a bride should be sure to feed the family pet CAT, if there is one, as this act of consideration will ensure her lasting marital happiness. If the cat should sneeze the day before the wedding, incidentally, this too constitutes a sign that the marriage will be happy (*see* SNEEZING).

As the bride leaves the house, it was once common in England for the doorstep to be washed with boiling water in the belief that this would hasten the marriage of the first single girl whose dress was dampened by it (usually one of the bridesmaids).

In times gone by, wedding parties generally made their way to the church on foot. Various superstitions concerned their route and events that might take place on the way, such as meeting certain animals or, if things went badly wrong, cross-eyed people and others suspected of having the power of the EVIL EYE. Among the most inauspicious persons to meet on the journey were members of the CLERGY, policemen, doctors, lawyers and blind men. In previous centuries, to keep evil spirits at bay attendants on both the bride's and the groom's parties fired guns into the air at regular intervals, or else a charge of powder was set off on the local anvil as they passed.

It was also thought unlucky for a bridal party to be obliged to cross running WATER; if this happened, someone in the party had to throw some object over their shoulder and into the water while reciting the charm 'Bad luck cleave to you' as a precaution. A version of the 'first foot' custom now confined to NEW YEAR also used to be observed by such wedding processions. This involved the groom giving a COIN or a gift of some food to the first person he met on the way to the church (and the bride doing likewise on leaving it).

According to weather lore, it is a good omen for the SUN to shine on a bride on her wedding day and also if it snows. If it is windy the marriage will be plagued by misunderstandings, and if it rains the couple concerned will be anything but happy (rain being more appropriate for FUNERALS). This superstition dates back to the days when marriage ceremonies were often conducted at the entrance to a church and brides risked getting a thorough soaking. A more ominous sign, though, is the sight of a newly dug open grave in the churchyard.

During the service itself a few tears from the bride are considered a good omen (though confusingly an alternative superstition warns that a bride who cries on her wedding day is fated to cry throughout her married life). Once safely in church, the happy couple may take heart if the service is interrupted by a child crying, generally held to be a good omen for the marriage. The groom and the best man should take care, however, not to drop the WEDDING RING, which is regarded as unlucky.

The throwing of CONFETTI (or RICE) as the couple leave the church is meant to promote their chances of having children in due course. A rarely revived custom that was once fairly common requires a cloth to be spread over the bride's hair as she leaves the church and an oatcake or a small plate to be broken above her head. This curious ritual is supposed to guarantee years of wedded bliss, providing the cake or plate do actually smash as intended (predictions about the future can also be made from the way in which the cake or plate breaks – the more pieces it breaks into, the better future the newly-weds have in store).

On leaving the grounds of the church, further ancient superstitions apply. The happy couple should not, for instance, take the same route that they took on arriving at the church and, in former times, were discouraged from walking through a LYCHGATE (*see also* BARRING THE WAY). Bad luck will also follow if they should happen to encounter a funeral procession or a PIG on their way to the reception, but good luck is certain if they encounter a CHIMNEY SWEEP (who is entitled to give the bride a kiss), a black CAT, a grey HORSE or an ELEPHANT. If the newly-weds are transported to the reception in a carriage (which should ideally be drawn by grey horses) it is crucial that the vehicle proceeds at a leisurely place, for anything faster suggests only ill luck.

The giving of presents to a newly married couple at their reception has its roots in the ancient custom of presenting them with fruit as a symbol of fertility. However certain presents, particularly KNIVES, should not be given as they are unlucky.

When the time comes for the newly-weds to depart on their honeymoon it is usual for the bride to toss her bouquet to the bridesmaids and other unwed females. This is a relatively recent tradition, probably invented in the USA in the early years of the twentieth century (in some regions the bride throws one of her SHOES). The idea is that the girl who catches the bouquet (or shoe) will be first to marry. Similarly, in the days when few happy couples went away after their wedding the bride used to allow one of the young men present to remove her loosened GARTER, which he would then wear in his hat before offering it to a girl of his choice for luck.

Bridegrooms to this day carry their new brides over the threshold, even if they are not entering their own home but spending their first night in a hotel somewhere. This tradition dates from Roman times, when it indicated that a bride sacrificed her VIRGINITY with becoming reluctance, though it has since become a 'lucky' act in a more general sense, meant in some unspecified way to protect the luck of the happy couple in their new home. One suggestion is that it is a legacy from primitive times when men were given to snatching and carrying off new wives against their will and had to carry them kicking and screaming into their future home. A rather pernicious tradition has it that a bride who steps over the threshold first will dominate the marriage from then on, as she also will if she manages to buy something for her husband before he buys her a gift.

For those single persons left behind when the happy couple disappear on their honeymoon comes the comforting tradition that 'one wedding brings on another'.

*See also* BRUSH; NAMES.

**wedding cake** A feature of WEDDINGS as far back as Roman times, the wedding cake symbolises both good fortune and fertility and brings good luck to all who eat it. It is important that the cake – which should be as rich as possible, to represent an abundance of the good things in life – turns out well: if it proves a disaster in the making then so will the marriage, according to one tradition. It is, moreover, thought to be most unlucky if the bride assists in the making of her own wedding cake and on no account must she be offered a taste of it before the actual wedding day.

It is essential that the bride and groom cut the first slice of cake as a sign that they will share all their possessions in the future. Should they fail to do so they run the risk of being unable to bear children. The bride may also care to set a slice of the cake aside for careful preservation, to guarantee that her new husband will remain faithful to her. Keeping a tier of the cake for possible use as a CHRISTENING cake, meanwhile, will ensure that the marriage is fertile. Everyone present at the reception should eat a little of the cake

– to refuse to do so is a very bad omen for the happy couple. Sending slices of cake to guests who are unable to attend the wedding is supposed to allow them to share in the luck of the whole party. According to time-honoured custom, unmarried girls among the guests may take a portion of cake home with them and sleep with it under their pillows, which may give them dreams of their own future husbands.

**wedding dress**  Bridal outfits must be put together with considerable care and no single item is as important in the ensemble as the dress. It is actually unlucky, according to ancient tradition, for a bride to wear any colour but white (symbolic of innocence and purity), though blue and pink are safe enough according to one old rhyme recorded in Warwickshire:

Married in white, you have chosen all right,
Married in green, ashamed to be seen,
Married in grey, you will go far away,
Married in red, you will wish yourself dead,
Married in blue, you will always be true,
Married in yellow, ashamed of your fellow,
Married in black, you will wish yourself back,
Married in pink, of you he'll think.

The all-white rule allows the exception of a sky-blue GARTER in order to satisfy the convention that all brides wear 'something old, something new, something borrowed, something blue'. It was once usual for the 'old' item to be the SHOES or a HANDKERCHIEF, but extra good luck will also attend a bride who wears the dress her mother wore. In some regions the 'something borrowed' may be varied as 'something stolen' or 'something golden'.

Many brides now make their own dresses even though this practice is frowned upon by superstition, which warns of great misfortune and further counsels against trying the outfit on before the wedding day (if the bride persists in doing so it is vital that she must not look at herself in a full-length MIRROR). One way round this inconvenient tradition is to try the dress on but not to wear the complete outfit, leaving off a shoe or glove. It is universally acknowledged that it is even more unlucky for the groom to see the wedding dress before his bride joins him at the altar (this holds true even as she comes up the aisle, when the groom must resist the temptation to turn round to see his wife-to-be approaching in all her finery).

On no account must the bride's dress be stained with blood (except by a dressmaker to counter evil on breaking her needle), for this is an omen that her own life will not be long, and no one should examine the dress by candlelight. Silk is the preferred material for bridal gowns; satin brings bad luck and velvet threatens poverty in the future. The dress must not be patterned, and pictures of BIRDS or vines must be avoided in particular. As a further measure for luck, it is suggested that a final stitch in the dress is left unfinished until the very last moment before the bride sets off for the service. Some brides also sew a HAIR or two into their dress for luck, or else slip a COIN into their stocking or shoe in the expectation that this will ensure their future prosperity.

The finishing touches to a wedding outfit are the veil and bouquet (though the veil should never be tried on with the dress before the wedding day). Veils are worn in order to conceal a bride's beauty from any evil spirits who might try to kidnap her on her journey to the church, and they should on no account be lifted until the marriage has been officially solemnised. The bouquet symbolises both sexuality and fertility and is by convention tied with luck-giving RIBBONS (*see also* MYRTLE; ORANGE).

**wedding ring**  Various superstitions surround the wearing of RINGS that have been presented during the marriage service as a physical symbol of a couple's union. Such rings, which usually take the form of a plain gold circle, should never be dropped during the service itself: this is very bad luck and warns that whichever of the couple dropped it will be the first to die. If the ring rolls on to the gravestone of a man the groom will die very soon, but if it comes to rest on the grave of a woman it is the bride whose death is at hand. It is important that neither of the happy couple attempt to retrieve the ring, for doing so would only further endanger their luck: it should be left to the person officiating. In Anglo-Saxon countries the ring should always, incidentally, be worn on the fourth finger of the left hand (the 'ring finger') – according to a very ancient tradition, a vein runs straight from this finger to the heart. In other parts of Europe (and in England until the sixteenth century) the ring is worn on the fourth finger of the right hand, the thumb and the first two fingers of that hand being sacred to the Trinity.

A wedding ring should never be removed once it has been put on, and its destruction or loss is widely thought to presage the collapse of the marriage itself. Should the ring be lost or broken, the consequences can only be avoided through the other party in the marriage presenting a replacement as soon as possible and renewing the marriage vows as the ring is slipped on. A regional variation of this prejudice against removing wedding rings, however, allows for their being taken off without any apparent ill effects any time after the first child of the marriage is born.

In the past, many couples could not afford a gold ring. A ring was therefore often borrowed for the ceremony and then returned to the rightful owner, or else the bride slipped her finger into the loop of the church KEY as a substitute. Rings were also removed from fingers on a fairly frequent basis for use in various love charms and so forth – perhaps the best preserved of which is the business of suspending a wedding ring over the belly of a pregnant woman to determine the sex of the unborn child (*see* PENDULUM).

**Wednesday**   *see* DAYS OF THE WEEK.

**weeds** Superstition claims that ground where weeds flourish can never be cleared, however hard a gardener or farmer works, because new ones will always spring up; this is in line with the old idea that such plants are generated from the SOIL itself and not by the usual means of seeds. This tradition, which runs counter to the modern contention that weeds are simply plants growing in the wrong place, echoes the ancient biblical belief that God created the first weeds as a deliberate punishment for Adam's disobedience. It is therefore both futile and irreligious to attempt to get rid of them. Those determined to attempt it anyway may consider the barbarous measure of burying three puppies in the ground, as this will apparently clear the whole area round about of weeds.

**well** Most superstitions concerning wells date from the days when they were a focal point of every community, crucial to the prosperity of people and animals alike and thus of great magical significance. Every well is supposed to have its guardian spirit, who must be treated with respect (as recalled today in the surviving ritual of 'well-dressing', notably in Derbyshire, in which certain wells that remained pure during the Black Death are gaily decorated). Some wells are reputed to have special powers of divination, making strange noises and filling or emptying as a warning of national disasters or other important events. Others are famed for their healing properties (it is said, for instance, that WATER drawn from a deep well at dawn will relieve TOOTHACHE). Rather more unusual is the well of St Elian at Llanelian-yn-Rhos in Wales, which is supposed to deliver curses: the curse must be written on a piece of paper and then lowered into the well in a lead casket.

Superstitions that apply to all wells include the notions that it is unlucky to spill any water from the bucket after it has been drawn up, and that to ensure a well does not run dry over the course of the year it should be offered a piece of bread at NEW YEAR. Anyone who drinks of the 'cream of the well' – that is, from the first bucket of water drawn up at the beginning of the year – will enjoy good luck or various 'marvellous' powers in the twelve months ahead.

*See also* WISHING WELL.

**werewolf**   In pan-European superstition, a man who in certain circumstances changes into a WOLF and then hunts down and feeds on human prey. Fear of werewolves is very ancient. People likely to become werewolves are said to include those who are born out of wedlock or have birthdays on Christmas Eve, and anyone who has unusually hairy HANDS and flat FINGERS or EYEBROWS that meet over the nose. In legend some people control their transformation, becoming wolves on donning wolkskin coats or belts.

Like the VAMPIRE, the werewolf is invulnerable to many forms of attack and can only be killed by a SILVER bullet, which should ideally have been blessed by a priest. Rather more simply, they may be cured by calling out three times the Christian name of the person who has thus been transformed. Some authorities have drawn a link between the werewolf of myth, as reshaped by Hollywood, with the medical condition known as lycanthropy, in which the patient develops a taste for raw meat and shows a tendency to howl and run around naked.

**whale**   Superstition generally regards whales as lucky creatures and warns that misfortune will befall those who kill them. It is, however, unlucky for a whale to appear in an area where these creatures are not usually seen. In times gone by, it was customary for the wives of whaling crews to stay in bed while their husbands were at sea, which was supposed to ensure that the men made a catch.

**wheatear**   Songbird, which usually frequents lonely places and is widely reputed to be unlucky, its appearance being seen as an omen of death. It is thought particularly ill omened in some regions to see a wheatear perching on a stone, though not so bad if it is sitting on the grass or on soft ground. The birds are especially feared in the Orkneys, where their nests are destroyed as a matter of course because, it is alleged, their eggs will be hatched by TOADS, which are themselves associated with the forces of darkness.

**whippoorwill**   *see* NIGHTJAR.

**whistling**   In certain circumstances, whistling is a taboo activity that risks the most dire consequences. Whistling in a theatre is absolutely forbidden among ACTORS AND ACTRESSES, and MINERS and SAILORS have a similar prejudice against hearing anyone whistling as they go about their work. Should this taboo be ignored while underground, an explosion or cave-in will quickly follow; if it is ignored at sea, a storm will be instantly 'whistled up'. FISHERMEN also dislike hearing anyone whistle after dark. A woman whistling is thought to be unnatural by some people and – like a hen crowing – is considered extremely unlucky (an old tradition has it that a woman stood idly by, whistling, while the NAILS that were destined for the Crucifixion were being made).

**white**   Superstition associates white with purity and holiness and the colour is therefore considered to have various protective properties, hence its popularity for WEDDING DRESSES and nightdresses. The fact that mourners in certain Eastern countries, such as Vietnam, wear white at funerals is in keeping with this notion of white representing wholesomeness and happiness, as the departure of loved ones for a better life beyond the grave is seen by these peoples as an occasion for rejoicing. In various regions, though, the colour has something of an unlucky reputation and many people fear the sight of white birds and animals, which they believe presage ill luck. To protect one's luck one should always spit on seeing a white CAT, COW, HARE, HORSE or PIGEON, among other white creatures – though strangely enough it is thought lucky to see a white DOG. Similarly, white flowers such as LILIES and LILAC should never be kept indoors or given to the sick, as they are associated with FUNERALS and may seal the patient's fate; it is, however, all right to mix them with blooms of any other colour except red (*see* HOSPITAL). FISHERMEN, meanwhile, have a prejudice against using white stones for BALLAST or to weigh down their NETS, and some people will refrain from picking up and keeping white pebbles that catch their eye for fear of the bad luck they may bring.

**Whitsun**  A time-honoured superstition of English origin insists that it is unlucky not to wear at least one item of new CLOTHING on Whit Sunday. As with the identical tradition associated with EASTER, people who ignore this custom run the risk of becoming a target for bird droppings. Another superstition maintains that those unlucky enough to be born at Whitsun are destined either to kill or to be killed (*see also* BURIAL).

**whooping cough**  Superstition offers many remedies for whooping cough, which is one of the most distressing of childhood illnesses to witness. Worried parents have a huge choice ranging from the relatively innocuous and possibly helpful to the totally outlandish. The more disgusting include feeding the patient OWL soup, a roast MOUSE or the slime of a SNAIL mixed with sugar; suspending a hairy CATERPILLAR in a bag around the sufferer's neck and keeping it there until it dies; hanging a live FROG in the chimney; coating the patient's feet with a mixture of chopped GARLIC and lard; and feeding the family dog a few

strands of the patient's HAIR in BREAD AND BUTTER. Alternatively, getting a person who was born a posthumous child and thus has special powers of healing to breathe into the mouth of the patient may do the trick, as it does in cases of thrush (*see* BREATH). If at a loss as to which treatment to adopt, one solution is to ask the advice of the rider of a piebald HORSE and to follow to the letter whatever is suggested, however unlikely it may seem.

**widdershins**  The direction opposite to the path of the SUN through the Heavens, which is often stipulated as the correct movement to make in raising the DEVIL and in the execution of various ill-intentioned spells. Taking such an anticlockwise direction when stirring a potion or moving from one point to another is held to be contrary to the natural and 'proper' way of doing things, and is therefore both unlucky and likely to attract the assistance of evil spirits in the making of malevolent magic. By the same token, witches and other sorcerers often recite PRAYERS backwards, reverse the symbols of Christianity and walk widdershins (or withershins) around their magic circles as a matter of convention. Persons innocent of such malicious intent should beware particularly of walking widdershins round a church or a place that is reputed to be haunted, as this might well provoke the attention of demons and ghosts.

*See also* SUNWISE TURN.

**widow**  Superstition generally regards widows as unlucky people and particularly warns against including them on the guest list for WEDDINGS, as their presence might damage the prospects of the happy couple. Meanwhile, the sudden appearance of a 'widow's peak' – a point where the HAIR grows lower down in the middle of a woman's forehead – may well be interpreted as a sign that the woman is fated to end her days a widow, and that the days of her widowhood may not be far away.

According to German folklore, if a widower remarries, the ghost of his first wife will turn up at the wedding, but will not interfere as long as her successor meets with her approval. Making a great deal of noise may have the desired effect of frightening away such a ghost if it decides to kick up a fuss. If a widow wishes to remarry and desires a glimpse of a future partner in her dreams, she should drip a few specks of blood on to her forehead, or wear a mixture of CORAL, magnate dust and DOVE's blood in a pouch around her neck, or slip a twig of POPLAR wrapped up in her stockings under her pillow when she goes to bed. If she succeeds in finding a new husband, it was once thought appropriate that she should wear a GLOVE when slipping on her new WEDDING RING.

**Wild Hunt** Spectral hunt, complete with hellish black hounds and demonic huntsman, that is said to haunt the skies over northern Europe. Stories about this Satanic hunt date back as far as pagan times and alleged sightings of it roaring across stormy winter skies have always inspired dread. According to legend, witnesses of the Wild Hunt risk being snatched away and carried off to some infernal region.

*See also* GABRIEL'S HOUNDS.

**will** In superstition it is unlucky to make a will, which supposedly hastens the hour of one's death. In the past, great offence was sometimes caused by the suggestion that someone should make a will and it was customary to read the document over the body of the deceased so that if they were dissatisfied they might make some sign of their feelings.

**will-o'-the-wisp** Glowing light of the type occasionally seen on marshy ground or near graves. The result of certain unusual atmospheric conditions or else created by burning marsh gases, these lights – otherwise called Jack-o'-lanterns – have often been considered of supernatural origin. Variously identified as GHOSTS or as malevolent imps and assumed to be omens of death or disaster, such lights are said by some to lure humans into bottomless bogs. To escape their attentions, the best remedy is to drive a NEEDLE into the ground – in which case the light will disappear into the eye of the needle. WHISTLING, meanwhile, should be avoided because it is said to increase the chances of their appearance. Some stories are told, however, of such will-o'-the-wisps that have actually led lost humans back to safety.

*See also* CORPSE-LIGHTS; ST ELMO'S FIRE.

**willow** The willow has long been associated with sorrow and lost love. In times gone by it was customary for people in MOURNING to wear sprigs of willow to indicate their loss, and also for lovers who had lost their partners to someone else to wear or to be sent, rather maliciously, garlands of willow. The idea behind this was that the tree, to which grieving comes as second nature, would relieve the pain of the loss by assuming it itself. In keeping with this reputation for melancholy, some say that willow catkins should never be brought indoors. Neither should willow wood be burned on the domestic hearth, nor children or animals be beaten with willow sticks, because it will stunt their growth or cause internal injuries. Anyone who reveals secrets beneath a willow tree, meanwhile, runs the risk of hearing the same secrets being repeated by the WIND.

Taking the opposite view, some people touch willows for luck and for the same reason are happy to bring willow catkins into the house on MAYDAY. Certain varieties are said to ward off WITCHCRAFT and the EVIL EYE, and carrying a willow switch is recommended for those who are particularly fearful of the threat of evil.

Many sorcerers favour wands made of willow when casting spells, and willow sticks may be used by girls for the purposes of divination in love. The procedure here is to take a stick of willow in the left hand and to turn round three times while intoning, 'He that's to be my good man, come and grip the end of it': if successful, the third time round the girl's future partner will appear at the other end of the stick.

In folk medicine, infusions of willow may be used in the treatment of ague and RHEUMATISM (in fact, the isolation of salicin in willow bark in chemical laboratories led to the discovery of salicylic acid and thus of aspirin). Children suffering from rickets and other ailments may also be passed through a fork in a willow tree to effect a cure.

**wind** Most superstitions relating to the wind are, for obvious reasons, of nautical origins. SAILORS becalmed at sea claim several ways of raising a helpful breeze. Scratching the mast of the ship with a FINGERNAIL may have the desired effect, as will breaking the taboo against WHISTLING, though this must be done very softly for fear of 'whistling up' a gale. Throwing a COIN or BRUSH into the waves is also supposed to help produce a healthy breeze. If all else fails, favourable winds may be bought in advance from a witch, usually in the form of a length of string with three KNOTS tied in it: when the purchaser of the string unties the first knot a breeze will spring up, when the second knot is untied there will a gale, and when the third is loosened there will be hurricane force winds.

*See also* STORM.

**window** Like a DOOR or CHIMNEY, a window can provide access to the household for evil spirits unless properly protected. The fact that the wooden frame of a window often makes a CROSS is itself enough to bar most malevolent agents, but nervous inhabitants may like to reinforce this protection by laying on the windowsill sprigs of various TREES and PLANTS that are reputed to repel witchcraft. Other precautions concerning windows include never watching a FUNERAL or gazing at a new MOON

through one. Furthermore, windows should always be opened when someone in the house is dying, to allow their soul free passage out of the house, and also when a STORM is raging, to allow any LIGHTNING that strikes the building to get out again. Fitting a window with a blind that has an acorn-shaped bobbin will further guard against bolts of lightning (a reference to the ancient though somewhat erroneous contention that OAK trees are never struck by lightning). A window blind that falls down without anyone touching it is a bad omen, thought by some to signify the imminent death of one of the family – an idea apparently inspired by the custom of drawing the blinds when someone in the house has died.

**wine** The preparation, serving and drinking of wine has its own time-honoured mythology. Among the most widespread superstitions are the beliefs that it is unlucky to pass a wine bottle in anything but a SUNWISE direction (particularly in the case of port) and that it is unlucky to spill wine – though the Greeks contend the opposite, that it is lucky to do so. Pouring libations of wine on the waves, meanwhile, is supposed to calm an angry SEA.

Many people sing the praises of wine as a medicine. Drinking wine is variously claimed to relieve COLDS, FEVERS and migraine HEADACHES. Rabies may be cured by drinking wine with a few strands of HAIR taken from the dog concerned, and mothers of underweight offspring who dip their WEDDING RING into a glass of wine and then give the child the wine to drink will see a rapid improvement. Wine used in church Communion services is also said to have special healing powers, particularly in treating the young.

To get a person drunk on just one glass of wine, all that is required is to add to the drink a few of their nail parings (*see* FINGERNAIL).

*See also* DRUNKENNESS.

**winking** A superstition recorded in the USA suggests that a girl may improve her chances of being lucky in love by winking at the largest star in the sky just before retiring for the night.

*See also* EYE.

**wish** Superstition delineates innumerable occasions on which a person may be granted a wish that it is almost certain to come true. Apart from getting the larger part of the WISHBONE or throwing coins into a WISHING WELL, other circumstances include spotting a black LAMB or the first STAR of the evening; a RABBIT, a black CAT, a dalmatian DOG, a cartload of HAY, a MAIL VAN or a CHIMNEY SWEEP; finding a HORSESHOE or a lump of COAL; saying the same thing as someone else at the same moment (*see* CONVERSATION); or experiencing an itchy PALM. Wishes may also be granted when dressing in new CLOTHING for the first time and when stirring the CHRISTMAS pudding. Perhaps most familiar of all, though, is the universal tradition that a wish may be made when blowing out the CANDLES on a birthday cake – though the wish will only come true if it is kept secret.

**wishbone** The forked bone, otherwise called the merrythought, that lies between a fowl's neck and its breast. When dried and then pulled between two people so that it breaks, the person holding the larger piece is granted a wish. For the wish to come true, it is crucial that neither party laughs or says anything while pulling on the bone and also that the wish itself remains secret. Alternatively, the person who gets the bigger piece is fated to marry first. The tradition probably has its roots in the fancied resemblance between the shape of a wishbone and that of a HORSESHOE.

A rather less well-known superstition relating to wishbones is sometimes encountered in the north of England. According to this, if a girl obtains the wishbone from the Christmas meal and nails it over the door at NEW YEAR, the first man to enter is destined to become her husband. In Scotland a man may find out how long he must wait to get married

by taking a wishbone and drilling a small hole in it, then placing it on his nose and trying to draw a thread through the hole: the number of attempts he has to make before he is successful equals the number of years he has yet to spend as a bachelor.

**wishing well** A WELL or pool of water into which coins, pins or pebbles are tossed in the belief that in so doing one will be granted a wish. If the wish remains unspoken it will be granted by the spirits who are supposed to dwell in such wells and pools. This practice is derived from the older custom of dropping stones into wells to divine the future: if the water threw up bubbles it was concluded that all would be well, but if it became cloudy then trouble lay in store.

**witchcraft** Superstition is much preoccupied with both the carrying out of witchcraft and the need to obtain magical protection from such activity. Distantly derived from various pagan religions and much altered after the introduction of Christianity and of the biblical DEVIL, witchcraft – a meeting-place between religion, folk medicine, and curiosity in and fear of the unexplained – takes many forms and is often intended to be beneficial, though it is the Satanic variety that has inspired the countless protective charms that superstition recommends. Most of these date from the late Middle Ages up to the eighteenth century, when the witchcraft hysteria was at its height and many suspected witches were tortured or put to death on the flimsiest of evidence.

Witchcraft has developed its own complex and detailed mythology, with no witch (in England at least) being complete without her FAMILIARS – in the form of CATS, OWLS and TOADS among other creatures – or without her broomstick, her black hat, her cauldron and her book of spells. The quintessential witch in the popular imagination is an old hag, bent upon evil and deriving pleasure from inflicting pain and misfortune upon others in the name of her diabolical master. Witchfinders of the seventeenth century tended to single out elderly women living on their own who were generally disliked or held in some mistrust by the local community, and the discovery of the 'Devil's marks' (such as WARTS or scars) about their person was often enough to convince any doubters of their guilt.

Alleged witches throughout the centuries have been blamed by the superstitious for all manner of ills that cannot otherwise be accounted for. These have ranged from plagues, storms and murders to such lesser problems as cattle failing to produce milk, horses lacking their usual vigour and crops failing to prosper. To provide protection against such misfortunes, many people used to wear special AMULETS and protected their homes in a variety of ways, ranging from concealing a pair of SCISSORS under the doormat to bringing in sprigs of various trees and plants, such as HOLLY or ST JOHN'S WORT, which are reputed to repel evil spirits.

Most spells that are intended to harm a person directly will only work if something incorporating the 'essence' of the victim is obtained first. This may be a little of their HAIR or nail parings (*see* FINGERNAIL) or a sample of their BLOOD, SALIVA or URINE – so taking extra care in the disposal of such items will go a long way towards foiling a witch's plans. To kill a witch outright, the surest way, so superstition dictates, is to shoot the suspect with a SILVER bullet.

**withershins**   *see* WIDDERSHINS.

**wolf**   Of all animals the wolf is perhaps the most feared in terms of superstition, being a favourite disguise of the DEVIL and everywhere linked with evil. In times gone by, the mere sight of a wolf was supposed to be enough to render a man dumb, assuming that the wolf saw the man first, and similarly even saying the word 'wolf' risked an imminent encounter with one. According to Welsh legend the wolf was created not by God but by the Devil and the creature has retained its

association with evil ever since, being blamed for attacking livestock and humans alike (though, curiously enough, it is also said to fear crabs and shrimps).

On a more optimistic note, the wolf has many uses in folk medicine. It is said that wrapping sufferers from EPILEPSY in a wolfskin will safeguard them from fits, and similar action will cure anyone suffering from rabies. In some parts of Europe wolfskins are also reputed to keep the house free of flies. Wolves' teeth may be rubbed against the gums to relieve TOOTHACHE in the young and may also be worn around the necks of young children to safeguard them from evil, according to the French. Hanging a wolf's tail over a barn door, meanwhile, will keep other wolves away, and eating a dish of wolf's meat will prevent a person from seeing ghosts. Sleeping with a wolf's head under the pillow will ward off NIGHTMARES, and applying wolf dung to the limbs will cure the colic.

*See also* WEREWOLF.

**wooden leg**   A superstition of obscure origins suggests that it is lucky to see a person with a wooden leg. A variation, however, qualifies this claim, warning that it is bad luck to see the back of a wooden leg, particularly early in the morning, and similarly unlucky to look over one's shoulder at a person with a wooden leg once they have passed.

**woodpecker**   Superstition in several countries associates the woodpecker particularly with RAIN. This tradition dates back to classical legend and survives in the English idea that hearing the noise of a woodpecker is a sure sign of showers in the offing; similar superstitions are shared by the French and Scandinavians. The Germans, meanwhile, claim that the woodpecker was condemned to peck wood and drink rain after refusing to help God dig holes for the world's lakes and oceans during the Creation because it did not wish to get its feathers dirty.

**work**   *see* BUSINESS.

**worm** An old superstition common to most European countries attributes TOOTHACHE to the activities of certain 'eel-shaped' worms. In order to cure toothache, therefore, one should inhale the fumes of powdered herbs placed over a glowing coal and then 'breathe' the aforesaid worm out into a cup of water. To extract a tooth without recourse to a dentist the sufferer can apply powdered worm to the affected tooth, when it will immediately drop out. To diagnose scrofula, the patient should lay a worm on the swollen skin and cover it with a leaf: if the worm turns to earth the disease is confirmed, but if it remains unchanged scrofula is not present. A person visiting a sick friend or relative should lift up a stone and see whether there is anything underneath – if a worm is found, the patient will definitely recover. People suffering from intestinal worms are recommended to consume a HAIR from a HORSE's forelock in a piece of BREAD AND BUTTER.

**wound** Superstition offers all manner of treatments for wounds, varying from the application of COBWEBS to help in knitting together cuts, to applying various potions and plant and animal extracts. Other measures include the dressing of fresh wounds with cow DUNG.

Perhaps the most curious treatment is the tradition of 'sympathetic medicine', which involves taking special care of the instrument that caused the wound, say a KNIFE, a SWORD or a fish hook, in the belief that this will ensure that the wound itself heals cleanly and properly. In the folk medicine of many cultures the wound is therefore left more or less alone, while the offending blade is cleaned, polished and treated with various magical preparations. If rusty nails are the culprit, tetanus may be avoided, it is alleged, by cleaning the nail, greasing it with special ointment and hanging it up in the chimney. In all such cases it is stressed that the guilty instrument must be kept clean and polished long after the actual wound has healed, for fear that the wound may open up again.

Preparations used in such cases included the famous 'Powder of Sympathy' that was devised by the English writer and diplomat Sir Kenelm Digby in the seventeenth century and, according to him in his *A Late Discourse Touching the Cure of Wounds by the Powder of Sympathy* (1658), was successfully applied in a number of instances. Other powders and ointments recorded in the same century include one particularly grisly example that incorporated powdered worms and bloodstones, stale boar fat and moss taken from an old human skull.

**wren** Superstition identifies the wren as the wife of the ROBIN, and the bird is generally regarded as lucky. Few people would dare to kill a wren, for fear of the bad luck this action would invite; in England, anyone who harms a wren or its nest will suffer a broken bone soon afterwards, while in France it is said that they will suffer a rash. More seriously, their house might be struck by LIGHTNING and the guilty hand might shrivel up. It was not always so, however, as the bird was frequently hunted and killed in the past so that its feathers might be sold, with due ceremony, to seafarers, who believed that carrying a wren's feather would preserve them from DROWNING.

A relatively little-known folk custom is the 'wren party'. The body of a wren (or a substitute) is taken in procession by groups of young boys in fancy dress on St Stephen's Day (26 December) to neighbouring houses in Ireland and other regions, the idea being to demand a few coins to pay for a party at the end of the day.

**wych elm** Superstition attributes to the wych elm a variety of protective properties. The tree is widely regarded as lucky, and carrying a stick of wych elm will ward off all manner of evil. In former times a twig of wych elm was often slipped into a churn to ensure that the milk 'turned' properly into BUTTER.

# Y

**yarrow** Herb, variously known as soldiers' woundwort, nose bleed, milfoil, devil's plaything, thousand weed and bad man's plaything, which is credited with various magical properties as a protective, as a means of divination and in medicinal applications. Legend has it that yarrow was the first herb that was held in the hand of the infant Jesus, and carrying a little of it about one's person will consequently safeguard one's luck and deter witches.

Intoning:

Good night, fair yarrow,
Thrice good night to thee,
I hope before tomorrow's dawn
My true love I shall see

and then sleeping with some yarrow beneath the pillow, meanwhile, will grant to the sleeper dreams of his or her future partner. Variations on this tradition insist that for these purposes yarrow taken from the grave of a young man is best. To establish whether a current lover is true, the procedure is to push a yarrow seed into the enquirer's nostril in the hope that this causes the nose to bleed – if it does not, the lover in question is unfaithful. Carrying yarrow at a WEDDING will ensure that the newly-weds remain faithful to each other for at least seven years.

In folk medicine, yarrow is alleged to be of some value in the healing of cuts and the staunching of nosebleeds (*see* BLOOD; NOSE), and in treating stomach upsets. It will also promote MENSTRUATION in a woman who has not had a period for some time.

**yawning** All actions to do with BREATH have their magical aspect. Most people are familiar with the rule of etiquette that a person should cover their mouth when yawning but may be unaware that this has its roots in medieval superstition, when it was thought that evil spirits could get inside a person's body when their mouth was opened so wide – though making the sign of the CROSS prevented this happening. Elsewhere in Europe it is suggested that yawning too long will allow the soul to escape the body and the habit should therefore be discouraged. In some cultures a yawn may be interpreted as a death omen, which must be countered at once by snapping the fingers.

**yellow** As one of the unluckiest of all colours, yellow is generally associated with cowardice, sickness and death (though some people connect it with the life-giving SUN). Yellow leaves that appear on peas or BEAN plants are supposed to presage a death in the household, and even evil spirits are said to avoid the colour. ACTORS AND ACTRESSES in particular sometimes show a reluctance to wear it.

**yellowhammer** Yellow-feathered bunting, which has a reputation as a relatively unlucky bird. The fact that its eggs bear serpent-like wavy markings means that it has long been associated with the DEVIL and the bird has suffered accordingly over the centuries from those seeking to destroy its nest, thinking it was hatching SNAKES (it is also said that the yellowhammer warns snakes of the approach of their enemies). According to Welsh folklore the bird feeds on the blood of VAMPIRES, while others claim that its irregular flight is the result of drinking the Devil's blood every MAY-DAY morning.

In folk medicine, the Welsh claim that JAUNDICE may be cured by holding a yellowhammer close to the patient's face – though the Danish insist that no fewer than three yellowhammers must actually be eaten for the cure to work.

**yew** Evergreen tree which is exceptionally long-lived and is therefore associated with life after death, which is why the tree is found in graveyards throughout Europe. The yew, with its poisonous leaves and dense timber, is respected for its protective properties and is supposed to safeguard the occupants of nearby houses from witchcraft and ghosts (despite the fact that its thick foliage may also provide a home for supernatural spirits and that cuttings of the tree should never be brought inside for fear of bad luck). Consequently, it is thought to be very unlucky to damage or cut down a yew tree, though its wood is prized for making dowsing rods and implements for use in casting spells. In fact, anyone who breaks this taboo and tears a branch off a yew is fated to die within twelve months.

More cheerfully, a girl who wishes to get a glimpse of a future lover in her dreams has only to sleep with a sprig of yew under her pillow, provided she picks the sprig herself from a graveyard she has never visited before.

Such is the yew's reputation that it has even been suggested that in past centuries churches were deliberately sited close to existing trees to benefit from their presence.

**yule log** A substantial log, ideally of BEECH wood, that was formerly burned in the hearth in homes as part of the CHRISTMAS festivities, traditionally on Christmas Eve. The arrival of the yule log was an occasion of great excitement, and only those with carefully washed hands were allowed to light it. Once burning, it was generally held to be unlucky to stir it at all while supper was being eaten that night and worse still if it burned in the presence of anyone who was cross-eyed (see EVIL EYE) or of any barefooted or flat-footed woman. Superstition dictated that keeping a piece of the burned Yule log safely under one of the beds would preserve the luck of the household over the following twelve months and would also prevent the house catching fire or being struck by LIGHTNING. It was further believed that mixing powdered yule log with some water constituted an excellent cure for CONSUMPTION, and that the ASHES mixed with corn seed would improve the harvest.

# Z

**zodiac** The twelve 'houses' into which the CALENDAR is divided, according to the pseudo-science of ASTROLOGY. Each house has its own unique character and people born between the dates each covers are supposed to share much the same traits, though further detail may be added by close examination of the precise time of birth and various other relevant circumstances. In brief, the twelve houses with their dates and allotted characteristics are as follows:

Aries: 21 March to 19 April (energetic, impetuous, self-reliant).

Taurus: 21 April to 20 May (stable, faithful, obstinate).

Gemini: 21 May to 20 June (clever, lazy, charming).

Cancer: 21 June to 21 July (changeable, ambitious, kind).

Leo: 21 July to 20 August (honest, friendly, athletic).

Virgo: 21 August to 20 September (reserved, kind, cautious).

Libra: 21 September to 20 October (fair-minded, artistic, charming).

Scorpio: 21 October to 20 November (determined, generous, brave).

Sagittarius: 21 November to 21 December (friendly, care-free, quick).

Capricorn: 21 December to 21 January (independent, precise, loyal).

Aquarius: 21 January to 19 February (sympathetic, reasonable, strong-willed).

Pisces: 21 February and 21 March (tolerant, lazy, good-natured).

The somewhat artificial division of the lunar calendar into twelve houses is questioned by some authorities, who have speculated, for instance, that there should be in reality a thirteenth house.

*See also* BIRTHSTONE.